Twentieth-Centur

Twentieth-Century Europe

A Brief History, 1900 to the Present

THIRD EDITION

Michael D. Richards
Paul R. Waibel

WILEY Blackwell

This edition first published 2014
© 2014 John Wiley & Sons, Inc.

Edition history: Harlan Davidson, Inc. (1e, 1999; 2e, 2005)
Harlan Davidson Inc. was acquired by John Wiley & Sons in May 2012.

Registered Office
John Wiley & Sons, Ltd, The Atrium, Southern Gate, Chichester, West Sussex, PO19 8SQ, UK

Editorial Offices
350 Main Street, Malden, MA 02148–5020, USA
9600 Garsington Road, Oxford, OX4 2DQ, UK
The Atrium, Southern Gate, Chichester, West Sussex, PO19 8SQ, UK

For details of our global editorial offices, for customer services, and for information about how
to apply for permission to reuse the copyright material in this book please see our website at
www.wiley.com / wiley-blackwell.

The right of Michael D. Richards and Paul R. Waibel to be identified as the authors of this work has been
asserted in accordance with the UK Copyright, Designs and Patents Act 1988.

Library of Congress Cataloging-in-Publication Data

Richards, Michael D.
   Twentieth-century Europe : a brief history, 1900 to the present / Michael D. Richards,
Paul R. Waibel. – Third edition.
      pages cm
   Includes bibliographical references and index.
   ISBN 978-1-118-65141-4 (paper)
1. Europe–History–20th century.   2. Europe–History–21st century.   I. Waibel, Paul R.   II. Title.
   D424.R517 2014
   940.5–dc23

                                         2013041082

A catalogue record for this book is available from the British Library.

Cover image: Funeral procession of former Czech President Vaclav Havel, Charles Bridge, Prague,
December 21, 2011. © David Brauchli / Getty Images
Cover design by Simon Levy Associates

Set in 11 / 13pt Dante by SPi Publisher Services, Pondicherry, India

Contents

Preface

Now that we are well into the twenty-first century, it has become necessary to change slightly the title of the third edition of what has been known for many years as *Twentieth-Century Europe: A Brief History*. Under its new title, it will remain a brief history and, as well, a readable and an accurate one.

As we have noted in previous prefaces, use of a brief but comprehensive survey permits one to assign outside readings and, we might add, other assignments that a feature-laden, very expensive textbook precludes. Readable is key, too. The more common ground students and their instructors have, the more likely class sessions can be exchanges of informed opinions and probing questions. Finally, accuracy is highly important. We have tried to create a text that will be a reliable introduction to European civilization from 1900 to the present.

Our approach is largely chronological. The book is divided into four parts. Two parts cover the period from 1900 to the outbreak of World War II. The third and fourth parts cover the period from the outbreak of the war to the present. Each part is introduced by an "Overview" summarizing the main themes of the period covered. Each part is then divided into three chapters. Two chapters, in parts two and four, respectively, provide a careful and thoughtful consideration of the most significant intellectual/philosophical currents and artistic trends of the twentieth century.

The carefully selected maps, tables, and illustrations aid the reader's comprehension of information in the text. Four maps show national boundaries at key points during the last 110 plus years. We have compiled tables to clarify certain events (such as the German inflation of 1923) or to provide an overview of key developments (e.g., the development over a half century of the European Community/European Union). Photographs, some from our own collections, are featured in every chapter to provide visual references.

Every chapter begins with a brief chronology to orient the reader and to serve as a reference. A list of "Further Reading" concludes each chapter. The titles featured are among the best and most interesting books available to the student or general reader who would like to pursue a topic in greater detail. A list of abbreviations and acronyms, which in this bureaucratic world grows longer with each edition, forms an appendix to the text. An extensive index, a valuable but often overlooked feature, rounds out the resources available in the text.

More than 30 years ago, Michael D. Richards, then a young professor at Sweet Briar College, published *Europe: 1900–1980: A Brief History*. Several years later, Paul R. Waibel came on board as co-author of the first edition of a new text, modeled on the original book but in its own right a careful, thoughtful reconsideration of Europe's experience in the twentieth century. The second edition contained a completely new chapter (Chapter 11) and a substantially revised chapter (Chapter 12). This third edition contains two substantially revised chapters (Chapters 11 and 12). As noted for the second edition, all other chapters have been carefully reviewed to reflect current scholarship and some parts have been extensively revised.

We have each taught thousands of students in careers stretching over several decades. In the course of our careers, we have accumulated debts to our teachers, colleagues, and students we can never repay. This book is in some large part the product of many conversations both within and outside the classroom. Through it we hope to have a continuing conversation with many more colleagues and their students.

It has been a great pleasure to work once again with our long-time editor, Andrew Davidson. He guided us through a careful and thorough review of the text, chapter by chapter. Thanks to him this edition is far more than an update here and there of the previous edition. We want to acknowledge as well the assistance provided by Linda Gaio-Davidson in securing permissions and selecting illustrations for the text. She was both resourceful and endlessly patient.

Georgina Coleby, Project Editor, helped to move the project forward in so many ways. We are very grateful for her prompt and gracious assistance with our many queries. Lindsay Bourgeois, Editorial Assistant, was also most helpful. Leanda Shrimpton supplied many, many possibilities for the cover, including the one we all agreed was just right. Velayutham Satheesh oversaw the massive and essential task involved in copy-editing the book and preparing it to be printed. We also want to thank Leah Thompson for her efforts in marketing the book.

We are grateful for the support and encouragement of our families. Dr. Richards wishes to thank John M. Richards; David, Jeanne, Will, and Wes Richards; Arie, Rebecca, John C., and Caroline Richards; and Nancy D. Potter and John, Blake, and Owen Crumbliss. Dr. Waibel wishes to thank Darlene, Elizabeth Joy, and Natalie Grace Waibel.

We sincerely hope readers will find this book both informative and enjoyable.

Michael D. Richards
Paul R. Waibel

Part 1

Overview: 1900–1919

THE TWO DECADES FROM THE DAWN of the twentieth century to the end of World War I formed the era during which European civilization peaked. It was also the period in which the very foundations of European civilization began to crack beneath the weight of inner contradictions and new challenges.

In 1900, Europeans could have said, somewhat paradoxically, that Europe was the world and the world was Europe's. For the first time in history, a world civilization existed, and that civilization was European. By 1914, "Europeans" controlled 84 percent of the world's land surface. Only Japan, which since 1871 had been pursuing a self-conscious policy of Westernization, was accepted as a "civilized" although non-Western nation.

The Europeans' sense of superiority seemed to be confirmed by history. The Scientific Revolution, Enlightenment, and Industrial Revolution gave to the West a scientific and technological advantage over the non-Western world. By the end of the nineteenth century, the lion's share of the world's wealth flowed into the Western nations.

In Europe itself, the remnants of the old aristocracy still occupied thrones and, in some countries like Russia, Germany, and Austria-Hungary, still possessed real or potential power. But the period from

Twentieth-Century Europe: A Brief History, 1900 to the Present, Third Edition.
Michael D. Richards and Paul R. Waibel.
© 2014 John Wiley & Sons, Inc. Published 2014 by John Wiley & Sons, Inc.

the end of the Napoleonic wars to the outbreak of World War I, the Great War, in 1914, was the golden age of the middle class, or bourgeoisie. They were the self-confident children of modernity, the Enlightenment tradition. Their ideology was classical liberalism, both political and economic. Their social status and, in some countries like Great Britain and France, political power derived from their growing wealth.

This Europe of Strauss waltzes and middle-class outings captured in impressionist paintings was being transformed just as it was reaching its fulfillment. Forces that had their origins in the nineteenth century were about to topple centuries-old dynasties and with them their archaic nobility. Likewise, the middle class, the real pillar of the existing order, was under serious attack. It was being challenged politically and economically by the emergence of a working class organized in increasingly powerful labor unions and political parties.

The Great War changed the course of European history. What began as a localized crisis resulting from the assassination of the heir to the Austro-Hungarian Empire rapidly escalated into a world war. All participants felt they would be fighting a defensive war to save their homeland from an aggressor. All felt that the war, when it came, would be a brief one of motion, concluded in time for them to be home for Christmas. All were disappointed. The enthusiasm that greeted the outbreak of war in August 1914 soon changed to morbid resignation.

Since no one had expected the outbreak of the war in 1914, none of the participants were prepared. By 1916, as the war at the front turned into one of attrition in which each side tried to bleed the enemy to death, governments began to organize their home fronts. Governments assumed a broader and more direct role in their economies and in the private lives of their people—to a level unknown before the war. Scarce economic resources vital to the war effort were carefully rationed, as were consumer goods. Government-sponsored propaganda, together with censorship, was employed to mobilize "human resources" for more than just military service. Civil liberties often received only a polite wink, as the need to combat the spirit of defeatism grew.

The year 1917 was a momentous year. In February, the German High Command persuaded the Kaiser to authorize a resumption of unrestricted submarine warfare. This move, intended to bring about the defeat of Great Britain, resulted in the United States coming into the war in April, thus assuring Germany's eventual defeat. In March, revolution broke out in Russia, where the Russian soldiers had voted against the war, as Lenin said, with their feet when they deserted in large numbers. But the Provisional Government of well-meaning liberals failed to govern effectively. In November, the Bolsheviks seized power in Russia, thus setting the stage for one of the dominant themes in twentieth-century European history.

The appearance of fresh American troops in large numbers tipped the scales in favor of the Allies on the Western Front. Allied armies broke through the Siegfried Line in July 1918. The Central Powers began to collapse. Revolution broke out in Germany. On November 9, the Kaiser abdicated and went into exile in Holland. Two days later, on November 11, Germany signed an armistice. The "guns of August" were finally silenced. The task of peacemaking lay ahead.

Germany had signed the armistice expecting to participate in the peace conference. It was not invited to do so. The victors who gathered in Paris to draft a treaty that they felt would be a fitting conclusion to the war fought to end all wars were divided between new world idealists and old world realists. What came out of the peace conference was a "victors' peace," one that was to poison the future and make a second world war almost a certainty, if not a necessity.

1

Before the Deluge
Europe, 1900–1914

Chronology

1899–1902	Boer War
1901	Death of Queen Victoria
1904–1905	Russo-Japanese War
1905	Revolution in Russia
	Tsar Nicholas II issues the October Manifesto
1906	Algeciras Conference
	Great Britain launches HMS *Dreadnought*
1908	Austria-Hungary annexes Bosnia and Herzegovina
1914	Assassination of Franz Ferdinand

AT 6:30 P.M. ON JANUARY 22, 1901, Queen Victoria died at Cowes on the Isle of Wight. Although her son Edward, the Prince of Wales, was present, she died in the arms of her favorite grandson, Wilhelm II. The German Kaiser had rushed from Berlin to be at her side.

Twentieth-Century Europe: A Brief History, 1900 to the Present, Third Edition.
Michael D. Richards and Paul R. Waibel.
© 2014 John Wiley & Sons, Inc. Published 2014 by John Wiley & Sons, Inc.

Deeply moved that the Kaiser conducted himself with such stately dignity at the Queen's funeral, the new king, his "Uncle Bertie," made him a British field marshal.

Victoria (1819–1901) was more than the queen of an empire upon which the sun never set. Many throughout the world viewed her as the beloved sovereign, at least symbolically, of the civilized world. Even those peoples who were not regarded as "civilized" by Europeans revered her. Four hundred million people spread over 12 million square miles of land were her subjects. Leaders from around the world paid homage to her memory. Even in the United States, flags flew at half-mast and newspaper editorials eulogized the late queen and the age to which she gave her name.

There was something very reassuring about Queen Victoria's funeral. Royalty and government leaders from all over Europe, including her grandson the Kaiser and his cousin Nicholas II, Tsar of Russia, gathered to say farewell. To have been present, or even to view the film footage of the funeral, was to be caught up in the solemn splendor of such a gathering of the world's political leadership. The observer might be pardoned for equating the pomp with power and concluding that the future was safe and secure. But such a feeling would have been only an illusion. The fabric of European civilization was already tearing at the seams and coming unraveled.

Europe and the World

Europeans before the Great War divided the world into "civilized" and "uncivilized peoples," much as we today speak of "developed" and "developing" nations. To be considered among the civilized nations meant being "Westernized," which in turn meant accepting the world view and lifestyle of Europeans. "Westernized" peoples included more than the residents of Europe itself but also those of such nations as the United States and Canada in North America and Australia and New Zealand in the South Pacific Ocean. The words "Western," "European," and "civilized" were often used interchangeably.

Despite the smug arrogance of the imperialists, to a certain degree, Europe's sense of moral superiority was justified. Europe's moral values, fundamentally religious in origin, were taken over and secularized by the eighteenth-century intellectuals. Emerging from the Enlightenment as inalienable human rights, these values were summarized by John Locke and Thomas Jefferson as the individual's right to life, liberty, and property (or happiness), the foundation of classical liberalism. In practice, during the nineteenth century, the enjoyment of these purportedly inalienable rights was often qualified by considerations of property and gender.

Westernization offered more than a few benefits. Europeans were better housed, better fed, and better clothed than people anywhere else in the world. They lived longer and their infant mortality rate was lower than in the non-Western world. Nearly 100 percent of the population of northwestern Europe was literate, whereas in much of the non-Westernized world, the literacy rate was barely above 0. Europeans no longer lived in fear of unseen forces. Scientific knowledge had given them mastery over nature, showering upon them a cornucopia of material blessings. They also governed themselves, while virtually the entire non-Western world was subject to the more advanced Europeans.

By 1900, the "relics of barbarism," such as slavery, infanticide, blood sports, and torture, were expunged from the European nations. Even women, who were still denied the vote and full equality with men in employment and education, possessed the same human rights as every other human being. And where human rights clashed with cultural or religious practice, human rights were deemed superior. European women were not subjected to such barbarous practices as genital mutilation or *suttee*, the burning of a Hindu widow on her husband's funeral pyre. Nor were they condemned to a lifetime of illiteracy and unquestioned submission to the arbitrary will of father or husband. This message of universal and inalienable human rights went, if not always practiced, wherever the might of European imperialism was felt.

There were, of course, other civilizations in the world whose ancestry reached further back than Europe's. China, India, Japan, and the Middle East all possessed the characteristics associated with being civilized, for example, literacy, cities, monumental architecture, a socioeconomic class structure, and systematic philosophical and religious thought. By the mid-1800s, however, all of the great non-European civilizations were but shadows of their past glory and vulnerable to an industrialized West in need of markets and resources to fuel its rapid development. Of the ancient non-European civilizations, only Japan survived the threat of the new imperialism from the West, and it did so only by rapid Westernization.

The humanitarian impulse was often used as a justification for imperialism. Although for some it was a sincere motivation, for many others, it served as an excuse for European domination and exploitation of the non-Western world. Christian missionaries brought Christianity to non-European nations, and they and other humanitarians built hospitals, orphanages, and schools for both boys and girls. Such people often saw the native peoples as child-like and backward, souls in need of "uplifting" from the darkness in which they seemed to exist and an introduction to the benefits of civilization, whether or not they wished such. This aspect of imperialism was romanticized by such ardent imperialists as the English writer Rudyard Kipling (1865–1936), many of whose works are set in India and relate the interactions of British colonials and subject Indians.

Kipling preached the "glories" of imperialism in his widely popular fiction and poetry. The best known of Kipling's proimperialist poems is *The White Man's Burden* (1899, pp. 290–291), composed to commemorate the United States' victory in the Spanish–American War (1898) and America's annexation of the Philippine Islands. In it, Kipling urged the United States to join Britain in the pursuit of empire and the spread of Western civilization:

> Take up the White man's burden –
> Send forth the best ye breed –
> Go bind your sons to exile
> To serve your captives' need;
> To wait in heavy harness
> On fluttered folk and wild –
> Your new-caught, sullen peoples,
> Half devil and half child.

However much one wishes to extoll the benefits of European imperialism enjoyed by subject peoples, there was a dark side, as imperialism's primary and most influential motivations always boiled down to economic exploitation and national prestige.

The rapid industrialization in the West increased the demand for raw materials, some of which, like petroleum and rubber, were necessary for the modernization of existing industries and the creation of new ones. As the standard of living slowly increased for the working classes, the demand for items from distant parts of the world such as coffee and tea increased. As mass production and distribution of products grew, so too did the need for reliable supplies of raw materials and new and expanding markets for finished goods. The seemingly insatiable need for new markets was in part due to the unequal distribution of wealth in the industrialized nations of the West. The concentration of wealth in fewer hands, combined with the inability of the working classes to purchase ever-increasing quantities of the goods they produced, pushed the investment of excess capital abroad.

The need to protect the profits of existing industries and protect those of emerging ones led the governments of turn-of-the-century industrialized nations to abandon free trade in favor of neomercantilism. The result was the creation of colonial empires that served as large, worldwide trading communities. Tariffs on imported goods, combined with restrictions on competition within the colonial empires, served to protect the luxurious lifestyle of the upper classes while providing limited improvements in the lifestyle of the working classes of the imperial powers. With the exception of the British Empire, however, the economic model fell short, as the cost of colonies often surpassed any economic benefit they provided for the mother country. More important, therefore, was what colonies meant in terms of national prestige and national rivalry among the great powers, themselves.

By the 1840s, steam-propelled ships equipped with the new screw propellers were revolutionizing both merchant and naval vessels. So-called tramp steamers were carrying goods from port to port around the world, often not returning to their home ports for a year or more. At first, the steam-powered ships were overshadowed by the fast-sailing and graceful clipper ships. But the opening of the Suez Canal in 1869, the very year that the most famous clipper ship, *Cutty Sark*, was launched, doomed the sailing vessels. As the colonial empires expanded, sea power became increasingly important. The growth of large navies, especially the naval race between Great Britain and Germany after 1898, was a major cause of the outbreak of the Great War in 1914.

One individual who clearly understood the interrelationship between seaborne commerce, large naval forces, and imperial expansion was US Admiral Alfred Thayer Mahan (1840–1914). Mahan presented his analysis of the importance of sea power in a series of lectures published in 1890 as *The Influence of Sea Power upon History, 1660–1783*. After reading Mahan's magnum opus, Kaiser Wilhelm invited Mahan to lunch aboard his yacht, the *Hohenzollern*, and then ordered that copies of the book be placed aboard every ship in the German navy. The Japanese adopted *The Influence of Sea Power on History* as a textbook in their military and naval academies.

In defending America's annexation of Hawaii (1898), Mahan argued that sea power was the key element in determining a nation's position in the world and its prosperity. Big navies, seaborne commerce, economic prosperity at home, and foreign colonies were all bound up together. Behind it all lay the influence of Social Darwinism. In this application of what was at the time a popular school of thought in the West, the greatness of a nation or a people was determined by struggle, ultimately struggle won or lost on the battlefield. The argument went that, naturally, the "fittest" people would triumph in any such conflict, to the betterment of both parties. To bring the supposition to its ironic—and ultimately tragic—conclusion, if peace were to prevail, then progress would stop, and Western civilization would stagnate.

Even though the colonial peoples were mere pawns in the high-stakes power struggle between the great powers, a significant majority of the citizens of the great powers were caught up in the romantic image of colonialism as preached by Kipling and others. Tales of explorers opening up the interior of Africa, still labeled the "Dark Continent" on many maps, or encounters with the mysterious ancient civilizations of Asia fed the popular imagination. One well-known example of how popular support for imperialism was encouraged, or even manufactured, was the highly publicized search to find the Scottish missionary and explorer David Livingstone (1813–1873), who was reported missing somewhere in Africa. Sir Henry Morton Stanley (1841–1904), himself an explorer, convinced the editors of the *New York Herald* and London's *Daily Telegraph* to sponsor his search for Livingston. The editors hoped to increase the daily circulation of their newspapers; Stanley sought both fame and fortune. Both were successful.

Europeans, as well as Europeans living abroad in North America and elsewhere, took pride in the fact that at the beginning of the twentieth century, the West's faith in progress and optimism was about to triumph over ignorance and darkness and usher in a new era of universal peace and prosperity. The humble peasant or laborer took pride in knowing that their country's flag was around the world, on the high seas and in the far corners of the globe. Their pride was nowhere more clearly voiced than the chorus of the popular hymn "Rule, Britannia" (http://www.hymns.me.uk/rule-brittania-lyrics.htm):

> Rule, Britannia! Britannia, rule the waves!
> Britons never, never, never shall be slaves.

But there was a not so romantic reality to the new imperialism, the best-known example of which was the Belgian King Leopold II's private rubber plantation in Central Africa, commonly referred to as the Congo Free State.

Leopold II (1835–1909) was a firm believer in the notion that a nation's greatness was tied to its possession of a colonial empire. When neither the Belgium government nor the Belgium people showed interest in Leopold's vision, he created a private holding company in 1876. With the help of Henry Morton Stanley, Leopold laid claim to 905,000 square miles of central Africa with an estimated population of 30 million. This chunk of territory was recognized internationally as Leopold's personal property. There were no legal restrictions on how he chose to exploit the Congo or its people. The methods employed by Leopold's agents, including forced labor and brutal mutilation, decimated the population and eventually aroused the conscience of many.

Among those who called attention to the methods employed to meet the demands for rubber were Joseph Conrad (1857–1924) and Sir Arthur Conan Doyle (1859–1930). Conrad published *Heart of Darkness* in 1902, a novel based on his personal experiences as a steamboat captain on the Congo River. He recorded in fiction the cruelty that characterized daily life in the Congo Free State. Doyle, best known as the creator of Sherlock Holmes, provided descriptions and photographs of the atrocities in *The Crime of the Congo* published in 1909. It was not until November 1908 that the government of Belgium ended Leopold's personal rule and made the Congo Free State a colony. The estimated death toll resulting from Leopold's rule between 1876 and 1908 is variously given as between 8 and 30 million. The Congo may well have been an extreme example of the new imperialism, but there were other such examples in colonies that were state controlled from the beginning.

Germany was a latecomer to the contest for colonies. Chancellor Otto von Bismarck (1815–1898) at first opposed ventures outside Europe but in 1884 yielded to popular clamor. The first German colony was Angra Pequena, later named German South-West Africa. Other possessions followed in Africa and the Pacific. Resistance to German rule was dealt with swiftly and decisively. When the Herero, a native pastoral people, revolted in 1904, the German forces suppressed the revolt and while doing so reduced the Herero population from an estimated 80,000 to an estimated 15,000. Similarly, in German South-East Africa, the Maji uprising of 1905–1907 was put down at the cost of between 80,000 and 100,000 African lives.

The "rules of the game," for the new imperialism, were agreed to at the Berlin Conference of 1884–1885, hosted by Bismarck. Representatives of 14 nations, including the United States and Turkey, attended the conference. One of the primary reasons for the conference was to assure all parties convened free access to the Congo Free State by recognizing Leopold's private ownership of the territory. But there was more. The so-called Principle of Effectivity was agreed to for further exploitation of Africa. In order to claim an area as a colony, the interested power had to make treaties with the local leaders, establish a police force, administer the area, and, perhaps most important, provide for the economic "development" of the area.

By 1895, Africa was carved up among the European powers. Only two states remained independent in 1900. On the west coast, Liberia, sponsored by the United States as a refuge for freed slaves who wished to immigrate to Africa, remained independent. In the northeast of the continent, known as the Horn of Africa, the ancient kingdom of Ethiopia (Abyssinia) remained the only independent, native-ruled nation on the African continent.

Asia suffered a similar fate. The kingdom of Siam (modern Thailand) maintained its independence by a clever diplomacy that argued the need for a buffer between British and French imperial expansion in southern Asia. In order to avoid being a victim of imperialism, Japan underwent a reform referred to as the Meiji Restoration that resulted in the modernization, or Westernization, of Japan. By the mid-1890s, Japan was itself an imperial power, one with expanding influence in Korea and Manchuria, as well as an emerging competitor with the United States for control of the Pacific Ocean.

No matter what standard one adopted, the world before the outbreak of the Great War in 1914 was Westernized. The traditional great powers of Europe, joined by the United States, were the masters of the world. But the changing power alignment and force of nationalism in Europe, exacerbated by colonial competition, were about to shatter the illusion of *La Belle Époque*.

The Great Powers

On the surface, at least, the European great powers in 1900 were the same powers regarded as such in 1815. They were the traditional five, Great Britain, France, Russia, Austria-Hungary (the Habsburg Monarchy), and Germany (formerly Prussia). Italy was considered by many in 1900 to be a great power, but as the events of the Great War were to demonstrate, this was more a clever ruse on Italy's part than an accurate assessment of its resources. And for that matter, there were, technically, only three great powers, since both Russia and Austria-Hungary lagged behind in those areas vital to maintaining great-power status into the twentieth century. Both had resisted the modernist ideas that came out of the Enlightenment, especially liberalism. There were some signs of industrialization and urbanization in the Austrian portion of the Habsburg lands and in Russia around St. Petersburg and Moscow, in Russian Poland, and the Donbas in the south. Still, both remained predominantly agrarian states of a few fabulously wealthy landlords and a multitude of poverty-stricken peasants.

Austria–Hungary

The Dual Monarchy, as Austria-Hungary was often called, maintained a cumbersome form of government with separate parliaments for Austria and Hungary. Common to both halves of the empire were ministries for war, finance, and foreign affairs. Uniting the vast multinational realm was the emperor, Franz Joseph (1830–1916), who had come to the throne in 1848 and who would stubbornly resist death until November 21, 1916. Like Queen Victoria, Franz Joseph was the much beloved symbol of a great historic tradition. The House of Habsburg was the oldest and most prestigious dynasty in Europe. But unlike Queen Victoria, Franz Joseph was committed to, and lived in, a world that no longer really existed.

Austria-Hungary did not possess an overseas empire. It was a multicultural land empire held together by soldiers, bureaucrats, parades, and a living symbol of past glory. It was being torn apart by nationalism. Poles, Czechs, Slovaks, Serbs, Croatians, and Ruthenians were only the more numerous of the minorities who inhabited the Habsburg lands. There were over 51 million inhabitants in 1911, who spoke at least 10 different languages. Among them were Roman Catholic and Greek Orthodox Christians, Jews, and Muslims.

Following defeat in the Austro-Prussian War (1866), Franz Joseph avoided dissolution of the empire by appeasing the Magyars (Hungarians). The result was the Dual Monarchy. By 1900, the Czechs were pressing for a further reorganization. Habsburg foreign policy was aimed at three goals: maintain and expand the empire at the expense of Turkey; prevent the spread of Russian influence in the Balkans; and combat the growth of nationalism among the South Slavs, especially the Serbian desire to create a Great Serbia.

One solution to the problem of trying to appease so many minority populations was a triple monarchy with the organization of an autonomous Yugoslav (South Slav) state from portions of Austria and Hungary. Another was a federal state composed of a number of largely autonomous units. The greatest obstacle to any of the various solutions proposed was Magyar intransigence. Magyar elites dominated Hungarian politics and opposed any reorganization of the empire. Many contemporary observers felt that only the aging emperor himself held the empire together.

Russia

Russia had much in common with Austria-Hungary. It, too, was a land-based empire after the sale of Alaska to the United States in 1868 for $7.6 million, slightly less than 2 cents per acre. Russia's status as a great power in 1900 rested upon its immense size—it stretched across the whole of Eurasia from the eastern border of Germany to the Pacific Ocean—and the fact that it had defeated the great Napoleon in 1812. Like Austria-Hungary, Russia was an old-fashioned agrarian state. The Romanovs, who ruled Russia since 1613, devoted their energies to the maintenance of autocratic rule. The current Tsar, Nicholas II (1868–1918), upon ascending the throne in 1894 promised: "I shall preserve the principle of autocracy as firmly and undeviatingly as did my father" (Sulzberger 1977). The ideas of the Enlightenment, especially any thought of liberal political reform, were dismissed by Nicholas II as simplistic nonsense. Handsome and devoted to his family but weak-willed and easily dominated by those around him, his one goal in life was to leave to his son and heir an unchanged Russia. He was not well suited to rule Russia in the troubled years before the Great War.

The century began badly in Russia with an economic recession, strikes, peasant disorders, and acts of terrorism. The government's difficulties increased after Russia became involved in war with Japan in 1904. Repeatedly defeated in battle by the Japanese, the Russian government faced a rising tide of discontent at home among workers, peasants, intellectuals, and members of minority nationality groups. The Revolution of 1905 was triggered by "Bloody Sunday" in January of that year. It involved a peaceful procession to the Winter Palace in St. Petersburg, organized by a Russian Orthodox priest, to present a petition by workers to the Tsar. As the peaceful crowd marched to the Winter Palace respectfully singing "God Save the Tsar," they were fired on by troops and dispersed with a great loss of life. The event touched off waves of strikes and disturbances that led eventually to the Tsar's issuing the October Manifesto (1905).

The October Manifesto, the document establishing the *Duma* or parliament, was seen by many as the beginning of a new era in Russian history. The revolutionary forces split. Most moderates and liberals were hopeful that a true parliamentary system would evolve. A party of moderates, the Octobrists, was founded on that hope. The major group of liberals, the Kadets, was more skeptical of the government, but it, too, hoped for the best. Some of the socialists, however, especially the Marxist revolutionaries, wanted to continue the revolution.

Liberal and moderate hopes were soon dashed. As the government regained confidence in 1906, it worked to limit the powers of the Duma and to repress any remaining signs of the revolution. In June 1907, the electoral laws were changed to disfranchise many workers and those persons from non-Russian parts of the empire. The various revolutionary groups were either destroyed or forced underground.

Pyotr Stolypin (1862–1911), the minister of the interior between 1906 and 1911, carried through an important series of measures that allowed a peasant to claim his land from the village commune as a unified, independent holding. The idea behind the measure was that the peasants would be more conservative politically if they had property of their own. Furthermore, if they farmed as independent farmers free of the restrictions of the commune, or *mir*, they would be more productive.

Some historians, in assessing Russia in 1914, point to the changes that the Stolypin land reforms were making, the spontaneous revival of the industrial economy, and the continued existence of institutions of parliamentary government, to justify an optimism about the solidity of the empire before the advent of its destruction with the Great War. Others, however, emphasize continuing problems in the countryside with low productivity and overpopulation, the precariousness and ineffectiveness of the Duma, the chasm between educated society and the government, and the hostility between urban workers and society to buttress their case that even had the war not come, the collapse of the empire was inevitable. They also point to the lack of political leadership in Russia after the assassination of Stolypin in 1911. As with Austria-Hungary, Russia's future did not appear bright.

Germany

Germany after 1900 was the dominant power on the continent and Great Britain's leading rival in the world. On the eve of war, Germany produced nearly a third more pig iron and twice as much steel as Great Britain and only slightly less coal. Having industrialized much later than Great Britain, German industry was able to take advantage of new sources of power and new techniques. Hence, its electrical and chemical industries flourished. German industry produced far more than could be consumed within the Reich. After 1880, Germany rapidly increased its share of world trade. By the outbreak of war in 1914, the nation's merchant marine was the second largest in the world behind Great Britain's.

Germany's surge to world-power status was not due only to its industrial development. Germany led the world in scientific development. Although no longer simply the land of "poets and philosophers," it still held a commanding lead in intellectual and cultural affairs. Its educational system from elementary schools through graduate universities was the model for, and envy of, all other developed countries. The number of German university students in 1911 was nearly twice the number of students enrolled in universities in any other of the European great powers.

In other areas, too, Germany appeared to be the most progressive nation in the world. Under Otto von Bismarck's leadership as the first chancellor (1871–1890) of the German Reich, Germany was the first nation to develop a system of social insurance. Designed to win the support of the working class, which it failed to do, the system provided for accident and sickness insurance, old-age pensions, and unemployment benefits. English workers would have to wait until 1906–1914, and American workers until Franklin Roosevelt's New Deal (1933–1939), to receive such benefits.

But Germany was far from being a liberal democratic country in the same mold of Great Britain and France. Political liberalism was defeated in Germany in the revolutions of 1848. After that, German liberals expended their energies on developing economic liberalism. The task of achieving national unity was carried out by conservatives with the enthusiastic support of the masses. Consequently, Germany emerged from the nineteenth century as one of the world's great industrial powers but with a governmental system that one might best describe as a pseudoconstitutional absolutism. Outwardly, Germany appeared to be a liberal constitutional monarchy, but this was only an illusion based upon the fact that the *Reichstag*, or parliament, was elected on the basis of universal manhood suffrage of all citizens over the age of 25. In fact, the Reichstag possessed little real power other than to refuse to pass the federal budget. Past experience in the Prussian parliament (1862–1866), however, left liberals with the conviction that this one "real" power was best left untested in the Reichstag.

The German Reich was in fact a federal union of individual German states in which real power was divided between Prussia, the largest state, and the *Bundesrat*, or federal parliament. Sovereignty was vested by the constitution in the Bundesrat, which was presided over by the Reich chancellor who was appointed by, and accountable to, the Kaiser (the King of Prussia). The delegates were appointed by the individual state governments and voted en bloc as directed by their governments. All really significant measures required approval by Prussia. Any attempt to amend the constitution could be defeated by 14 votes in the Bundesrat—and Prussia had 17 votes.

The period from 1890 until Germany's defeat in 1918 is referred to as the "Wilhelmian era," for it was the Kaiser who determined the course of events in Germany. In foreign policy, Wilhelm II

The German crown prince Wilhelm stands over a tiger he shot in a big game hunting trip to Ceylon, c. 1912, a fitting symbol of European dominance in the world before the Great War. © ullsteinbild/TopFoto

(1859–1941) charted a "new course" meant to achieve for Germany a commanding role in world affairs or, as he put it, a "place in the sun." Wilhelm II's new world policy, or *Weltpolitik*, brought Germany into conflict with France and Great Britain, especially the latter.

The "new course" meant colonies, and colonies meant a great navy capable of a commanding presence throughout the world. For Germany, the greatest military power in Europe, to build a fleet capable of challenging British naval supremacy was a direct challenge to Great Britain. It was to prove a dangerous, and ultimately disastrous, course. As in Austria-Hungary and Russia, in Germany, the emperor possessed real power. Whatever the constitutional trappings, Wilhelm II ruled Germany. What made the situation dangerous for world peace was the fact that, unlike Austria-Hungary and Russia, Germany possessed the economic power and national unity to make the Kaiser's wildest dreams possible. Without responsible leadership, the German Reich was a real threat to the peace of Europe.

In the minds of many, responsible leadership was precisely what Germany lacked in the years before 1914. Special interest groups achieved positions of influence in Germany. The Bülow tariff of 1902, a protective tariff, was brought about by the cooperation of industrialists from the Rhineland and Junkers, landed nobility from East Prussia. The combination of rye and steel was powerful in Germany. Similarly, the Navy League, an organization composed of merchants, businessmen, and the military, supported and encouraged the Kaiser's commitment to naval construction. Finally, the general staff of the army increasingly usurped the government's prerogatives in voicing opinions or making commitments.

Nine of Europe's sovereigns gathered for a group picture while attending the funeral of Britain's King Edward VII. Standing fourth from left is Kaiser Wilhelm II. Seated in the middle is Britain's George V. Royal Collection Trust/© Her Majesty Queen Elizabeth II 2013

In the 1912 elections, both the Social Democratic Party (SPD) and Catholic Center Party made strong showings. If they had banded together with the Progressive Party, a majority on the left and left-center might have been created to press for a revision of the political system. Such a coalition was unthinkable, however, and Germany continued into 1914 without leadership except for that provided by nationalists and militarists.

France

France, too, was an industrialized nation, although on the eve of the Great War, it lagged far behind Germany, Great Britain, and the United States. Unlike its competitors, France was a nation of small businessmen, small farmers, and small manufacturers, a nation of petit bourgeoisie rather than giant industrialists. More than half of the French still made their living from agriculture.

Of the great powers, France was the most democratic. Like Great Britain, it had a parliamentary system, but in France, members of the upper house, or Senate, were elected. Also, unlike in Great Britain with its two large political parties, in France, politics found expression in numerous small parties. The proliferation of parties meant that every government was a coalition, often only briefly in office. Between 1890 and 1914, a period of only 24 years, France had 43 different governments and 26 different premiers. At the turn of the century, French politics and French society were plagued by a sharp polarization between Left and Right. In part, this was historic. Those on the Left saw themselves as the heirs of an anticlerical, democratic revolutionary tradition reaching back to 1789. Those on the Right were conservatives, who, from their base within the church and army, called for more order while blaming France's decline in power on too much democracy. In short, it can be said that the Third Republic, a republic born of France's defeat in the Franco-Prussian War of 1870–1871, was divided between those who favored a republican form of government and those who desired a restoration of monarchy but were unable to determine the "rightful" monarch.

The divisions within French society intensified as a result of the Dreyfus Affair between 1894 and 1906. In 1894, Captain Alfred

Dreyfus (1859–1935) was accused of selling military secrets to the Germans. Tried and convicted, Dreyfus was sentenced to life imprisonment in the infamous penal colony on Devil's Island. Believing Dreyfus was falsely charged, a group of noted politicians and intellectuals waged a public campaign for his release. Until his final exoneration in 1906, France was bitterly divided by an often violent controversy that involved anti-Semitic, anticlerical, and antirepublican issues.

Between 1906 and 1911, a period in which the Radicals (a left-center party devoted to the preservation of the French Republic and the advancement of the interests of the "little man" in French society) were dominant, two developments unfurled. One was the emergence of a radical right movement centered on the opinions espoused in the newspaper *Action Française* and the writings of Charles Maurras (1868–1952) and Leon Daudet (1867–1942). *Action Française* favored a return to strong government at home and a highly nationalistic and aggressive policy abroad. Its views were shared by many who were not royalists but still found the Third Republic lacking. At the same time that a sizable opposition arose on the right, labor militancy increased on the left. Strikes among vineyard workers took place in 1907 and again in 1911. A major strike by postal workers in 1909 was followed by a strike of railroad workers in 1910. The railroad workers returned to work unconditionally when the premier, Aristide Briand (1862–1932), a former socialist, threatened to mobilize the workers. The criticisms and demands of neither the left nor the right had been met; they had only been sidestepped. France in 1914 possessed a workable system of government provided not too many demands were placed on it.

Great Britain

In contrast to the other European great powers, Great Britain at the turn of the century appeared to be the shining example of Western civilization in its golden age. It possessed the world's largest empire and the world's largest navy to protect it. Although its rate of economic growth was slipping behind that of Germany and the

United States, especially in the key industries of steel, iron, and coal, Great Britain nevertheless lay at the center of world trade, with vast, highly profitable foreign investments. London remained the financial capital of the world.

In contrast to the appearance of political and social fragmentation in France, Great Britain possessed a stable, two-party parliamentary system. The trend in Great Britain through the nineteenth century had been in the direction of steady, if at times slow, social and political reform. Beginning with the Great Reform Bill of 1832 and including the Reform Bill of 1867 and the Franchise Bill of 1884, the Parliament had gradually extended the suffrage until virtually every adult male could vote. By 1900, it appeared that Great Britain, of all of the European great powers, would make a smooth transition to democracy.

It was the Liberal Party, which came to power in 1906 and remained in power until after the Great War, that actually presided over the transition from aristocratic conservatism to popular democracy and the first signs of the emergence of a welfare state. In 1909, David Lloyd George (1863–1945), chancellor of the exchequer and leader of the radicals within the Liberal Party, presented a budget that proposed a revision of the tax system so as to place the burden for financing the new social legislation upon the wealthiest classes. It was a radical new departure, one that foreshadowed the future British welfare state. The proposed budget led, not unexpectedly, to a showdown between the two houses of Parliament. The outcome severely curtailed the power of the House of Lords to veto legislation passed by the House of Commons, making the House of Commons unequivocally the center of political affairs in Britain.

The Liberals remained in power between 1906 and 1914, partly through agreements with the Labour Party and the Irish delegation to the Parliament. By 1914, these agreements were fast becoming liabilities. The Labour Party was increasingly dissatisfied with its alliance with the Liberals, despite the gains made. Even more important, the working-class militancy grew enormously from 1911 to 1914. A series of strikes in 1911 and 1912 reflected the influence of the idea that change would come only through direct action. In the spring of 1914, a "triple industrial alliance" of transport workers, railwaymen, and miners was formed. Beyond the control of the moderate union officials or the Labour Party, it was watched nervously in the summer of 1914.

That same spring, the question of home rule for Ireland, promised to the Irish delegation in return for their support, came before the House for the third time and passed. Ireland was to receive home rule with no separate provision for Northern Ireland (Ulster). Volunteer armies in Northern and Southern Ireland were already in existence. Many in the British army had indicated that they would not act to enforce home rule. Civil war seemed a possibility. A militant suffragist movement completed the forces, making for what has been described as "domestic anarchy" in 1914. That summer, Britain faced its worst crisis in decades.

The United States of America

In the period before the Great War, the United States of America was emerging as a major power in world affairs. Its population stood at 76 million in 1900. An additional 13 million immigrants, including 1 million Jews, were added prior to 1914, mostly from Central and Southern Europe. The immigrants provided an energetic and willing labor force for the burgeoning northeastern industrial complex that was rapidly becoming the most productive in the world. Between 1900 and 1914, manufacturing replaced agriculture as the nation's chief source of wealth. The great captains of American industry and finance, like J. Pierpont Morgan (1837–1913), Andrew Carnegie (1835–1919), and John D. Rockefeller (1839–1937), were every bit as worthy of note as any of Europe's "robber barons." Blessed with abundant natural resources, a democratic yet business-friendly environment, and a vision of America's destiny, the United States was becoming the world's greatest industrial power.

America's rising status was not due solely to its industrial growth. The same spirit of nationalism that drove Europe's great powers was propelling the United States to establish its place in the sun. The belief in "Manifest Destiny" that drove America's expansion across the continent from the Atlantic to the Pacific oceans was thrusting the United States onto the world stage during the late nineteenth and early twentieth centuries. Albert J. Beveridge (1862–1927), the expansionist senator from Indiana, proclaimed:

> Fate has written our policy for us. . . . The trade of the world must and shall be ours. . . . We will cover the ocean with our merchant marine. We will build a navy to the measure of our greatness. . . . (Tuchman 1966, p. 154)

In 1890, America's navy was little more than a collection of "wash-tubs," as one congressman put it. But that soon changed.

Theodore Roosevelt (1858–1919), the flamboyant Progressive politician, became one of Mahan's fans and disciples, prompting "TR," or "Teddy," as he was affectionately known, to write a book of his own the subject, *The Naval War of 1812* (1882). When he became president in 1901, following the assassination of President William McKinley (1843–1901), TR took every opportunity to make America's presence felt in world affairs. In 1905, Roosevelt offered to mediate between Russia and Japan and hosted the peace conference at Portsmouth, New Hampshire, that ended the Russo-Japanese War. In the following year, Roosevelt was instrumental in persuading his admirer, the Kaiser, to agree to an international conference at Algeciras, to relieve tensions over the Moroccan crisis. In 1907, he sent the new American navy on a cruise around the world, just to show the flag. It was standard TR theatrics, a bit of bluster perhaps, but with a serious purpose.

A booming industrial plant and a great navy were two signs of great-power status or at least the aspiration to such status. Another sign was the acquisition of a colonial empire. Here, too, the United States was taking action that earned it membership in the ranks of the world's imperialist powers at the beginning of the twentieth century.

The Hawaiian Islands were formally annexed to the United States in July 1898. One month later, the Spanish–American War ended, with the United States gaining portions of the old Spanish Empire in the Caribbean and the Pacific. Puerto Rico, Guam, and the

Philippines became American possessions, while the island of Cuba became, in essence, an American protectorate. In 1899, America's demand that China be opened to commercial exploitation by all (the so-called Open Door Policy) was accepted by other Westernized nations with interests in China. Within the Western Hemisphere, the United States asserted a kind of informal sovereignty. With the Roosevelt Corollary (1904) to the Monroe Doctrine, the United States asserted the right to intervene at will in the matters of any Latin American state. When Columbia refused an offer of $10 million for America's right to build a canal through Panama, the United States encouraged the Panamanians to revolt, gaining independence from Columbia. Like Cuba, Panama then became a virtual protectorate of the United States, to whom it "leased" the Canal Zone.

The United States was emerging as a great power before the Great War but was not yet a member of the club. In 1917, it would enter the war to decide its outcome in favor of the Allies but afterwards would retreat into isolation. Not until the second Great War, World War II, would America reenter world affairs. During the Cold War that followed World War II, the United States would be the dominant power in the West. By the end of the century, it would emerge as the dominant power in the world, with no apparent challenger on the horizon.

Japan

The United States forced the opening of Japan to trade with the West in 1854. At first, it appeared that Japan would suffer the same fate as China, but in 1868, a small group of Samurai and noblemen instituted a reform movement known as the Meiji Restoration (1868–1912). The new leadership undertook a program of rapid Westernization, restructuring Japan using what were considered the best of the West as models in each area.

Compulsory education was introduced as was military conscription. At first, France served as the model for restructuring the educational system. Later, Germany replaced France as the inspiration. Germany served also as the model for the new army and Britain for the new imperial navy. A constitution providing for a parliamentary system was introduced in 1889. Once again, Germany provided the model, perhaps because the German Constitution allowed for the outward appearance of a true constitutional system while in fact leaving real power in the hands of a few. One notable difference was the fact that whereas the German Kaiser could rule as well as reign, the Japanese emperor was never much more that the symbol of sovereignty.

Japan followed the Western example in another area. The combination of government-sponsored economic reforms, including industrialization, allowed Japan to become an imperialist power. Japan was the victor in both the Sino-Japanese War (1894–1895) and the Russo-Japanese War (1904–1905). The latter in particular gained international respect for the Japanese army and navy. As early as 1902, Japan entered into an alliance with Great Britain, the first non-Western nation to be recognized as an equal. Korea became a Japanese protectorate in 1905 and was annexed in 1910. Clearly, imperial Japan was a rival of the United States in the Pacific by the beginning of the Great War in 1914.

The Class Structure

The Upper Class

The class structure of Europe before the Great War was still a pyramid, with a handful of very wealthy at the apex and a great multitude of poor at the base. The ruling aristocracy at the turn of the century was a union of the old landed wealth and the new industrial wealth. Titled, land-owning families with pedigrees that stretched back for centuries formed marriage alliances of convenience with the wealthy new plutocrats of commerce and industry. This new elite shared a common pattern of education and consumption and similar economic and political views. Generally, the greater the industrialization of a nation, the more closely tied was the upper middle class to the government. Peers of the realm and the giants of industry and commerce (the "robber barons") often had the same values, the same political interests, and the same condescending attitude toward the propertyless classes at the base of the pyramid.

The Working Class

Most of those at the base of the pyramid were better-off in 1900 than at the beginning of the century. At least this was true for those living in the industrialized nations of Great Britain, France, Belgium, Germany, and the United States. For them, the quality of life was improving. Not only had real wages risen, but purchasing power had almost doubled in the decade before 1914. Even so, poverty was a reality for most Europeans, even for those in the most prosperous nations.

Out of a population of 44.5 million in Great Britain before the war, 15.5 million earned less than £50 a year, this at a time when the "poverty line" was estimated as £55 a year for a family of five (Tuchman 1966). One study of London households in 1899 revealed that almost one-third of the inhabitants of the world's richest city lived in poverty. Poverty was even more pervasive in the less industrialized areas of Eastern and Southern Europe. Life expectancy in the Balkans and in Spain remained at less than 35 in 1900 (Carr 1979).

Politically, the laboring classes were attracted to ideologies that, in contrast to liberalism, emphasized equality of reward over equality of opportunity. The two most attractive political ideologies were anarchism and Social Democracy (i.e., Marxism). Anarchism sought the violent overthrow of all existing order and the establishment of a stateless, voluntary order in its place. Anarchism was most appealing to the urban and rural unemployed in the more backward regions of Eastern and Southern Europe.

More important than anarchism was the appeal of Social Democracy for the working class in the more industrialized nations of Northern and Western Europe. Grounded in Marxism, Social Democracy was undergoing a transformation by 1900. Known as "revisionism" in Germany, the emphasis was shifting away from revolution to evolution. Also, like the Fabian socialists that influenced the Labour Party in Great Britain, the revisionist Social Democrats in Germany looked more and more to a future welfare state as their goal, rather than the classless utopia of Marx's dreams. The desire for "gas and water" socialism was replacing the ideology of class struggle.

The German Social Democratic Party (SPD) was the strongest in Europe. Publicly, it defended Marxist orthodoxy on the need for revolutionary overthrow of bourgeois society and the state. At the same time, many within the party worked for limited improvements through legislative action. This was undoubtedly the goal of the German trade union movement. Although acceptance of the industrial system was never made explicit by the SPD or the trade unions, there were numerous indications that it was tacitly accepted by large numbers within both groups.

The SPD and the German working class have been characterized as existing in a state of "negative integration" with German society in the early part of the twentieth century. Mutual hostility and suspicion prevailed; integration was only partial in that the SPD and the working class did not (and often were not allowed to) participate fully and positively in all aspects of German life. Yet the SPD was set firmly in the framework of German society and German workers participated in national life in many ways. Examples might include the veneration of the Kaiser or working-class fascination with the growth of Germany as a world power.

In general, the working class in Europe reacted to changing circumstances less according to national characteristics than according to the stage of industrialization reached in a particular area. Where experience was lacking, hostility and friction were vented in radical and often violent protest. Where experience with industrial life reached back over two or three generations, a durable if not always satisfying relationship between working class and industrial order emerged. For workers in Britain, France, Belgium, and Germany, the industrial system was becoming increasingly acceptable, even if expectations always seemed to race ahead of fulfillment.

Socialism never gained a significant following in the United States. Part of the reason was the multicultural nature of the working class. In some areas, for example, the South, racism helped to divide the working class. Of all the attempts at organizing a socialist party in America, the Socialist Labor Party was perhaps the most successful, especially under the charismatic leadership of Eugene V. Debs (1855–1926). Debs ran for president as a socialist candidate in 1900,

1904, 1912, and 1920. His share of the popular vote varied from 0.6 percent in 1900 to 3.5 percent in 1920. He conducted his 1920 campaign while a prisoner in the Atlanta Federal Penitentiary.

Another reason for socialism's failure to attract a large following in America was the Progressive Movement of the 1890s through the 1920s. Many historians interpret the period as one of struggles: that between the agricultural West and South and the urban and industrialized East, as well as one between small farmers and urban laborers against Big Business such as railroads and trusts in steel, oil, and other industries. Much of the era's political struggles were waged over the issue of silver versus gold. The debt-ridden farmers hoped that coining silver and gold, a bimetallism of "16 to 1," would lead to an increase in the money supply, thus lowering interest rates and enabling the farmers to pay back their loans and sell their agricultural products more profitably. "Free silver" and "16 to 1" were popular campaign slogans used by those who favored bimetallism.

The Democratic Party embraced the cause of the farmers and free silver in the presidential campaign of 1896, in which the Democratic Party ran the Nebraskan Populist William Jennings Bryan (1860–1925), the "Silver Knight of the West," as its presidential candidate. Bryan was one of the most gifted orators of his time, referred to as the "Boy Orator of the Platte." He often invoked biblical imagery in his speeches, not uncommon in that era. In what was perhaps his greatest moment, Bryan rallied the Democratic Party by identifying the free silver movement as a righteous cause. Concluding a speech before the 1896 Democratic National Convention in Chicago, Bryan thrust his arms out to his sides invoking the dramatic image of Jesus Christ on the cross and proclaimed, "You shall not press down upon the brow of labor this crown of thorns; you shall not crucify mankind upon a cross of gold." Bryan and free silver lost the election of 1896, and again in the 1900, and 1908 presidential elections as well. By 1914, the Progressive Movement was merging with the middle-class movement for reform. The focus shifted to the East and such prominent politicians as Robert La Follette (1855–1925), Theodore Roosevelt (1858–1919), and Woodrow Wilson (1856–1924).

The Middle Classes

In later decades, the middle classes were to view the era before 1914 largely as a golden age, *les bon vieux temps*, "the good old days" in Europe or the "Gilded Age" in American history. In retrospect, it seemed that there had never been a better time for the well-to-do than the two decades before the Great War. A prosperous middle-class family with an annual income of $10,000 could employ a staff of 10 full-time servants for only one-quarter of that income. One measure of middle-class standing was the ability to employ one full-time maid.

Economic opportunities abounded, political influence was increasing, and even social prominence was on the rise. The changing economic structure offered few opportunities for individuals or families to own and control their own enterprises, but this was compensated for by an expansion of positions within management and the civil service. Wider educational opportunities also made it possible for many to enter the professions or the upper reaches of government bureaucracies. Possibilities, especially in Western Europe and America, of achieving a comfortable income and a commensurate status were good.

The middle class was not a unified group. The views of one group of businessmen often conflicted with those of professionals or other business groups. The middle class was, nonetheless, a formidable political power in states where parliamentary government was well established. Politics was increasingly the preserve of professionals, both elected and unelected, and the middle class supplied more and more of these people. At the same time, the middle class furnished the leadership of most major political parties in Europe and America. This was true even of some socialist parties, in which renegade members of the middle class formulated most of the policies and interpreted doctrine for the rank and file. Governments were increasingly sympathetic to middle-class views, as demonstrated by the trend toward protective tariffs and other legislation favorable to business.

The middle class was beginning to set the tone for all of society. The activities of the aristocracy and particularly the royal families of

Europe were still of great interest to many, but, increasingly, standards were set by a new elite drawn from both the middle class and the aristocracy. The upper class with its vast wealth became an important source of patronage for the arts and had a significant influence on fashion and style.

The lower middle class, like the middle class, was not a unified group. One component, the independent lower middle class of shopkeepers, merchants, and artisans, had long been a part of European and American society. It had emphasized familiar middle-class ideals of family, property, and respectability. A second, largely dependent, component was a product of recent structural changes in the economy. The expansion of distribution and sales together with the increased complexity of organization required vast numbers of clerks, salespeople, and technicians. Governments also began to require larger and larger numbers of clerical and technical personnel.

Both the independent and dependent elements of the lower middle class had in common a sense that in terms of status and behavior, they were distinct from the working class. As regards income, however, the lower middle class no longer earned a great deal more than the working class. Lower-middle-class people spent their money differently, however, either buying or saving mainly for items connected with social status, such as a piano; the working class tended to spend on immediate pleasures. The intense consciousness of status was reflected not only in the behavior but also in the politics of the lower middle class, which was usually conservative, antisocialist, and sometimes also anti-Semitic. In politics, the lower middle class favored parties such as the Radical Party in France or the Christian Social Party in Austria, parties that catered to the "little man" and stressed the importance of order, property, and attachment to the nation.

Like the middle class, the lower middle class enjoyed the good times of the era before 1914 including a new measure of prosperity, status, and political power. Living in close proximity to the lower classes, the lower middle class tended to take the good times less for granted than the middle class as well as remain more anxious about any developments that might threaten their position in society.

Swan Song

The West's dominate position in the world was based upon a number of illusions, chief among them the belief that history can somehow be made to stand still. Imperialism is never more than a momentary advantage. It nourishes resentment and envy: resentment because the human spirit can never endure humiliation indefinitely and envy because human beings naturally desire to imitate what symbolizes a better life.

The long history of the rise of Western civilization peaked during the first decade and a half of the twentieth century. Many of the era felt they were living at the dawn of new age of world peace and progress. Others in Europe and abroad in the colonies sensed they were living on the verge of history-making change such as occurs from time to time in world history. Was it like the period of the fourteenth through sixteenth centuries, a waning of the old or the birth something new? Storm clouds were gathering in the sky above. In the spring and summer of 1914, the storm broke, and Europe and the world were plunged into the most destructive war since the collapse of the Roman Empire in the West:

> The silver Swan, who living had no Note,
> when Death approached, unlocked her silent throat.
> Leaning her breast against the reedy shore,
> thus sang her first and last, and sang no more:
> "Farewell, all joys! O Death, come close mine eyes!"
> "More Geese than Swans now live, more Fools than Wise."
> (Orlando Gibbons [1583–1625], *The Silver Swan*.
> http://rpo.library.utoronto.ca/poems/
> silver-swan-who-living-had-no-note)

References

Carr, William. 1979. *A History of Germany, 1815–1945*, 2nd ed. New York: St. Martin's Press.

Kipling, Rudyard. 1899. "The White Man's Burden," *McClure's Magazine* 12 (4): 290–291.

Sulzberger, C. L. 1977. *The Fall of the Eagles*. New York: Crown Publisher.

Tuchman, Barbara W. 1966. *The Proud Tower: A Portrait of the World Before the War: 1890–1914*. New York: Macmillan.

Further Reading

Miranda Carter, Wanda. 2010. *George, Nicholas and Wilhelm: Three Royal Cousins and the Road to World War I*. New York: Alfred A. Knopf. Reveals how powerful but incompetent personalities blundered into a war that brought down the curtain on their world.

Hale, Oron J. 1971. *The Great Illusion, 1900–1914*. New York: HarperCollins and Tuchman, Barbara W. 1966. *The Proud Tower: A Portrait of the World Before the War, 1890–1914*. New York: Macmillan. Both are classic, very readable overviews of the period before the Great War.

Hardwick, Mollie. 1976. *The World of Upstairs, Downstairs*. New York: Holt, Rhinehart and Winston. A lively illustrated social history of Britain from the turn of the century to the Great Depression based upon the popular BBC series.

Hochschild, Adam. 1998. *King Leopold's Ghost: A Study of Greed, Terror, and Heroism in Colonial Africa*. Boston: Houghton Mifflin. A well-written, much-praised case study of the dark side of European imperialism in Africa and the Belgian king whose plantation in the Congo triggered the "scramble of Africa."

Morton, Frederic. 2001. *Thunder at Twilight: Vienna, 1913/1914*. New York: De Capo Press. Life in Vienna on the eve of the Great War is portrayed in very readable and interesting fashion.

Olusoga, David and Casper W. Erichsen. 2011. *The Kaiser's Holocaust: Germany's Forgotten Genocide and the Colonial Roots of Nazism*. London: Faber and Faber. A recent and thorough examination of German imperialism in German South-West Africa (modern day Namibia).

Taylor, A. J. P. 1980. *The Struggle for Mastery in Europe, 1848–1919*. New York: Oxford University Press. Still the best scholarly study of the diplomatic background to the war.

2

The Great War, 1914–1918

Chronology

1914	Archduke Franz Ferdinand assassinated
	Italy defects from the Triple Alliance
	Fighting begins with German invasion of Belgium
	First Battle of the Marne and failure of the Schlieffen Plan
	Battles of Tannenberg Forest and Masurian Lakes
	Turkey enters war on the side of the Central Powers
	Western Front established from English Channel to Switzerland
1915	Beginning of trench warfare along the Western Front
	First use of poison gas at the Second Battle of Ypres
	Italy declares war on Austria-Hungary
	Ill-fated Gallipoli Campaign

Twentieth-Century Europe: A Brief History, 1900 to the Present, Third Edition.
Michael D. Richards and Paul R. Waibel.
© 2014 John Wiley & Sons, Inc. Published 2014 by John Wiley & Sons, Inc.

1916	Battle of Verdun and the Somme
	Sykes–Picot Agreement
	Battle of Jutland
	Woodrow Wilson reelected president of the United States
1917	Zimmerman Telegram
	Germany resumes unrestricted submarine warfare
	Russian (March) Revolution
	United States enters the war against the Central Powers as an Associated Power
	Balfour Declaration
	Russian (November) Revolution
1918	Treaty of Brest-Litovsk; Russia leaves the war
	Major German offensive on the Western Front fails
	Kaiser Wilhelm II abdicates
	Germany asks for armistice
	War ends on November 11

Otto von Bismarck once prophetically said that someday a general European war would result from some foolish incident in the Balkans. The war that Bismarck predicted did result from an event in the Balkans, the assassination of Archduke Ferdinand, heir to the throne of Austria-Hungary. It was known as the "Great War" until the beginning of World War II in 1939, after which it was called World War I. Indeed, some historians suggest that the Great War was only the first round of a truly great war that began in 1914 and did not end until 1945, with a ceasefire between 1918 and 1939.

Some of the very elements that had made Europe master of the world worked in the Great War to destroy it. Industrial productivity and the capacity to mobilize troops and money made possible the horrific carnage few people could have anticipated before 1914. The five years of war and revolution damaged the fabric of European life beyond repair. The contradictions of the prewar period, more or less successfully repressed at the time, emerged to challenge old certainties. It was the end of one era and the beginning of another, and darker, one.

The Coming of the Great War

The long-term causes of the war included the economic and imperial rivalry between the great powers and the armaments race, especially the naval race between Germany and Great Britain. The holding of two peace conferences at The Hague in 1899 and 1907 belied the fact that the participants were arming for war. Many of the tensions between the great powers resulted from the loss of a balance of power in Europe following the Franco-Prussian War and unification of Germany in 1871.

A system of defensive alliances substituted for the balance-of-power principle as the mechanism for maintenance of peace in Europe after 1871. The alliance system was largely the work of German chancellor Otto von Bismarck. According to Bismarck's reasoning, France was the major threat to peace because of its defeat in the Franco-Prussian War and its desire to avenge that affront to French national honor. It became Bismarck's goal in foreign policy to isolate France. Referring to the traditional five great powers of Europe, Bismarck said: "The key was always to be in a majority of three in any dispute among the five great European powers."

The first and most enduring of Bismarck's coalitions was the Dual Alliance between Germany and Austria-Hungary concluded in 1879. The Dual Alliance provided that one partner would aid the other in the event that either was attacked by Russia. The Triple Alliance, concluded in 1882 between Germany, Austria-Hungary, and Italy, bound the three to act together in the event that either Germany or Italy was attacked by France. To allay Russian fears of a hostile Austro-German alliance, Bismarck signed the Reinsurance Treaty with Russia in 1887. It provided for one partner assuming a policy of benevolent neutrality was the other partner attacked. Thus, France was left isolated, while Germany was neatly allied with the other great powers on the continent. Peace was maintained, that is, until Bismarck's retirement in 1890, when his alliance system began to unravel.

Now, Wilhelm II's "new course" in foreign policy, which aimed at elevating Germany to world-power status, stood as a direct challenge to Great Britain's position as the world's leading power. The threat of a great German navy that would rival Britain for control of the seas irked the British. This, coupled with a growing feeling of diplomatic isolation resulting from international criticism of the British for their atrocious treatment of Dutch settlers (including women and children) during the Boer War in South Africa (1899–1902), led the British to abandon its "splendid isolation" and begin to seek allies of its own. In 1902, Britain concluded the Anglo-Japanese Alliance, followed in 1904 and 1907 by two informal "understandings," or "ententes," that resolved outstanding imperial disputes with France and Russia, respectively. Autocratic Russia was already in a formal defensive alliance with democratic France, one concluded in December 1894. Russia, one might justly say, had been pushed into the waiting arms of France by Wilhelm's decision in 1890 not to renew the Reinsurance Treaty. The new alliances between France, Russia, and Britain, when considered together, comprised what became known as the Triple Entente. By 1907, Europe was divided into two increasingly hostile camps, the Triple Alliance and the Triple Entente.

The existence of a potentially dangerous new power alignment in Europe was evident to all parties gathered at the Algeciras Conference in January 1906. The conference had been called after Wilhelm II of Germany provoked a crisis over Morocco in North Africa. He had done so to drive a wedge between France and Britain, by declaring his support of the Sultan of Morocco in the latter's bid to resist French imperialism, and make a public demonstration of Germany's claim to world-power status. In the conference, however, Germany found itself outmaneuvered. In the end, Britain and France stood together against Germany and even were joined by Germany's ally in the Triple Alliance, Italy. With this, Bismarck's alliance system unraveled.

Germany, now supported only by Austria-Hungary, was isolated, much as France had been in 1890. Rather than demonstrating Germany's world-power status, the move had exposed its vulnerability. For the last time, the European great powers would meet together in congress before the outbreak of the Great War.

Just as the continent was polarizing into two hostile camps, the Balkans emerged as the new "hot spot" in Europe. In 1908, Austria-Hungary annexed Bosnia and Herzegovina, which it had been administering since 1878 on behalf of Turkey. Austria's action, supported by Germany, inflamed Serbian nationalism. The Serbs had hoped to create a Great Serbia in the Balkans, and they regarded Bosnia, with its large Serbian population, as a necessary part of such an independent state. Serbian nationalism was encouraged by the Russians, who, following their defeat in the Russo-Japanese War (1904–1905), turned their attention once again to their opportunity in the Balkans, over which region Turkish power and influence was disintegrating. The Balkans was fast becoming the focus of European great-power diplomacy.

As predicted decades before by Otto von Bismarck, the Great War started over an incident in the Balkans, the whole of which, he had contended, was not worth "the healthy bones of a single Pomeranian musketeer." The event that served as the impetus for war was the assassination of Archduke Franz Ferdinand (1863–1914), heir to the throne of Austria-Hungary, by a 19-year-old Serb named Gavrilo Princip (1894–1918). But it was not for the Archduke that the "Guns of August" were unleashed.

Upon hearing of the death of his nephew, of whose marriage he disapproved, the aging emperor Franz Joseph expressed relief—it was, he believed, divine judgment. He did not even bother to attend the funeral. Nonetheless, the British monarch, King George V (1865–1936), expressed his concern for what a terrible shock the news must have been "for the dear old Emperor." Wilhelm II was entertaining a visiting squadron of British battle cruisers at the Kiel naval base when he received the news. "This cowardly, detestable crime," he exclaimed, "has shaken me to the depths of my soul." Franz Ferdinand was a close friend of the Kaiser. They had been hunting together only a week earlier. The most disturbing news of the day for Tsar Nicholas II was word that a madwoman attempted to assassinate Grigori Rasputin (1869–1916), an Orthodox monk believed by many to exercise a dangerous influence over the Tsarina, and, through her, the Tsar. The key players in the drama about to unfold were all shocked by the assassination of the Archduke, but none really wanted a war, none that is except Austria.

If Austria had acted promptly to punish Serbia for its part in the assassination, the rest of the world would no doubt have accepted its decision. But Austria hesitated. Austrian prestige demanded some military action against Serbia, but prudence, or perhaps fear, demanded that Germany's backing be secured first. The delay allowed time for Russia to conclude that Russian prestige could not allow Austria to crush Serbia. Similar crises had occurred in the past but were resolved through diplomacy. In the final analysis, what transformed the July crisis into the cause célèbre for the Great War was a breakdown of diplomacy.

On July 5, Austria obtained assurance of German support for whatever action it chose to take against Serbia. Germany believed that the so-called blank check was justified, in part, because it feared for its own position in Europe should Austria decline as a power. Germany did, however, expect Austria to act while world opinion was still favorable. But Austria delayed further, first to win over Count István Tisza (1861–1918), prime minister of Hungary, and then to launch an investigation into Serbia's actual role in the assassination. In the meantime, Russia's position had begun to harden, and it warned Austria that it would not tolerate the humiliation of Serbia.

Austria ignored the warning and presented an ultimatum to Serbia on July 23. Most of the demands called for the Serbian government to suppress all public criticism, or other activity, that might incite the Serbs against Austria-Hungary. Serbia accepted all but one or two clauses that would have allowed the Austrians to take part in the Serbian investigation of the assassination plot; this, Serbia contended, would infringe on its sovereignty. Serbia's reply was seen by all the powers, Germany and Austria included, as remarkably conciliatory. Yet Austria went ahead with mobilization and a declaration of war on July 28. Although Germany was by this time already beginning to have second thoughts, it did not effectively apply pressure to halt Austrian preparations for war.

Also on July 28, the Russians ordered a partial mobilization and then, for technical reasons, on July 30, ordered full mobilization. Otherwise, Russia had concluded, it would have no chance of influencing Austria. Full mobilization by Russia made it imperative that Germany put the Schlieffen Plan into effect. Since this plan called for Germany to deal with France first, then quickly turn back to the east, each day that the Russians spent mobilizing before the Germans launched their drive to the west further jeopardized the success of the plan. Now, it was all a matter of railroad timetables. Germany attacked France, violating Belgian neutrality in the process. Britain came into the war to aid the French and to defend the principle of neutrality. Of all the great powers, only Italy remained, for the time being, out of the conflict.

The Great War, 1914–1917

The war that the diplomats failed to prevent in July 1914 was not the war the generals were prepared to fight. During that fateful month, they had assured their reluctant monarchs that the conflict would be a brief and glorious little war, not unlike the wars of German unification, in which the rapid deployment of troops on open battlefields had decided the day. Indeed, the military strategies in which the generals of the day were schooled differed little from those employed by their counterparts who waged the Napoleonic wars a hundred years earlier. However, a century of remarkable technological "progress"— one that included the development of railroads, telegraphs and telephones, airplanes, submarines, machine guns, tanks, poison gas, flame throwers, and a great many other wonders of modern civilization—shortly transformed a little conflict in the Balkans into what was up to that time one of the most gruesome wars in history, the Great War, World War I.

The blustery saber-rattling monarchs of those ancient and soon-to-be vanquished empires of Germany, Austria-Hungary, and Russia tried to avert war in the final hours before the first gun sounded.

There was a rapid exchange of notes between Wilhelm II and his cousin, Tsar Nicholas II. Nicholas pleaded with Wilhelm to restrain Austria, for he was being "overwhelmed by pressure" and would soon "be forced to take extreme measures" leading to war.

Neither was the Kaiser, Germany's supreme warlord, in command of the snowballing events. As the German Chancellor Theobald von Bethmann-Hollweg (1856–1921) related to the Prussian Council of Ministers on July 30, despite the peaceful intentions of everyone concerned, events were progressing under their own momentum. If anyone was in control of the direction of those events as the crisis deepened, it was the generals. They, themselves, however, were captive to concrete plans for mobilization and war, plans with which they felt unable to tinker, even in the minutest detail.

The Failure of the Schlieffen Plan

The fateful role played by the war plans was particularly evident in the case of Germany. The German plan for war, known as the Schlieffen Plan after General Alfred von Schlieffen (1833–1913), chief of the German General Staff from 1891 to 1905, presupposed a two-front war with France and Russia. It was a bold plan that called for the rapid movement of German forces through neutral Belgium, to the north and west of Paris, in a sweeping arc that would encircle and crush the French armies. Once this had been accomplished, German forces would turn back to the Eastern Front in time to deal with the Russian armies, which would just then be completing mobilization, according to German calculations. Within six weeks, the war would be over and Germany's position as a world power secured. The Schlieffen Plan was a daring gamble.

While the Schlieffen Plan looked good on paper, a number of miscalculations and unforeseen exigencies undid its successful execution. On July 31, Germany refused a British demand that Belgium neutrality, guaranteed by international treaty since 1839, be respected. Three days later, Belgium rejected a German demand for free passage across its territory. By the afternoon of August 3, German troops were pouring into Belgium. On August 4, Germany declared war on Belgium, referring to the 1839 treaty as "a scrap of paper." Although no match for the swiftly advancing Germans, the Belgians put up a valiant fight, slowing the German advance and costing the German army time critically needed were the Schlieffen Plan to succeed.

Belgian resistance was not factored into the Schlieffen Plan. Neither was the speed with which the Russians managed to throw an army into East Prussia on August 17. To meet the Russian threat, and believing the war against France already won, General Helmuth von Moltke (1848–1916) detached two corps from his vital right wing and sent them east. It was a fatal error. With other corps already detached to hold the Belgians at Antwerp, von Moltke's move seriously weakened the German army's right wing, upon which the Schlieffen Plan depended. On August 30, with the Schlieffen Plan days behind schedule, Moltke began to have doubts, turning his right flank south while still east of Paris. This maneuver opened the door for the French commander-in-chief, Joseph Joffre (1852–1931), to launch a counterattack against the German left flank along the Marne River. The First Battle of the Marne, September 5–9, remembered as the "Miracle of the Marne," saved France from a swift defeat by halting the German advance. General von Moltke resigned in disgrace.

Meanwhile in the East, the Germans had managed to halt the Russian advance at the Battles of Tannenberg Forest (August 30) and Masurian Lakes (September 15). General Aleksandr Samsonov (1859–1914), the Russian commander at the Battle of Tannenberg, attempted to redeem his honor by committing suicide, while Field Marshal Paul von Hindenburg (1847–1934) and General Erich Ludendorff (1865–1937), the victors of Tannenberg, emerged as heroes. As the war progressed, the two men became virtual military dictators of Germany.

A great many volumes have been written by historians trying to explain what caused the Great War; who, if anyone, was to blame for it; as well as why the Schlieffen Plan failed. With respect to the former, it is true, as the German historian Fritz Fischer has alleged, that Germany ambitiously pursued world-power status. It is also true, as the English historian A. J. P. Taylor has demonstrated, that

Europe in 1914

the German plan for mobilization was tantamount to a declaration of war, since the said mobilization was to be completed outside Germany—inside France and Belgium. When all the arguments and counterarguments have been considered, however, the comment of the British prime minister, David Lloyd George, that the European great powers simply slithered over the brink into a war no one desired remains the best explanation. Diplomacy had failed. In a similar vein, the historical consensus today is that the Schlieffen Plan was a desperate gamble that, even under the best of circumstances, had little chance to succeed.

In the wake of the failed Schlieffen Plan in the West, the so-called race to the sea ensued. The opposing armies, French corps joined by the British Expeditionary Force (BEF) and the Belgium army against the German army, tried to outflank each other, as they steadily moved north to the English Channel. By December 25, the soldiers, who went into battle with expectations of being home for Christmas, stood opposite each other in a line of trenches that stretched from the English Channel in the north to Switzerland in the south, a distance of about 400 miles. There followed nearly four years of stalemate, wherein the line of trenches remained virtually unchanged despite the expenditure of millions of casualties in futile attempts to break through the lines and turn the stalemate into a war of motion the generals could understand. This "troglodyte world" of trench warfare would later strain the imaginations of artists, writers, and poets, as they tried to depict it for those who had not experienced the horror of it firsthand.

Trench Warfare

The Great War was like no other war before it, although there were some hints of what this first industrial war might entail. The American Civil War (1861–1865), the Boer War (1899–1902), and the Russo-Japanese War (1904–1905) each foreshadowed in some way what "industrialized warfare" would mean. Even "Queen Victoria's little wars" in the colonial world should have provided some insight. The effectiveness of rapid-firing machine guns at, for example, the Battle of Omdurman in the Sudan (1898) had demonstrated the obsolescence of massed cavalry or infantry charges in modern warfare. But these lessons were lost on the generals who planned the battles of the Great War. Unlike the campaigns of Julius Caesar or the great Napoleon, the more recent battles were not in the textbooks studied at Europe's prestigious military academies. In response to the machine guns, the soldiers went underground.

Siegfried Sassoon (1886–1967), a British infantry officer and war poet, once commented that "when all is said and done the war was mainly a matter of holes and ditches." And in the Great War, these

Along the Western Front from the English Channel to the Swiss border was an elaborate complex of zigzagging trenches in parallel lines. Courtesy Dayton Castleman

holes and ditches were enormously complicated. For example, the French system, with a frontage of about 270 miles, contained approximately 6,250 miles of trenches of one sort or another. Trenches usually were arranged in three roughly parallel lines: first came the frontline trench; several hundred yards behind which lay the support trench; and, finally, another few hundred yards behind the support trench ran the reserve trench. In addition to the three parallel lines of trenches, the firing trenches from which attacks were launched and enemy attacks repulsed, there were various trenches running perpendicular to some or all of the firing trenches. Behind the front, there were communication trenches through which ammunition, reinforcements, and food were brought up to the front. Running out from the front line into "No Man's Land" (the space between the front lines of the opposing armies) were "saps," shallow ditches leading to forward posts for observation, listening, grenade throwing, and machine-gun placements. Dimensions of firing trenches varied, but they would almost always be deeper than a man was tall, with, on the enemy side, a parapet of earth or sandbags rising another 2 or 3 feet off the ground. Trenches were built in a zigzag fashion to minimize damage from shelling and to make it difficult for an attacking enemy to clear a trench. In the sides of the trenches were one- or two-man holes, "funk holes," and deeper dugouts. There was something of a national style in trenches: German trenches tended to be deeper, drier, and more elaborate than British or French systems; the British systems seemed the most provisional and least carefully worked out.

With the digging of the trenches, the war of motion, the traditional war the generals understood, ended. Throughout the Great War, the generals on both sides hoped to break the stalemate on the Western Front and turn the conflict back into a war of motion. The strategy for the great breakthrough was the same on both sides. Large numbers of troops were massed at some spot along the front. Artillery bombarded the enemy trenches unceasingly (for seven days and nights at the Battle of the Somme) to "soften up" the enemy's position. Then, the artillery fell silent, and the command was given for the infantry to "go over the top" and across the No Man's Land of 100–500 yards before meeting the first line of the enemy's trenches. Trudging through a barren waste of barbed wire, shell holes, and rotting bodies from previous failed assaults, the advancing infantrymen typically were cut down by enemy machine guns. Perhaps the first line of trenches would be taken, but eventually, the assault failed, and the advancing columns, or what was left of them, fell back to their own trenches to await counterattack. And so it continued, without significantly altering the line of the opposing trenches.

The sights and sounds of trench warfare were enough to change forever those who experienced it. The sight of mass mutilation was everywhere. Ernst Jünger (1895–1998), a novelist who won Germany's highest decoration, described a scene near the front at the Somme after enemy artillery made a direct hit on a house where German soldiers were quartered:

We grabbed the limbs sticking out of the rubble and pulled the corpses out. One was missing its head, and the neck sat on the torso like a large bloody fungus. On another shattered bones protruded from the stump on an arm, and the uniform was sodden with blood from a huge chest wound. On a third the innards flowed forth from a body that had been slit open. As we were pulling this one out, a splintered board that had stuck in the terrible wound gave resistance, making gruesome sounds. (Eksteins 1990, p. 152)

An Englishman whose dugout was hit with a shell took a photograph of his dead comrade lying next to him, his body "laid open from the shoulders to the haunches like a quartered carcass in a butcher's window" (Eksteins 1990, p. 152). Such scenes were not easily forgotten when the war was over.

Between assaults, life in the trenches was an incessant struggle against boredom, extremes of weather, and the pitiless assault of the vermin that infested the trenches. At Flanders, rains transformed the battlefield into a quagmire of mud into which a fallen soldier could disappear from sight and drown. Winter along the Western Front could be so cold that wine froze in November, and rations turned into chunks of ice. To such discomforts were added the ever-present battle against vermin attracted by the stench of the trenches and the men and corpses that occupied them.

Some of the pests, such as flies, fleas, and mosquitoes, were a nuisance that the battle-hardened warrior could get used to, but the lice and the rats were different. Lice laid their eggs in the soldiers' clothing and multiplied with terrifying speed. Nothing helped. Hot baths and washing clothing, when possible, brought only temporary relief. Soldiers on both sides took consolation in the belief that the lice afflicting the enemy were larger.

Rats were everywhere, attracted by the rotting corpses in the trenches. Soldiers reported rats as large as cats or small dogs. The battle against the rats, fought with spades, clubs, or whatever was readily at hand, was an unceasing one. For some, "rat hunting" became an obsession, vented during the interludes between assaults. The only relief from the rats and other vermin came as a result of a gas attack, which temporarily cleared the trenches of vermin. But, like the enemy across No Man's Land, the rats and the lice returned.

The enthusiasm that greeted the call to arms in July–August 1914 died in the trenches. In addition, the trenches bred a sense of alienation and estrangement from civilian life and values that endured long after the war. The life the soldiers lived before the war seemed distant and unrecoverable. Life in the trenches had to be experienced to be understood. If the civilians back home could somehow see it, wrote Wilfred Owen (1893–1918), one of England's greatest poets, who died one week before the Armistice, then

> My friend, you would not tell with such high zest,
> To children ardent for some desperate glory,
> The old Lie: Dulce et decorum est
> Pro patria mori.
> ("It is sweet and becoming to die for one's country,"
>   a quotation from the Roman poet, Horace.)
>   (Walter 2006, pp. 141–142)

The Course of the War: 1915

Though the Schlieffen Plan had failed, the Germans were in a strong position at the beginning of 1915. They had gained control of Belgium and the industrialized northern regions of France. General Erich von Falkenhayn (1861–1922) assumed command from the failed Moltke and launched a major offensive against the British in April at Ypres, in Belgium. The battle, known as the Second Battle of Ypres (April 22–May 24), is primarily remembered for the use of poison gas by the Germans. Taking advantage of favorable winds, the Germans released the gas from canisters in their own trenches. (The first recorded use of poison gas in the war was in August 1914, when the French used tear gas containing xylyl bromide to slow the German advance in Belgium.) The surprise gas attack opened a large gap in the British lines, but the Germans were not prepared to take full advantage of it. They broke off the attack in late May. After the failure at Ypres, the Germans assumed a defensive posture on the Western Front while simultaneously attempting to defeat the Russians on the Eastern Front and rescue their beleaguered ally, Austria–Hungary.

Austria, who many believed had started the war, was on the verge of collapse by the end of May 1915. A Russian offensive in 1914 had captured Galicia and threatened Hungary. Italy, having defected from the Triple Alliance in 1914 by declaring neutrality, succumbed to Allied bribes and declared war on Austria-Hungary on May 23, 1915. (Italy did not declare war on Germany until August 28, 1916.) Also, Austria's conscripts from among its polyglot empire's minorities were deserting in large numbers. To save the situation, the Germans launched a major offensive on the Eastern Front. The Russians fell back, abandoning not only Galicia, but Poland. The Germans, however, were unable to achieve their objective of trapping the Russian armies.

If victory eluded the Germans in 1915, so too did it elude the Allies. The Italians entered the war militarily unprepared. Otto von Bismarck once observed that the Italians had a big appetite but not

Millions of soldiers died on the Western Front along the "Path of Glory." Here a German soldier lies among the barbed wire after a night raid. © The Print Collector/Alamy

the teeth to match it. As the war dragged on, they proved to be more of a burden than an asset to the Allies.

After Italy's defection to the Allies in August of 1914, Turkey entered the war on the side of the Central Powers two months later, in October 1914. In an effort to relieve pressure on the Western Front and open a supply route to Russia, the Allies launched a campaign against Turkey aimed at capturing Constantinople. The campaign, known as the Battle of Gallipoli, the Gallipoli Campaign, or the Dardanelles Campaign, was the brainchild of Winston Churchill (1874–1965), first lord of the admiralty, supported by David Lloyd George, chancellor of the exchequer, and Field Marshal Horatio Herbert Kitchener (1850–1916). An allied force of Australian, New Zealand, and French troops began landing at Sula Bay in present-day Turkey on August 8. Poorly planned and executed, the campaign was a disaster.

Direction of Allied war efforts in the West remained in French hands during 1915. Joffre, no longer believing that one great victory would end the war, hit upon a plan to bleed the enemy to death, a grim strategy the French called "war of attrition." The phrase later took on a surrealistic life beginning with the Battle of Verdun in February 1916. Meanwhile, Joffre launched a series of offensives beginning in May. By the end of the year, despite great losses, the Allies had gained nothing. The front remained virtually in the same place where it had lay at the beginning of the year.

Sausage Machine: 1916

The common soldier, we are told by the British novelist and poet Robert Graves (1895–1995), spoke of the front as the "sausage machine," because "it was fed with live men, churned out corpses, and remained firmly screwed in place" (*Observer* 1950). A sausage machine was an appropriate image for the major battles fought along the Western Front during 1916. Each side began the year believing that the elusive great breakthrough could be achieved by massing enormous quantities of men and firepower along a limited sector of the front.

The Germans set the example at the Battle of Verdun. Verdun was of no strategic importance to either side, but General Falkenhayn believed, correctly, that the French would defend it doggedly. Falkenhayn reasoned that if the Germans could kill five French soldiers for every two Germans the French killed, it was possible to bleed the French white at Verdun.

The battle opened on February 21, with a German artillery bombardment that rained two million shells down on Verdun and its ring of forts. General Henri-Philippe Pétain (1856–1951) was sent in to take command of the defense of the fortress. "They shall not pass," Pétain declared, which became a famous motto. Falkenhayn forgot his original intentions and became as obsessed with capturing Verdun as Pétain was with saving it. When the bloodletting finally halted almost 10 months later, on December 16, half a million men had perished in the sausage machine. Nearly one-half of them were Germans. Total casualties (killed and wounded) were reckoned at 400,000 for the French and over 350,000 for the Germans. Clearly, Falkenhayn had miscalculated. Verdun was the longest battle of the war.

In an effort to relieve pressure on Verdun and to end the war, the Allies planned a major, three-pronged offensive for the summer of 1916. The British were to attack along the Somme River. The Italians were to attack Austria along the Isonzo River, and the Russians were to launch a major offensive into both Poland and Galicia.

The Russian offensive opened on June 4, but after some initial success, the Russian steamroller ran out of steam and stalled without having achieved its objectives. The Italians attacked the Austrians on August 6 with their usual results. Despite heavy casualties, they were able to capture only the town of Gorizia. Meanwhile on July 1, the British began the bloodiest battle of the war along the Somme.

The site chosen by the British command was heavily fortified by the Germans and of no strategic importance. An impressive arsenal of heavy and light artillery, tanks, and airplanes was assembled along a 23-mile front. The British had a record number of artillery pieces, a total of 1,500, or an average of one for every yard of the front for which they were responsible. The British began the battle on June 24 with a seven-day-and-night bombardment of the German trenches.

Four million rounds were fired by the British guns on the first day. Sir Douglas Haig (1861–1928), commander of the Allied forces, expected the artillery bombardment to win the battle before the infantry, and possibly even cavalry, would move in to "mop up" whatever resistance remained.

The Allied artillery barrage failed to do its job. It did not, for example, cut the barbed wire as expected. The German machine gun crews simply went underground and waited. When the British and French infantry went "over the top," on July 1, the Germans emerged from their dugouts and manned the machine guns. The slaughter that ensued was made all the more certain by orders that the advancing infantrymen attack in formation while carrying 66 pounds of equipment each. The result was the highest casualty rate in the history of modern warfare. The British alone suffered 60,000 casualties, including 40 percent of their officer corps, on the first day of the offensive. Not one yard had been gained. When the battle ended on November 18, the British had sacrificed over 400,000 men and the French over 200,000. German casualties stood at about 450,000.

The inconclusiveness of the campaigns of 1916, including the only major naval battle of the war, the Battle of Jutland in May, led to changes in the German and French commands, but not that of the British. Falkenhayn was replaced by the team of Hindenburg–Ludendorff. On the French side, Joffre was replaced by General Robert Nivelle (1856–1924), whose inept leadership brought on the massacre of French soldiers at the Second Battle of the Aisne in April 1917 and the subsequent mutiny of some 54 divisions.

Away from the front, the Austrian Emperor Franz Joseph died on November 21, 1916, after 68 years on the throne. His successor and grandnephew, Karl I, began looking for a way out of the war. More auspicious for the future perhaps was the reelection of Woodrow Wilson (1856–1924) as president of the still neutral United States.

The costliest calendar year of the Great War, 1916, had been a bloodbath during which human lives had been reduced to a matter of statistics, just like any other material resource. The civilians on the home front, too, were beginning to feel the intensive stress of prolonged industrialized war.

The Home Front

Unless there is a decisive victory early in the war, a modern industrial war will be decided on the home front. In a prolonged war, the advantage lies with the side that is best able to organize its economic and human resources. Otherwise, the heroism of the soldiers at the front is in vain. This was one of the lessons the leaders of 1914 should have learned from, for example, the American Civil War, but had not. None of the belligerents was prepared for so prolonged a war. By the end of 1915, each government was taking steps in order to wage "total war." As a result, the role of government in regulating economic life and manipulating public opinion reached heights from which it has never fully descended.

Germany was the first to mobilize its economic resources. As early as 1914, Walther Rathenau (1867–1922), one of the nation's leading industrialists, began to organize each branch of production so that raw materials were allocated to producers who were the most efficient and involved with work of the highest priority. Rathenau also pushed efforts to develop substitute products and to manufacture some items synthetically. His *Kriegsrohstoffabteilung* (KRA or War Raw Materials Administration) became a model for state organization and regulation of the economy. It was not until the end of 1916, however, that a comprehensive attempt was made to mobilize the human resources of Germany through the Auxiliary Service Law, which placed all males between the ages of 17 and 60 at the disposal of the war effort.

Germany's eastern ally was less successful at organizing the home front. In Austria-Hungary, the competition of the two halves of the empire for food thwarted any attempt to set up a unitary agency such as Germany's KRA or Britain's Ministry of Munitions. As the war deepened, the inherent ethnic conflicts within Austria-Hungary crippled all such efforts at organizing the economy or public opinion. Indeed, urged on by Allied propaganda, the various nationalities and ethnic groups of the empire did what they could to undermine the war effort.

If the outlook in Austria-Hungary was grim, in Russia, it was virtually hopeless. No belligerent suffered more from a failure of leadership than Russia, which did the least of any of the warring nations to mobilize the home front. The Tsar and his officials greeted with suspicious hostility all efforts at cooperation between the government and citizenry to bring together resources and solve the problems of supply and distribution plaguing the Russian war effort. Everywhere, Russian officials saw civilian attempts to help as efforts to bring in reform and revolutionary change by the back door, thereby undermining the autocracy. Apparently, Russia's leaders feared constitutional change more than military defeat.

The British and French faced fewer problems than the three empires in the east, but both nations still had to struggle to improvise the means for conducting war on an unprecedented scale. Rumors of a shortage of shells led to a broadening of the Liberal cabinet in Britain into a nonpartisan regime in May 1915. Following this, in July of that year, a Ministry of Munitions was created, headed by David Lloyd George. He quickly turned the ministry into the British equivalent of Germany's KRA, controlling the allocation of resources and men and the level of profits from the manufacture of arms. Through his control of the munitions industry, Lloyd George was increasingly involved in the regulation of the entire economy.

In France, the government (i.e., the military) had extensive authority to commandeer resources in time of war, a tradition going back to the revolution. France, like Britain, benefitted from the Royal Navy's blockade of Germany. Both allies could draw upon imperial resources, as well as those of the United States. Everywhere, the increased role of big government in the regulation of the economy was one of the most important legacies of the Great War.

The United States Congress declared war on Germany on April 6, 1917 and began putting in place a massive mobilization of the American economy and its people. A military draft was introduced in 1917, resulting in a military force of almost five million men, including both volunteers and draftees. Bernard Baruch (1870–1965), a leading financier, was at the head of the newly created War Industries Board and charged with aiding private industry to produce for the war effort. Among the goals was to assure peace between labor and management so as to maintain high levels of industrial output. In order to assure an adequate food supply for the new army and to help feed the European Allies, President Wilson created the United States Food Administration (USFA) and appointed the future president, Herbert Hoover (1874–1964), United States Food Administrator. Farmers were assured of a fair price for what they produced. Civilians were encouraged to conserve food and resources for the war effort by planting "Victory gardens" in backyards and going along with called-for "wheatless" Wednesdays, "meatless" Tuesdays, "fuel-less" Mondays, and "gasless" Sundays, and much more. By such efforts, domestic food consumption was reduced by 15 percent, agricultural yield increased by 25 percent, and exports of food to the Allies was increased more than threefold.

In the atmosphere of total war, civilians, no less than soldiers, were an important resource that had to be mobilized. Each nation introduced conscription, not only to assure adequate fighting forces but to ensure that skilled workers remained in the factories. The war benefitted the working classes. Unemployment virtually vanished and the increasing importance of the labor force, together with its loyalty, led to an increased acceptance of worker's rights in general and trade unions and collective bargaining in particular.

The demand for soldiers also opened up employment opportunities for women at home. Women stepped in to fill the slots left in the factories by men in training camps and on the front. In Britain alone, approximately 1.5 million women obtained jobs previously not open to them or in which they had only nominal representation. As with labor, the role played by women in the war effort helped to advance women's efforts for equality. It was much harder after the war for society to resist, for example, the demand for women's suffrage.

On the negative side of the ledger, civil liberties suffered as opposition to the war mounted. As enthusiasm for the war among the general populace slackened with so many men and boys away and bombarded by one dreary newspaper headline after another, governments stepped up the level of war propaganda they generated in attempts to shore it up. Atrocity stories about the enemy, often false or exaggerated, helped to transform the war into a moral crusade for justice.

Opposition to the war on moral or other grounds was viewed as treasonous. In England, the Defense of the Realm Act (1914) permitted the arrest of dissenters as traitors and the censorship of newspapers or even their outright suspension. In France, after Georges Clemenceau (1841–1929) became virtual dictator in November 1917, civil liberties were suppressed. Newspaper editors were drafted for publishing negative reports on the war or, in at least one case, executed for treason.

The United States, land of freedom and liberty, was no less vigorous than the European powers in suppressing all signs of opposition to the war and perfecting the use of propaganda to build support for America's entry into the conflict. Scholars, clergymen, and entertainers of every sort were recruited to shape public opinion. The popular evangelist and former baseball player, William Ashley "Billy" Sunday (1862–1935) combined salvation with patriotism in his highly popular sermons. He portrayed the war as a struggle between Heaven and Hell. If Hell were turned upside down, said Billy, "Made in Germany" would be found stamped on the bottom.

Citizens' civil liberties, guaranteed by the US Constitution, were openly and "legally" violated. Private patriotic organizations (vigilantes) worked together with the FBI to find draft dodgers, spies, or any person or organized group who opposed America's war effort. The Espionage Act of 1917, together with the Sedition Act of 1918, made any criticism of the military, government, or even the American flag a federal offense. Violations were punishable by fines, imprisonment, or even death. War led to fear and hysteria in all of the warring nations, often calling into question the very ideals they were fighting—and dying—to guarantee.

The War around the World

The European great powers were imperial powers with, at least in the case of Great Britain, France, and Germany, colonial possessions around the world. Hence, the Great War was fought all over the world, not just in Europe. Also, the British and French used native colonial troops in Europe. The fact that the Ottoman Empire was one of the Central Powers, and the fact that Russia stretched from Central Europe across Eurasia to the Pacific Ocean, also globalized the war.

Except for Gallipoli, the war against the crumbling Ottoman Empire was largely overshadowed by the war in Europe. The British mobilized an army of two million, including a large number of troops from India, Australia, and New Zealand. The Turks wanted to capture the Suez Canal in order to cut Britain's lifeline to India. The British meant to defend the canal and secure the supply of oil. The heavy use of airplanes, trucks, and tanks in the prosecution of the war turned oil into a vital resource. The British forces were not prepared for the desert environment near the canal. Temperatures there reached 125 degrees Fahrenheit, and monsoon-like rains and extended supply lines caused much suffering among their troops. There was an Arab saying that when the Devil created Hell, he found it too pleasant; therefore, he created Mesopotamia and added flies. Filth and disease combined with intense heat, blowing sand, and the scarcity of water to create a nightmare in the Middle East to some extent comparable to the nightmare being experienced by the entrenched troops in Europe.

The war in the Middle East was, at least, a brand of war the generals understood. It was one of motion in which cavalry still played an important role. Colonel T. E. Lawrence (1888–1935), a British army intelligence officer serving in Cairo, Egypt, in 1914, was instrumental in effecting an Arab revolt against the Turks. The Arab irregular forces led by Colonel Lawrence captured the strategically important port of Aqaba on the Gulf of Aqaba in July 1917. A British force under the command of General Edmund Allenby captured Jerusalem in December 1917 and Damascus in October 1918.

In order to bring the Arabs into the war against Turkey, Sir Henry McMahan (1862–1949), British high commissioner in Egypt, made certain commitments to Sharif Hussein bin Ali of Mecca (1853–1949). In an exchange of correspondence between McMahan and Sharif Hussein (July 1915–January 1916), McMahan offered, or appeared to offer, British support for an independent Arab state that, if the war went their way, would include all of the Arab lands then under Turkish rule. Sharif Hussein understood those lands to include Palestine. However, the British were simultaneously seeking the support of the Jewish people. In a letter dated November 2, 1917, to Lord Walter Rothschild (1868–1937), a leader of the Jewish community in Britain and pro-Zionist, British Foreign Minister Arthur James Balfour (1848–1930) stated that Britain would use its influence to secure in Palestine a national home for the Jews. The letter was made public and is referred to ever since as the "Balfour Declaration."

The Balfour Declaration obviously lay at odds with promises made to the Arabs. So, practically speaking, promises were just that, promises. On May 19, 1916, Britain and France reached an agreement known as the Sykes–Picot Agreement, according to which the Arab lands belonging to the Ottoman Empire would be divided among the two. Neither the promises made to the Arabs nor the Balfour Declaration was to be implemented in the manner in which the Arabs or the Jews expected. The European great powers did not envision a postwar world significantly different than that of the period before the Great War. They did not realize that arousing nationalist feelings among colonial peoples would have fatal consequences for their empires.

The outcome of the war in Africa, however, came as no surprise. With the exception of German East Africa, the German colonies were all taken by British and French military forces, assisted by Portuguese and South African forces. Although of no great significance for the outcome of the war in Europe, the struggle for German East Africa was one of the most interesting of the whole war. In it, Colonel (later General) Paul von Lettow-Vorbeck (1870–1964) fought a guerilla war with a mixed force of German and African (Askari) soldiers. Always greatly outnumbered and forced to depend on captured supplies or what could be found at hand, Lettow-Vorbeck was nonetheless able carry on the war in German South East Africa from November 1914 until a telegram arrived informing him that the war was over in Europe. He surrendered undefeated to British forces on November 25, 1918, two weeks after the fighting ended on the Western Front in Europe. His remaining army consisted of 155 Germans, 1,168 Askari, and approximately 3,500 porters.

Minor battles were fought elsewhere in the world. When hostilities began in 1914, the Japanese, allied with Britain since 1902, seized German possessions in China and some minor islands in the

Pacific. German Samoa surrendered in August 1914 to a small force from New Zealand. German New Guinea surrendered to a small force from Australia after a brief skirmish. Two minor naval battles were fought in 1914, the Battle of Coronel off the coast of Chile in November and the Battle of the Falklands off the coast of Argentina in December. The Germans won the first and lost the second.

Decision, 1917–1918

When 1917 opened, all of the belligerents were at the point of exhaustion. For each side, 1917 was unquestionably the low point in the war. Yet the scales were not clearly tipped in anyone's favor. As the momentous events of 1917 unfolded, it seemed possible that either side might snatch victory from the jaws of defeat. What eventually assured an Allied victory was the entry of the United States into the war on April 6, 1917, as an "Associated Power" of the Allies.

The American entry into the war, although seemingly inevitable when viewed with the benefit of hindsight, was not a foregone conclusion in January 1917. In December 1916, President Wilson asked the belligerents to state their war aims in an attempt to bring about a negotiated peace. It is astonishing to recall that after more than two years of bloodletting, neither side had actually formulated any specific aims. In December 1916, both sides felt no need to be conciliatory, and hence, the demands of each amounted to nothing short of complete victory. On January 24, just over two weeks after Wilson stated his Fourteen Points as a basis for negotiations, Germany and Austria-Hungary declined a joint American–British peace proposal. Wilson, who had recently campaigned for reelection (1916) on a slogan of "he kept us out of war," was rebuffed in his crusade to end the hostilities.

On January 17, 1917, British naval intelligence intercepted a telegram from the German foreign minister, Arthur Zimmermann (1864–1940), to the German envoy in Mexico, suggesting a possible alliance between Germany and Mexico. The American public opinion, already angered by Germany's decision of January 31 to resume unrestricted submarine warfare, was further aroused by release of the telegram to the public on March 1. It was the renewal of unrestricted U-Boat attacks, however, that compelled President Wilson to seek a declaration of on Germany.

The Germans' attempt to starve Britain—long dependent upon its world trade—into submission by sinking, without warning, all ships on their way to Britain was a desperate gamble. When the Kaiser pointed out that such a move would surely bring the United States into the war against Germany, he was assured that not a single American soldier would set foot on the continent before England surrendered. It was a fatal miscalculation.

Believing that the German crimes against American lives on the high seas were of such a nature that they could only be addressed by the United States becoming a belligerent, Wilson asked the Congress for a declaration of war. On April 6, 1917, the Congress complied with the president's request. With the vast human and material resources of the United States available to the Allies, it appeared only a matter of time before the Central Powers would be defeated. But the outcome was not yet certain.

The American entry into the war was made more plausible by events unfolding in Russia during early 1917. Between March 8 and 14,[1] a revolution broke out that toppled the autocratic tsarist regime (see Chapter 3). A Provisional Government was established by former deputies of the Duma as a first step toward the creation of a liberal-democratic government. This initial phase of what would prove to be a two-part Russian Revolution had two immediate influences: the end of the autocratic rule of the Tsar and the promise of a constitutional government in Russia helped move American opinion in favor of intervention in the war. It was simply easier for Americans to enter a war "to make the world safe for democracy" if they would be fighting alongside a constitutional rather than tsarist Russia.

A second immediate influence of the March revolution in Russia was to energize the German command with new hope, perhaps the

---

[1]   Russians were still using the Julian calendar in 1917, which was 13 days behind the Gregorian calendar used in the West. Hence, the events are often referred to as the "February" and "October" revolutions.

last hope, for a German victory in the war. If Germany could bring the war with Russia to an end and transfer significant numbers of troops from the Eastern Front to the Western Front, it was possible to achieve victory before American troops began to arrive in Europe. The decision of the new Provisional Government of Russia to defy popular demand and remain in the war caused further deterioration of the Russian home front and a second revolution on November 7, led by the Bolsheviks. The Bolshevik Revolution brought to power a communist government committed to an immediate end to the war. Russia requested an armistice on December 5 and began negotiations on March 5, 1918. Germany was victorious on the Eastern Front. Still, the outcome of the Great War itself remained to be decided on the Western Front.

In a final desperate effort to achieve victory on the Western Front, Germany launched the last major offensive of the war, on March 21. Ludendorff threw everything he had left into the offensive. The Allies were taken by surprise. The Germans made significant gains against the British sector, briefly turning the war back into a war of motion. On March 23, the Germans began bombarding Paris from 75 miles (120 kilometers) using the so-called Paris Gun (a.k.a., the "Williams Gun"), the largest artillery piece of the Great War. On May 30, the Germans were within 55 miles of Paris. As in 1914, the French government made preparations to leave the capital. Time, however, was running out for the Germans.

On July 18, buttressed by nine fresh American infantry divisions, the Allies counterattacked. A surprise British assault on August 8, assisted by 450 tanks, gained 5 miles in half a day, as the German lines began to crack. Ludendorff called it "the black day" of the German army. On September 4, the Germans retreated to the Siegfried Line, a defensive line from Lens to Rheims. With military defeat imminent, and in an effort to prevent a "revolution from below" as had just occurred in Russia, Ludendorff and Hindenburg informed the Kaiser on September 29 that they needed to reach an armistice immediately.

The news of the impending defeat stunned the Kaiser. After admitting that he could not work miracles, he appointed his cousin, the liberal Prince Max von Baden (1867–1929), chancellor. On the following day, the Prince asked President Wilson for an armistice as preliminary to a peace conference to negotiate a settlement on the basis of Wilson's Fourteen Points.

With Germany's allies already suing for peace, and with a mutiny among the sailors at Kiel, the Kaiser yielded to advice from Hindenburg and abdicated on November 9. At the request of the British royal family, he was granted exile in the Netherlands. Two days later, at 5 A.M., a German delegation signed the armistice. In accordance with the terms of the agreement, the fighting stopped at 11 A.M. on November 11, 1918. At long last, "all quiet on the Western Front."

References

Eksteins, Modris. 1990. *Rites of Spring: The Great War and the Birth of the Modern Age*. New York: Anchor Books.

Observer. "What Was That War Like, Sir?" London. November 9, 1950.

Walter, George, ed. 2006. *The Penguin Book of First World War Poetry*. London: Penguin Books, pp. 141–142.

Further Reading

Cobb, Humphrey. 2010. *Paths of Glory*. New York: Penguin Classics; Jünger, Ernst. 2007. *Storm of Steel*. New York: Penguin Classics; and Remarque, Erich Maria. 2011. *All Quiet on the Western Front*. New York: Ballantine Books. Three passionate fictional accounts of the war experience.

Eksteins, Modris. 2000. *Rites of Spring: The Great War and the Birth of the Modern Age*. Boston: Houghton Mifflin. The experience of trench warfare and how it altered the psychology of Europe.

Englund, Peter. 2011. *The Beauty and the Sorrow: An Intimate History of the First World War*. New York: Knopf. An exceptionally well-written narrative history of the Great War that follows the lives of 20 individuals.

Fussell, Paul. 2013. *The Great War and Modern Memory*. New York: Oxford University Press. A new edition of a classic study of the Great War that draws upon the literature of the war era to go beyond the military aspects and find the deeper meaning of the war experience.

Horne, Allister. 1994. *The Price of Glory*. New York: Penguin. Especially good account of the Battle of Verdun.

Howard, Michael. 2007. *The First World War: A Very Short Introduction.* New York: Oxford University Press;Strachan Hew. 2003. *The First World War.* New York: Penguin; Meyer, C. J. 2007. *The World Undone: The Story of the Great War, 1914 to 1918.* New York: Random House;Hochschild, Adam. 2011. *To End All Wars: A Story of Loyalty and Rebellion, 1914–1918.* Boston: Houghton Mifflin; and Beckett, Ian F. W. 2013. *The Making of the First World War.* New Haven: Yale University Press. All are very fine surveys of the Great War.

Joll, James and Martel, Gordon. 1984. *The Origins of the First World War.* New York: Pearson; Lafore Laurence. 1997. *The Long Fuse: An Interpretation of the Origins World War I.* Lake Zurich: Waveland Press; Mombauer Annika. 2002. *The Origins of the First World War: Controversies and Consensus.* New York: Pearson; andTuchman, Barbara W. 2004. *The Guns of August.* New York: Macmillan. Excellent studies of the causes and early fighting of the Great War.

Leed, Eric J. 1981. *No Man's Land: Combat and Identity in World War I.* Cambridge, UK: Cambridge University Press. A scholarly look at the impact of trench warfare.

Palmer, Svetlana and Sarah Wallis, eds. 2003. *Intimate Voices from the First World War.* New York: HarperCollins. The Great War as told through the diaries and letters of those who experienced it.

Williams, John. 1972. *The Other Battleground.* Washington, DC: Henry Regnery. War on the home front in England, France, and Germany.

3

Revolution and Peacemaking, 1917–1919

Chronology

1917	Russian (March) Revolution
	Russian (November) Revolution
1918	Woodrow Wilson's "Fourteen Points"
	Treaty of Brest-Litovsk; Russia leaves the war
	Armistice on the Western Front, November 11
	German Republic proclaimed
	Russian Civil War (1918–1920)
1919	Paris Peace Conference
	Weimar Constitution adopted in Germany
	Versailles Peace Treaty with Germany
	League of Nations Covenant signed

THE EUROPE, INDEED THE WORLD that welcomed the armistice in November 1918 was very different from the Europe that enthusiastically greeted the outbreak of war in August 1914. The "old order" had fallen, but no one was quite sure what the "new order" would be like. At its outset, the war was an old-fashioned affair of kings,

Twentieth-Century Europe: A Brief History, 1900 to the Present, Third Edition.
Michael D. Richards and Paul R. Waibel.
© 2014 John Wiley & Sons, Inc. Published 2014 by John Wiley & Sons, Inc.

emperors, and statesmen defending dynastic and/or national honor against the aggressor. By 1916, it had become a war for territorial expansion. In 1917, the Russian Revolution and the entry of the United States transformed the Great War into an ideological struggle, a crusade for a new world order. Woodrow Wilson, the president of the United States, and V. I. Lenin (Vladimir Ilyich Ulyanov, 1870–1924), the Bolshevik leader of the new Russia, personified two different visions of the future, at least initially. Each proposed a new world order entirely different from what Europeans had known before the war. Each vision, in its own way, held out the hope that the Great War might not have been waged in vain.

Wilson's vision took shape partly in response to Lenin's call for an immediate peace of justice without victors or vanquished. Wilson, who as late as 1916 campaigned for reelection on his record as an isolationist, began to speak of a new democratic international order based upon the abstract "universal principles of right and justice." Before a joint session of Congress in January 1918, he outlined in his "Fourteen Points" the principles on which a just peace settlement must be negotiated. They included "open covenants openly arrived at," the principle of national self-determination, and a "general association of nations" in order to assure the political independence and territorial integrity of each nation. In the ensuing months, as the peace conference unfolded, Wilson's "general association of nations," the League of Nations, became his chief goal, the essential basis of his new world order.

Wilson and Lenin had much in common. Both were products of Enlightenment thought. Both believed in the innate goodness of man. Hence, they were both humanitarians, but with a difference. Wilson's belief that man is by nature good, possessing certain inalienable natural rights, led him to become a liberal-democrat, for whom the loss of American lives to U-Boat attacks was a crime that had justified American intervention in the Great War. Lenin's sense of humanitarianism was more abstract. He had great compassion for humanity in general, but as a Marxist, he viewed individuals as expendable cogs in the wheels of history. And although Lenin defended orthodox Marxism as objective truth, he did not adhere, as Marx did, to historical determinism. Lenin was, much like Hitler, a

Lenin mobilized the raw energy of the masses to bring the Bolsheviks to power in the second Russian revolution. Above: Lenin (center) at the unveiling of a monument to Marx and Engels. © Pictorial Press Ltd / Alamy

voluntarist for whom will power (the will of the leader) was the decisive factor in determining the flow of history.

Wilson's vision appealed mainly to middle-class liberals, who wished to replace the old world of aristocratic privilege and secret diplomacy with a new international order of democratic nation-states cooperating in a League of Nations. This was a free and democratic, but not a classless, world order. None of Wilson's Fourteen Points dealt with Lenin's most pressing concern: the need for a new *social* order. In Lenin's view, imminent world revolution, for which the Russian Revolution was a catalyst, would sweep away both nation-states and classes to liberate mankind from the corruptive influence of past historical development. Although Lenin's program appealed to millions, millions more feared it. Those who feared his ideas did so because behind them lay the fact of the Russian

Revolution and the forces it had unleashed. No one, however, Bolshevik or bourgeois democrat, quite knew what might develop from the events of 1917 in Russia.

Revolution in Russia

The Russian Revolution of 1917 was actually two revolutions. The first occurred in March (February, according to the Julian calendar then in use in Russia) and resulted in the creation of a liberal Provisional Government. The Provisional Government was organized by former deputies of the Duma, suspended by the Tsar in September, 1915. The second, or Bolshevik Revolution, occurred in November (or October)[1] and was carried out by the Bolsheviks, a radical Marxist faction within the Soviet of Workers' and Sailors' Deputies, or *Petrograd Soviet*. The Petrograd Soviet came into existence on the very same day as the Provisional Government. From its beginning, the Petrograd Soviet functioned as a shadow government, issuing decrees of its own and countermanding decrees of the Provisional Government.

That there was a revolution in Russia at all was due to the failure of the Tsar's government to deal adequately with the demands of the war. This in turn was the result of a number of factors. Russia was the most effectively blockaded of the belligerents. At the same time, it was unable to exploit its vast natural resources due to its general economic backwardness and the government's unwillingness to organize the economy and society for a total war effort. In short, it was an abdication of authority by the Tsar's government that led to the creation of the Provisional Government and the Petrograd Soviet.

There were three different coalition governments during the period of the Provisional Government from March 18 to November 7, 1917. The first consisted of middle- and upper-middle-class liberals from the *Kadets* (Liberal Constitutional Party) and *Octobrists* (moderate

---

[1] Many accounts of the Russian Revolution refer to the "February Revolution" and the "October Revolution."

constitutionalists) and Aleksandr Kerensky (1881–1970), a member of a moderate Labor Party, the lone socialist. In May, several *Mensheviks* (the moderate wing of the Social Democratic Labor Party) and *Socialist Revolutionaries* (a radical party with a peasant base) joined the coalition. Kerensky became minister of war and began preparation of an attack intended to contribute to the allied war effort. After the July Offensive failed, Kerensky took the post of minister-president and formed a second coalition government on August 6. Kerensky also led the third and final coalition cabinet that lasted from October 8 to November 7, when the Bolsheviks seized power.

Why the Provisional Government failed (and why there was a second revolution in November) is one of the great historical questions of 1917. But the reason the Provisional Government failed is not as simple as sometimes believed. It is true that the Provisional Government forgot the first duty of any government: to govern. But there were both ideological and practical reasons why the Provisional Government failed to act decisively. It was a coalition of liberals committed to defending civil liberties, but none of them felt they had the right to make any far-reaching changes in Russian society until a constitutional assembly had been elected and met to draft a constitution. In short, they believed that the fundamental issues of how to interpret the inalienable rights of the individual and define the limits of governmental authority must be decided by a duly elected Constituent Assembly. Until then, the Provisional Government saw itself as just that, "provisional," the transitory caretaker of national sovereignty.

This overly cautious and legalistic approach, more than anything else, crippled and then doomed the Provisional Government. It had claimed authority but then was both unwilling and unable to exercise authority. Faced with growing economic problems and the pressures of continuing an increasingly unpopular war, it could not provide the firm leadership for which the Russian masses were desperate in 1917.

The expectations of the people were a major challenge faced by the Provisional Government. Tsarism had ended and "democracy" was now established, or being established, but "democracy" meant something different to each group within Russian society. It was not possible for the Provisional Government to address these expectations, given its legalistic interpretation of its provisional status. Its failure to respond to the peasants' demand for land with some sort of land reform program is an example of the Provisional Government's overly cautious approach to governing. Rather than address the demands of the masses, it made the fatal decision to continue the war, and even launched a new, major offensive in July. And it was the decision to continue the war that doomed the already floundering Provisional Government. In part, it was a matter of honor. While many in the Provisional Government felt that Russia had to fulfill certain obligations to its allies, there were other, more selfish, reasons for continuing the war. In May, 1917, the Provisional Government continued to pursue acquisition of Constantinople and the Turkish Straits, two of primary war aims of the Tsarist government. Despite widespread and very vocal public opposition, the Provisional Government failed to see the necessity of extricating Russia from the war, a hard reality that Lenin forced the Bolsheviks to accept in 1918.

The arrival of Lenin in Petrograd in mid-April altered the course of the revolution. Lenin was living in exile in Switzerland when the March Revolution occurred. It was the German military who facilitated Lenin's return to Russia as a "secret weapon" in the war with Russia. As early as 1915, Lenin had been openly advocating a revolution in Russia as a prerequisite to peace. He and his fellow Bolsheviks argued for peace at any cost, even the defeat of Russia if necessary. The German High Command decided in April of 1917 to secure Lenin's return to Russia, along with 31 other prominent Bolsheviks. The Germans provided Lenin and his coconspirators with an estimated 50–60 million marks to fund, what they no doubt hoped would be, the overthrow of the Provisional Government and an end to the war with Russia.

Upon his arrival in Petrograd, Lenin began immediately to persuade the Bolsheviks to embrace his interpretation of the revolution. In what came to be known as the "April Theses," Lenin called for immediate peace, a transfer of governmental authority to the Soviets, and a nationalization of land. Lenin argued that the second stage of the revolution, the "proletarian revolution," was at hand, and it was the task of the Bolsheviks to take the lead. The April

Theses were initially rejected by the Bolshevik leadership, although published in *Pravda* on April 7 as Lenin's personal interpretation. Lenin presented the theses to the seventh All-Russia Conference of Soviets of Workers' and Soldiers' Deputies, which adopted them as its program (Marxists Internet Archive 1917).

The Bolsheviks grew rapidly in the spring and early summer of 1917, in an atmosphere of increasing anarchy. At the same time, the Provisional Government was losing even the limited power it once had. Aleksandr Kerensky, minister of war after May 19, attempted to rally the troops for a new offensive. On July 1, the Russian offensive began against the Austro-Hungarian and German lines in Galicia. After some initial success, the Russian offensive collapsed, and on July 19, the Germans counterattacked, all but destroying the Russian army as an effective fighting force. Meeting little resistance, the German army pursued the retreating Russians through Galicia and Ukraine as far as the Zbruch River. Now, the Russian troops began deserting in large numbers. Lenin correctly observed that "The army voted for peace with its feet."

The failure of the July Offensive was disastrous for the Provisional Government. The cabinet resigned, and a new government was formed with Aleksandr Kerensky as prime minister, succeeding the liberal Prince Georgi Lvov (1861–1925). Growing chaos caused fear among some liberal and conservative army officers, businessmen, and political leaders who feared that Russia was drifting toward civil war. This liberal–conservative coalition found a champion in the colorful Cossack general, Lavr Kornilov (1870–1918), Kerensky's new commander-in-chief.

Fearing that his commander-in-chief was plotting a coup, Kerensky dismissed Kornilov on September 8. Kornilov refused to obey and ordered army units to begin marching on Petrograd. Swift action by the Petrograd Soviet, however, robbed Kornilov of the support of the troops. The soldiers simply deserted as they approached Petrograd. The Kornilov "coup," if indeed it was ever meant to be such, fizzled out. The Provisional Government was saved, but by the action of the Petrograd Soviet, not its own.

What existed in Russia in September 1917 was a kind of organized anarchy. No single organization could really speak for all the people.

A process of fermentation was at work within the armed forces, among the peasantry and the industrial workers, and within various national and ethnic groups. The aspirations of these many different groups could not be adequately expressed in conventional political terms, as Kerensky was trying to do by patiently preparing for the election of a Constituent Assembly. The energies of the masses had been unleashed by the destruction of the traditional authorities. No government could succeed unless it tapped those energies or, at the least, managed to ride their currents.

From his hideout in Finland, where he fled in mid-July when the Provisional Government cracked down on the Bolsheviks, Lenin sought to direct the raw energy of the masses to the goal of seizing power. He saw the possibility of combining the anarchistic rebelliousness of the masses with the revolutionary efforts of the vanguard of the proletariat, the party. In September, he wrote to the Central Committee of the Bolshevik faction: "the Bolsheviks must seize power at this very moment."

Lenin's proposal met with opposition from some of his closest associates, who argued that the time was not right. The differences were resolved at a secret meeting of the Central Committee attended by Lenin on the night of October 23. Lenin prevailed, and the Central Committee agreed to prepare for a coup. Since Lenin wished to remain in hiding, leadership of the coup was given to Leon Trotsky (Lev Davidovich Bronshtein, 1879–1940).

The seizure of power by the Bolsheviks took place on November 7 (October 25), 1917. Actually, "seizure of power" is too glorious a phrase to convey the reality of the confused situation in Petrograd. It would be more accurate to say that once the Provisional Government failed in its attempt to destroy the Bolsheviks and the Military Revolutionary Committee, power was dumped into the lap of the Bolshevik faction. Trotsky's preparations made it appear that power had been seized in the name of the Soviet movement. Not all members of the Second Congress of Soviets, meeting at that time in Petrograd, accepted that notion, but the delegates who remained at the meeting, although a minority voted to accept a Bolshevik government. For the time being, it was also accepted in Moscow and other important cities. Perhaps more important, it was accepted in most areas at the front. In the provinces, distant from central authority in any case, a watchful attitude was adopted. At the same time, centers of resistance sprang up, but the Bolsheviks managed to retain power without great difficulty in the last months of 1917.

The situation became much graver in 1918. The revolutionary government faced several difficult situations. First, it had to contend with the Constituent Assembly, elected in November after the revolution. The Bolsheviks were badly outnumbered, notably by the Socialist Revolutionaries who had received strong peasant support. At the initial meeting of the Constituent Assembly in January 1918, delegates began immediately to criticize the government sharply. The government responded by dispersing the assembly at the end of the first day; there was not even enough organized support for parliamentary rule to counter this move.

The second problem could not be dealt with so easily. It involved ending the war with Germany. Trotsky led the Russian delegation in negotiations with Germany and Austria beginning in December, but he was not able to moderate the harsh demands laid down by the German general staff. Lenin, as he had so often in the past, used his powers of persuasion and prestige to persuade the Bolsheviks to accept the German terms, harsh as they were. With great reluctance, Russia signed the Treaty of Brest-Litovsk on March 3, 1918, abandoning Poland, Lithuania, the Ukraine, the Baltic provinces, Finland, and Transcaucasia. Russia lost major portions of its industrial capacity and food-raising capabilities but gained time in which to attend to internal problems without the constant demands of war impinging. It was a substantial but necessary sacrifice. Otherwise, it is difficult to imagine how the Bolshevik government could have survived the three years of civil war that followed.

Civil War in Russia

The Bolsheviks moved quickly to consolidate their control. They moved the capital from Petrograd (St. Petersburg) to Moscow, a more secure location in the interior and farther away from

Europe. Leon Trotsky resigned as foreign minister to become war commissar in March 1918. The Red Army, created in January by Trotsky, had become a formidable force, one ready to defend the Bolshevik government from those within Russia as well as possible intervention from Russia's former allies or Japan. Some former Tsarist generals joined the Red Army of their own free will; others served because the Bolsheviks held their family members as hostages. In July 1918, the Bolsheviks expelled the Left Socialist Revolutionaries, a splinter group that had broken off from the Socialist Revolutionaries, from the government. That same month, the Russian Soviet adopted the Constitution of Federated Socialist Republic.

Meanwhile, the Tsar, along with his wife and children and their doctor and servants, were imprisoned in the town of Yekaterinburg, on the eastern side of the Ural Mountains where Europe and Asia meet. All of them were executed on the night of July 16/17 by their captors, who feared they might be liberated by a White[2] Army that was closing in on Yekaterinburg. There remain many questions concerning the fate of the Tsar and his family, but certainly, the execution of the entire Romanov family served as a sort of notice that there was no turning back. Tsarist Russia was history. It remained for the victor in the civil war, either the Reds or the Whites, to determine the future of Russia. On September 2, the Bolshevik government proclaimed a "Red Terror" against all those considered counterrevolutionaries.

The Reds enjoyed certain advantages over the Whites. The Reds were unified geographically, as well as ideologically. They controlled the most important provinces of the former Russian empire, which gave them control of the economic resources, including the railroads, and internal lines of supply and defense. To insure that the Red Armies received the necessary supplies and manpower, the government introduced a set of policies commonly referred to as "War Communism." Factories were nationalized; strikes were prohibited; vital resources, including food, were rationed; and the

---

[2] Those who opposed the Bolsheviks (Reds) were collectively referred to as the Whites.

peasants were forced to fulfill quotas for the production of grain and other agricultural products. Throughout the areas controlled by the new government, what amounted to a military discipline was implemented. These measures enabled Leon Trotsky to raise a Red Army that totaled around five million soldiers by the end of the civil war.

In contrast, the Whites were never unified ideologically or with regard to military strategy. They attacked the Reds from the north, east, and south with armies that never totaled more than a quarter-million. They lacked leadership, both military and ideological. Whereas the Reds were able to unify their armies as well as the civilian population in the areas under their control, the Whites were never able to do so. They lost the struggle for the hearts of the people, who came to fear a White victory more than a Red victory. The final battle of the civil war was fought in the Crimea, around the town of Perekop, between November 7 and 15, 1920. The Russian Civil War ended in a victory for the Red Army, but at the expense of an estimated 10 million lives.

It is noteworthy that the Whites lost the civil war despite assistance from imperial Russia's allies during the Great War. Great Britain, France, Japan, and the United States all became embroiled in the civil war. Allied involvement was, however, never coordinated and largely limited to material support for the White Armies. The British and French governments decided on intervention with three goals in mind. The first was to safeguard stockpiles of military supplies provided to the Tsarist government and stored at Archangel. Second was a desire to use the Czech Legion located along the Trans-Siberian Railroad against the Bolsheviks. Finally, they hoped to revive an Eastern Front against Germany and Austria-Hungary. In July, President Wilson agreed to commit 5,000 American troops to the effort.

Once the Great War ended in November 1918, the Allies faced numerous and complicated global issues resulting from their victory. Interest in what was happening in Russia declined rapidly, and those interventionists that still remained in Russia began seeking an honorable exit. By the end of October 1922, the last of the foreign troops (Japanese) departed, leaving the Russian people a deep and lasting distrust of the Western powers. At the same time, fear that communism might spread beyond Russia was growing in Europe and the United States.

Revolution in Germany

The revolution in Germany was, like the Russian Revolution, actually two revolutions, or attempted revolutions. Forces on the left attempted a "revolution from below" but were checkmated by forces on the right, who attempted a "revolution from above." The result was the establishment of an "accidental" republic that lacked popular support. The traditional elites of the army, judiciary, bureaucracy, church, and wealthy landowners and industrialists remained entrenched and hostile toward the republic. During the republic's brief existence, the forces of extreme right and left struggled to achieve their respective revolutionary goals until the final victory of the extreme right in January 1933.

Once the Allied armies broke through the Hindenburg Line on September 29, 1918, even General Erich von Ludendorff, commander of Germany's last offensive, had to accept reality. The main challenge facing Ludendorff and the High Command in October 1918, once it became clear that Germany had lost the war, was how to save the old order. Guilt for the defeat had to be spread as broadly as possible, but without including the military leadership. The solution was to create a broadly based civilian government of center-left parties that would be burdened with the task of asking for an armistice and making the necessary peace. Hence, Prince Max von Baden was appointed chancellor; ministers became responsible to the Reichstag; the Prussian three-class voting system was abolished; and the Kaiser lost much of his control of the armed forces. Germany became a constitutional monarchy, but not a republic. All of this was to create a responsible civilian government capable of accepting the burden (or blame) of defeat while at the same time preventing a possible Bolshevik-style revolution from below.

Nevertheless, Germany seemed ripe for a revolution from below in November 1918. On November 3, the sailors at the Kiel naval base mutinied. It was a spark that ignited revolutions across Germany. On November 8, Kurt Eisner (1867–1919), an Independent Socialist,[3] established a Constituent Workers', Soldiers', and Peasants' Council in Munich and proclaimed a Republic of Bavaria. Revolt also broke out in Berlin, on November 8. On the following day, Prince Max von Baden announced both the Kaiser's abdication (to which the Kaiser had not yet agreed) and his own resignation. As he resigned, he transferred his powers to Friedrich Ebert (1871–1925), leader of the Majority Social Democrats. The transfer of power gave an aura of legitimacy to Ebert's government, although Prince Max had no actual constitutional authority to do so. The "Ebert Cabinet," which called itself the "Council of Peoples' Deputies," derived its authority from the Workers' and Soldiers' Councils of Berlin and from the two parties on the left, the Social Democratic Party (SPD) and the Independent Social Democratic Party (USPD). The Independent Social Democrats originated as a small fraction of Social Democrat delegates who in 1915 voted against additional funding for the war.

The moderate socialists in the SPD and USPD were willing to accept government responsibility, and with it the burden of making peace, because they, as well as the trade union leaders and a majority of the people they represented, feared a revolution from below as much as did the traditional elites. Initially, the socialists intended to help preserve a constitutional monarchy. The abdication of the Kaiser and the proclamation of a republic by Philipp Scheidemann (1865–1939), deputy leader of the SPD, on November 9, were not a part of the original plan. Once it was a fact, however, Ebert and his supporters felt the immediate need to establish order first and then to elect a Constituent Assembly that would draft a constitution, which in turn would determine the nature and extent of reform.

Ebert was very upset when he first learned that his deputy had proclaimed a republic. Scheidemann had reacted more or less instinctively

---

[3]   The Independent Socialists split off from the Majority Socialists (SPD, or Social Democratic Party of Germany) in 1915 to protest the SPD's continued support of the war. In 1917, the Independent Socialists formed the USPD, or Independent Social Democratic Party of Germany. The *Spartakusbund*and and KPD (Communist Party of Germany) evolved out of the USPD.

to a momentary crisis. He was having lunch, eating a bowl of potato soup at the Reichstag on November 9, when he was informed that Karl Liebknecht (1871–1919), a radical leader of the *Spartakusbund*, a splinter group from the SPD, was about to proclaim a Soviet Republic from the balcony of the imperial palace. The Spartakusbund originated as a group of radicals who opposed war with Russia. After aligning themselves with the USPD between 1916 and 1918, they renamed themselves the Communist Party of Germany (KPD) in January 1919. Attempting to preempt Liebknecht's announcement, Scheidemann went to the window and made a brief speech to the crowd outside, which he concluded with, "Long live the new! Long live the German Republic!" Hence, Germany became a democratic republic because the alternative, a Soviet Republic, was simply too frightful.

Much ink has been spilt by historians trying to explain why the Social Democrats, a party whose historical roots and party program were Marxist, did not initiate fundamental changes in Germany once they achieved governmental responsibility. The reasons given are varied. Certainly, one reason is that a radical revolution lacked a mass base of support. Also, the radicals in Germany faced strong opposition from the conservative traditional elites. The army, even if it had been defeated on the battlefront, was still a formidable force in German internal affairs. The bureaucracy continued to function efficiently. And even though the old government had collapsed, most of the other institutions in Germany were still sound and committed to preventing any real change in German society. Finally, the more radical forces found little sympathy for their demands among the Majority Socialists.

Any chance that the Majority Social Democrats would lead a "real" revolution in Germany was short-circuited by the so-called Ebert–Groener Pact on November 9 and the Stinnes–Legien Agreement on November 15. In the former, General Wilhelm Groener (1867–1939), Ludendorff's successor, offered the Ebert government the support and protection of the army in exchange for Ebert's promise to "suppress Bolshevism," that is, to suppress the soldiers' councils and recognize the authority of the officer corps.

The Stinnes–Legien Agreement was one concluded between employers and trade union leaders on November 15. The employers agreed to recognize the unions as the only legitimate representatives of labor, abolish company unions, hire returning soldiers, and implement codetermination in all firms employing at least 50 workers. In return, the trade unions agreed not to push for any changes in the existing property structure of Germany.

Many have argued ever since November of 1918 that the real "stab in the back" occurred when, as a result of the Ebert–Groener Pact and the Stinnes–Legien Agreement, the Majority Social Democrats allegedly were taken captive by the forces on the right. Caught between a revolution from above and a revolution from below, they opted for the former. Whatever the truth, the leftist uprisings during 1919 were swiftly put down by the army and the *Freikorps*, paramilitary associations of former soldiers. A Spartakus-led revolt in Berlin in January 1919 also was crushed. Rosa Luxemburg (1871–1919) and Karl Liebknecht, leaders of the Spartakusbund, were murdered by the Freikorps, right-wing militia groups called upon by Ebert to put down the revolt. Further uprisings in February and March in Berlin, Munich, and other areas and a brief Soviet Republic proclaimed in Bavaria in April were all likewise suppressed. The German Revolution, unlike the revolution in Russia, stopped halfway.

Elsewhere in Central Europe, defeat in war, the disintegration of old, prewar governments, and the powerful example of 1917 in Russia created potential revolutionary situations. In Austria, there were disorders throughout 1919, but no revolutionary accomplishments. In Hungary, a revolution in October 1918 created a government of socialists and communists, but in March 1919, that government became a communist dictatorship under Béla Kun (1886–1936). Communist Hungary did not last long. Romanian troops invaded in April. At the same time, a counterrevolution began, and by August 1, Béla Kun fled the country. Miklós Horthy (1868–1957), a former admiral in the Austro-Hungarian Navy, ruled as regent and head of state until 1944.

Despite setbacks, by the end of 1919, the fate of world revolution was still undetermined. Revolutionaries remained optimistic but, as events played out, much of their optimism was unfounded. Success in Russia was based on two factors, the utter collapse of the old regime and widespread rebellion among the lower classes in the cities and especially in the countryside. Neither factor led to success in Germany, where the empire collapsed but the institutions and traditional elites undergirding it remained. There was no German equivalent to the Russian peasantry on which the small, isolated radical groups could base their activity. In Central Europe, a large peasantry existed, but it was fragmented by ethnic and national differences and kept under control by great landowners, the aristocracy, and the military who, sometimes with difficulty (as in Hungary), managed to dominate politics after the Great War in every Central European state except Czechoslovakia. The only successful revolution outside Russia in the immediate postwar period occurred in Turkey, where army officers and nationalists rallied in 1919 and 1920 to prevent the victorious Allied Powers from imposing peace terms on their nation.

Revolution, if relatively unsuccessful by 1919, still had an enormous impact on postwar Europe. As in the United States, in Europe there was considerable and often irrational fear of a Bolshevik menace. A good deal of energy and time was spent at the Paris Peace Conference working out methods by which the Russian Revolution might be quarantined or possibly destroyed. An informal counterrevolutionary movement developed that led to dictatorships, initially in Eastern and Southeastern Europe, then in Italy and the Iberian Peninsula, and finally in Germany.

Peacemaking, 1919

In the midst of the disorder and turmoil, when the threat of revolution looked a good deal more imposing than it did by the end of 1920, the Paris Peace Conference opened on January 18, 1919. It lasted until January 21, 1920. The victorious powers met not simply to end the Great War but also to reconstruct the world. One cannot avoid the temptation to compare the Paris Peace Conference with the Vienna Congress (1814–1815) that concluded the Napoleonic Wars. Both came at the conclusion of major Europe-wide conflicts, and both attempted to set right the map of Europe and draft a peace that would last indefinitely. However, the Vienna Congress seems to have succeeded, whereas the Paris Peace Conference failed. Apart from the brief wars of German unification, there was general peace in Europe for 100 years following the Vienna Congress. The Paris Peace Settlement lasted only 20 troubled years before Europe, and the world, was plunged into a second and even more devastating war.

The Europe of 1919 was very different from the Europe of 1814–1815. The diplomats who went to Vienna represented monarchies and were answerable only to their sovereigns. Hence, they enjoyed a freedom of action not allowed the diplomats of 1919, who represented liberal-democratic governments, which in turn were answerable to the people. Ideology was enlisted as a weapon during the Great War to mobilize whole nations. Such had been true only of France in the Napoleonic Wars. Furthermore, the peacemakers at Vienna met at the end of a revolutionary cycle and the beginning of a century of modern ideology. The peacemakers at Paris were meeting at a time when Europe was erupting with turmoil and revolution fed by the new "isms" that had emerged during the intervening century.

The Vienna Congress was guided in its decision making by a set of principles: balance of power, legitimacy, and compensation. Every decision was weighed against the guiding principles. Hence, there was an agreed-upon basis for peace. Not so at Paris.

The only guiding principle at Paris in 1919 was the desire of the victors to contain their differences of opinion and present a united front to the defeated powers. There was no agreed-upon basis for peace. Thus, every decision was a political compromise among the victors. Wilson's Fourteen Points (see Table 3.1), which the Germans expected to be the basis of a negotiated peace, were shunted aside as a victors' peace emerged.

The treaty with Germany is commonly referred to as the Versailles Treaty, because it was signed in the Hall of Mirrors at the Palace of Versailles. There were four additional treaties signed with the other members of the Central Powers and named after the Paris suburb in which each was signed. The Versailles Treaty was the work of the "Big Four" (France, Great Britain, Italy, and the United States),

Table 3.1   Wilson's Fourteen Points

1. No more secret agreements ("open covenants openly arrived at")
2. Free navigation of all seas
3. An end to all economic barriers between countries
4. Countries to reduce weapon numbers
5. All decisions regarding the colonies should be impartial
6. The German army is to be removed from Russia. Russia should be left to develop her own political setup
7. Belgium should be independent like before the war
8. France should be fully liberated and allowed to recover Alsace-Lorraine
9. All Italians are to be allowed to live in Italy. Italy's borders are to be "along clearly recognizable lines of nationality"
10. Self-determination should be allowed for all those living in Austria-Hungary
11. Self-determination and guarantees of independence should be allowed for the Balkan states
12. The Turkish people should be governed by the Turkish government. Non-Turks in the old Turkish Empire should govern themselves
13. An independent Poland should be created which should have access to the sea
14. A League of Nations should be set up to guarantee the political and territorial independence of all states (History Learning Site 1918)

actually the "Big Three," following Italy's noncooperation after being denied the territorial compensation it demanded for its participation in the war. France, represented by Georges Clemenceau, wanted a treaty that would assure French national security and require Germany to pay for war damages. France's desire for a harsh treaty was somewhat mitigated by a willingness to compromise in order to achieve assurances of American cooperation in postwar Europe.

David Lloyd George, Britain's representative, was compelled by the results of the December 1918 elections to side with Clemenceau and thus support harsher peace terms than he personally felt were justified. Lloyd George, a leader of the Liberal Party, campaigned for "a country fit for heroes to live in." As

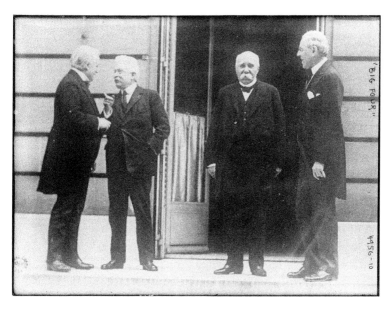

The "Big Four" enjoy a cordial chat at the Paris Peace Conference, 1919 (left to right), British Prime Minister David Lloyd George, Italian Premier Vittorio Orlando, French Premier Georges Clemenceau, and American President Woodrow Wilson. Courtesy of the George C. Marshall Foundation, Lexington, Virginia

chancellor of the exchequer, Lloyd George authored the People's Budget of 1909 that introduced social welfare programs in the United Kingdom. The promise of "a country fit for heroes to live in," given the new economic realities at the end of the war, required a hard line on reparations from Germany.

The role of President Woodrow Wilson, who personally represented the United States, has been analyzed in great detail by historians. His idealism clashed with the realism of his European counterparts, especially that of Clemenceau. The extent to which his unwillingness to make the treaty a bipartisan political issue at home resulted in the US Senate's, and the people's, ultimate rejection of it also has been examined at length. What remains indisputable is Wilson's sincere commitment to a just peace as a basis for building a new world order. He believed that the League of Nations was the essential cornerstone of that new order, but its existence required the postwar cooperation of the victors. To see the League become a reality, Wilson was forced to compromise, often at Germany's expense. He justified this compromise in the sincere belief that whatever defects the treaty contained could be repaired in later years by international cooperation through the League.

Perhaps the most glaring defect of the peace conference was the failure to include representation from Russia (now the Soviet Union) and Germany, especially the latter. Russia was not represented both because the Bolsheviks, if in fact they were the legitimate government, had little interest in what seemed to them a meaningless farce and also because of the fear that the very notion of the Bolshevik revolution caused among the delegates of the "civilized" nations gathered at Paris. They feared, as the British historian A. J. P. Taylor has pointed out, that Soviet Russia represented a "genuine element of social change," which threatened to spread: hence, the need to at least quarantine, or if possible snuff out, Bolshevism.

That Germany was not allowed to join the conference was a serious flaw. As the treaty took shape, however, it became clear that it would effect a victors' peace. The demand that Germany pay the costs of the war necessitated an admission of guilt by Germany for having started the war, thus the inclusion in the treaty of the infamous Article 231, or "war-guilt clause." To accept the burden of reparations, the amount the treaty left unspecified, was an injustice. But to accept responsibility for a war for which the Germans felt they were not in fact to blame was a burden that could only be imposed, as it could never be willingly accepted. Had Germany participated in the peace conference, as a defeated France had at the Vienna Congress, it would have meant a deadlock at the conference and deepening political crisis at home for the diplomats of the victorious Allies.

Germany was seriously weakened by the terms of the Versailles Treaty, although not fatally so, as the French had initially wanted. It lost a little territory in its west: Alsace-Lorraine was returned to France and a part of Schleswig was ceded to Denmark after a plebiscite (or popular vote). In addition, a few border communities were transferred to Belgium (but restored to Germany in 1926). The coal mines of the Saar were placed under French control for 15 years

Europe Between the Wars

after which a plebiscite would determine the national status of the area. The Rhineland remained a part of Germany, despite extensive French efforts, but the area west of the Rhine and a strip 50 kilometers to the east were "demilitarized." Allied troops were to occupy the west bank of the river for 15 years. In the east, Germany lost a good deal more territory. A large part of Posen and West and East Prussia were ceded to Poland. Danzig was declared a free city within the Polish customs union. Memel was ceded to the Allies and later taken over by Lithuania. Upper Silesia's fate was to be determined by plebiscite. Germany also lost its colonies.

As a military power, Germany was much reduced in size. It was allowed an army of no more than 100,000 men with limitations on the types of weapons that they might have. Its navy was reduced in size and was forbidden to have submarines. Furthermore, Germany was not allowed to have an air force.

The Treaty of Versailles was regarded by most Germans as extremely unfair and harsh. They had, of course, forgotten their own treaty making efforts at Brest-Litovsk. The "war-guilt clause," reparations, unilateral disarmament, the loss of territory in Europe, and colonies outside Europe all furnished texts for German nationalists in the next decade.

Had the Treaty of Versailles been the only product of the Paris Peace Conference, Europe might have maintained political stability in the 1920s and 1930s. There were, however, four additional treaties and the League of Nations Covenant. The failure of several of these agreements, combined with the limited success of the Treaty of Versailles, created an extremely volatile situation in the 1930s. Of the four treaties, two can be disregarded: the Treaty of Sèvres with Turkey never went into effect; the Treaty of Neuilly with Bulgaria had no important repercussions. The other two, the Treaty of St. Germain with Austria and the Treaty of Trianon with Hungary, created problems that were never fully resolved between the two world wars. Instead, two different problems were created. First, Austria and Hungary, before the war semiautonomous parts of the Habsburg Empire and each dominant in its own sphere, became small, relatively weak states. Austria particularly was an anomaly, a landlocked state of over six million, of whom two million lived in Vienna. The state was lopsided in every imaginable way, but especially economically. Unfortunately, Austria was not allowed to join with Germany for fear that this would unduly strengthen the latter.

The other problem involved the creation of a series of new or reconstituted states in Eastern Europe and conflicting claims over territory and population. The idea of national self-determination was extremely difficult to apply in this area with any fairness. Czechoslovakia, for example, included areas in which the majority of the population was German or Polish; these areas had been included for strategic reasons, as was the Sudetenland with its majority of Germans, or for historic reasons, as was Teschen with its Polish majority. Poland included areas with German majorities. Romania and Yugoslavia had large concentrations of Magyars. Numerous other examples could be cited of the impossibility of a simple, completely fair division of territory according to the principle of national self-determination.

The irony of the settlement in Eastern Europe is that the frontiers established by the treaties and the quarrels arising from them had torn apart what had been an important economic unit. Factories were now in one state, their sources of raw materials in a second, and their traditional markets in a third. This contributed to the weakness and instability of the area and nullified any possibility that the states of Eastern Europe could serve as a proper counterbalance to either a resurgent Germany or the strengthening Soviet Union.

The League of Nations

The Paris Peace Settlement, as mentioned, failed to provide a lasting peace. With the benefit of hindsight, we can see that its failure was due in part to an inability to recognize, or perhaps an unwillingness to accept, the new realities of 1919. By the end of the war, the economic and financial center of the world had shifted from Europe to the United States. The Pax Britannica ended with the Great War, but no one, least of all Great Britain, wanted to admit it. Neither was the United States ready to assume the new responsibilities being thrust upon it.

Wilson fought hard to have the League of Nations[4] made a part of each of the treaties that together comprised the Paris Peace Settlement. The European Allies saw in the League a means by which to involve the United States in postwar Europe. In order to secure French support for the League and to soften France's demands for a harsh and punitive treaty with Germany, Wilson agreed to a

---

[4]   The full text of the Treaty of Versailles and the League of Nations Covenant is available as a PDF file online at http://foundingdocs.gov.au/resources/transcripts/cth10_doc_1919.pdf.

defensive alliance with Great Britain and France. But the US Senate refused to ratify the Versailles Treaty without alterations to protect United States' sovereignty, changes Wilson refused to accept. Therefore, the United States rejected the treaty and with it both membership in the League of Nations and the defensive alliance.

Blame for America's failure to ratify the treaty or join the League has often been laid at the feet of Wilson. There can be no doubt that Wilson, at the time suffering the aftereffects of a major stroke, completely mishandled the whole affair back home. But much of the blame must be assigned to the American public. Many Americans felt that participation in the war in Europe had been a mistake. The war over, most Americans wanted to return to a policy of isolationism (except when it came to collecting war debts), or as the popular slogan of the time put it, "back to normalcy."

The United States turned its back on Europe, but to say that in so doing it doomed the peace is too severe. Problems arising from the imperfect treaties might have been minimized, or entirely avoided, if the League of Nations Covenant was successfully implemented. The Covenant contained adequate machinery for maintaining peace in the world. It made provisions for an International Court of Justice, submission of disputes to arbitration or to the Council or Assembly of the League, and even the use of force to resolve disputes.

Apart from America's refusal to participate, the League was made ineffective by the absence of both Germany (which did join in 1926) and the Soviet Union (which joined in 1934, shortly after Germany had left). There were other pertinent factors, also. In the formative period, Britain and France, each having a different idea of how the League should be run, canceled each other out. Later, in the early 1930s, the League failed some crucial tests (e.g., the Italian invasion of Ethiopia), perhaps because the issues involved were not seen as central to European politics.

Given the ineffectiveness of the League, all that was left to maintain the peace was a return to the old-fashioned principle of the balance of power. But that was not possible so long as Soviet Russia remained ostracized and Germany held down by the Versailles Treaty. One of the neglected realities of the 1920s was the fact that

Germany was still potentially the most powerful nation on the continent. All it needed was to get out from under the restrictions of the treaty.

Europe and the world faced an uncertain future in the spring of 1919, as Germany, bowing before the inevitable, signed the Versailles Treaty. Both Europe and its relationship to the world had changed, but much of this was ignored. Scattered groups and individuals recognized the changes. Their voices were sometimes heard in the first troubled years of the 1920s, but they were soon overwhelmed by the refusal of the majority to acknowledge the full extent of change in Europe.

Perhaps the best contemporary assessment of the peace comes from the French poet Romain Rolland (1866–1944), who ended his wartime journal on June 23, 1919, with the comment: "Sad Peace! Laughable interlude between the massacres of peoples!"

References

History Learning Site. 1918. "Woodrow Wilson's Fourteen Points." Accessed February 3, 2013. http://www.historylearningsite.co.uk/woodrow_wilson1.htm

Marxists Internet Archive. 1917. "Vladimir Ilyich Lenin: The Tasks of the Proletariat in the Present Revolution." Accessed February 3, 2013. http://www.marxists.org/archive/lenin/works/1917/apr/04.htm

Further Reading

Bailey, Thomas A. 2010. *Woodrow Wilson and the Lost Peace*. New York: Cambridge University Press. A very readable review of the compromises Wilson had to make at Paris and how he lost the peace at home.

Fitzpatrick, Sheila. 2008. *The Russian Revolution*. New York: Oxford University Press. An excellent brief survey of the Russian Revolution.

Harman, Chris. 2003. *The Lost Revolution: Germany: 1918–1923*. Chicago: Haymarket Books. A history of the German Revolution by a socialist who laments the failure of the revolution.

Kuhn, Gabriel, ed., trans. 2012. *All Power to the Councils: A Documentary History of the German Revolution, 1918–1919*. Oakland: PM Press. A collection of manifestos, speeches, articles, and letters from those who participated in the German Revolution.

Lincoln, Bruce. 1999. *Red Victory: A History of the Russian Civil War, 1918–1921*. New York: Da Capo Press.

MacMillan Margaret. *Paris, 2003 1919: Six Months that Changed the World*. New York: Random House. The best study of the Paris Peace Conference now available.

Nicolson, Harold. 2011. *Peacemaking, 1919*. London: Faber and Faber. A classic and very human appraisal of the conference by a member of the British delegation.

Pipes, Richard. 1996. *A Concise History of the Russian Revolution*. New York: Knopf. A thorough and very readable survey of the Russian Revolution.

Reed, Jack. 2007. *Ten Days that Shock the World*. New York: Penguin Classics. Reed was one of the leading radical American intellectuals, and one who participated in the Russian Revolution. This is the original version as written by Reed.

Sharp, Alan. 2008. *The Versailles Settlement: Peacemaking in Paris, 1919*, 2nd ed. New York: Palgrave Macmillan. A well-written brief history of the peace conference.

Trotsky, Leon. 1980. *History of the Russian Revolution*. Ann Arbor: University of Michigan Press.

Part 2

Overview: 1919–1939

THE TWENTY YEARS FROM 1919 TO 1939 form a crucial period in the history of Europe. Those Europeans who assumed that the world they had known before 1914 would resume after war's end had to face the reality that the Europe of 1919 was already a different place from prewar Europe. The ancient empires of Germany, Russia, Austria-Hungary, and Turkey had vanished. In their places were newly proclaimed republics struggling to survive in a hostile environment. Everywhere communist parties emerged to champion a third alternative to both the old order and the new liberal idealism advocated by the likes of Woodrow Wilson and his supporters.

Among the former great powers, there were signs of serious troubles ahead. Great Britain, the world's superpower in 1914, was suffering from the economic impact of the war, from which it would never fully recover. France, another of the so-called victors, remained politically confused and fragmented. The defeated Germany, the key to European recovery, was a republic without republicans. Burdened by the harsh terms of the Versailles Treaty and dependent upon anti-republican forces for its survival, the future looked grim for the Weimar Republic. Italy, also a victor in the Great War, suffered from an injured national pride and, like the rest of Europe, was troubled by economic and social problems. Italy would be the first of the former

Twentieth-Century Europe: A Brief History, 1900 to the Present, Third Edition.
Michael D. Richards and Paul R. Waibel.
© 2014 John Wiley & Sons, Inc. Published 2014 by John Wiley & Sons, Inc.

great powers to succumb to the lure of fascism. In Soviet Russia, a new style of authoritarian government was taking shape, one that would present a serious challenge to the historic values of Western civilization until the last decade of the twentieth century.

In addition to the political and economic disruptions of the prewar order, a pervasive disillusionment and intellectual uncertainty called into question the very foundations of European civilization. A generation that experienced four years of trench warfare and the monstrous battles of the Western Front found it hard to believe any longer in a rational order to the universe. If people are reasonable and by nature good, as the Enlightenment thinkers postulated, then how did the Great War happen? Was it a failure of diplomacy, or a chance event in a universe of random chaos? Novel theories were emerging to explain the human predicament, and modern prophets were waiting in the wings, as Friedrich Nietzsche predicted, to offer fresh myths for the birth of a new order.

Yet by 1925, there were hopeful signs for the future. The Dawes Plan in 1924 dealt with the reparations issue in such a way as to stimulate economic recovery in Germany and throughout Western Europe. The Locarno treaties signed in 1925 seemed to herald an era of rapprochement between Germany and France. A "spirit of Locarno" was in the air as many Europeans began to believe that a lasting peace was, after all, possible. Prosperity and optimism suffered a fatal blow, however, as the Great Depression that originated in the United States hit Europe in the early 1930s.

Much was changed by the Depression. It discredited liberalism, both politically and economically, especially for the middle class, the traditional bastion of the liberal order. The failure of the liberal-democratic governments to deal effectively with the stunningly high rates of unemployment and accompanying miseries caused by the Depression also created grave doubts among the working class. They, like the middle class, began to look for alternatives to liberalism, increasingly viewed as a failed idea from the past that had brought them to their current state.

Most European countries contended also with political crises intimately connected with the economic difficulties. The Weimar Republic fell apart in the early 1930s, creating conditions that made it possible for Adolf Hitler and the Nazi Party to come to power. Hitler, like Joseph Stalin (1879–1953) in the Soviet Union, constructed a new authoritarian dictatorship in Germany that was the very antithesis of liberalism. Unlike the traditional conservative dictatorships that sought merely to defend the status quo, the new authoritarian dictatorships sought a wholly new ideological order based upon a "born again" believer, the citizen-subject.

The major issue of the late 1930s was imminent threat of another world war and how best to meet this threat. The League of Nations proved to be useless in this regard. Britain and France failed to meet Nazi Germany's challenges, even when the Soviet Union seemed to be offering its support, until after the destruction of Czechoslovakia at the Munich Conference in 1938. When Hitler early in 1939 broke promises he had made in Munich, the stage was set for Nazi Germany's invasion of Poland, sparking the crisis that pushed the Western powers over the brink and into World War II in September 1939.

Changes in all areas of life had been extraordinarily rapid and pervasive in what, in hindsight, became known as the interwar period. Europe remained the center of world civilization during this time, but there were already signs that Europe's problems could not be solved without the intervention, once again, of the United States in European affairs. But America, battling the Depression and awash in a renewed spirit of isolationism, was not yet willing to assume the responsibilities that, ironically, would result in its newfound economic resources and military strength. That development would have to wait the outcome of a second great war. As Europe entered World War II, many could not help but feel that life as they had always known it would not survive a second major conflict. What most did not realize was the extent to which life had already changed.

4

Aftershocks of the Great War

Chronology

1859	Charles Darwin defines human beings as thinking animals
1882	Friedrich Nietzsche's "God is dead" philosophy cuts humanity adrift in a meaningless universe
1917	Albert Einstein's Theory of Relativity
1918–1922	Oswald Spengler predicts the death of Western civilization in *The Decline of the West*
1922	T. S. Eliot portrays postwar European culture as a wasteland
1930	Sigmund Freud and José Ortega y Gasset see civilization as an artificial creation

Twentieth-Century Europe: A Brief History, 1900 to the Present, Third Edition.
Michael D. Richards and Paul R. Waibel.
© 2014 John Wiley & Sons, Inc. Published 2014 by John Wiley & Sons, Inc.

THE GREAT WAR WAS PERHAPS the most traumatic event in Europe's history since the fall of the Roman Empire in the West. The twentieth century is often termed the "Age of Anxiety" because it was a century of change that left the future of European civilization in doubt. But the Great War did not cause the Age of Anxiety. It only acted as a catalyst for trends established well before 1914.

Intellectually, philosophers and theologians, as well as natural and social scientists, had been actively questioning the presuppositions (or axioms) that undergirded Western civilization before the Great War. The works of artists, writers, poets, and musicians, in short, the creators and guardians of culture, reflected these questions. Finally, the emergence of the "masses" into political life (e.g., growth of liberal democracy) and the development of a "mass culture" (e.g., organized sports, vaudeville) as distinct from "high culture" were already well advanced before 1914. Likewise, the economic forces that would undermine the dominant position of the middle class had been afoot long before the onset of the Great War.

Intellectual Trends

According to the Enlightenment tradition, autonomous reason could discover the natural laws that governed society as well as nature. Assuming that humans were by nature good (although perhaps corrupted by history), the eighteenth-century intellectuals believed that by the application of reason, humans could build a better world, perhaps even a utopia. Theories put forth by the leading philosophers (e.g., John Locke's environmentalism in *Essay Concerning Human Understanding* [1689]) created a faith in progress and a sense of optimism about the future. Setting themselves free from all accepted authority (especially Christianity), they created a vision of a future humanity guided by the light of reason. History had meaning. It was going somewhere. The individual was meaningful, for the individual was a thinking, reasoning creature, and thereby the master of his or her own fate and of history.

During the decades before the Great War, a second scientific revolution and a new set of intellectuals brought forth new theories and scientific discoveries that called into question whether the individual human being was, after all, a reasoning, rational being in an orderly, meaningful universe and suggested that, instead, a human being might be simply an irrational animal adrift in a universe of random chaos. For many thinking individuals, the experience of the Great War made more urgent the need to find new answers to the most basic questions of ultimate meaning. The Great War merely accelerated the movement away from the fundamental assumptions of the Enlightenment tradition.

A Second Scientific Revolution

The popular acceptance of Charles Darwin's (1809–1882) theory of the evolutionary origins of life as presented in *Origin of the Species* (1859) and the *Descent of Man* (1871) was a key development. The theory of the evolutionary origin of life was as ancient as the Greek philosopher Anaximander (610–ca. 547 B.C.) of Miletus, who first suggested it in the sixth century B.C. Darwin benefitted from the acceptance of Charles Lyell's (1797–1875) principle of uniformitarianism (*Principles of Geology* [1830–1833]), by which the earth was thought to be millions of years old. Lyell's theory provided the immense time span required by Darwin's theory, if it was to have any credibility.

Although Darwin did not directly attack Christianity, the implications of his theory called into question the truth of biblical revelation, and hence Christianity. Also, according to Darwin, humans were no longer a special creation, but just a higher form of animal life, albeit thinking animals. And history still had meaning, for, as understood from the assumptions of the Enlightenment tradition, evolution implied progress toward some goal, whatever that might be. Life may have begun as a chance event in some primeval slime, but by Darwin's day, evolution of life had progressed to the stage of a reasoning biped (e.g., Darwin).

The human being as a reasoning animal, however, was soon under attack, as was the validity of scientific reasoning. The German philosopher Friedrich Nietzsche (1844–1900) more than any other thinker of the nineteenth century saw clearly where autonomous reason was leading. He argued that the discoveries of modern science

No one better symbolized the changing views of reality during the twentieth century than Albert Einstein. © Keystone Pictures USA/Alamy

and philosophical reasoning had led to the conclusion that the "myth" of God was no longer tenable, that is, "God is dead." Since the Judeo-Christian understanding of God was the essential basis of Western civilization, his absence cut humans adrift in a universe without meaning (e.g., the parable of the madman in *The Gay Science* [1882]). The Enlightenment's rejection of Christianity while trying to retain Christian ethics was a hoax. There were no absolute values. The universe is not governed by rational principles. Humans, said Nietzsche, were driven by dark instinctual drives, not motivated by reason.

Other intellectuals like Henri Bergson (1859–1941) and Georges Sorel (1847–1922) also questioned the validity of scientific reasoning as a guide to truth (positivism) and claimed that humans were irrational by nature. None, however, was more influential than Sigmund Freud (1856–1939), the founder of psychoanalysis. Although Freud clung to the Enlightenment's belief that reason and scientific inquiry made civilization possible, his conclusion that humans are motivated by primitive, irrational drives hidden deep in the subconscious tended to undermine the Enlightenment's image of humanity. Also, Freud rejected both the Christian belief that evil was essentially a moral problem and the Enlightenment's assumption that it was an environmental problem. Rather, Freud believed that evil was rooted in human nature. For him, there was no utopia in the future. Faith in progress and optimism about the future no longer had a basis. Human beings as the thinking (reasoning) higher animals of Darwin's vision, like human beings created in the image of God, were now obsolete.

What threw the Enlightenment tradition into total disarray was the revolution in physics from the 1890s to the 1920s. The discoveries of Max Planck (1858–1947), Niels Bohr (1885–1962), Werner Heisenberg (1901–1976), and especially Albert Einstein (1879–1955) challenged, and for many effectively overthrew, the Newtonian view (classical physics) of the universe upon which the Enlightenment tradition rested. Classical physics taught that the universe was a three-dimensional, objective reality, whose properties could be measured from an absolute reference point. The new physics taught that there was no objective reality. Space and time did not exist independent of the observer. There is no fixed (absolute) reference point anywhere in the universe. The Enlightenment's view of the individual as an autonomous being capable of making rational choices in a universe of meaning was gone. Its departure heralded the end of optimism about the future of Western civilization. The individual was now cut adrift in a cold, mysterious universe without any coherent answer to the question "Who am I?" At best, the individual was a random chance "happening," thrown up by an impersonal universe, whose ultimate reality was only the molecules of which he or she was composed.

Postwar Despair

The new view of reality destroyed the foundational premise of classical liberalism and democracy, as well as humanitarianism. The experiences of the Great War together with the economic crises and social dislocations that followed, and in part resulted from, it further deepened anxiety over the future. Those who had experienced the "troglodyte world" of trench warfare might well agree with the view that Western civilization was dying.

The French writer Paul Valéry (1871–1945) expressed the disillusionment and despair felt by the postwar intellectuals. The storm that was the Great War had passed, leaving those who survived restless and uneasy, "as if the [next] storm were about to break" and fearful of the future. The atmosphere was filled with anxiety and darkness. All the fundamental assumptions were irreparably damaged by the war. The damage done to the mind, observed Valéry and other intellectual guardians of civilization, cast a shadow over the future.

Paul Bäumer, the main character in what is perhaps the best-known novel of the Great War, *All Quiet on the Western Front* (1929), while visiting a military hospital reflects on how the war dehumanized the generation that experienced it. The cumulative knowledge of the past, Bäumer concludes, "must be all lies and of no account when the culture of a thousand years could not prevent this stream of blood being poured out. . . ." (Modern History Sourcebook 1997). For those who survived the war in the trenches, their knowledge of life is limited to "despair, death, fear, and fatuous superficiality cast over an abyss of sorrow." What can the future hold for a generation whose calling for the past four years has been killing one's fellow human beings?

"The war," wrote Ernst von Salomon, a former *Freikorps* member, "will never discharge them; they will never return home; they will always carry the trenches in their blood" (Salomon, p. 87). How could the soldier of the Great War ever return to life as a civilian, take up once again the daily routine of a peaceful citizen? The war would end for some, but for the veteran, it will never end. The warrior is forever marching, forever haunted by memories that can never be exorcised.

No one better expressed the postwar mood than the German school teacher and philosopher Oswald Spengler (1880–1936). Spengler's *The Decline of the West* (1918–1922) was the most famous postwar prophecy of impending doom. Spengler viewed Western civilization as a living organism which, like any other living organism, must pass through the stages of life from birth to death. The signs of degeneration were everywhere, said Spengler. Western civilization was on its deathbed, its demise unavoidable.

Spengler's ideas were widely spread, especially in Germany, where they were often discussed and cited. Those on the extreme right exploited them by claiming to construct a new order upon the ruins of a dead civilization. Nietzsche had prophesied the rise of supermen (*übermenschen*) who would create new myths to take the place of God, who had been murdered by the advance of civilization. In a sense, Hitler can be understood as one such "superman," and the Nazi racial state as one such myth. Likewise, Lenin, Stalin, and the Soviet Union may be understood as fulfillments of Nietzsche's prophecy.

Other writers used the theme of apocalypse to emphasize the possibility of renovating European civilization from a new Dark Age. This approach culminated in two remarkable books that appeared at the end of the 1920s: Sigmund Freud's *Civilization and Its Discontents* (1930) and José Ortega y Gasset's (1883–1955) *The Revolt of the Masses* (1930). Both men emphasized that civilization was an artificial product of human effort, maintained only by work and sacrifice. Freud, in line with his research before the Great War, stressed the idea that civilization was based on the repression of natural instincts, so that one paid a psychic price for living in a civilized society. However, from his vantage point at the end of the 1920s, Freud saw the failure to maintain civilization exacting an even higher cost in the long run: the destruction of all human values.

In *The Revolt of the Masses*, Ortega argued that civilization was being eclipsed by a new age of barbarism. The postwar era was witnessing the emergence of new "mass" mentality, "the commonplace mind," one that knows no standard by which to judge the legitimacy of anything, one that demands conformity and the annihilation of all those who refuse to become just like everyone else. There can be no culture where there are no ruling principles or standards by which to define culture. The average individual claims to have ideas, but in reality, what he claims to be ideas are "nothing more than appetites in words. . . ." Such are the masses upon which the new authoritarian dictatorships are based.

The new Bolshevik order in Russia also benefitted from the despair of the postwar years. There too, a Nietzschean prophecy was apparently being fulfilled. The new socialist individual and a new Marxist doctrine of progress toward a future utopia on earth were attractive to many, especially leftist intellectuals, who sought to escape despair by a leap of faith. Many took the pilgrimage to the Soviet Union during the 1930s. Some, like the American journalist Lincoln Steffens (1866–1936), returned convinced that they had been to the future and that it worked. Others, like the British journalist and Fabian socialist Malcolm Muggeridge (1903–1990) and the anarchist Emma Goldman (1869–1940), came back thoroughly disillusioned. Muggeridge expressed his disillusionment in a novel, *Winter in Moscow*, published in 1934, and Goldman in a memoir not so subtly titled *My Disillusionment in Russia* (1923). The Soviet Union was not an answer to despair, but rather a symptom of postwar demoralization.

The fine arts were powerful ideological weapons in the mission to construct a new culture in Nazi Germany, Fascist Italy, and Marxist–Leninist Russia. Hitler, himself an artist, understood how the arts could be the key to unlock the conscious and subconscious mind and thus further the inner conversion of the individual. Both the visual and performing arts have the power to transform dry ideology into the images and myths that move the individual emotionally. Like one who experiences a religious conversion, the newly born-again believer will follow he who embodies the "gospel" to which he or she has been converted.

Many intellectuals, artists, and writers of various sorts during the 1930s took one side or the other in the great ideological struggle between fascism and communism. The "Auden Generation," for example, which included the poets W. H. Auden (1907–1973) and C. Day Lewis (1904–1972); important continental writers such as André Malraux (1901–1976), Ignazio Silone (1900–1978), and Arthur Koestler (1905–1983); and artists such as Max Beckmann (1884–1950) and Max Ernst (1891–1976) lent their talents in one fashion or another to the defense of democracy and the criticism of fascism. The support offered to fascism by intellectuals and artists was less substantial. Scattered examples, such as the playwright Gerhart Hauptmann (1862–1946) in Germany or the novelist Louis-Ferdinand Céline (1894–1961) in France, come to mind. By and large, however, commitment by artists and intellectuals meant a defense of democracy (and often a defense of the socialist democracy of the Soviet Union) and a condemnation of fascism.

The experiences of the Great War also helped promote the careers of the utopian demagogues of the 1930s and 1940s in other ways. Not only were the new discoveries of science and the new philosophical theories beyond the comprehension of the masses, so too was the carnage of the war. The social and economic dislocations resulting from the collapse of the old order drove large numbers of people to seek answers. It was easy for the new demagogues to direct the resentment of the masses to an identifiable enemy, be it the Jews, capitalists, communists, or simply the establishment. Somewhere, some personified evil force was to blame for the chaos from which it benefitted.

It was also possible to preach the mass extermination of the enemy race or class. The Great War had cheapened life. It left behind images of mass death previously unknown. If millions of lives could be sacrificed to gain a few yards of churned-up earth, did it not make more sense to sacrifice millions of lives to create a classless or racially pure utopia? The Holocaust of Nazi Germany and the "GULAG" of Soviet Russia were to some extent conceivable because of the images left by the Great War.

Culture

The new world view that took shape even before the Great War was given expression by the artists, writers, poets, and musicians. The new emerging world view assumed that there is no truth, not even in science. Instead of truth, there are only truths. Instead of order, there is only chaos. Indeed, there is no value for humans and history (although the post-World War II existentialists, covered in Chapter 11, would say that the individual can give his or her life and history value through action). The new world view was a fragmented view of reality. Great art is the merger of technique with world view. The purveyors of culture after the Great War developed a technique of fragmentation to fit the new world view.

In art, the transition began with the impressionist painters in the 1870s. In the name of "realism," they rebelled against the practice of portraying the world around them with camera-like realism. The impressionists (e.g., Claude Monet [1840–1926], Pierre Auguste Renoir [1841–1919], Camille Pissarro [1830–1903], Alfred Sisley [1839–1899], and Edgar Degas [1834–1917]) emphasized the play of light as they perceived it. In so doing, they abandoned objective reality (portraying the world around them) for a subjective response to the real world. Now, the question was: what was "real," the object or the artist's mental "impression" of it?

The impressionists were succeeded by a group known as the postimpressionists. They sought reality in the recesses of the mind. Reality was now the observer's (i.e., individual artist's) mental reflections upon the sensory images coming into the mind as light waves. Among the leading postimpressionists were Paul Cézanne (1839–1906), Vincent Van Gogh (1853–1890), Paul Gauguin (1848–1903), and Georges Seurat (1859–1891). By 1910, postimpressionism yielded to abstract art.

The abstract artists totally abandoned reality. No longer did the artists see as their task simply painting, in any form, the objective world around them. As with the new physics, there was no fixed reality. Reality was what the artist said it was. A painting was not a portrait or even an impression of reality. Rather, it "created" reality. Also, there could no longer be an objective standard by which to judge what was good art or bad art. Art had become a vehicle for the new world view.

As in any age, only a relatively small segment of the population was aware of the changing intellectual and artistic understanding of reality or wrestled with the implications of an acceptance of the new view of humans as irrational animals in an impersonal, morally neutral universe. The masses only slowly absorbed the new world view and then only passively and in cursory form through the mass media (e.g., radio, motion pictures). They would borrow "sound bites" from the new physics or psychology and speak of "relativity" or the "unconscious," much as in an earlier period they spoke of "survival of the fittest" or "natural selection," without any real understanding of the meaning or implications of these "buzzwords." The average individual does not sit down and try to systematically define and analyze his world view, or the presuppositions underlying it. Still, everyone has a world view and acts according to it, as much as artists, philosophers, or politicians do.

The message of most artistic movements of the interwar years was one of anarchy, even nihilism. In responding to the disillusionment of war, the Dadaists rejected all order and reason. Believing that the Great War revealed the absurdity of all of life, the Dadaists embraced nihilism. The life span of Dadaism, the first "anti-art art," was brief. Beginning in the midteens, it ended in the midtwenties, when it yielded the field to surrealism. Influenced by Freudianism, surrealism sought reality in the unconscious, beyond the reach of reason. Both Dadaism and surrealism were responses to the apparent chaos of the time, but without any hint of an answer.

In the skilled hands of artists like Otto Dix (1891–1969), George Grosz (1893–1959), Pablo Picasso (1881–1973), Max Beckmann, Käthe Kollwitz (1867–1945), and others, the new fragmented technique was employed to make paintings powerful statements against the insanity of war and the decadence of postwar society and politics.

The message that passed through the artist's brush onto the canvas also passed through the poet's or novelist's pen onto the page, and thence into the mind of the reader. James Joyce (1882–1941) used the literary technique known as "stream-of-consciousness" in *Ulysses* (1922) to portray a single day in the lives of middle-class Dubliners. In both the title and the style of *The Waste Land* (1922), T. S. Eliot (1888–1965) used a fragmented form of poetry to convey a fragmented message:

> Le Prince d'Aquitaine à la tour abolie.
> These fragments I have shored against my ruins
> Why then Ile fit you.
> Hieronymo's mad againe.
> Datta. Dayadhvam. Damyata.
> Shantih shantih shantih. (p. 50)

Joyce and Eliot were among the avant-garde. Interwar literature aimed at mass consumption consisted largely of realistic novels and accepted poetic styles. The same was true of music and the new art form, the cinema.

Jazz was a peculiarly American contribution to both popular and high culture between the wars. It first appeared as a distinct form of music in New Orleans around the turn of the century, where it was "composed" and performed without written music by African American street musicians who had no formal training in music. From New Orleans, it spread to Chicago and Harlem. After the war, the "Jazz Age" was born, as white jazz bands began to appear across America and in Europe. Jazz music found a home in Paris, one of the two centers of European culture during the 1920s. There, and later in Berlin, the other locus of cultural life in the 1920s, Josephine Baker (1906–1975), an African American from St. Louis, delighted audiences dancing the Charleston wearing only a string of bananas around her waist, as she sang jazz favorites. The first talking motion picture was *The Jazz Singer*, starring Al Jolson (1927).

Berlin, where "life was a cabaret," was a Mecca for those from all over Europe seeking a decadent lifestyle that included jazz, night-clubs, drugs, liquor, prostitution, and homosexuality. One of the keenest observers of the Jazz Age culture was Count Harry Kessler (1868–1937), also known as the "Red Count." His detailed diaries from the period are an invaluable source for the cultural life of Berlin during the Weimar era.

At one o'clock in the morning of February 13, 1926, Count Kessler was invited to a party at a Berlin apartment. He arrived to find Max Reinhardt and the other gentlemen dressed in tuxedos, surrounded by naked girls. As Kessler describes the scene,

> Miss Baker was also naked except for a pink muslin apron, and the little Landshoff girl [the host's mistress] was dressed up as a boy in a dinner-jacket. Miss Baker was dancing solo with brilliant artistic mimicry and purity of style. . . . The naked girls lay or skipped among the four or five men in dinner-jackets. The Landshoff girl, really looking like a dazzlingly handsome boy, jazzed with Miss Baker to gramophone tunes.

Berlin was also the center of the motion picture industry prior to the Nazis' ascent to power. Not all of the films produced were meant only for entertainment. In Weimar, Germany, film became a serious art form. Pictures like *The Cabinet of Dr. Caligari* (1920) and *The Golem* (1920) merged technique and message to produce works of expressionist art. Perhaps the best-known, and perhaps the most significant, film produced in Weimar Germany was *The Blue Angel* (1930), starring Marlene Dietrich (1901–1992). Some critics have seen in it an allegory of the triumph of the new (and decadent) Germany over the old. Through their music and atmosphere, *The Blue Angel* and Bertolt Brecht's (1898–1956) stage play, *The Threepenny Opera*, captured the mood of Weimar Germany's cultural life. *The Threepenny Opera* premiered at the Schiffbauerdamm Theatre in Berlin, with a musical score influenced by jazz and composed by Kurt Weill (1900–1950).

It was in the 1920s, and especially the last half of the decade, that one could begin to speak of a "popular culture" as distinct from "high culture." Of course, the popular culture of postwar Europe had its roots in the last half of the nineteenth century. But it was in the 1920s that it developed into what we know today. Originally, the property of the working classes and class-oriented, popular culture had become by the late 1920s largely a matter of entertainment, recreation, fashions, and fads which, for a short period of time, might bind people from different social backgrounds together and blur the still significant differences that existed.

Whether good or bad, popular culture in the affluent and vital late 1920s developed most of the attributes familiar in today's society. Entertainment became increasingly commercialized and built on changing fashions. New songs, new dance steps, and new movie stars followed one another in an accelerating pace. The growth of spectator sports was only one example of the trend toward passive involvement in culture. In all areas of entertainment, the lowest common denominator was sought in order to attract as wide an audience as possible.

The masses were the passive consumers of culture during the interwar years. The disintegration of the Enlightenment tradition and its consequences, which preoccupied the scientists and philosophers and found anguished expression in the creative works of the artists and poets, did not immediately affect the masses. It was not until after World War II that the assumptions of the new world view

Josephine Baker (1906–1975) symbolized the vitality of Afro-American, or Jazz, culture to her admiring audiences in Paris and Berlin during the 1920s. © AF archive / Alamy

(in the form of, e.g., existentialism) would filter down to the masses through the mass media. Catalyzed again by war and economic dislocations, they would find violent expression during the 1960s and 1970s, before giving way in the last quarter of the century to an individual quest for personal peace and affluence, one troubled still by a vague feeling of anxiety.

The Social Impact

Even in the best-run war efforts, there was much dislocation and suffering among civilians, but one of the most important ways in which the Great War changed social relations was to reduce the importance of class or status. The emphasis from the beginning had been on the cooperation of all layers of society in the war effort. Each country had its own equivalent of the French *union sacrée* (French for "Sacred Union") or the German *Burgfrieden* (German for "castle peace," or a political truce agreed to by the political parties in Germany during the Great War). Governments erased many distinctions through rationing and other efforts to make the burdens of war somewhat equitable. Governments also erased distinctions by the first efforts toward the standardization of life, an example of which were the form postcards that civilians received from the front: on the cards were only a few standard messages from which the soldier could choose. If anything other than a signature was added, stated a printed warning at the top of the postcard, "the post card will be destroyed."

In a more positive manner, the comprehensive mobilization of each population during the war created a sense of participation in the affairs of the nation and a sense of individual self-respect that many had never before felt. Many were thrust into new responsibilities and discovered in themselves abilities and aspirations that had previously lain dormant. One such person was Rosina Whyatt (1888–1971), a household servant before the war, who went to work in a munitions plant and after the war became a labor organizer. Many felt that after the war, they could not accept a return to the old society and that, in any case, they had earned a reward for their sacrifices. These feelings were reinforced by returning soldiers who, after living through the horrors of trench warfare, would not willingly stand mutely in awe of their "betters" again. Leonard Thompson, a farm worker from Suffolk, came back after serving in the war to organize a branch of the Agricultural Labourers Union. Others in Britain and on the continent followed similar paths.

One group in particular took on new roles during the war. Women found positions in industries that had traditionally been closed to them, as well as expanded opportunities in areas in which they were already active. It became far more acceptable than ever before for women to have their own apartments, to go out unescorted, and, generally, to make their own decisions about their lives. It was no longer possible after the war to deny women the vote. Women's suffrage was granted in the Soviet Union in 1917, in Germany in

1918, and in the United Kingdom in 1918 with certain qualifications and on equality with men in 1928. In the United States, women were granted the right to vote with the passage of the Nineteenth Amendment to the US Constitution in 1920.

Some people, of course, returned to an older concept of "the place" of women once the unusual situation created by the war had ended. Many women, however, found it impossible to give up the independence and responsibility to which they had become accustomed. The era of the flapper in the twenties would not have been possible without the changes in attitudes, in both males and females, caused by the Great War.

Peasants and Agriculture

The peasantry was perhaps the class least affected by the Great War, and the one class that did not share in the general prosperity of the later 1920s. Food prices, on which the income of farmers depended, were low throughout the 1920s and competition from abroad was stiff. Many peasants in Western Europe had borrowed either during or right after the war to purchase land or equipment. These debts were difficult to repay in the later 1920s.

Many peasants had served in the army or had in other ways become more aware of the nature of life beyond their own region. They expected more in the 1920s and in some cases were willing to work in new and different ways to obtain their demands. In Britain, many agricultural laborers joined organizations to improve pay and working conditions. The interwar period was one of bitter struggle as organized agricultural laborers tried to persuade their fellow laborers to join and fight to gain recognition from the landlords. In Italy, an attempt in the early 1920s to reform landholding patterns was defeated in the postwar violence that led to Fascism. In Germany, many peasants left the land for the cities; those who remained on the land began to support movements such as the Nazi Party, which promised to protect the farmer and the small agricultural enterprise. Although some French and German peasants resorted to lobbying groups, cooperative movements, and the promise of technology to improve their condition, little changed in terms of agricultural practices and lifestyles. Peasants continued to lead largely isolated, family-centered existences. The peasants in Western Europe had been brought into contact with the modern world before the Great War through the development of the market economy, the spread of public education, expansion of national institutions like the army, and the improvement of transportation and communication facilities, but their contact was still slight and episodic even in the late 1920s.

In Eastern Europe, the process of rural adaptation—which had taken place in Western Europe and America before the Great War—had barely begun by the end of the 1920s. The power of the landed elites and traditional aristocracies was still formidable. In some countries, Bulgaria, for example, the small peasant landholders remained an important group. In most countries, Hungary being perhaps the best example, the large estate owners dominated agriculture. In every case, rural populations continued to grow, placing additional pressure on the agricultural economy. In much of Eastern Europe, poverty, superstition, ignorance, and isolation were the rule among the peasantry. Some new ideas circulated as a result of service in the war, the impact of the Russian Revolution, and the work of peasant political movements, but most peasants lived in ways scarcely different from those of their ancestors in the early 1800s. Only in the Soviet Union was a large-scale effort made to introduce the peasant to the modern world, an effort that took on revolutionary proportions in the early 1930s.

The Working Class

In general, the working classes benefitted from the war. Labor supported the war effort in each country by ensuring labor stability and thus war production. In return, the working classes received higher wages, recognition of the right to unionize and bargain collectively, and even participation by labor's leaders in government decision making. When the war ended, labor was determined not to yield any of its newly won status or influence.

Although in the 1920s the organized working class was stronger and more influential than it had been before the war, it was not as strong as it might have been. This was due to two related developments. First, the organized working class split in the immediate postwar period into a communist movement that centered on the Communist International (Comintern) and a socialist movement that continued the policies of the old Second International. The German Social Democratic Party (SPD) faced competition from the left in the Communist Party of Germany (KPD); and there were similar divisions elsewhere in Western Europe. The split was also reflected in the trade union movement and many other specialized organizations. Precisely because the Communist and the Socialist Parties referred to the same Marxist heritage to interpret political and social events and because both appealed to the same social group—the working class—they were bitter rivals. The communists in particular thought competition with the socialists caused the working class to divide into mutually hostile groups. The split also made it difficult for Social Democratic Parties to moderate their stance toward bourgeois society and government. Even in Germany, where the SPD was often a crucial element in coalition governments, the official line was unremitting hostility to the existing order. Any serious compromise of Marxist doctrine might have driven even more of the working class into the Communist Party.

Although a united working class would have been stronger than a divided one, a divided one was still impressive. Socialists were not only represented in large numbers on the national level, but they also played important roles in municipal and provincial governments in Italy (until the Fascists came to power), Germany, and France. Unfortunately, despite generally responsible attitudes and actions, working-class representatives never gained the trust and full cooperation of their middle-class counterparts. Particularly in Germany, most members of the middle class resented the new political power of the workers on the local and state levels.

Organized labor faced even stronger resistance to its influence in the economic sphere. At the end of the war, the labor movement had pushed hard for economic changes, including higher wages, better working conditions, shorter hours, and worker participation

in the management of industry. The dislocation of national economies (e.g., Great Britain) made it difficult for organized labor to
maintain its wartime gains. This, together with the determination
of returning veterans to gain what they believed was fairly theirs
and promises of a better life by politicians and business leaders,
fueled strike movements in 1919 and 1920 in France, Britain,
Germany, and Italy.

Efforts to resolve these economic and social problems in the
immediate postwar period met with little success. In part, this
failure was due to the short depression that Europe experienced at
the beginning of the 1920s. The split within the labor movement
at the same time also weakened it. Employers rapidly organized
groups in the early 1920s to influence the government and to provide
mutual aid against strikes; the rate of defeat of strikes went up.
Governments became less sympathetic to labor goals and in some
cases, notably that of Fascist Italy, obviously hostile. Still, by 1924,
general prosperity led to better conditions for most groups of
workers. Many worked eight-hour days with Saturday half-holidays.
Real wages rose between 1924 and 1929. Workers participated with
other groups in the new possibilities for entertainment and recreation.
The major exception to the general labor peace in the latter part of
the 1920s was the British General Strike in 1926, but Britain was
plagued by high levels of unemployment in the 1920s and by a particularly troubled but important sector of the economy, the coal mining
industry. Perhaps the main result of the resounding defeat of the coal
miners, who had stayed out on strike after other groups involved in
the General Strike had gone back to work, was the reduction of overt
labor unrest in Britain despite the troubled economy.

The Middle Class

Historically, the middle class (or bourgeoisie) was the driving force
and backbone of liberalism. Indeed, the nineteenth century was the
"golden age" of both liberalism and the middle class. But the stability of the middle class rested upon its ability to accumulate wealth
and pass it on to the next generation. The validity of its world view

was based on traditional morality. Middle-class people believed that by their industriousness, frugality, and defense of the nuclear family and traditional values, they played a major role in creating a better world. The middle class had retained its faith in progress because of its self-confidence. One of the most important effects of the Great War was that it undermined that self-confidence.

The spiritual crisis confronting Western civilization at the turn of the century (as noted above) undermined the religious foundations of middle-class morality. Since the middle class traditionally viewed everything in moral terms, the emergence of a new world view had serious implications for it. Likewise, the emancipation of women (e.g., greater employment opportunities, loosening of divorce laws and traditional moral codes) furthered by the war effort, together with the growth of public education and a mass culture, undermined the importance of the family. Individuals increasingly sought their fulfillment outside of the home.

The financial base of middle-class ascendancy was also weakened by the war and its economic repercussions. Some historians have speculated that one of the most important effects of the Great War was the financial impoverishment of the middle class due to taxes, inflation, and the expropriation of wealth through nationalization, land reform, and rent controls. Taxes, virtually nonexistent or very light before 1914, became burdensome after 1919. Inflation was often devastating for the middle class. In France, for example, a capital investment of 500,000 francs in 1914 would allow one to live in style off the annual interest income. That same capital investment in 1924, although producing a higher annual income, was not sufficient to maintain the same standard of living. The cumulative impact was demoralizing for the middle class, who began to question the value of its work and its other contributions to civilization. Also, the middle class began to question the validity of liberalism, both economic and political.

Businessmen, for example, tended to believe that parliamentary democracy was a weak and ineffectual means of government. A strong national state required a more authoritarian kind of leadership and, in any case, one sympathetic to business. Those who lived in small towns and provincial centers identified Europe's problems with the increase of urbanization. It was the city, especially Berlin in Germany and Paris in France, where all that was wrong and dangerous was spawned. For the middle class, the late 1920s were good times, but, having experienced war, revolution, depression, and inflation in recent memory, this segment of the population was wary and somewhat insecure. Waiting in the wings to benefit from that sense of insecurity during the 1930s were the demagogues, those who considered themselves the supermen of Nietzsche's vision.

References

Eliot, T.S. 1980. *The Complete Poems and Plays, 1909–1950*. New York: Harcourt Brace Jovanovich, Publishers, p.50.

Modern History Sourcebook. 1997. "On European Civilization and the European Mind, c. 1919, 1922." Accessed October 12, 2012. http://www.fordham.edu/halsall/mod/valery.asp

Ortega y Gasset, José. 1930. *The Revolt of the Masses*. London: G. Allen & Unwin, ltd.

Remarque, Erich Maria. 1929. *All Quiet on the Western Front*. New York: Fawett World Library.

Salomon, Ernst von. 1931. *Die Geachteten*. Translated as *The Outlaws* by Theodor H. Von Laue, in *Sources of Twentieth-Century Europe*, edited by Marvin Perry. 1999. Boston: Houghton Mifflin.

Further Reading

Friedrich, Otto. 1972. *Before the Deluge: A Portrait of Berlin in the 1920's*. New York: Harper and Row. A very readable and entertaining history of the cultural life of Weimar Germany.

Graves, Robert and Alan Hodge. 2001. *The Long Week-End: A Social History of Great Britain, 1918–1939*. New York: W. W. Norton. The ever-popular account of everyday life in interwar Britain.

Johnson, Paul. 2007. *Intellectuals: From Marx and Tolstoy to Sartre and Chomsky*, revised ed. New York: Harper Perennial. Short, well-written biographies of important cultural figures including Bertolt Brecht, Bertrand Russell, and Jean-Paul Sarte.

Pais, Abraham. 2005. *Subtle is the Lord: The Science and Life of Albert Einstein*. New York: Oxford University Press. A look at the life and ideas of the man who "reordered" the universe.

Rookmaaker, H. R. 1994. *Modern Art & the Death of a Culture*. Wheaton: Crossway Books. Discusses art as a vehicle for worldview.

Sontag, Raymond J. 1972. *A Broken World, 1919–1939*. New York: Harper Torch books. A very good introduction to Europe during the 1920s.

Stromberg, Roland N. 1991. *Makers of Modern Culture: Five Twentieth-Century Thinkers*. Wheeling: Harlan Davidson. A concise examination of five individuals—Sigmund Freud, Albert Einstein, Ludwig Wittgenstein, James Joyce, and Jean-Paul Sartre—who transformed the world.

5

Recovery and Prosperity, 1919–1929

Chronology

1919	German National Assembly drafts the Weimar Constitution
1920	"Kapp Putsch" led by Wolfgang Kapp
1921	Russian Civil War ends
	Lenin introduces the New Economic Policy (NEP)
1922	Washington Naval Conference
	Rapallo Treaty between Germany and the Soviet Union
	Mussolini's so-called March on Rome
1923	"Beer Hall (Munich) Putsch" led by Adolf Hitler
	Ruhr occupation (June 1923–August 1924) triggers Great Inflation in Germany

Twentieth-Century Europe: A Brief History, 1900 to the Present, Third Edition.
Michael D. Richards and Paul R. Waibel.
© 2014 John Wiley & Sons, Inc. Published 2014 by John Wiley & Sons, Inc.

1924	Lenin dies; power struggle between Leon Trotsky and Joseph Stalin
	Stalin proclaims the possibility of "Socialism in One Country"
1925	Locarno treaties between Germany, France, and Belgium
1926	General Strike in Great Britain
1928	Kellogg–Briand Pact
1929	Joseph Stalin succeeds Lenin as the leader of the Soviet Union
	Lateran Accord between Italy and the Papacy

THE GREAT WAR HAD BEEN FOUGHT to "make the world safe for democracy." It also had been hailed as the "war to end all wars." To some perceptive individuals in 1919, these were hollow utopian slogans that concealed the approach of the grim reaper to harvest the bitter seeds of resentment and hatred sown and watered at the Paris Peace Conference. Looking back after a second and more destructive world war, it is tempting to view the events of the 1920s and 1930s with the clarity of historical determinism. But if one views the events of the 1920s without the benefit of hindsight, it is possible to sympathize with those who chose to see the Great War as a brief and unfortunate interruption in the forward march of civilization. The Great Depression would abruptly end the "Roaring Twenties" and reveal how fragile the foundations of the return to "normalcy" were, but a look at international relations and the internal affairs of the major European states reveals a collection of mixed signals.

The most obvious outcome of the Great War was the passing of the ancient empires of Germany, Russia, Austria-Hungary, and Turkey. With the departure of those antique dynasties, and with them a host of lesser princely houses, a new era appeared to be dawning, when, as President Woodrow Wilson had foretold in 1917, those who submitted to authority would have "a voice in their own government." Where in 1914 there had been 17 monarchies and 3 republics, in 1919, there were 13 monarchies and 13 republics. Germany, Austria, Hungary, Czechoslovakia, and Turkey were all proclaimed republics. In Russia, the autocratic rule of the Tsar was replaced by what Lenin called "democratic centralism," a Soviet republic that was soon revealed as more autocratic than tsarist Russia. In nearly every country, a communist party emerged from the old social democratic and trade union movements to challenge what communists termed "bourgeois democracy." The various communist parties were connected with one another in an organization called the Communist, or Third, International (the Comintern), which seemed, potentially at least, very dangerous to democracy. Attempts to establish the new Soviet-style "democracy" in Germany (1919, 1921, and 1923) and Hungary (1919) were defeated by the army, assisted in Germany by paramilitary forces (the Freikorps, sometimes called the Black Reichswehr) and in Hungary by the Romanian army.

A constitutional and parliamentary government, republican more often than monarchical, was the norm by the mid-1920s. Universal male suffrage was generally accepted; some nations had adopted female suffrage as well after the war. On the continent, socialist parties had to face the question of active participation in government. In Germany, the Social Democratic Party (SPD) formed a major component of the coalition government. In France, the Socialists backed away from full participation. Everywhere the centrist parties formed the backbone of the ministries. It was still nearly a decade before William Butler Yeats's prophetic line "Things fall apart; the center cannot hold" would come true.

There were several examples of cooperation in international relations during the 1920s. In 1922, the Washington Naval Conference made progress toward limiting the size of navies among the five postwar great powers. Some 70 ships were scrapped; a 10-year moratorium on the construction of any new battleships was declared; and the 5 signatories agreed to limit the tonnage of capital ships to a ratio of: 5, Great Britain; 5, United States; 3, Japan; 1.75, France; 1.75, Italy. In April 1922, Germany and Soviet Russia signed the Rapallo Treaty, by which they reestablished diplomatic relations, renounced all financial claims against each other, and pledged cooperation. It initiated five years of close cooperation between the two ostracized powers. Also in 1922, the "Little Entente" of Czechoslovakia, Yugoslavia, and Romania was formed under French auspices to dampen the fears of both France and the East European successor states of a revived Germany.

Perhaps the most promising development was the Locarno treaties concluded in December 1925. In the principal treaty signed by France, Belgium, and Germany and guaranteed by Great Britain and Italy, Germany accepted as final its western borders with France and Belgium as fixed by the Versailles Treaty. The inviolability of the demilitarized Rhineland was also confirmed. The Locarno treaties were the work of German Foreign Minister Gustav Stresemann (1878–1929), French Foreign Minister Aristide Briand, and British Foreign Secretary Austen Chamberlain (1863–1937)—all of whom received the Nobel Peace Prize—three men committed to international cooperation based upon the fulfillment of the Paris Peace Settlement. A new spirit of conciliation swept through Europe in the wake of the Locarno agreements. Even the French were beginning to suspect that the Germans were becoming civilized. The fact, however, that Germany specifically refused to accept as permanent its eastern borders should have cast a shadow over the "spirit of Locarno."

Perhaps the best expression of the widespread optimism engendered by the spirit of Locarno was the Kellogg–Briand Pact of 1928, which outlawed war as an instrument of national policy. Proposed to US Secretary of State Frank B. Kellogg (1856–1937) by Briand, it was signed by 64 nations. The Kellogg–Briand Pact was given more immediate significance due to the fact that Germany and the two leading non-League members—the United States and Soviet Union—signed it. As the following decade was to demonstrate, outlawing war and calling for peaceful resolution of international disputes while not providing any means for enforcement was only a pious gesture or, as one US senator put it, an "international kiss." In 1928, spirits were high amidst economic prosperity and international conciliation. No one could see the Great Depression waiting ominously in the wings to shatter the illusion. A closer look inside the European powers during the 1920s reveals disturbing signs of future distress.

Great Britain

On the eve of the Great War, three major problems had threatened to overwhelm the British government: 1) the question of Irish home rule, 2) the vote for women, and 3) a broad-based dissatisfaction among workers. At the end of the war, the first two issues were resolved, although not to everyone's complete satisfaction. Agreements in 1920 and 1921 resulted in the division of Ireland into Northern Ireland, which remained attached to Great Britain as an autonomous area, and the Irish Free State, which gained Dominion status. It was a far-from-definitive solution, but one which largely removed the Irish problem from British politics for the first time in over a century. The second issue was resolved when women over the age of 30 were given the vote in 1918 (10 years later, women received the vote on the same terms as men).

The third issue was more intractable. Great Britain's problems between the wars were rooted in the economic impact of the Great War. As an island nation with an empire upon which the sun never set before 1914, British prosperity, and with it British influence, depended upon foreign trade. But Britain's dominant position in world trade was severely shaken by the war. Many old reliable trading partners either developed their own industries and reduced imports or established new trade relations with other nations (e.g., the United States and Japan). Still others were themselves too impoverished by the war to continue as major trading partners. An example of the latter was Germany, Britain's leading continental trading partner before 1914. At the same time, the cost of the war had increased the national debt by about 1,000 percent. In the course of the war, Britain had exchanged its position of creditor for that of debtor.

In some important ways, Britain had become less competitive industrially. It did not participate to the same extent as Germany in the rapid development of electrical and chemical industries. A large part of its industrial base consisted of the older coal, iron, steel, textiles, and shipbuilding industries. It was in these key labor-intensive industries that Britain had lost the competitive edge. When in 1925 the Exchequer put Britain back on the gold standard, the problem was only exacerbated. British goods became too expensive, resulting in decreased exports. For a while, the "invisible exports" (e.g., income from shipping and foreign investments) offset the losses. But the drop in exports hit especially hard those traditional industries that employed large numbers of workers. The result was chronic unemployment of at least one, often two or more, million persons during the 1920s.

Chronic unemployment led to frequent strikes that culminated in the General Strike of May 3–12, 1926. The broader labor conflict began with a strike by the coal miners. The miners' wages had dropped by one-third in the previous seven years. Mine owners suffered from Germany's providing "free" coal to France as reparations, a part of the Dawes Plan (1924) that helped assure reparations would be paid and the Ruhr occupation ended. Britain's return to the gold standard in 1925 contributed to the mine owners' problems by inhibiting exports and raising interest rates.

In solidarity with the miners, the Trades Union Congress (TUC) called for a general strike, which most of Britain's organized labor heeded. At its peak on May 4, more than 1.5 million workers were out on strike. Leaders of the Labour Party began to fear that the radical elements among the unions threatened to derail the party's growing acceptance in the public's eyes as a legitimate alternative to the Conservative Party. The Conservative-led government of Stanley Baldwin (1867–1947) saw the general strike as a threat to the very principles upon which parliamentary government rested, which could lead to anarchy. On May 11, the Chancery Division of the High Court ruled that the General Strike was not protected by the Trade Disputes Act of 1906, thus opening the way for the employers to seize the unions' assets. The unions capitulated on the following day, ending the strike without achieving their goals.

The dominant theme in British politics during the 1920s was the decline of the Liberal Party and the rise of the Labour Party amidst a generally conservative political mood among voters. Until 1922, the Liberal Party governed with the support of the Conservatives. In the parliamentary elections of 1922, Labour emerged for the first time as "His Majesty's Loyal Opposition." Twice during the 1920s Labour led a minority government headed by Ramsay MacDonald (1866–1937) and supported by the Liberals. Neither during their first tenure in office, from January to October 1924, nor their second, from May 1929 to August 1931, did the Labour government attempt anything radical. Rather, by governing very timidly, largely in line with the policies set by the Conservatives, they earned respect among middle-class voters, the key to becoming the normal alternative to the Conservatives. The most daring action taken by the Labour governments was to establish diplomatic relations with the Soviet Union. The Conservatives, with their belief in deflation, strict economy in government spending, and a passive foreign policy, best represented the mood of most British voters during the 1920s.

France

During the 1920s, France was preoccupied with Germany. This was due to both economic and security considerations. France had suffered greater proportional losses than any other country in the Great War. Northeast France had been a battlefield for almost four years. Much of the nation's prewar industry was devastated. It borrowed heavily in order to rebuild the war-ravaged areas. Plagued with inflation, a rising national debt, and an unbalanced budget, the French looked to war reparations from Germany for financial relief.

The hard line toward Germany also seemed necessary because of France's feelings of insecurity. When both the United States and Great Britain refused to ratify the defensive alliance with France, the French were left to fend for themselves. Thus, France adopted an intransigent attitude toward Germany, determined to keep Germany weak and isolated. At the same time, it sought to replace the old prewar Franco-Russian alliance with alliances with the new Eastern European states (e.g., the Little Entente in 1922). It was a dangerously shortsighted policy that could only hope to succeed so long as both Germany and the Soviet Union remained prostrate.

The political situation in France remained confused and unstable during the 1920s. The Socialist Party split in 1920 into the French Communist Party, affiliated with the Comintern, and the Socialist Party. In May 1924, the Left Cartel, a coalition of Socialists and Radicals, assumed control of the government from the National Bloc, a coalition of centrist and rightist parties. The Socialists and Radicals disagreed on how to deal with the troubled economy. Between April 1925 and June 1926, six cabinets came and went as Socialists and Radicals remained deadlocked.

In July 1926, Raymond Poincaré (1860–1934) returned to power at the head of a National Union ministry that governed France until July 1929. With the support of the Radicals and the centrist and rightist parties, Poincaré pursued a conservative economic policy. Poincaré headed the government between 1922 and 1924, when France (together with Belgium) occupied the Ruhr industrial district of Germany with disastrous results for the Weimar Republic and France. Between 1926 and 1929, however, Poincaré's conservative policies restored financial stability to France.

In 1928, with the franc worth about one-fifth its prewar value (as opposed to one-tenth at its low point two years before), France went on the international gold standard. The devaluation of the franc was a disguised repudiation of much of the national debt, which had been contracted in terms of the prewar franc. It was a difficult blow for many in the middle classes, the value of whose savings and investments was undermined. The determination grew never to allow the franc to be touched again. Devaluation brought financial stability, however, and "normalcy" to France. In fact, mainly because of Poincaré's measures, France was better prepared than most European countries for the worldwide economic difficulties that began in 1929.

Weimar Germany

In January 1919, while Berlin was in revolution, German voters elected a National Assembly to draft a constitution. Because the delegates to the constitutional convention met in the town of Weimar, the German Republic served by the new constitution became known as the Weimar Republic. The National Assembly chose as president Friedrich Ebert, the leader of the Social Democratic Party and former saddle maker, bartender, journalist, and party bureaucrat. The constitution drafted at Weimar was the very model of a democratic constitution. Two aspects of the constitution were to prove fatal for the Republic, however. Article 48 allowed the president to rule by decree during times of national emergency. Also, the lower house of the Reichstag was to be elected by universal suffrage but according to a system of proportional representation that made it virtually impossible for any one party to achieve a majority. Indeed, during the life of the Republic, no party ever achieved a majority.

The survival of the Republic became dependent upon the cooperation of the so-called Weimar parties—Social Democratic Party (SPD), Catholic Center Party (Z, or Zentrum), and German Democratic Party (DDP). These parties were ideologically incompatible but willing to collaborate because the alternative was too frightening to contemplate. Important differences of opinion on both economic and political questions were merely papered over. Most Germans did not prefer the Republic and even associated it with defeat and betrayal. The traditional elites of army, judiciary, bureaucracy, church, and landed and industrial wealth remained openly hostile to it. Symptomatic of German feeling toward the Republic was the election in 1925 of Paul von Hindenburg, war hero and supporter of the monarchy, as president, following the death of Ebert.[1]

One way in which the threat from the right saw expression was in the form of attempted coups in 1920 and 1923. On March 13, 1920, Wolfgang Kapp (1858–1922) attempted to seize power in Berlin in what became known as the Kapp *Putsch* (carefully plotted, sudden attempt to overthrow the government). Kapp was an extreme nationalist who, together with Alfred von Tirpitz (1897–1916), grand admiral and commander of the German navy between 1911 and 1916, founded the Fatherland Party in September 1917 in an effort to revive the "spirit of 1914" and snatch victory from impending defeat

[1] Wilhelm II formally abdicated the thrones of Prussia and the German Empire on November 28, 1918. He lived in exile in Doorn, the Netherlands, where he died on June 3, 1941.

in the Great War. The Fatherland Party was dissolved in December 1918. After the war, Kapp joined General Ludendorff and other extreme nationalists in the National Union dedicated to a counter-revolution that would overthrow the Weimar Republic and establish a conservative militaristic government. He became a member of the conservative National People's Party and was elected to the Reichstag in 1919. Kapp blamed socialists, communists, and Jews for Germany's defeat.

The attempted coup began on the morning of March 12, when a group of Freikorps known as the Ehrhardt Brigade occupied Berlin. Kapp, supported by Ludendorff, proclaimed himself chancellor. The government left Berlin and called upon the army to suppress the coup. General Hans von Seeckt (1866–1936), chief of staff of the army, declined the government's command. "German soldiers do not fire on German soldiers," he replied. The army and Freikorps cooperated when it came to suppressing the Spartacus revolt in January 1919 or any other communist revolt, but they were not quick to defend the Republic from threats from the right.

Kapp and his followers did not, however, have the support of the citizens of Berlin. The bureaucrats did not obey Kapp's orders, and they kept the official state seal from Kapp, thus leaving him without the authority to withdraw funds from the Reichsbank or conduct any official state business. He did issue a couple of decrees, including one to confiscate supplies of matzo flour needed for the upcoming Jewish holidays. The Social Democratic Party called for a general strike. For four days Berlin was at a standstill. Unable to govern, Kapp "resigned" and went to Sweden. The Ehrhardt Brigade marched out of Berlin, but not before firing a volley directly into a crowd of spectators.

Also from the right came the attempt by Adolf Hitler (1889–1945) to seize control of the government in Munich, on November 8–9, 1923, preliminary to a "march on Berlin." The National Socialist German Workers Party (NSDAP or Nazi) was a minor right-wing party based in Bavaria in 1923. Bavaria, in which there was widespread support for a separation from Germany, was ruled by a triumvirate led by Gustav von Kahr (1862–1934). Kahr organized a meeting of Bavarian nationalists for the evening of November 8, at the Bürgerbräukeller, a large beer hall in Munich. Kahr and his supporters intended for Kahr to make a speech in which he would announce Bavaria's secession from the Germany. Bavaria was once again to become an independent state.

When Kahr was only minutes into his speech, Hitler suddenly jumped onto a chair, fired two shots into the ceiling, and announced that he was forming a national government. Armed Nazis took control of the crowd. On the following day, Hitler joined by General Ludendorff led a march down Ludwigstrasse in the direction of the Feldherrnhalle, a mid-nineteenth-century monument honoring the Bavarian army. Hitler had envisioned the affair as the beginning of a Mussolini-style "march on Berlin," but before long the group was confronted by a cordon of armed Bavarian police who fired on them. Eighteen individuals, fourteen demonstrators, and four policemen were killed. Hitler fled the scene and was later arrested. Only Ludendorff continued the march, walking unopposed through the police cordon. He, too, was later arrested.

Ludendorff and Hitler were both tried for treason. Ludendorff was acquitted and Hitler was sentenced to five years of imprisonment, of which he served only nine months. The failure of the Kapp Putsch and Hitler's "Beer Hall Putsch," as well as separatist revolts in the Rhineland and communist revolts in Saxony and Thuringia during October, indicated a relative lack of strength among extremist groups by 1923. A greater threat to the stability of the Republic was the hyperinflation caused by the Franco-Belgian occupation of the heartland of German industry, the Ruhr.

War reparations were the main sticking point in Franco-German relations and the foremost issue in German domestic politics in the early 1920s. France believed that Germany could pay enough in reparations to finance the reconstruction of France and other costs related to the war. The Germans doubted this. In January 1923, the French and the Belgians occupied the Ruhr in order to force Germany to pay. The German government encouraged a program of passive resistance, which it tried to finance by printing more and more money. Currency quickly lost all value other than the value of the paper for pulping.

In July 1914, one US dollar was worth 4.2 marks. In January 1919, one US dollar would purchase 8.9 marks. When the Ruhr occupation began in January 1923, the figure had risen to 17,972 marks, an unbelievable sum, but nothing compared to the 4.2 trillion marks that a single US dollar would bring on November 15, 1923. Examples of the inflation are numerous. One university student recalled ordering a cup of coffee listed on the menu for 5,000 marks (Table 5.1). When he finished the first cup, he ordered a second. After drinking the second cup, the price of two cups of coffee had risen to 14,000 marks. Factory workers and teachers were paid daily at 11:00 A.M., the very hour that the banks closed for the day. A worker described payday at a factory:

> At 11:00 in the morning a siren sounded, and everybody gathered in the factory forecourt, where a five-ton lorry was drawn up loaded brimful with paper money. The chief cashier and his assistants climbed up on top. They read out names and just threw out bundles of notes. As soon as you had caught one you made a dash for the nearest shop and bought just anything that was going (Public Broadcasting System 2013).

The material impact was significant; the psychological shock was even greater. Hardest hit was the middle class, whose financial base was wiped out.

The American author Pearl S. Buck (1892–1973) was in Germany during 1923. She wrote later of how the German people were

Table 5.1   Inflation in Weimar Germany

1914	$1 = 4.20 marks
1919 (July)	$1 = 14.00 marks
1921 (Jan.)	$1 = 64.90
1922 (Jan.)	$1 = 191.80
1922 (July)	$1 = 493.20
1923 (Jan.)	$1 = 17,972.00 marks
1923 (Sept.)	$1 = 100 million marks
1923 (Oct.)	$1 = 1 trillion marks
1923 (Nov.)	$1 = 4.2 trillion marks

The inflation of 1923 left many Germans badly prepared for the next great crisis, the Great Depression. © Mary Evans Picture Library / Alamy

dazed, confused, wondering how such a thing could happen. "Yet they had lost their self-assurance," she remembered, "their feeling that they themselves could be the masters of their own lives if only they worked hard enough; and lost, too, were the old values of morals, of ethics, of decency." How could such a thing happen? Many began turning to the rightist parties for an explanation and a solution.

Finally, the government reorganized under the leadership of Gustav Stresemann from the German People's Party (DVP). A new mark, the Rentenmark, was issued at the rate of one new mark for one trillion of the old inflated marks. Soon the mark stabilized at its old prewar value of 4.2 marks to the dollar. Stresemann, who served as foreign minister from 1923 until his death in 1929, carried through a policy of "fulfillment" with regard to reparations.[2]

---

[2] The fact that much of the positive diplomacy of the 1920s was the result of the personal relationship between Stresemann and Aristide Briand made Stresemann's untimely death all the more tragic.

"Fulfillment" was based on the assumption that the surest route to revision of the Versailles Treaty was to avoid open confrontation and to work with existing possibilities. Positive results were not long in coming. In 1924, the Dawes Plan provided a realistic scale for the payment of reparations and a foreign loan (largely provided by American banks) of 800 million gold marks. These measures, together with the end of the Ruhr occupation, enabled the German economy to recover rapidly. By 1928, German industrial production was second only to that of the United States, and unemployment was reduced to 650,000.

In contrast to its own early years of strife and turmoil, the Weimar Republic passed the last half of the decade in relative tranquility. Hitler, following his attempted putsch, spent his time in prison writing his political credo, *Mein Kampf* (1925). After his release, he was able to rebuild the Nazi Party so as to make it stronger organizationally and more intensely loyal to him personally. Yet, he was not able to make much headway in the late 1920s. He was the best-known figure of the extreme right, but not a major politician until his cooperation with the German National People's Party (DNVP) in the 1929 referendum on the Young Plan for the reorganization of reparations. This move brought him into national prominence. The DNVP, based on the hostility of the aristocratic large landowners and some industrialists toward the Weimar Republic, seemed a much more substantial threat to the Republic than any group on the extreme right.

Nonetheless, the major danger to the Republic in the late 1920s lay not without but within. The army had achieved a position of almost complete autonomy and was even more isolated from the mainstream of life in the Weimar Republic than the imperial army had been before the Great War. The civil service remained largely composed of people technically competent but uncommitted and often actively disloyal to the Republic. Business interests combined and organized to the point where they possessed enormous powers that the government could not begin to control. The 1925 election of Paul von Hindenburg as president—a man unsympathetic to parliamentary control of government—created another problem for the Republic. A republic with such a president and with so many groups antagonistic toward it could hope to survive only if it avoided the necessity of dealing with serious problems.

Italy

Although Italy was on the winning side in the Great War, its military performance was less than impressive. The peace conference awarded Italy much less than it felt entitled to by the Treaty of London between the Triple Entente and Italy (1915). The secret treaty promised Italy territory along the Aegean Sea that was part of the Austro-Hungarian Empire in exchange for it declaring war against Germany and Austria-Hungary. Injured national pride was exacerbated by economic and social problems. The aftereffects of the war included a massive national debt, rapid inflation, and increasing unemployment. Between 1919 and 1921, angry workers and peasants began occupying factories and land. Italy appeared to some Italians to be on the verge of a "Bolshevik" Revolution.

The political system offered little hope for the future. The two largest parties, the Socialists and the Catholic *Popolari*, were each deeply divided. In 1921, the Socialist Party split into socialist and communist factions. The *Popolari* remained united in its support of the Catholic Church but divided over economic and social issues. Neither the Socialists nor the *Popolari* were able to govern alone or able to imagine governing with the other. The smaller Liberal and Radical parties were unable to deal with the political and social crisis of 1919–1922, even when they possessed a working majority in the parliament.

Into this confused situation stepped the small Fascist Party, formed in 1921 by Benito Mussolini (1883–1945), a former school teacher and editor of the Socialist Party newspaper, *Avanti*. Mussolini was expelled from the Socialist Party in 1914, when he called for Italy's entry into the war on the side of the Allies. After the war, Mussolini organized the Fascist Party in 1921 and began denouncing Marxism and liberal democracy while talking vaguely of social and economic reform.

The fatal attraction between Benito Mussolini and Adolf Hitler eventually led both to defeat and infamy. National Archives and Records Administration (ARC no. 540153)

From the beginning, Italian Fascism lacked any coherent doctrine or concrete program of reform. Rather, the emphasis was on action. It was a mass movement akin to a religious revival. Like both National Socialism (Nazism) and Marxism–Leninism, it claimed to abolish class distinctions and fuse the masses into an organic whole. Once asked to describe the kind of order he was attempting to establish in Italy, Mussolini coined the term "totalitarianism." It must be noted, however, that Mussolini never achieved such total control in Italy. Italian Fascism was in fact a blend of ideas drawn from Friedrich Nietzsche, Georges Sorel, Henri Bergson, and other pre-1914 intellectuals, dynamic and even romantic.

Mussolini organized a Fascist Party militia, the Blackshirts, which was used to terrorize peasants, organized labor, socialists, and communists alike. In fact, while much of the disorder caused by workers and peasants ended by 1921, the Fascists continued their work and became in that year the actual source of the largest part of the continuing unrest. They were perceived by many, though, as saving Italy from Bolshevism.

Matters came to a head in October 1922. Mussolini demanded that a Fascist cabinet be formed. The premier refused and wanted to declare martial law. King Victor Emmanuel III (1869–1947) would not agree to this, evidently fearing the power of the Fascists and believing also that they might govern responsibly if given the opportunity. The premier resigned and Mussolini was asked to form a government. The "March on Rome" that the Fascists had threatened against the government turned out to be only a train ride into the capital for Mussolini and some of his colleagues.

In the course of the next few years, Mussolini and the Fascists moved rather slowly to gain control of the government. The elections of 1924, held on the basis of the 1923 Acerbo election law which gave the party with the largest number of votes two-thirds of the seats, gave the Fascists an overwhelming position in the Chamber of Deputies. It was not, however, until the murder in 1924 of Giacomo Matteotti (1885–1924), a socialist deputy who had strongly criticized the Fascists, that the party broke with parliamentary and constitutional government in a decisive way. Shortly after the murder, most of the non-Fascist minority of the chamber left in the Aventine Secession. They were not allowed to return. The Fascists took control of both houses of parliament.

Mussolini dreamed of creating a corporate state at home and a new Roman Empire in the Mediterranean. According to theory, the corporate state harmonizes capitalism and socialism through a system of corporations (22 in Fascist Italy), each of which had councils of employers and workers. Strikes by workers or lockouts by employers were forbidden. Ideally, labor and management worked together to resolve disputes, set wages, determine working conditions, and set production levels. Although a National Council of Corporations was established to make policy, the corporate state was a fraud. All decision making remained firmly in the hands of the government, which favored the interests of the industrialists over those of the workers.

Neither Mussolini's domestic nor foreign policy was successful. The only real success he enjoyed in either was the Lateran Accord of

February 1929, which resolved the "Roman Question" that had plagued Italy since the Kingdom of Italy seized Rome in 1870. According to the agreement, Italy paid financial damages to the Catholic Church, recognized the Vatican City as a sovereign state ruled by the pope, Roman Catholicism as the state religion, church marriages, and approved compulsory instruction in the Catholic religion in the nation's schools. In return, the state received the right to veto the appointment of Italian bishops, and, perhaps most important, the church agreed to refrain from any involvement in politics. With the Lateran Accord, Mussolini effectively neutralized what was potentially the most effective opposition to Fascism. Hitler carried out a similar coup with the Reich Concordat in 1933. During the 1930s, Mussolini's belligerent and unsuccessful foreign policy eventually drew Italy into a fatal alliance with Hitler's Germany.

The Soviet Union

The Soviet Union[3] was the nation that faced the most difficult tasks in bringing about recovery from the war. Interest among Europeans in its fate was probably greater than interest in any other nation except Germany. The Allies did intervene in the Russian Civil War (see Chapter 3) but only halfheartedly and without any coordination or clear objectives. Despite the allied intervention in support of the White armies, the Reds were victorious. It was during the Civil War, however, that the Communist Party under Lenin's leadership consolidated its control through implementation of what was called "War Communism."

Historians disagree about whether War Communism was a series of emergency measures necessitated by the Civil War, or a means by which the political independence of the people was undermined by eliminating their economic independence. It was an attempt at

---

[3]   The constitution of 1918 referred to the state as the Russian Soviet Federated Socialist Republic (RSFSR). In 1924, when additional territory was added, a new constitution was drafted which created the Union of Soviet Socialist Republics (USSR). In 1918, the Bolsheviks began to refer to themselves as the Communist Party.

ignoring the requirements of orthodox Marxism by destroying the market economy and immediately replacing it with state-controlled socialism. It involved the nationalization of all property, beginning with church, monastic, and crown lands and eventually including all personal property. All banking and commerce, both internal and external, became a monopoly of the state. At one point, money was temporarily replaced by an official barter system. Workers' control of industry was ended by decree in 1918, and industry was nationalized over the next two years. At first, agricultural products were requisitioned from the peasants. Then, in November 1918, all land was nationalized. Workers were forbidden to strike, and in 1920, compulsory labor was introduced.

No one disputes that War Communism was disastrous. Industrial production fell below prewar levels; agricultural production to less than half. Without counting deaths caused by the war or including those who emigrated, the population dropped by an estimated 16 million between 1917 and 1922. People fled the cities for the countryside. The two largest cities, Moscow and Petrograd (St. Petersburg), lost just more than 58 percent of their prewar population in the two years from 1918 to 1920. Both Lenin and Trotsky later admitted that War Communism failed to achieve its goal. War Communism clashed with reality, concluded Trotsky, and reality won.

By 1921, several serious rebellions took place in protest against the harsh policies of War Communism. War Communism was abandoned that year, when delegates to the Tenth Party Congress accepted the New Economic Policy (NEP), sponsored by Lenin. The NEP allowed peasants to sell their surplus grain on the open market after payment of a tax based on a percentage of the harvest. Retail trade and private enterprise were partially restored, while what Lenin called the "commanding heights" of the economy—banking, large industry, transport, and foreign trade—remained under government control.

The NEP did not come quickly enough to prevent a severe famine in 1921–1922, but it did result in fairly rapid economic recovery over the next few years. By the mid-1920s, standards of living improved and illiteracy was reduced. By this time, however, Lenin was dead. His death in 1924 marked the beginning of a struggle for power which by 1929 resulted in the emergence of Joseph Stalin (Iosif Vissarionovich Dzhugashvili [1878–1953]) as the most powerful figure in the party and government, and in turn to new experiments with the society and economy of the Soviet Union.

In his "testament," dictated by Lenin in December 1922 following his first stroke, and in a postscript added in early January 1923, Lenin first criticized Stalin and then recommended his removal from the post as general secretary of the party. For a time, Stalin seemed a rather obscure figure, without much power, but he had, in fact, acquired considerable power through a series of bureaucratic posts.

The power struggle within the Soviet leadership between Stalin and Leon Trotsky soon focused on two opposed views regarding the future of the Soviet Union. In 1924, Stalin put forth the idea of "Socialism in One Country." According to this concept, the Soviet Union could create the conditions for socialism, an industrial economy, by itself, without the aid of revolutionary states elsewhere in Europe. This was contrary to Trotsky's ideas about "Permanent Revolution," which called for aid from other centers of revolution. By 1925, Stalin had stripped Trotsky of much of his power and moved into an alliance with the "right" group, while using his position to bring a number of people personally loyal to him to key posts in the government and party.

In 1928, having completely crushed the "left" opposition of Trotsky, Grigori Zinoviev (1883–1936), and Lev Kamenev (1883–1936) the year before, Stalin adopted some of the ideas long associated with the left, ideas concerning economic planning and rapid industrialization based on the control of agriculture. Essentially, Stalin believed that state control of agricultural production was necessary for the rapid industrialization of the Soviet Union. Collectivization of agriculture and industrialization had to be accomplished simultaneously.

At this point, Stalin was extremely powerful but far from all-powerful. His ideas were accepted because they appeared to meet the needs of the Soviet Union as the Communist Party perceived them. Many at the time viewed Stalin as an efficient bureaucrat who could get things done. Stalin's first Five-Year Plan, in its original form, was ambitious but not unrealistic. Only later, through Stalin's arbitrary modifications, did the Five-Year Plan and collectivization become overly ambitious and even utopian. In 1929 and 1930, Stalin and his colleagues implemented plans that would change drastically the lives of four-fifths of the population—those living in the rural areas—and make the Soviet Union into a major industrial and military power.

The Smaller States

Outside the three major democracies of Britain, France, and Germany, democracy was also firmly established in the Lowlands (Belgium, Luxembourg, and the Netherlands), the Scandinavian countries (Denmark, Sweden, Norway, and Finland), and Czechoslovakia. Belgium was severely affected by the Great War but managed a rapid recovery under the popular King Albert I (1875–1934). The most troublesome question concerned the division of the country between the French-speaking Walloons in the south and the Dutch-speaking Flemish in the north. The Dutch largely escaped the problem of postwar adjustment that most other European nations experienced. Under Queen Wilhelmina (1880–1962), the Netherlands enjoyed considerable prosperity in the 1920s, much of it based on the great empire of the Dutch East Indies.

In the Scandinavian countries, the 1920s and 1930s were times in which parliamentary governments, universal suffrage, and the welfare state became firmly rooted. Each country instituted a range of social services including various plans to provide for old age, illness, accident, and unemployment. Another characteristic of the Scandinavian societies was the mixed economy, in which some government-run enterprises coexisted with many privately owned businesses and a few others in which both government and private capital actively cooperated. Many developments in the Scandinavian countries between the wars foreshadowed general trends after World War II. However, neither the Scandinavian nor the Lowland countries were strong enough, individually or collectively, to affect the course of European affairs in the 1920s and 1930s.

Eastern Europe

The collapse of the Habsburg Monarchy at the end of the Great War created a very unstable situation in Eastern Europe. The Dual Monarchy of Austria-Hungary was formally dissolved on October 31, 1918. In the final battle against a combined Italian, British, and French force, the imperial army fought without a supply of either food or munitions for an empire that no longer existed. At the Paris Peace Conference in 1919, the Treaty of St. Germain was signed with Austria and the Treaty of Trianon with Hungary. Among the provisions of the former was a clause that prohibited the union of Austria and Germany.

In general, the Eastern European states that emerged from the old Habsburg Empire began the 1920s with constitutional and parliamentary governments. With the exception of Czechoslovakia, all turned to authoritarian governments by 1930. Each was plagued by a combination of a lack of experience with parliamentary forms of government, severe economic problems stemming from largely agrarian economies no longer in touch with prewar markets and resources, and problems between ethnic minorities.

Poland, perhaps the most important state in the area in terms of potential influence, experienced all the difficulties typical of the Eastern European states following the Great War. Caught between the Soviet Union and Germany, it was plagued by comprising many different ethnic minorities. Its parliamentary system was crippled by a plurality of 59 parties, which made achieving a parliamentary majority virtually impossible. In May 1926, a coup led by Józef Pilsudski (1867–1935) abolished the republic and established a dictatorship behind the facade of a constitutional system.

Hungary had a very brief experience with a republican form of government. The republic, declared in 1918, was transformed by Béla Kun in 1919 into a communist dictatorship which, in turn, was destroyed by a Romanian invasion and the appearance of a counter-revolution. In 1920, Admiral Miklós Horthy (1868–1957), commander-in-chief, became regent and head of state. He declared Hungary a monarchy with the throne vacant. Principal governmental efforts in the 1920s were devoted to maintaining the status quo, which meant reinforcing the power of the great landowners over the peasantry and that of the majority Magyars over the ethnic minorities.

The State of Slovenes, Croats and Serbs, the Kingdom of Serbia, and the Kingdom of Montenegro were combined to form the Kingdom of Serbs, Croats and Slovenes. In 1929, King Alexander I (1888–1934) established a dictatorship and changed the country's name to Yugoslavia. He attempted to create a unified nation out of the diverse ethnic populations. In reality, Yugoslavia was only a smaller version of the former Austria-Hungary, plagued by all of the same problems. Only some form of dictatorship was able to maintain the fiction of national unity in what was really a Great Serbia.

Czechoslovakia was a major exception to the rest of Eastern Europe in the 1920s. What is now referred to as the First Republic of Czechoslovakia came into being on October 28, 1918, with the union of the Czech lands with Slovakia. Tolerant of its ethnic minorities, heavily industrialized, and possessing a large urban population in comparison to other states in the area, Czechoslovakia was the only Eastern European nation with a deeply rooted liberal tradition. The nation was clearly a success by the end of the 1920s and entered the 1930s able to withstand the rigors of the Depression. In large part, its success was due to the constant efforts of the liberal Tomás˘ Masaryk (1850–1937) and the enormous prestige and respect he had acquired within the nation.

The two Balkan kingdoms of Romania and Bulgaria were on opposite sides in the Great War. Romania chose the Allies, while Bulgaria joined the Central Powers. Romania emerged from the war nearly twice its prewar size. In fact, between the wars, the kingdom was often referred to as *România Mare*, or "Greater Romania." Its government was a liberal constitutional monarchy from 1918 to 1930, when Carol II who had renounced the throne in 1925 returned to Romania and established a dictatorship. Its acquisitions merely increased the problem of ethnic minorities that plagued virtually all of the so-called successor states of Eastern Europe.

During the Great War, Bulgaria declared war on France and Great Britain but resisted pressure to declare war on Russia. Still, having been one of the Central Powers, it emerged from the war a defeated power.

The Treaty of Neuilly (1919) burdened Bulgaria with a reparations debt of $4.5 million, in addition to reparations in kind. Boris III (1894–1943) inherited the throne on October 3, 1918, just as the war was ending. A land reform program immediately after the war set a limit of 60 acres on all estates. The remaining land was distributed among the peasants. Bulgaria was economically a century behind Czechoslovakia. Its chief exports were tobacco and the "star of roses," used to make perfume. Bulgaria did enjoy one advantage over the other Eastern European countries during the interwar period, a largely homogenous society: 81 percent of its population was Bulgarian.

On the whole, the instability of Eastern Europe stemmed from the strength of the older centers of power—the landholding aristocracy, the military, and the dominant ethnic groups—when confronted by some newer forces for democratic forms of government and more modern social and economic arrangements. Exacerbating this were economic problems caused by the breakup of the old economic unit formed by the Habsburg Empire and diplomatic tensions brought on by its location between two rival powers that bordered the region west and east, Germany and the Soviet Union.

Turkey (Ottoman Empire)

Fighting between the Ottoman Empire and the Allies ended on October 30, 1918, with the Armistice of Mudros. As with the Habsburg Empire of Austria-Hungary, the Ottoman Empire was rapidly dissolving. The fate of the non-Turkish portions was decided at the Paris Peace Conference in accord with the Sykes–Picot Agreement of 1916 between Great Britain and France. The Ottoman government under the sultan signed the Treaty of Sèvres in 1920, but it was never ratified. A war for Turkish independence broke out that thwarted efforts by the British and French to partition Turkey into spheres of influence. Also, the Turkish forces led by Kemal Pasha (1888–1938), the hero of the Battle of Gallipoli (1915), were able to defeat a Greek invasion aimed at separating Anatolia from Turkey. Gold and arms were provided by the Soviet Union during the Turkish War of Independence (1919–1922).

The Republic of Turkey gained international recognition with the Treaty of Lausanne in 1923. The treaty took the place of the Treaty of Sèvres. The capital was moved to Ankara from Constantinople (the name of the city officially changed to Istanbul in 1930). Mustafa Kemal Pasha was given the title Atatürk, "Father of the Turks." Under his leadership, Turkey became a modern nation-state. Education was emphasized, including for girls, Western-style dress introduced, and the state declared secular. Turkey was the only member of the Central Powers during the Great War that was treated as an equal when negotiating a treaty with the Allies (Treaty of Lausanne).

United States

President Woodrow Wilson hoped that the Versailles Treaty and the League of Nations would be the crowning achievements of his administration. However, for various reasons, including the president's unwillingness to compromise with the Republicans in the Senate, the Senate refused to ratify the treaty on March 19, 1920. Technically, the United States remained at war with Germany until the Treaty of Berlin in 1921. The Senate had already voted against joining the League on January 17, 1920. The mood of the American people that lay behind the nation's return to isolationism was summed up in the slogan "back to normalcy," coined by the Republican Warren G. Harding (1865–1923) during his campaign for the presidency in 1920.

Many Americans felt that it had been a mistake for the United States to enter the Great War. Signs of a desire to a return to isolationism in foreign affairs were evident in increased tariffs on foreign imports to protect the postwar economic boom. In 1921, Congress passed an emergency immigration act that established a quota system on new arrivals. Immigration from any one country was limited to 3 percent of the number of people of that nationality living in the United States at the time of the 1910 census. The total number of immigrants allowed entrance fell from just over 800,000 in 1920 to just under 200,000 in 1921–1922.

What is referred to as a spirit of nativism and provincialism characterized the decade. Fear of Bolshevism led to America's first "Red Scare," a grim foreshadowing of the McCarthyism that would appear in the 1950s. Some Americans even blamed the Germans for the Spanish flu epidemic of 1918–1919 that claimed around 700,000 lives in the United States.[4] Rumors spread that German agents were sent by the Kaiser to "seed" Boston Harbor with influenza germs. The Ku Klux Klan spread from the South to the North and Northwest, where it was largely anti-Jewish, anti-Catholic, anti-immigrant, and anti-Communist.

After a brief period during which the US economy readjusted to peacetime demand, it entered a boom period that would last until the stock market crash in 1929. The United States emerged from the Great War the richest nation in the world. The financial capital of the world moved to New York City. Wages increased. At the beginning of the century, the average worker earned approximately $675 per year for a 59-hour week. That figure rose to $750 by 1919 and finally to $1,236 on the eve of the Great Depression. Millionaires were made seemingly overnight through speculation in the stock market. The belief that prosperity would continue was expressed by Herbert Hoover (1874–1964) in his acceptance of the Republican nomination for the presidency at the convention in August 1928:

> We in America today are nearer to the final triumph over poverty than ever before in the history of any land. The poor-house is vanishing from among us. We have not yet reached the goal, but given a chance to go forward with the policies of the last eight years, and we shall soon with the help of God be in sight of the day when poverty will be banished from this nation. (About.com American History 2013)

China and Japan

Although China was declared a republic in 1912, there was no real central government in China during the 1920s. The period between 1916 and at least 1928 is known as the Warlord Era, during which

---

[4]   It is hard to determine how many people died worldwide. Some estimates go as high as 100 million; most estimates are around 50 million. Seventeen million died in India, alone.

powerful generals turned provinces into their personal domains. What was theoretically the national government was located at Beijing until 1926, when it was moved to Nanjing. Nanjing was controlled by Chiang Kai-shek (1887–1975), de facto leader of a non-functioning Republic of China. In reality, Chiang Kai-shek was one of the more powerful warlords and the one who commanded what he called the National Liberation Army. Meanwhile, a militant communist movement under the leadership of Mao Zedong (1893–1976) strengthened during the 1920s. As a result, Chiang Kai-shek gained greater recognition in the West as the leader of the "legitimate" government of China.

Japan made territorial gains as a result of the Great War. German rights in Shandong, China, were transferred to Japan. Germany's holdings in the Pacific north of the equator also were transferred to Japan as mandate territories under the League of Nations. During the 1920s, Japan appeared to be a democratic state in which democratic forces balanced the influence of the military. During the 1930s, both the army and the navy pursued their own foreign policy objectives without approval of the civilian government. More and more Japan fell under the spell of militarism. It could be said that the independent actions of the military leaders drew Japan deeper into conflict in China and ultimately led to war with the United States in 1941.

Conclusion

Taken as a whole, the late 1920s were times of economic prosperity and political stability for the United States and large parts of Europe. The liberal, parliamentary governments of the period in Europe were, however, seldom more than modestly successful. The experiences of Weimar Germany were a good measure of the lack of strength and popularity of parliamentary government. There were also some resounding failures in Eastern and Southern Europe, where authoritarian regimes came into power. Two important tendencies, which became much more influential in the early 1930s, were the decline of the liberal center in politics and, quite closely related, the growth of extremist movements on the margins of parliamentary life.

The prosperity of the later 1920s was already showing signs of faltering before the spectacular crash of the American stock market in 1929. Particularly important was the precarious base for the credit structure in Germany and other areas in Central Europe, dependent as it was on American loans. There were indications, even in 1928, that Europeans might have to face a period of economic readjustment. That readjustment turned out to be more severe than anyone had predicted, involving political and cultural ramifications of great significance. The resources for meeting such a serious crisis were lacking. Beneath the glitter lay areas of great vulnerability. Europe and much of the world entered a time of trial that would extend for the better part of two decades.

References

About.com American History. 2013. Herbert Hoover Address Accepting the Republican Presidential Nomination. Accessed February 9, 2013. http://americanhistory.about.com/library/docs/blhooverspeech1932.htm

Public Broadcasting System. 2013. "Commanding Heights: The German Hyperinflation, 1923." http://www.pbs.org/wgbh/commanding-heights/shared/minitextlo/ess_germanhyperinflation.html. Accessed February 9, 2013.

Further Reading

Boyce, Robert. 2012. *The Great Interwar Crisis and the Collapse of Globalization.* New York: Palgrave Macmillan. Very helpful in understanding the relationship between economics and politics leading up to the outbreak of war.

Koestler, Arthur et al. 2001. *The God That Failed.* New York: Columbia University Press. A collection of "confessions" by Western writers who were attracted to the Soviet experiment and subsequently disillusioned by it.

Margaret, MacMillan. 2003. *Paris 1919: Six Months That Changed the World.* New York: Random House. A detailed but very readable look at the Paris Peace Conference and the end of the Great War.

Neilson, Keith. 2009. *Britain, Soviet Russia and the Collapse of the Versailles Order, 1919–1939.* New York: Cambridge University Press. Neilson suggests that the underlying cause of the outbreak of war in 1939 was the intellectual failure to find a way of maintaining the new order established at Versailles.

6

From Depression to War, 1929–1939

Chronology

1928	Soviet Union abandons Lenin's NEP and implements the first Five-Year Plan (1928–1932)
1929	Great Depression begins in the United States
1930	Beginning of presidential dictatorship in Germany
1931	Japan invades Manchuria
1932	Second Five-Year Plan in the Soviet Union (1932–1937)
1933	Hitler appointed as chancellor in Germany. The German Reichstag passes the Enabling Act.
1935	Hitler repudiates the disarmament clauses of the Versailles Treaty

Twentieth-Century Europe: A Brief History, 1900 to the Present, Third Edition.
Michael D. Richards and Paul R. Waibel.
© 2014 John Wiley & Sons, Inc. Published 2014 by John Wiley & Sons, Inc.

1936	John Maynard Keynes publishes *The General Theory of Employment, Interest, and Money*
	Spanish Civil War (1936–1939)
1937	Japan invades China
1938	Third Five-Year Plan begins in the Soviet Union
	Munich Conference
1939	Nazi–Soviet Nonaggression Pact
	Hitler invades Poland
1941	Japanese attack on Pearl Harbor

WHILE SOME PROSPERED during the Great Depression, most suffered to one degree or another. George Gelies was a New Yorker who worked as a janitor for 40 years. Over the many years, Gelies deposited extra coins and an occasional dollar into a savings account until his balance reached $1,000 in 1930. When informed that the bank had failed and his savings were lost, Gelies went home and hanged himself from a steam pipe. There were many stories of wealthy speculators jumping from windows or otherwise ending their lives after losing their fortunes. In Berlin in 1930, there were five cases of businessmen committing suicide in a single week. Still, some prospered as the Depression deepened. One example was the American millionaire, Andrew Mellon (1855–1937), who paid Leningrad's Hermitage Museum seven million dollars for 21 paintings. The Soviet government needed the cash; Mellon coveted the artworks.

On Tuesday October 29, 1929, the bottom fell out of the New York Stock Exchange. In that single day, stocks traded lost a total value equal to more than twice the value of all currency in circulation in the United States. Despite a steady rise in the stock market during the last six weeks of the year, the crisis deepened and became international during 1930. The rapid economic decline in most countries brought into question social structures and political systems as well as economic policies. It has been argued that the Great Depression, not only in America and Europe but all over the world, had an even more pervasive impact than the two world wars of the twentieth century and from it, at least in large part, proceeded a whole chain of consequences that, added to other developments, did not stop until well into the 1950s. Both the middle and working classes began to wonder if liberalism, economic and political, was not obsolete. Perhaps the crises of the 1930s required new theories, new ideologies accompanied by action.

The American Connection

The failure of the New York stock market sent shockwaves through Europe. Even before the New York crash, the European economy was experiencing difficulties. Agriculture had been a troubled sector since at least the mid-1920s. Wartime demand had resulted in vastly increased production of agricultural products in North America, some areas of South America, and Australia. But after the war, prices dropped steadily as cheap foreign grain poured into Europe. Canadian or Australian grain could be shipped to Europe cheaper than grain could be shipped from the Eastern European agricultural states to Western Europe. In 1930, the price of wheat was at its lowest level since the Reformation.

There were other danger signs, largely ignored. As noted above, the British economy was greatly disrupted by the war, leading to chronic unemployment in such key industries as coal and steel production. In Eastern Europe, the breakup of the Habsburg Monarchy resulted in the creation of several competing national economies, wherein high tariff walls hindered economic recovery.

A hidden weakness in the postwar European economy was its dependence upon American finances. The great prosperity of the period 1924–1929 was financed by American loans, while the prosperity of America itself was financed by credit. In 1924, the American financier Charles Dawes (1865–1951) chaired a committee that produced the Dawes Plan for the payment of reparations by Germany. Included in the plan were arrangements for an immediate loan of 800 million gold marks. By 1925, American banks had loaned

Germany three billion gold marks. More money flowed into
Germany between 1924 and 1929 in the form of loans than flowed
out as reparations payments. The German economy prospered, and
that prosperity bubbled over into the rest of Europe, as money
flowed in a circle from the United States to Germany in the form of
loans, to France and Great Britain in the form of reparations
payments, and back to the United States as payment of war debts.
European prosperity in the "Roaring Twenties," like that of America,
was based more on speculation than on production and consumption of goods and services. If anything should disrupt the flow of
credit, the whole edifice would collapse. And so it did between 1929
and 1932.

The prosperity of the 1920s was based upon speculation in stocks,
often purchased on "margin" (on credit) with the stocks themselves
serving as collateral. Although even some working-class people
speculated in stocks, most workers did not share in the prosperity.
Wages remained low for workers, which, together with the
depressed agricultural sector, meant that the purchasing power of
the masses could not keep up with production—in short, workers
did not earn enough to afford to purchase the products they made.
The collapse of the stock market set in motion a vicious cycle,
as the financial crisis became an industrial crisis. Bank failures led to
the closing of factories and rising rates of unemployment. As
unemployment spread, further reductions in production and plant
closings followed. Factories cannot produce what the public cannot
afford to purchase.

The Great Depression spread from America to Europe. Already in
1928, Americans were withdrawing funds from Europe to invest
in stocks. As the Depression struck, Americans ceased investing in
Europe and began to withdraw funds from European banks in great
quantities. Hardest hit were banks in Germany and Central Europe.
The decline in American industrial productivity, the withdrawal of
American capital from the world market, and the low prices paid for
agricultural products and raw materials combined to reduce production, trade, and the movement of capital everywhere.

The crisis was international, but not much was done at that
level to deal with the problem. In 1931, President Herbert Hoover

A group of unemployed men in England entertain a theater queue in 1932. The hatless man slightly to the right of the center of the photograph appears to be holding a hat or cap into which people might drop money. Photo by General Photographic Agency/Getty Images

of the United States proposed a moratorium of one year on all intergovernmental debts, in recognition of the problems of transferring sums of money for payment of reparations or war debts. This was accepted by European leaders and regarded as an acknowledgment of the connection between reparations and war debts, that is, the latter would not be paid unless the former were paid. That this was not the American understanding became all too clear the following year, when Americans refused to include a plan for setting aside reparations in an agreement on war debts. The question was never resolved by agreement. In the next few years, Germany repudiated reparations, and most European states owing money to the United States made only token payments. In 1933, a third international effort floundered when the United States, by then set on a path of economic nationalism, declined to cooperate. Most other countries had already begun their own efforts to find a way out of the morass.

Responses

The Great Depression, or "World Slump," was made all the more severe by the near universal commitment to classic (or orthodox) liberal economic theory. According to classic economic theory, the problem was a loss of confidence in the monetary system and the need to become more competitive in the world market. The solution, then, was what is called "deflation," balancing government budgets and reducing the cost of production by, for example, lowering wages. Believing that the economy had to "right" itself, the liberal economists, together with the majority of politicians and businessmen, were prepared to tolerate a high level of public misery. They were convinced by accepted theory that any attempt by governments to maintain wages, or maintain unemployment benefits by deficit financing, would only insulate inefficient sectors of the economy, leading to a worse economic disaster in the future.

What the classic liberals feared was just what others, who saw underconsumption as the root problem, believed necessary in order to save capitalism by making it work. Unlike the liberals, these advocates of a "middle road" saw the necessity of some public management and planning of the economy. In addition, they advocated what economists call "deficit spending," that is, the use of public funds raised by borrowing. Unlike the socialists, they were committed to preserving private property. Like the economic policymakers of the post-World War II era, theirs was a program that would allow as much planning as necessary and as much freedom as possible. The leading advocate of this new consumer-based economic theory was the Englishman John Maynard Keynes (1883–1946), who expressed his ideas in his *The General Theory of Employment, Interest, and Money* (1936).

Keynes's belief that governments could, in effect, spend their way out of economic slumps found many advocates. In Britain, Sir Oswald Mosley (1896–1980), one of the most talented members of the Labour Party, authored a memorandum in 1930 that called for ending the Depression through government intervention and deficit spending. When his ideas were rejected, he bolted the party and founded the British Union of Fascists. Perhaps the best application of what has since become known as Keynesian economics was Franklin Roosevelt's New Deal in the United States. In the end, however, it was the massive spending for defense during World War II, rather than the New Deal programs, that brought an end to the Depression in America. Likewise, it was the massive spending for rearmament after Hitler came to power in 1933 that ended the economic slump in Germany.

The Depression in Germany: The Nazis Come to Power

The Great Depression helped make possible the Nazi "seizure of power" in 1933 by discrediting liberalism, both political and economic, especially for the middle class. It also caused serious doubts among the working class as to the ability (or even desire) of the liberal-democratic government to deal with the unemployment, and its accompanying miseries, caused by the Depression. As both deserted the middle, pro-Republic parties for the extremes, the Weimar Republic, which never really commanded the enthusiastic support of the German people, fell victim to Hitler and the Nazi revival.

On October 3, 1929, just three weeks before "Black Tuesday" at the New York Stock Exchange, Gustav Stresemann died. Stresemann was perhaps the only German statesman who could have led a coalition to resist Hitler. During the previous six years, Stresemann led Germany out of the Great Inflation of 1923, through the Dawes Plan and Locarno treaties, and to an acceptance of the Young Plan (for the reorganization of reparations) just two months before his untimely death. As the Depression began to strike Germany, the Republic was left without a pilot at the helm.

Recession and rising unemployment at the beginning of 1930 led to the fall of the Republic's last truly parliamentary government, the Grand Coalition (1928–1930), led by Chancellor Hermann Müller (1876–1931), a Social Democrat. As unemployment rose, available funding for unemployment insurance proved inadequate. Müller's proposal to reduce benefits while raising the unemployment insurance rates met with strong opposition from both industry and organized labor. The result was the fall of the Müller government and its replacement by a new government headed by Heinrich Brüning (1885–1970) of the Catholic Center Party. Unable to govern through the Reichstag, Brüning resorted to rule by presidential decree. Germany became, in effect, a presidential dictatorship.

The economic and political crisis continued to deepen under Brüning. Germans went to the polls in national elections no fewer than four times in 1932. Twice in 1932, the people elected delegates to the Reichstag, in July and again in November. The results of both elections were similar. Of the old Weimar coalition parties, the Democratic and the People's Parties did badly. From a total of nearly 14 percent of the vote in 1928, they declined to under 3 percent in 1932. The Center Party largely maintained its electorate, but the Socialists, while remaining a major party, lost heavily. They dropped from nearly 30 percent of the vote in 1928 to just over 20 percent in 1932. The center of the political spectrum had won about 55 percent in 1928 but only around 35 percent in 1932. Yeats's line, "The centre cannot hold," had come true.

The extremes gained at the expense of the middle. On the left, the Communists had steadily increased their share of the vote from about 10 percent in 1928 to nearly 17 percent in 1932. On the right, the Nazis became a major political force, rising from under 3 percent of the vote in 1928 to 37.8 percent in July 1932, the largest percentage ever received by a party during the Weimar Republic. With 230 seats, the Nazis were now almost twice as large as the second largest party, the Social Democrats.

The growing strength of the Nazi movement was evident also in the presidential elections of March and April 1932. In March, Hitler came in second behind President Hindenburg in a campaign featuring four candidates from the extreme right to the extreme left. In the runoff election in April, Hitler again came in second. Hindenburg's reelection was credited to his having received the support of the left-of-center voters, who saw him as the only means of preventing Hitler's election.

On May 30, 1932, Hindenburg replaced Brüning as chancellor with Franz von Papen (1879–1969), a conservative Catholic aristocrat best known for political intrigue. Although Hindenburg hoped that Papen could put together a majority in the Reichstag, he did not. On September 12, the Reichstag, by a vote of 512 to 42, passed a vote of no confidence in the chancellor. Papen dissolved the Reichstag and called for new elections for November 6. The Nazis lost two million votes, dropping from 37.8 to 33.1 percent of the votes cast. The government crisis continued. Rejecting Papen's suggestion of a military dictatorship, Hindenburg dismissed Papen and replaced him on December 2 with General Kurt von Schleicher (1882–1934). Schleicher's chancellorship lasted only until January 28, when the 85-year-old, and possibly senile, President Hindenburg yielded to the advice of Papen and the president's son, Oskar, and offered Adolf Hitler the chancellorship on January 30, 1933.

It is perhaps appropriate to note that the Weimar Republic had been "hollowed out" even before Hitler came to power by those constitutionally responsible for the republic but actually very much opposed to it as a political system. Hindenburg was a committed monarchist, who assumed the presidency out of a sense of duty to the Kaiser. He saw himself as a caretaker head of state until the exiled Kaiser returned to assume his rightful place.

Article 48 of the Weimar Constitution gave the president, the constitutional head of the state, the power to rule by decree during a national emergency. From the chancellorship of Heinrich Brüning to the end of the Republic in 1933, each chancellor (appointed by, and responsible to, the president, not the Reichstag) governed through emergency decrees issued by President Hindenburg. Since neither Brüning, Papen, Schleicher, nor Hitler was able to command a majority in the Reichstag, the Weimar Republic became a presidential dictatorship after March 1930.

With Papen as vice chancellor, the old elites thought they could control, even "use," Hitler. They were badly wrong. On February 27, 1933, the Reichstag building was mysteriously set on fire, destroying the central chamber in which the parliament met. Claiming that there was sufficient evidence that communists were responsible and intended that the fire should be a signal for a communist uprising, Hitler convinced President Hindenburg to issue the Decree of the Reich President for the Protection of People and State

(German: *Verordnung des Reichspräsidenten zum Schutz von Volk und Staat*). Civil liberties, including freedom of the press and speech, were suspended. The law was aimed at silencing opposition to the Nazis, especially from communists and social democrats. The Communist Party (KPD) was suppressed and some 4,000 of its members arrested. Among them were the party chairman, Ernst Thälmann (1886–1944), and party founders, Wilhelm Pieck (1876–1960) and Walter Ulbricht (1893–1973).

On March 5, against a backdrop of fear and violence, Germans again went to the polls once again. Despite efforts to suppress the communist and social democratic vote, the Nazis failed to win a majority. They received 43.9 percent of the votes cast. With support from the German National Peoples' Party (DNVP), the Nazis were able to command a majority but less than the two-thirds needed to legally establish a dictatorship.

The inglorious end of the Weimar Republic came on March 23, when the Reichstag passed the Enabling Act granting Hitler dictatorial powers for four years. The necessary two-thirds majority was achieved by preventing the Communists and 21 Social Democrats from attending. Also, the Catholic Center Party voted for the Enabling Act. Only the remainder of the Social Democratic delegates led by Otto Wels (1873–1939) was courageous enough to vote against it. When the final vote was announced, the Nazi delegates rose to their feet and sang the "Horst Wessel Song," the party anthem.

The New Dictatorships

What followed the Nazi seizure of power in Germany, like what followed the Bolshevik Revolution in Russia and to a lesser degree Mussolini's March on Rome, was the emergence of a new type of authoritarian state peculiar to the twentieth century. These new authoritarian dictatorships[1] were very different from the traditional

---

[1] We are deliberately avoiding the use of the term "totalitarian." Although the term was originally coined by Mussolini, its usefulness for the 1930s and 1940s was compromised by its employment during the Cold War.

conservative dictatorships that arose as attempts to salvage something of the old order from the threat of advancing liberalism. So long as the citizen-subject paid his taxes and served in the military when called upon, in short was obedient or at least gave passive support, he was allowed considerable personal freedom. Such "garden variety dictatorships" arose during the 1920s and early 1930s in Portugal and the East European "successor states," for example, Poland, Hungary, and Yugoslavia. Their goal was basically conservative, to maintain the status quo. They did not seek a wholly new ideological order based upon a following whose total being, mind and body, were subject to the authoritarian leadership.

Although Mussolini's Fascist regime had many characteristics in common with the Hitler and Stalin regimes, it was more akin to the traditional dictatorship. *Il Duce*, the leader, as he was known, never achieved total power. For example, he did not interfere with the judiciary and himself remained subject to the Fascist Grand Council, which could in theory, and did in fact, dismiss Mussolini in July 1943.

The new authoritarian dictatorships of Hitler and Stalin were very different. They were the very antithesis of classical liberalism. Conceived during the total war effort of the Great War and given birth during the Russian Civil War,[2] they reached maturity in the Nazi Third Reich and Stalinist dictatorship. Like a great religious revival, the new dictators harnessed the masses in an idolatrous worship of the state (or party, or leader) and a never-ending violent struggle against enemies, both within and without. The individual as a rational being who possessed certain inalienable natural rights ceased to exist, becoming instead a mere faceless object at the disposal of the state. Not only was individualism denied but also the traditional liberal belief in reason, progress, and the basic harmony of human society. Loathing the middle class, the mainstay of classical liberalism, the new dictators promised a classless state (never achieved). Employing a large state police apparatus and a carefully crafted program of systemic terror, the masses were recruited for a permanent revolution.

---

[2] Some see its origins as far back as Rousseau's social contract with its emphasis on the general will arising from the masses and to which the individual must submit.

What made possible the success of the new dictators in Germany and the Soviet Union was the fateful confluence of several trends already discussed above. This included the weakening of the Enlightenment tradition in European thought. As mentioned, Nietzsche, Georges Sorel, Vilfredo Pareto (1848–1923), Sigmund Freud, and others chose to view humans as irrational beings who could be manipulated and motivated by myth and violence. The middle class, the mainstay of liberalism, saw its financial security eroded by taxes, inflation, and various forms of expropriations. Finally, the failure of the liberal-democratic governments to deal effectively with the suffering caused by the Great Depression caused the working class, like the middle class, to abandon its faith in both political and economic liberalism.

Once legally installed in power by presidential appointment and passage of the Enabling Act, Hitler spent the next two years bringing every aspect of life in Germany under control of the Nazi party, a process referred to as the *Gleichschaltung*, or coordination of society. It was meant to alter totally the relationship between the individual and the state and also between individuals. It worked as well to alter the way people thought. Joseph Goebbels (1897–1945), Hitler's Minister of Propaganda and Public Enlightenment, summed it up best at the end of 1933, when he said: "If liberalism took as its starting point the individual and placed the individual man in the center of all things, we have replaced the individual by the nation and the individual man by the community" (Pipes 1981). The Nazi dictatorship was meant to be a rejection of European history since the Enlightenment. Germany was to become a *Volksgemeinschaft*, a national or racial community in which traditional social classes would be replaced by a mass of "folk (i.e., racial) comrades."

During the course of 1933, all independent organizations were abolished and/or absorbed into Nazi-led organizations. Thus, for example, all labor unions were abolished and workers required to join the German Labor Front. A Reich Chamber of Culture under Goebbels was established to oversee all aspects of media production and dissemination. In January 1934, the *Reichsrat*, the upper house representing the state governments, and all state legislatures themselves were abolished. For the first time in its history, Germany became a centralized national state.

At the end of 1933, only two key institutions remained outside party (i.e., Hitler's) control—the *Reichswehr* (army) and the churches. To secure the support of the army and to remove any opposition within the party to his personal control, Hitler purged the party leadership in the "Night of the Long Knives" (June 29). Ernst Röhm (1887–1934) and several hundred SA (*Sturmabteilung*, or storm troopers) were shot. The Reichswehr had feared the SA as a potential rival. Now nothing stood in the way of the Reichswehr giving its loyalty to Hitler. After Hindenburg's death on August 2, all in the army swore their personal loyalty to Hitler, now *Der Führer* (the leader).

The "coordination" of the churches proved more difficult. Attempts to establish a National Reich Church under Ludwig Müller (1883–1945) as Reich Bishop were less than successful. Evangelical Christians, including Karl Barth (1886–1968), Dietrich Bonhoeffer (1906–1945), and Martin Niemoller (1892–1984), formed the Confessing Church in opposition to the Reich Church. Many of the Confessing pastors, including Bonhoeffer, subsequently suffered martyrdom at the hands of the state.

Hitler was somewhat more successful in neutralizing the Catholic Church as a center of organized opposition. In what was one of his most spectacular foreign policy successes, Hitler signed the Reich Concordat with the papacy on July 20, 1933. By the terms of the concordat, the Catholic Center Party was disbanded, and the Catholic clergy were required to give up all political activity. Henceforth, Catholics who opposed the Nazi state and its policies (e.g., the Holocaust) had to do so as individuals. Although there were courageous individuals among both Catholics and Protestants, the organized institutional churches generally capitulated to and openly supported the regime and its policies.

The Stalinist Dictatorship

Old Bolsheviks, members of the Communist Party before the October Revolution in 1917, called the events of the early 1930s "the great change." Western historians have labeled them the "Stalinist revolution." Whatever label one might choose, it was revolution more profound than the revolution of 1917. The primary goal of the second revolution was to transform the Soviet Union into a major industrial power, which in turn would be the basis for a modern military machine capable of securing the Soviet Union from the threat of annihilation by hostile capitalist powers.

The Stalinist dictatorship was constructed between 1928 and 1938. During the first period, from 1928 to 1933, the emphasis was on economic development. Stalin's aim was to make the Soviet Union a major industrial power within 10 years through rapid industrialization. In 1928, Lenin's strategic retreat from socialism (NEP) was abandoned in favor of economic planning. The first Five-Year Plan, begun in 1928, aimed at developing heavy industry. Backed by a mixture of dedicated enthusiasm and physical and psychological coercion, the results were impressive. Capitalism was eliminated, a socialist economy established, and agriculture collectivized.

The brutal process of collectivization of agriculture was meant to destroy the independence of the peasants while assuring the food supply necessary for industrialization. The peasants were forced into collective farms, where they were given production quotas to meet. The quotas were often greater than the farmers could produce. When the peasants resisted by burning their crops and farm buildings and slaughtering their livestock, they experienced severe repression. Estimates of the number who died as a result of the collectivization and the famine in the Ukraine (1932–1933) vary widely. Around 15 million for the period 1929–1930 is a likely figure. Many died when planning failed to produce expected results. Some deaths may have been intended. Many believe that Stalin deliberately caused the great famine of 1932–1933 in the Ukraine, during which millions perished. Millions more were sent to labor camps in Siberia and the Arctic regions of the Soviet Union. Some concessions were made to the peasants during the second Five-Year Plan (1932–1937).

A third Five-Year Plan was launched in 1938 but had to be suspended due to the German invasion of the Soviet Union in 1941. The basis for a modern industrial economy was created in the period of the first Five-Year Plan. At the same time, the basis for the Stalinist state was formed. By 1933, Stalin could not be seriously questioned without also calling into question the right of the Communist Party to rule. Those who challenged Stalin in any fashion had to be eliminated. This Stalin set out to do, beginning in 1934, in a series of actions that made Hitler's "Night of the Long Knives" seem benign by comparison.

In the winter of 1934–1935, Stalin began a reign of systematic terror aimed at physically eliminating all individuals and groups who might challenge his regime. The murder of Sergei Kirov, leader of the Communist Party in Leningrad, at the end of 1934 signaled the beginning of Stalin's purge of party leaders who he perceived to be a threat to his control. A series of show trials was staged in 1936, 1937, and 1938 to convict and execute key party officials (usually close associates of Lenin) on preposterous charges to which the accused confessed following extreme physical and mental torture. Millions were arrested by the secret police (NKVD), often at random to fill quotas, and either executed without trial or sent off to the slow death of the GULAG, the growing network of prisons and labor camps. When the purges ended in 1938, millions of innocent citizens languished in the GULAG; the government and party bureaucracies and the military high commands were decimated; and the population of the Soviet Union lived in fear, but Stalin enjoyed a level of power that would have caused the most autocratic Tsar to blush.

The Road to War in Europe

Virtually, all reputable historians agree that World War II in Europe was the result of Hitler's aggressive foreign policy. There can be no doubt that Hitler included a war in his plans for the creation of a greater German Reich that would last a thousand years. The war he got, however, was not the limited war in Eastern Europe that he desired. Remove Hitler from the equation, and World War II was not inevitable.

During his first two years in power, the years of the *Gleichschaltung*, Hitler pursued a cautious foreign policy. It was necessary to secure his position at home and begin secret rearmament without alarming

Great Britain and France. From hindsight, it may be concluded that if Hitler were to be removed from power and war avoided, he would have to have been stopped before 1936. After 1936, his position in Germany was secure and rearmament sufficient that only military defeat could oust him from power. But the aversion to war, the understandable commitment to avoid a replay of the Great War, was so strong among the Western democracies (England and France, not to mention the United States) that appeasement seemed the most logical foreign policy. Certainly, it was the policy that best represented the wishes of the populace of Britain and France in the 1930s.

Hitler removed Germany from both the League of Nations and the Geneva Disarmament Conference in October 1933 while giving assurances of his desire for peace and pledging peaceful cooperation with all countries that treated Germany as an equal. In 1934, to isolate France while also appearing to desire peaceful change, Hitler signed a nonaggression pact with Poland.

Hitler's first overtly aggressive move came in March 1935, when he denounced the disarmament clauses of the Versailles Treaty, introduced military conscription, and announced the existence of an air force. Although the League of Nations condemned Hitler's unilateral action, the British and French took no action to enforce the treaty. In fact, Britain signed the Anglo-German Naval Treaty with Germany in June 1935, implicitly legitimatizing Hitler's violation of the Versailles Treaty. Neither did Britain nor France do any more than protest when Hitler remilitarized the Rhineland in March 1936.

Until November 1936, when Hitler and Mussolini formed what Mussolini called the "Rome–Berlin Axis," Hitler was without an ally. In fact, before that time Fascist Italy stood with Britain and France against Hitler. Mussolini had been alarmed by an attempted coup by Austrian Nazis against the government of Engelbert Dollfuss (1892–1934) of Austria in July 1934. Then, when Hitler announced that Germany would rearm, Mussolini joined with Britain and France in the so-called Stresa Front to oppose Hitler: this was the last act of unity involving the three Allies of the Great War. What shattered the Stresa Front and sent Mussolini rushing into the waiting arms of Hitler was Italy's attack on Ethiopia in October 1935.

The attack on Ethiopia was in part an attempt by Italy to avenge its defeat at the Battle of Adowa in 1896. It was also meant to connect Italian Somaliland and Eritrea. In attempting to understand why Mussolini attacked Ethiopia, one must not overlook his megalomaniacal dreams of rebirthing the Roman Empire. No doubt he felt Ethiopia was an easy kill. Ethiopia's air force consisted of a mere 12 outdated fighter planes. The Ethiopian army included tribal warriors armed with spears and shields. Still, they bravely resisted the Italians, who resorted to using both mustard and phosgene gas against the Ethiopians.

Both Italy and Ethiopia were members of the League of Nations. Despite that fact, and Italy's use of outlawed chemical weapons, the League limited its action to condemning Italy's aggression and imposing some minor economic sanctions. It stopped short of placing an embargo on oil to Italy. Only by cutting off Italy's source of the oil it needed to prosecute its invasion could the League have saved Ethiopia. By taking only a weak-willed stand, the League merely offended Mussolini, pushing him into an alliance with Hitler, while effectively ending the League's role as an agent for collective security.

Mussolini and Hitler found an opportunity for cooperation when civil war broke out in Spain in July 1936. Nationalist forces led by Francisco Franco (1892–1975) reacted against increasing bloodshed at the hands of the Republicans and political chaos following the election of a left-wing Popular Front government in February. The Nationalists were aided by materiel and some military forces from Italy and Germany. The two dictators used the war in Spain to refine military techniques, strengthen national pride, and test the resolve of the democratic powers. The Republicans were aided by volunteers, including the International Brigades, but the bulk of the assistance they received came from the Soviet Union. For its part, the Soviet Union hoped to divert Hitler and Mussolini from a possible thrust into Eastern Europe and to rally the democratic powers to a strong antifascist position. Britain and France chose to remain neutral. The subsequent victory of Spain's Nationalists was seen as a victory for Mussolini and Hitler and as a defeat for the Western democracies.

On November 5, 1937, Hitler met with his generals. He informed them that Germany's need for living space (*Lebensraum*) in the east would necessitate a war not later than 1943–1945. In the meantime, he meant to destroy both Austria and Czechoslovakia in order to protect Germany's flank. Two weeks later, Hitler met with Lord Halifax (1881–1959), British Foreign Secretary and a leading appeaser. After Hitler spoke of Germany's need to deal with various border disputes and minority problems in the east, Lord Halifax informed Hitler that Britain would accept peaceful change in the status quo. Hitler took Halifax's response as a sign that he could proceed.

First on Hitler's agenda was the annexation of Austria, the so-called Anschluss. In February 1938, Hitler summoned the Austrian chancellor, Kurt von Schuschnigg (1897–1977), to Berchtesgaden. Hitler demanded concessions, including Austrian Nazi participation in the government. When Schuschnigg called for a plebiscite on Austrian independence, he was forced to resign and replaced by Arthur Seyss-Inquart (1892–1946), an Austrian Nazi. Seyss-Inquart invited the German army to enter Austria. On March 13, Austria's union with Germany was proclaimed to cheering crowds. Again, the Western democracies protested but did nothing.

Hitler was ready to move against Czechoslovakia, the only one of the "successor states" created by the peace settlement still a democracy in 1938. In fact, Czechoslovakia was the only model of democratic government, fair treatment of minorities, and industrial progress in Eastern Europe. Also, both France and the Soviet Union had treaties with Czechoslovakia, committing them to the maintenance of Czechoslovakia's integrity. Britain favored appeasement.

The Czechoslovakian crisis centered on the fate of the German minority living in the Sudetenland, the region along Czechoslovakia's border with Germany. Encouraged by Hitler, the pro-Nazi Sudeten German party under Konrad Henlein (1898–1945) demanded autonomy for the Sudetenland. The crisis intensified during the summer of 1938; then, on September 12, Hitler threatened intervention unless the Sudeten Germans were allowed to decide their own fate. On the following day, Konrad Henlein called for annexation with Germany.

As war appeared increasingly likely, Britain's prime minister, Neville Chamberlain (1869–1940), flew to Berchtesgaden on September 15, and to Bad Godesberg one week later, in order to assess Hitler's demands and find a way to satisfy them without risking a war. When the Czechs refused Hitler's terms, and war seemed inevitable, Mussolini proposed a conference at Munich. Britain, France, and Germany were invited, but not Czechoslovakia or the Soviet Union. The Soviet Union urged the Allies to resist Hitler's demands and offered military assistance to Czechoslovakia in the event of war.

The Munich Conference convened on September 29. Hitler presented the western Allies with a choice between sacrificing Czechoslovakia or an almost certain war. They chose to sacrifice Czechoslovakia. Czechoslovakia, the only democracy in Eastern Europe, had been sold out. Hitler once again triumphed over the Western democrats and his opponents at home, the generals and the resistance, who were urging the appeasers to reject Hitler's demands. Neville Chamberlain returned home to a cheering crowd, waving a piece of paper with Hitler's signature guaranteeing "peace in our time." The former premier of France, Leon Blum (1872–1950), who opposed the Munich Agreement signed by his successor, Edouard Daladier (1884–1970), was more clear-sighted and spoke of a sense of "cowardly relief" that war had been averted.

Several key developments followed the Munich Conference. In mid-March 1939, Hitler destroyed what was left of Czechoslovakia. Bohemia and Moravia were annexed, while Slovakia became a separate satellite of Germany. It was the first time Hitler had taken territory not containing a German population. Even Chamberlain had to acknowledge this act as aggression (Table 6.1). When Hitler then began making demands on the free city of Danzig and the Polish Corridor, Chamberlain reacted by writing out in his own hand a guarantee of Polish sovereignty. Britain's pledge of military assistance for Poland if attacked by Germany was endorsed by France. But Hitler, reckless in the glow of his string of successes, did not take the warning seriously. On April 3, *Der Führer* ordered his generals to prepare for war with Poland.

Table 6.1 Timetable of German Aggression

1935 (Mar. 16)	Hitler repudiates disarmament clauses of Versailles Treaty, restores conscription, announces founding of *Luftwaffe* (the air force), and expands the army to over half a million
1936 (Mar. 7)	Hitler sends troops into demilitarized Rhineland (Oct. 19) Two-year compulsory military service introduced (Nov. 1) Rome-Berlin Axis formed. Germany and Italy recognize Franco's government and begin intervention in Spanish Civil War. Anti-Comintern Pact between Germany and Japan
1938 (Mar. 11)	*Anschluss* (joining) between Germany and Austria (Sept. 30) Munich Conference. Germany occupies the Sudetenland
1939 (Mar. 15)	German troops occupy Bohemia and Moravia; Slovakia becomes German puppet state (Sept. 1) Germany invades Poland. Great Britain and France declare war on Germany two days later

Another by-product of the Munich Conference was a shift in Soviet policy toward Germany. Apparently, Stalin felt that the West's sellout of Czechoslovakia at Munich was evidence of a capitalist plot to direct Hitler's aggression toward the Soviet Union. Perhaps as a countermeasure, Stalin began to appease Hitler. The result was the Nazi–Soviet Nonaggression Pact signed on August 23, 1939. A secret portion of the pact divided Eastern Europe into German and Soviet spheres of influence. The Soviet Union was to receive two of the Baltic States (Latvia and Estonia), as well as Finland, Bessarabia, and eastern Poland.

The Nazi–Soviet Nonaggression Pact left Hitler free for his desired little war in Poland. He apparently expected not only an easy victory but also for Britain and France to conclude that there was nothing to be done about it. After taking Poland, he could then look for another angle to work. Thus, on September 1, German forces invaded Poland and annexed Danzig. Two days later, on September 3, Britain and France declared war on Germany. On September 17, the Soviet Union invaded Poland from the east. By the end of the month,

German forces invade Poland on September 1, 1939, thus beginning World War II in Europe. Poland surrendered on September 27. © Image Asset Management Ltd./Alamy

Poland fell and was partitioned between Germany and the Soviet Union, and a British Expeditionary Force of 158,000 men was on its way to France.

The Road to War in the Pacific

What transformed the war with Germany in Europe into a second world war was the emerging conflict with Japan in the Pacific. Since the end of the Great War, indeed even before, there was rivalry between the two new great powers, Japan and the United States. Each country felt its vital interests in the Pacific threatened by the other. For Japan, at least, the conflict increasingly took on the nature of a struggle for expansion and survival of the Japanese empire.

Events around the turn of the twentieth century increased tension between the United States and Japan. The Sino-Japanese War (1894–1895), the Russo-Japanese War (1904–1905), and the Spanish–American War (1898) revealed both nations as imperial powers with a growing conflict of economic interests in China and the Pacific. Japan's defeat of Russia in 1904–1905 removed Russia as a major player in the Pacific. As a result of the Spanish–American War, the United States acquired Guam and the Philippine Islands.

Acquiring the Philippine Islands increased American involvement in China and in securing its share of the lucrative Chinese trade. The Open Door Policy proposed by Secretary of State John Hay (1838–1905) in 1899–1900 was meant to secure American access to China while preserving the fiction of China's territorial integrity and independence.

Great Britain had already reduced its role in the area, when it concluded the Anglo-Japanese Alliance in 1902. The rising threat of the German High Seas Fleet compelled Britain to turn policing of the Pacific Ocean over to Japan in order to concentrate its naval forces in the North Sea and the Atlantic Ocean. Japan became the dominant naval power in the western Pacific. This fact led some in the United States to conclude that Japan had become the major threat to American interests in the Pacific. The result was America's "War Plan Orange" (1911), a plan for a possible war with Japan that remained valid until 1939.

Japan's seizure of the German territory of Kiaochow in November 1914, and its Twenty-One Demands (January 1915) aimed at gaining a virtual protectorate over China, further aroused suspicions of Japanese imperialism among Americans. Japanese suspicions of American motives were, meanwhile, heightened by developments at the Paris Peace Conference (1919) and the Washington Naval Conference (1921–1922).

At the Paris Peace Conference in 1919, Japan requested that a declaration on racial equality be included in the League of Nations Charter. Woodrow Wilson, fearing that such a declaration would assure defeat of the Versailles Treaty (which included the League Charter) in the Senate, refused to agree. As a kind of consolation prize, Japan was awarded a lease on the Shantung (Shandong) Peninsula in China, formerly belonging to Germany.

Additional gains during the Great War in the central Pacific of the former German Caroline, Marianna, Marshall, and Palau islands meant that Japan threatened American supply lines through the Pacific Ocean. To meet the threat, the United States prevailed upon Great Britain to end its private alliance with Japan and join with the United States, Japan, and other great powers to limit the size of their navies and define their interests in the Pacific region. Japanese military leaders would later see the agreements reached at the Washington Naval Conference (November 12, 1922–February 6, 1923) as an affront to Japanese national pride and an attempt to artificially limit legitimate Japanese imperial interests. The conference did, however, afford international recognition of Japan as a major power, if not the major power, in eastern Asia.

Relations between Japan and the United States remained cordial during the 1920s. Both enjoyed immense prosperity. Japan was the only nation, other than the United States, whose investments exceeded its foreign debt. The United States was Japan's number one trading partner, with 40 percent of its industrial product going to the United States. Another 25 percent went to China. As with the world's other industrial nations, the Great Depression brought an end to the prosperity and set the two great powers of the Pacific on a collision course.

The arrival of the Great Depression brought an end to prosperity in Japan, as it did elsewhere. The effects of the depression in Japan were made worse by an increase of 25 percent in the American tariff on Japanese goods. Wages fell one-third by 1931, rice prices fell below cost, and silk prices collapsed. Soon one-half of Japan's rural population was living in abject poverty. As conditions worsened, real power within Japan's government passed into the hands of a small clique of military leaders, who saw Japan's salvation in an aggressive foreign policy. Under slogans like a "Greater East Asia Co-Prosperity Sphere," Japan set out to establish economic control of China and Southeast Asia and military domination of the whole region. Such an aggressive imperialism meant conflict with both the Soviet Union and the United States.

In 1931, Japan invaded Manchuria, an act of unprovoked aggression which was condemned by the League of Nations. Condemnation by the League and its attempt to impose sanctions provoked the Japanese into withdrawing from the League and renouncing the Washington Naval Conference agreements. The United States also condemned Japan's aggression, but did not join in the sanctions. Manchuria was reconstituted as Manchukuo in 1932, under Japanese "protection," and with Henry P'u-i (1906–1967), the last emperor of China, as its (puppet) regent.

Japanese forces invaded China in July 1937. Once again, the League of Nations condemned Japan's aggression, but the deteriorating situation in Europe prevented effective action and even encouraged Japan's militarist leaders. Japanese and Soviet forces clashed along the border between Siberia, Manchukuo, and Korea, despite a nonaggression treaty between the powers, signed in August 1937. Relations with the United States grew more tense when in December 1937 Japanese bombers attacked the American gunboat *Panay* near Nanking, followed by Japan's rejection of the Open Door Policy in November 1938.

The United States pursued a cautious policy toward Japan in hopes of avoiding war, until the summer of 1940. With the steady success of German forces in Europe (see Chapter 7), Japan occupied Indochina in 1940–1941. President Roosevelt responded by freezing Japanese assets in America and imposing an embargo on trade with Japan, including oil. When the Dutch East Indies complied with the oil embargo, Japanese imports of the vital resource dropped by 90 percent. Faced with either withdrawing from Indochina and China, as demanded by the United States, or exhausting its oil reserves within two years, Japan saw a solution in gaining control of the Dutch East Indies. That, however, necessitated first defeating, or at least disabling, the American and British fleets in the Pacific. On December 7, 1941, Japanese forces attacked the American Pacific Fleet at Pearl Harbor. On the same day, the Japanese attacked American and British installations at Wake Island, the Philippines, Guam, Hong Kong, and Malaya. On December 8, the United States declared war on Japan. In an act of reckless abandon with few parallels in history, Germany and Italy declared war on the United States on December 11. The war in Europe and the war in the Pacific became World War II, a global conflict that lasted until September 1945, leaving thinking people in the world wondering what had become of civilization.

Reference

Pipes, Richard. 1981. *Modern Europe*. Homewood: Dorsey Press.

Further Reading

Allen, William Sheridan. 1985. *The Nazi Seizure of Power: The Experience of A Single German Town, 1922–1945*, rev. ed. Danbury: Franklin Watts. A classic study of why one small German town succumbed to Nazism.

Bracher, Karl Dietrich. 1991. *The German Dictatorship*. New York: Penguin Books. A scholarly study, and still the best on the origin and structure of the Hitler regime.

Fallada, Hans. 2009. *Little Man, What Now?* Translated by Susan Bennett. Brooklyn: Melville House Publishing. Depicts the tragedy of the Great Depression in Germany.

Greenwood, Walter. 1990. *Love on the Dole*. New York: Penguin Classics. Depicts the tragedy of the Great Depression in a small English town.

Gilbert, Martin and Martin Gott. 2000. *The Appeasers*. Burlington: Phoenix Books. Still a good survey of England's foreign policy during the 1930s.

Kershaw, Ian. 2008. *Hitler: A Biography*. New York: W. W. Norton. Perhaps the best biography of Hitler available.

Koestler, Arthur. 2010. *Darkness at Noon*. New York: Vintage Books. A classic novel of Stalin's purge trials of Old Bolsheviks.

Kindleberger, Charles P. 1986. *The World Depression, 1929–1939*. Berkeley: University of California Press. A standard survey of the Great Depression.

Thomas, Hugh. 1977. *The Spanish Civil War*. New York: Harper & Row. Widely acclaimed history of the Spanish Civil War.

Tucker, Robert C. 1992. *Stalin in Power: The Revolution from Above, 1928–1941*. New York: W. W. Norton. A fascinating picture of Stalin and the creation of the Soviet Union.

Part 3

Overview: 1939–1967

FROM THE START OF WORLD WAR II IN 1939 to the appearance of the European Community in 1967, Europe experienced a historical roller-coaster ride. The sickening plunge into global war was followed by a painful climb to recovery. The Europe emerging from wartime destruction and postwar hardships was, however, a different Europe from that which had gone to war.

World War II was a continuation of the Great War, now styled World War I, but it was also a global war, involving the United States, Japan, and China, among others. The outcome of the conflict completed Europe's descent from its dominant position at the start of the century and pushed two new great powers, deemed the two "superpowers," to center stage, the Soviet Union and the United States.

Barbarism on the one hand and technical brilliance on the other marked World War II. The Manhattan Project, the Anglo-American effort to construct an atomic bomb, reflected both facets. Building the bomb, a nuclear weapon of unprecedented power, required assembling gifted scientists and coordinating their work. The American use of the "A-bomb" on civilian populations, although possibly a factor in the Japanese decision to surrender, horrified large segments of the world population.

Twentieth-Century Europe: A Brief History, 1900 to the Present, Third Edition.
Michael D. Richards and Paul R. Waibel.
© 2014 John Wiley & Sons, Inc. Published 2014 by John Wiley & Sons, Inc.

The Holocaust, the systematic genocide of millions of people at the hands of the Nazis, caused many to question whether European civilization had not completely lost its bearings in the twentieth century. There was no military justification for the Final Solution. There was no rational way to understand the Holocaust despite the methodical, businesslike manner that sometimes characterized it. That the Holocaust originated in Germany, seemingly the most civilized of European countries, was particularly disturbing. Was this the result of a *Sonderweg*, a special historical path, or something any nation might be capable of doing?

Other aspects of the war offered hope. Advances made originally for military application in such areas as medicine and communications could be transferred to civilian life. Many became convinced during the war of the need for social and economic changes that would provide a better life for the masses. There was also a new desire to establish an international system to prevent future wars.

Three basic developments marked the period from 1945 to 1967. First, Europe found itself in the middle of the so-called Cold War. It also contended with waves of decolonization, as first Asian then African colonies gained independence. Finally, a divided Europe struggled to recover economically, socially, and spiritually. By 1967, when the European Economic Community, the European Coal and Steel Community, and the European Atomic Energy Commission joined to form the European Community, recovery was complete, at least in Western Europe.

The Cold War began to take shape in 1945 and 1946. Already at the Potsdam Conference (July–August 1945), there was an atmosphere of suspicion. The main sources of disagreement were European: the new Poland and occupied Germany. The Soviet Union was anxious to secure a Poland that would defer to Soviet strategic interests. It desperately wanted assurance that Germany would not again be able to wage aggressive war.

The year 1947 proved to be a crucial one. First, President Harry Truman of the United States proclaimed the Truman Doctrine, a promise to help governments in danger either from internal subversion or from external aggression. The same year saw the extension by the United States of the Marshall Plan, a package of economic aid to a war-ravaged Europe. Some saw the Marshall Plan as an economic counterpart to the Truman Doctrine. It was, however, meant to be simply an American initiative to help the peoples of Europe and restart European economies, west and east. In the new Cold War atmosphere, however, the Soviet Union saw it as an American plot to gain economic advantage.

Several events—among them a communist coup in Czechoslovakia, the Berlin Blockade (and Airlift), the formation of the North Atlantic Treaty Organization (NATO), the appearance of West Germany and East Germany, and, finally, the victory of the Chinese Communists over the Chinese Nationalists—convinced Europeans and Americans the so-called Cold War was a real and ongoing conflict. The American response to the Korean War in 1950 and the decision to aid the French in Indochina (Vietnam) made the Cold War global, even though the essential issues remained Soviet concerns in Europe.

Colonial empires in Asia were, generally, quickly dismantled in the decade following World War II. The British left the Indian subcontinent. America granted independence to the Philippines. The Dutch failed in their efforts to retain the Dutch East Indies. The French withdrew from Indochina after a bitter war against the Vietnamese communists.

In Africa, decolonization began in the 1950s. With some exceptions, it took place in an orderly manner. A major exception was Algeria, where a million European residents opposed independence. The French army, defeated in 1940 and in 1954, also resisted independence. The British experienced a difficult situation in Kenya with the Mau Mau Movement. Rhodesia and South Africa, white settler colonies, resisted efforts by the black majority in each country to come to power. The Belgians granted the Congo independence without, however, making an effort to insure its success. The Portuguese, however, clung to their colonial holdings until the mid-1970s.

In Eastern Europe, the interests of the Soviet Union were paramount. It undertook yet another Five-Year Plan emphasizing defense and heavy industry. After Stalin's death in 1953, there were more efforts to meet the needs of the people. Under the Soviet umbrella, each satellite country experienced a variation on the

Soviet model of industrialization in the 1950s: central planning, concentration on heavy industry, and collectivization. By the end of the decade, some were finding a national path to economic development. Yugoslavia, balanced precariously between East and West, since the late 1940s experimented with forms of economic organization, neither completely communist nor capitalist.

In the West, the Marshall Plan did indeed play an important role in restarting economies. Each country helped by the plan pursued its own brand of capitalism. The French emphasized planning and government-directed investing. The German *Wirtschaftswunder* (economic miracle) was largely the product of industry and the banks. The major development in the European economy in this period entailed cooperation and integration, first with the European Coal and Steel Community (ECSC) and then with the European Economic Community (EEC).

By the 1960s, a divided Europe no longer seemed a novelty. Europeans had also discovered the possibility of life without colonial empires. Europeans, especially in the West, enjoyed a material abundance that only a few had known earlier. The war was a distant memory, the Cold War a threat with which one had learned to live. The situation was not ideal, but the future for Europeans, for the first time in a long while, looked bright.

7

Armageddon
Europe in World War II, 1939–1945

Chronology

1939	Germany invades Poland; the Soviet Union invades Poland later that September
	Great Britain and France declare war on Germany
	Winter War between the Soviet Union and Finland
1940	Germany invades Denmark and Norway
	Germany invades the Netherlands, Belgium, and France
	Battle of Britain
1941	Atlantic Charter
	Germany invades the Soviet Union
	Japan attacks the United States at Pearl Harbor
	United States declares war on Japan
	Germany declares war on the United States

Twentieth-Century Europe: A Brief History, 1900 to the Present, Third Edition.
Michael D. Richards and Paul R. Waibel.
© 2014 John Wiley & Sons, Inc. Published 2014 by John Wiley & Sons, Inc.

1942	Wannsee Conference
	Battle of Midway
	Battle of Stalingrad
	Allied victory in North Africa
1943	Allied invasion of Sicily and Italy
	Mussolini deposed
	Italy joins the Allies
1944	D-Day invasion of German-occupied Europe by the Allies
	Battle of the Bulge
1945	Yalta Conference
	Germany surrenders
	Potsdam Conference
	Atomic bombs dropped on Hiroshima and Nagasaki
	Japan surrenders

IN THE SPRING AND SUMMER OF 1939, the Soviet Union and Nazi Germany carried out a complicated diplomatic dance that led eventually to the Nazi–Soviet Nonaggression Pact. Stalin had given up on the idea of collective security. Instead, he cynically used negotiations with England and France as a means by which to encourage Hitler to agree to a nonaggression pact. Hitler, for his part, was eager to begin the invasion of Poland at the start of September, before the fall rains began, and did not want to take a chance on becoming involved in a two-front war.

Midway through August, the tempo of the dance increased rapidly. Stalin invited Joachim von Ribbentrop (1893–1946), the German foreign minister, to Moscow on August 23. Negotiations took very little time, after which the participants promptly signed the nonaggression treaty. They attached a secret protocol to the treaty that indicated each country's sphere of interest in Eastern and Central Europe.

In the early morning hours of August 24, Stalin hosted a late supper for Ribbentrop at which he toasted Hitler. Ribbentrop joked that "Stalin will yet join the Anti-Comintern Pact" (an agreement between Germany and Japan in 1936, with Italy joining in 1937, that was directed against the Soviet Union [as quoted in the record of the conversation of Stalin and Ribbentrop in the online Avalon Project 2013]). According to Nikita Khrushchev (1894–1971), then a member of the Politburo, Stalin said a couple of days later that he had tricked Hitler. The treaty would keep them out of the war and allow them to save their strength.

The years of war and diplomacy that began with the invasion of Poland in September 1939 completely changed Europe's position in the world. From apparent dominance before World War II, Europe fell in 1945 to a position of near impotence before the two great world powers, the Soviet Union and the United States. Furthermore, 1945 marked the beginnings of a process by which the European colonial empires were gradually and painfully dismantled. Of course, part of the explanation for this startling reversal of fortune lies in the realities that prevailed in 1939: World War I and the Depression in the 1930s had hollowed out European civilization. World War II in many ways only confirmed what some had already noticed. The world was rapidly changing and Europe's easy dominance of it had effectively ended.

Blitzkrieg

The German invasion of Poland, which began on September 1, 1939, made brilliant use of the strategy of *Blitzkrieg* (lightning war). This involved combining mechanized spearheads of troops, motorized artillery, tanks massed in groups, and close tactical support by fighters and dive-bombers, all closely controlled by radio. It was a strategy that emphasized surprise and the use of overwhelming force. It both demanded and usually resulted in a rapid, decisive victory. Easy victories in 1939 and again in 1940 led Germany to believe it need not prepare for a protracted war. This failure to grasp the fundamental reality of modern warfare proved fatal over the next few years.

In the meantime, however, Germany was encouraged by its own military prowess. Blitzkrieg tactics resulted in the rapid defeat of Poland. By September 8, the German forces were outside Warsaw. Soviet forces invaded Poland from the east on September 17. Caught between two massive armies, Poland surrendered on September 28, less than a month after the beginning of the German offensive.

A strange interlude known as the "Phony War" occurred during the eight months following the fall of Poland. Technically, a state of war existed between Germany and the two Western democracies of Britain and France, yet no military engagements took place. Hitler expected Britain and France to accept his offers of peace. While Britain and France did not pursue these offers, they had few ideas about how to respond to Germany's recent conquest.

On November 3, the Soviet Union demanded several small areas from Finland to enhance the defenses of Leningrad. When the Finns refused, Soviet forces invaded Finland, beginning what came to be called the "Winter War," November 1939–March 1940. The Finns did surprisingly well against their much larger opponent, but the massive resources of the Soviet Union eventually prevailed. After beating the Finns, the Soviet Union moved to incorporate the Baltic States of Estonia, Latvia, and Lithuania, as well as Bessarabia and Northern Bukovina from Romania.

Germany returned to the offensive in April 1940. Once again, Blitzkrieg tactics brought swift results as Denmark and Norway fell victim this time. In May, a massive German effort was launched against the Netherlands, Belgium, and France. The Netherlands and Belgium were quickly beaten. On May 14, Rotterdam's center was flattened by German bombers and 40,000 civilians died, an early indication the new war would be even more senselessly brutal than the previous one.

France crumbled with unexpected quickness after German forces drove all the way to the English Channel, cutting off the British Expeditionary Force and thousands of French troops. In a daring rescue operation at Dunkirk undertaken between May 26 and June 4, the British turned defeat into a kind of victory by evacuating more than 300,000 troops, of which more than 100,000 were French,

Belgian, and Dutch, with the help of an armada of small boats and ships. An essential part of the remarkably successful evacuation was a calm sea. By mid-June, the French cabinet voted to ask Germany for terms of a ceasefire. The armistice was signed on June 22 in the same railroad car in which the Germans had signed the armistice ending World War I. By terms of the agreement, France was divided into a Nazi-occupied zone in the north and an unoccupied zone in the south, which the French were allowed to govern. The latter became known as Vichy France, after its capital in the resort town of Vichy. The head of state of the new regime was Henri-Philippe Pétain (1856–1951), the great hero of the battle of Verdun in World War I.

The Fall of France was due primarily to military mistakes. In preparing to meet the Germans in the new war, French generals had prepared to fight the last war. A reliance on the Maginot Line, a series of heavily fortified and well-armed barriers the French had built in the wake of the Great War to safeguard their nation's borders with Germany and Italy—symbolic of France's emphasis on defense—is often seen as the cause of the French defeat. This, however, oversimplifies the situation. The Maginot Line did what it was supposed to do. The Germans, however, did something no one anticipated. They largely ignored the Maginot Line and invaded France by going through the hilly and heavily wooded terrain of the Ardennes, to the north of the line. French and British forces in the meantime waited for the Germans to follow the invasion route of World War I, along the coast of Belgium. The German invasion caught them by surprise, a surprise compounded by their inability to grasp the techniques of Blitzkrieg. One French commander, the then-Colonel Charles de Gaulle (1890–1970), had long advocated techniques of tank warfare which, had they been employed in 1940, might have made a significant difference. His colleagues had largely ignored him, but German officers had paid close attention.

The Fall of France reflected the dislike many French felt for the Third Republic, the lack of a clear-cut national purpose, and the paucity of leaders of imagination and daring. Nevertheless, while the defeat was "strange," as Marc Bloch (1886–1944), a historian and later hero of the French resistance, put it, it did not result from treason, as some have argued, but rather from bad judgment and failure of nerve.

By midsummer 1940, only Britain remained to carry on the struggle against Nazi Germany and Fascist Italy. Italy had joined the war against France at the last minute but proved to be a burden rather than an asset. As of May 10, the veteran politician Winston Churchill had begun to lead Britain as prime minister. Over his long career, Churchill had known many ups and downs, but true greatness had escaped him. Now, the new prime minister became the man to match the hour. More than any other single individual, he became associated with the Allied cause in World War II and generally with its more memorable moments.

If that summer was, as Churchill later put it, Britain's "finest hour," it was also a very dark hour. Before the start of July, Hitler engaged in planning for Operation Sea Lion, an invasion of the British Isles. The commander of the German *Luftwaffe* (air force), Marshal Hermann Goering (1893–1945), believed he could bomb the British into surrender. The British responded to the air attacks by evacuating urban areas, organizing air-raid defense systems, and sending up squadrons of Spitfire and Hurricane fighter planes to meet the bombers. By fall, Goering had to acknowledge failure, and Hitler had to call off the invasion. The British had won the Battle of Britain.

Several factors help to explain the British success. Perhaps most important was the nature of the Luftwaffe and the way in which it was commanded. It had been designed more for tactical support of the Blitzkrieg than for extended bombing runs. Indeed, the German bombers were slow and their level of fighter protection often inadequate. Goering, improvising without a clear plan of attack, changed targets from the planes of Britain's Royal Air Force (RAF) to the terror bombing of London. This was, at least in part, in response to RAF attacks on Berlin on August 25, 28, and 29. Had the Luftwaffe concentrated on destroying the RAF on the ground, they might have won. British advantages included new, improved versions of Hurricanes and Spitfires that gave them an advantage in one-on-one combat. Radar, which the British had made a great deal of progress with in the 1930s, provided a crucial few minutes warning. As Wing Commander Max Aitken (1879–1964) remarked, "Radar really won the Battle of Britain. . . . We wasted no petrol, no energy, no time" (as quoted in Roberts 2011). At this point in the war, simply surviving to fight another day was a victory in itself.

Operation Barbarossa

Germany, primarily because of its defeat in the Battle of Britain, decided against attempting an invasion of Britain. Possibly, Hitler thought the British would eventually accept peace terms. Probably, he and his advisers realized the odds against success were very high since Germany lacked command of the air and could not challenge Britain's naval strength. In any case, he had already been thinking about invading the Soviet Union. Ideologically, the decision accorded with Hitler's pronouncements in *Mein Kampf*. The east was where Hitler intended to find *Lebensraum*, space for the rapidly growing Germany he envisioned in the near future. Additionally, Slavs were second only to the Jews as objects of Hitler's hatred. As *Untermenschen* (subhumans), they would serve as slaves in the Third Reich or be left to starve. Hitler regarded the defeat of the Soviet Union as crucial not only for *Lebensraum* but also for the elimination of what he termed "Jewish Bolshevism." The decision was taken to launch Operation Barbarossa in the late spring of 1941. Looking back on that fateful decision, it seems odd Germany would take on a country with such vast resources. At the time, however, there were practical considerations that seemed significant and appeared to reinforce ideological objectives. The Soviet Union appeared still disorganized by the purges and the Five-Year Plans. In addition, the Russian army had performed poorly in the war against Finland. The Nazis knew the Soviet Union would only become stronger as time went on, and they were well aware it had taken actions conflicting with Germany's interests in Central and in Eastern Europe. Nonetheless, the invasion of the Soviet Union must be counted as one of Hitler's major miscalculations.

In the meantime, Stalin had been warned repeatedly of plans for a German invasion. Richard Sorge (1895–1944), a German Communist working in Japan, actually provided the date of the invasion. Stalin finally decided to send an alert message, which came too late to do any good, early on the same day on which the invasion began, June 22, 1941.

Initially, Operation Barbarossa was even more successful than German strategists had hoped it would be. The Russian military, kept from making adequate preparations for a possible invasion by Stalin's fearful insistence on adhering fully to the terms of the Nazi–Soviet Nonaggression Pact, was caught off guard. Whole armies collapsed and were cut off. Attempts to retreat and regroup turned into routs. Much of the Russian air force was lost in the first days of the invasion. Stalin fell apart and sank into depression. It was two weeks before he finally spoke on the radio. Within weeks, Leningrad was under siege, German troops were advancing rapidly toward Moscow, and most of the rich croplands and important industrial complexes of the Ukraine had been conquered.

Yet the Soviet Union did not surrender. Stalin created the State Defense Committee (GKO), which he chaired. The general headquarters of the Soviet supreme command reported to the GKO. It was in charge of basic strategy while the army general staff developed operational plans. Perhaps even more important, the Soviet Union turned to the old traditions and, in particular, to the experience of Napoleon's invasion of Russia in 1812, giving ground but slowly bringing to bear its enormous resources. Now, Stalin called on the patriotism of the masses. The Russian Orthodox Church was pressed into service. Able young leaders emerged in the military and also in the party and government.

The resilience of the Russian people found an unexpected ally in the weather. First came the rains, a time the Russians called *rasputitsa* (the time when the roads dissolve into mud). Then, winter came early and caught the German military totally unprepared. As before, they had counted on a quick victory and therefore were not provisioned for a winter campaign. They had come close to gaining it, but had failed largely because Hitler insisted on mounting three major campaigns simultaneously: against Leningrad in the north, Moscow in the center, and the Ukraine in the south. The campaign in the south was particularly important as the efforts to take the city of Kiev used men and resources badly needed in the campaign to conquer Moscow.

Strategic errors were compounded by tactical errors. Rather than regroup and establish winter quarters, Hitler demanded the army to push on until, in some cases, major units were cut off and lost. By the end of 1941, if the Soviet Union had only a precarious lease on life, at least it could claim to have stopped the German army short of victory. In fact, on December 6, it launched a major counterattack.

The fatal flaw in Nazi strategy was now apparent. Like Nazi politics, Nazi war making had been a matter of improvisation. Neither the German economy nor society had been mobilized for the kind of prolonged warfare World War II demanded. Germany had learned nothing from its victories. Britain and the Soviet Union, for their part, had been forced by disastrous defeats to accept the fact that only an extended and long-term effort could possibly lead to victory. American aid to the British and Russians, who had immediately allied in the wake of the German invasion of the Soviet Union, was restricted in the beginning mainly to supplies and money.

In the last month of 1941, the Japanese attack on Pearl Harbor, December 7, 1941, catapulted the United States into the war. In response to President Roosevelt's request, Congress declared war on Japan on December 8. Although the attack had been highly successful, its architect, Admiral Isoroku Yamamoto (1884–1943), worried that the United States would soon recover and overwhelm Japan. As he had noted the year before, "If I am told to fight regardless of the consequences, I shall run wild for the first six months or a year, but I have utterly no confidence for the second or third year. . . ." (as quoted in Kennedy 1999).

On December 11, 1941, Hitler made what many historians regard as one of his greatest mistakes of the war. In a speech to the Reichstag, he declared war on the United States. Germany was under no obligation to do this. In fact, Japan had not informed Germany beforehand of its plans. By declaring war on the United States when Germany was already involved in a massive campaign against the Soviet Union, Hitler committed an act of hubris of gigantic proportions.

In May 1942, Admiral Yamamoto hoped to involve the US Navy in a decisive battle by attacking Midway Island, some 1,100 miles west of Hawaii. In the meantime, American code breakers, their efforts called "Magic," had begun to decipher the Japanese naval code. Many of the Japanese naval messages referred to "AF." Guessing that "AF" was Midway Island, the US Navy instructed the garrison at Midway to transmit by radio in early May a phony message that the distillation plant was malfunctioning, and they were running short of fresh water. The Japanese took the bait, sending coded messages that "AF" was low on water.

Admiral Chester Nimitz (1885–1996), commander-in-chief of the US Pacific Fleet, reinforced the garrison at Midway and sent every ship possible to protect the island—including a strategic aircraft carrier that the Japanese admirals assumed was temporarily out of commission. When the aircraft carrier USS *Yorktown* made its way into Pearl Harbor to repair heavy damage it had sustained in a recent clash with the Japanese at the Battle of Coral Sea early in May, mechanics estimated the work would take several weeks to complete. Nimitz gave them three days. Working around the clock, workers carried out the most essential repairs. The *Yorktown* was ready in time to depart with the rest of the task force.

The Japanese attacked Midway on June 4, 1942. As the Japanese bombers were being refitted for a second-wave attack on the US installations on the island, a Japanese scout plane spotted the American task force. The Japanese commander reversed the refitting process so that the planes could be instead sent against the arriving American task force. American planes had been attacking his fleet, but not one had scored a hit up to that point. Then, as the redirected Japanese fighters, the Zeros, were preoccupied trying to thwart torpedo planes dispatched from *Yorktown*, a squadron of USS *Dauntless* dive-bombers slipped through and in five minutes mortally wounded three Japanese carriers, their decks covered with flaming aircraft, fuel hoses, and ordnance.

As Kennedy (1999) notes:

> Before Midway, the Japanese had six large fleet-class carriers afloat in the Pacific and the Americans three (four with Saratoga, which was

returning from repairs on the west coast at the time of the battle at Midway). With the loss of just one American and four Japanese carriers, including their complements of aircraft and many of their superbly trained fliers, Midway precisely inverted the carrier ratio and put the Imperial Japanese Navy at a disadvantage from which it never recovered. (p. 543)

Although it took three more years and many casualties, Admiral Yamamoto's nightmare came true. America used its immense resources to push the Japanese steadily back toward the home islands, even while it contributed significantly to the war in Europe. The Battle of Midway, June 4–7, 1942, was the turning point in the Pacific, just as Stalingrad, which began on July 17, would be the turning point in Europe.

Stalingrad and D-Day

In 1942, two questions of vital importance appeared on the allied agenda. The first concerned whether the Russian military could hold Stalingrad, a city on the Volga River important both for reasons of strategy and prestige. The other vital question concerned the possibility of the United States and Britain establishing a second front in the European Theater that year.

Hitler pressed the German military to capture Stalingrad at any cost, while the Russian military was determined to resist the German assault with all the resources it could muster. The struggle, which began on July 17, 1942, was an intense one waged block by block, house by house, and, in some cases, room by room. German soldiers referred to the vicious struggle for Stalingrad as a "Rat War (*Rattenkrieg*)." Snipers, both men and women on the Soviet side, were also closely associated with Stalingrad.

While one part of the Russian army held the bulk of the German forces in front of it, other portions of the Russian military massed to the north and to the south of Stalingrad. On November 19, 1942, the Russians launched a gigantic pincers movement, cutting off a large German force in the now-ruined city. The German military could

Russian soldiers preparing to cross the Volga River and take part in the Battle of Stalingrad (1942–1943), a major turning point in the war in Europe. Reproduction of a painting by V. K. Dmitrievskii. Library of Congress, LC-DIG-ppmsca-18531

neither break through and reestablish contact with the surrounded troops nor adequately supply them. Hitler refused to give the cutoff troops permission to try to fight their way out of the encirclement. He also gave orders not to surrender. Nevertheless, on February 2, 1943, the remaining German forces, perhaps one-third of the original force, did surrender. Hitler felt he had been betrayed. German soldiers, he said, rather than surrender, should have fought to the death or ended their own lives.

While the Russian victory at Stalingrad was the turning point of the war in Europe and probably the greatest military campaign of the war, in 1943 another battle of gigantic proportions took place at Kursk. This battle, a German counterattack that failed, ended any realistic hope the German military might have had in the possibility of victory.

The numbers of men, tanks, and airplanes involved in the Battle of Kursk were staggering. The Germans fielded some 900,000 troops, 2,700 tanks and self-propelled guns, and 2,600 aircraft. The Russians threw nearly two million men, 3,800 tanks and self-propelled guns, and 2,100 aircraft into the battle. The German effort was another example of Blitzkrieg. This time, however, the difference lay in the fact that there was no element of surprise. By 1943, the Russians had seen their share of Blitzkrieg and had learned how to defeat it. Not only had the Russians rebuilt their army on the ruins of the force of 1941, but they had learned to use it much more effectively. It was still a war of attrition but one in which the Soviet Union had all the advantages and Nazi Germany none. In the remainder of 1943, the Soviet Union began steadily advancing on all fronts. In January 1944, the siege of Leningrad was lifted and Soviet forces were nearing several key cities in Eastern Europe.

Continuously in 1942 and 1943, the Soviet Union pressed their Allies to open a second, Western, front in Europe as a means of easing the enormous burden they were shouldering in fighting off the Germans. The United States was largely preoccupied in that period with the war in the Pacific. For its part, Britain spent most of 1942 dealing with General Erwin Rommel (1891–1944), the "Desert Fox," in Libya and Egypt. The closest thing to a second front in 1942 was the occupation of French North Africa. This was as much a diplomatic as a military maneuver in that the area was nominally controlled by Vichy France. The Allies risked the possibility that Germany would sweep the Vichy government aside or force it to join Germany as an active combatant in retaliation for the invasion. On the plus side, the successful takeover of French North Africa helped the now-General Charles de Gaulle emerge as undisputed leader of the Free French, a military organization created after the French government had signed the armistice with Germany.

The Soviet Union was not satisfied with the Allied occupation of French North Africa. Nor was it satisfied the following year with the Anglo-American invasion of Sicily and the Italian mainland. The invasion of the Italian mainland took Italy out of the war. The Fascist Grand Council deposed Mussolini, and King Victor Emmanuel III (1869–1947) appointed Marshal Pietro Badoglio (1871–1956) as premier to replace Mussolini. Badoglio, after disbanding the Fascist Party, opened negotiations with the Allies, which resulted in Italy switching sides on September 3, 1943. In the meantime, German paratroopers had carried out a daring rescue of Mussolini. The Nazis established the Italian Social Republic with Mussolini as head of state, but it was a puppet regime. Mussolini had no power and seemingly little interest in the course of the war. The "republic" lasted only from September 23, 1943, until April 25, 1945, just over 19 months.

A large number of German troops were committed to the defense of Italy. These troops, combined with the mountainous terrain, made the Allied campaign as it made its way up the peninsula a difficult and bloody one. For the Soviet Union, however, this was still not the major diversion they sought. They did not consider it the long-awaited second front.

Only with D-Day, June 6, 1944, did the Soviet Union get what it had wanted all along. Operation Overlord, the landings on the beaches of Normandy by American, British, and Canadian forces, was as much a feat of logistics as anything else. Simply to amass and coordinate the equipment and men needed for the cross-Channel invasion was a tremendous achievement. Waiting for the right combination of weather and tides, and preventing German intelligence from discerning the nature of preparations, constituted additional formidable tasks.

The weather was the first great question mark. Overlord was originally scheduled for June 5. US General Dwight David "Ike" Eisenhower (1890–1969), supreme commander of the Allied Expeditionary Forces, ordered a 24-hour postponement until June 6. Although, in theory, he could have postponed the invasion one more day, the reality was either June 6 or wait until June 19. As it turned out, June 19 saw the worst summer storm in the Channel in 40 years.

The British and Canadian troops landing on Sword, Juno, and Gold beaches met limited resistance and linked up with airborne troops that had dropped earlier. American troops landing on Utah beach overwhelmed the defenders. Omaha Beach, however, was another matter. The film *Saving Private Ryan* (1998) provides some idea of the deadly chaos American soldiers encountered when they stepped off the landing crafts. Yet the sheer weight of numbers pushed the German defenders back.

By nightfall on D-Day, more than one hundred thousand troops had come ashore. Many more came ashore in the following days, as did an avalanche of materiel. The German response was hampered by Hitler's insistence that the real invasion would come far to the east along the French coast, at the Pas de Calais, and by his refusal to order a timely relocation of Panzer divisions. Nonetheless, German resistance was surprisingly effective and delayed the "breakout" from the linked beachheads south and east into central France by approximately a month. Once the allies achieved breakout, they moved rapidly. The French Forces of the Interior were the first troops to enter Paris. General de Gaulle gave a speech at the Hotel de Ville (town hall) on August 25, the day the Germans surrendered. The rapid advance of allied troops across France and the liberation of Paris created a wave of optimism that the war might be concluded by the end of the year.

Instead of a collapse of the German war effort, the Germans, in what was seen later as a last-ditch effort, counterattacked the relatively thin center sector between British armies in the north and the American forces in the south. Coming once again out of the forests of the Ardennes on December 16, the Germans created a "bulge" in the allied line, hence the Battle of the Bulge. Eisenhower asked US Lt. General George Patton (1885–1945) to swing his troops ninety degrees to hit the flank of the German salient. Early in January, the Battle of Bulge was over, the most costly battle of the war for the United States. Of greater importance, however, Hitler's gamble had failed, using up in the process his last reserves of men, armor, and aircraft in the West.

Home Fronts

Germany lost the war in large part because it failed to make a commitment to an all-out effort until it was too late. Throughout 1941, this kind of commitment had seemed unnecessary. Quick victories made it possible to reequip the German military without placing much strain on the civilian economy. Occupied countries had the tops of their economies skimmed off for the German war effort.

Additionally, Sweden and Switzerland, both neutral during the war, were important factors in the German war effort. When the Soviet Union did not collapse as expected in 1942, however, it became clear something had to be done to coordinate the economy for military purposes. Goering, who had been in charge of the Four-Year Plan (1936) before the war, made efforts in this direction, as did army personnel. Fritz Todt (1891–1942), minister of armaments and munitions, began a more successful effort that, after his death in 1942 in an airplane accident, Albert Speer (1905–1981) carried on. Speer, Hitler's personal architect, demonstrated considerable managerial ability in reorganizing the German economy. Parallel efforts by Heinrich Himmler (1900–1945) and the Schutzstaffel (SS) hampered Speer's effort. The SS, originally a protective guard for Hitler and other Nazi leaders, evolved to become a virtual state within a state; it possessed its own military units and used vital resources for purposes such as the Holocaust that had little to do with the prosecution of the war. Nevertheless, Speer tripled the production of munitions and weapons between 1942 and 1944. However, Allied bombing raids and a lack of raw materials and manpower resulted in a precipitous decline in production in 1945.

Britain, its back against the wall, worked to organize its resources and transform a peacetime economy into one fully mobilized for war. Taking cues from the experience of World War I, Winston Churchill reorganized the War Cabinet and turned over direction of the economy to a small ministerial group called the Lord President's Committee. From 1940 on, Britons suffered materially from the war, but this was borne by most with good grace. It was, first of all, a necessity. Additionally, there was the expectation the postwar period would usher in a new social order, equitable if not egalitarian.

The Soviet Union had the advantage of a tightly controlled command economy from the beginning. Under the Five-Year Plans of the 1930s, some industries had been shifted to the east. When war began, entire plants were dismantled, relocated, and put back into production in a matter of weeks. Until 1943, however, Germany controlled large amounts of Russian farmland and significant parts of Russian industry. As the German army retreated, it destroyed as much as possible. Still, the Soviet Union, with its population completely mobilized for the war effort and with considerable American aid in the form of the Lend-Lease Program, built up its productive capacity. The standard of living for the individual Russian dipped below even the previous lows reached in the days of the civil war or the early 1930s, but the war effort was sustained. Like the British, the Russians faced both an unavoidable necessity and the prospects of a much-improved situation after a victorious end to the war.

Behind the successful allied war effort stood the enormous resources of the United States, its productive capacity freed from the Depression by the demands of war. America became, as President Franklin Roosevelt put it, "the arsenal of democracy." Within a year of the late 1941 attack on Pearl Harbor, American production of armaments equaled that of all Axis powers combined. By 1944, the amount of armaments produced in the United States was double that of the Axis.

As the United States entered the war, it faced the question of what to do with groups it regarded as potentially subversive. It quietly rounded up 14,000 German and Italians regarded as security risks. It also arrested more than 2,000 Japanese. In Hawaii, where the Japanese community constituted nearly half the population and was vital to the economy, internment was out of the question. In California, however, the Japanese constituted barely 1 percent of the state's population. In February 1942, the chief of the army Western Defense Command requested authority to remove all Japanese, including Japanese Americans who were native-born US citizens, from their homes and farms on the West Coast. Although the Justice Department argued against this move, President Roosevelt signed an executive order on February 19 that permitted designation of military areas from which certain unspecified people might be excluded. Soon after this, more than 100,000 Japanese were imprisoned in relocation camps staffed with armed guards, where they remained until the US government in December 1944 declared there was no longer a need for the camps and began to empty them.

Collaboration and Resistance

The Third Reich made little attempt to use the situations they had created to construct a "new order" in Europe. Even those among the occupied nations who wanted to collaborate with Germany were forced to do so under disadvantageous conditions. Some groups, Ukrainian nationalists, for example, who were eager to help in the destruction of the Soviet regime, were treated so badly that they had little choice but to resist the Nazis.

In occupied Europe, it was frequently difficult to draw a clear distinction between resistance and collaboration. For instance, how should a state functionary see his position? What he did was largely for the welfare of the people in his country, but some of what he did might aid the German war effort. This was the essential dilemma of those governing Vichy France. Pierre Laval (1883–1945), premier during much of the existence of Vichy, argued after the fact that his policies were necessary in order to keep the German occupation at a distance. It was better for Vichy authorities to supervise the recruiting of workers for labor in the German war industry than to turn this task over to the Germans themselves. Similarly, Laval argued, it was important for the French police to function as fully as possible, even if this meant cooperating with the Gestapo (*Ge*heime *Sta*atspolizei or Secret State Police) in tracking down Jews or in dealing with the resistance.

Not many of those involved in the Vichy government could be accurately labeled as fascists. Most were conservatives who practiced collaboration because it seemed unavoidable and also because it appeared to offer the chance to carry out a "National Revolution." Between June 1940 and April 1942, members of the Vichy government believed they were working to replace the shopworn values and institutions of the Third Republic with something far better. By 1943, however, Henri-Philippe Pétain, Laval, and the rest of the Vichy government found it possible to do only what Germany allowed or required them to do. What may have been a sensible policy in the shock of defeat in 1940 had become, through a series of almost imperceptible changes, no longer justifiable by 1943 and 1944.

Elsewhere in occupied Europe, there was even less possibility than in Vichy France of convincing oneself one was working out a national regeneration within the context of the German occupation. The pressure to supply the Nazi occupiers with food, workers for the factories, and Jews for the death camps was too great. Here and there, efforts were made to save the young men from labor service and the Jewish population of the country from exportation. Perhaps the best-known effort to hide Jews was that undertaken by the Frank family and their friends in Amsterdam. Although the effort failed, the diary left behind by Anne Frank has inspired millions in the years since its publication. Corrie ten Boom (1892–1983) and her family were more successful in their efforts to hide Jews in Haarlem, the Netherlands. Oskar Schindler (1908–1974), whose story has been told in Steven Spielberg's (1946–) film *Schindler's List* (1993), protected a large number of Polish Jews by employing them in his business. The extraordinary efforts of the Protestant community of Le Chambon in France also saved the lives of many Jews. Some countries did a better job of protecting their Jewish populations than others. Denmark was amazingly successful in this endeavor, eventually sending most of its Jewish citizens to safety in neutral Sweden. Ironically, the record of Fascist Italy was also quite good in this respect.

Organized resistance movements in Europe have often been romanticized and their importance exaggerated. There is a poignant scene in Marcel Ophül's documentary on Vichy, *The Sorrow and the Pity* (1970), in which a man talks about being part of the resistance: he kept a gun hidden under a woodpile throughout the war. This was, of course, dangerous in that he might have been shot had the gun been discovered, but it meant, in reality, his role in the resistance had been played out only in his mind and probably after the fact at that. Many in France and elsewhere, once the war ended, repressed any instance of collaboration and blew up out of all proportion anything that might be interpreted as resistance. For those who played an active part, there was always the question of whether it did any good. The moral ambiguity involved in ambushes and assassinations is examined, for example, in Harry Mulisch's powerful novel, *The Assault* (1985), which is about one such incident in Haarlem, the Netherlands.

Nonetheless, the resistance movements accomplished much of crucial importance. They furnished intelligence, helped downed pilots and escaped prisoners of war, and, in some cases, severely hampered the German war effort. The most successful resistance movement in the war was the Communist resistance movement in Yugoslavia led by Josip Broz (1892–1980) or Tito. Tito's partisans defeated not only the German occupiers of the country but also their rivals, the conservative Chetniks, who had hoped to restore the monarchy. The liberation of Yugoslavia without outside help was vitally important in the postwar period.

In various other ways, the resistance movements left important legacies. Communists played large roles in most movements because of their previous experience with underground work. Even the noncommunists among the resistance workers tended to reject the old order, which they held responsible for the problems of the 1930s and for the war itself. Many members of the resistance movements hoped to find different ways of organizing society, politics, and the economy after the war. For some, this took the form of a "European" approach that would counter the dangers of nationalism. For others, the emphasis was on social justice. Various resistance "charters," such as the Charter of the National Council of Resistance in France, provided guidelines for postwar reconstruction programs.

The tendency to overestimate the importance of the resistance is perhaps most notable in Germany. Much has been made of the circles, composed largely of military officers and aristocrats, which on several occasions attempted to assassinate Hitler. By 1943, these circles realized that Hitler's plans were leading Germany to disaster. There was also considerable uneasiness about the activities of the SS and the Gestapo. Efforts to assassinate Hitler and stage a coup were delayed in part by the reluctance of some to break their oath of loyalty sworn to Hitler as supreme commander and by fears for the integrity of Germany after the coup. Most of those involved in the plot did not envision Germany changing much and were reluctant to open the way to victory by the Allied Powers.

Hitler seemed to lead a charmed life, as attempt after attempt on his life miscarried. The effort by Count Claus Schenk von

Stauffenberg (1907–1944) on July 20, 1944, nearly succeeded, leaving Hitler wounded but alive. The plotters, thinking he had been killed, started the coup. Joseph Goebbels, Hitler's minister of propaganda, kept the coup contained until it could be confirmed Hitler was alive. The failure of the plot resulted in the destruction of the German resistance movement. For his loyalty and swift action, the Führer rewarded Goebbels with the office of General Plenipotentiary for the Mobilization of Total War.

The Holocaust

While some Germans had been involved in one capacity or another in the resistance, many more had been active in planning an unprecedented program of genocide. Anti-Semitism had long been a major point in the Nazi program. In the 1930s, this had been expressed mostly through quasilegal measures designed to exclude German Jews (less than 1 percent of the population) from public life and force them to emigrate. With *Kristallnacht* ("the Night of Broken Glass"), November 9, 1938, the regime seemed to head in a more violent direction. The SA used the assassination of a German diplomat in Paris by a young Polish Jew as a pretext for a night that included beatings, rapes, killings, the torching of synagogues, and the breaking of Jewish shop windows (hence the "Night of Broken Glass"). The event is often seen as marking the beginning of the Holocaust. Once the war began, the Nazis gained control over millions of Jews. They also realized that actions could be taken in wartime that would be publicized and criticized in times of peace.

At first, emigration, perhaps to some far-off place such as the French colony of Madagascar or, after the defeat of the Soviet Union, some corner of Siberia, was suggested. Large numbers of Jews were placed in ghettos. In the meantime, the euthanasia campaign in Germany in the 1930s, designed to eliminate mentally and physically disabled people, so-called worthless life, provided the occasion for some experiments in killing people efficiently.

The turning point in Nazi efforts to deal with what they termed "The Jewish Problem" came with preparations for the campaign against the Soviet Union. First, the SS created task forces, the *Einsatzgruppen*, which followed the German army as it moved across the Soviet Union. The task forces were instructed to round up communist officials and Jews and to kill them. Thousands of people were forced to dig their own graves and then killed by machine guns. The best-known example of this campaign of slaughter is Babi Yar, near Kiev, where, in September 1941, over a period of two days, an estimated 35,000 Jews were killed. Although more than a million Jews were killed in this fashion, it was an inefficient process and difficult for some of the perpetrators to stomach. Late in 1941, plans began to be made for a more organized and coordinated process of slaughter. The Wannsee Conference in January 1942, held in a suburb of Berlin, was partly an effort to resolve remaining logistical problems and other issues, but more importantly it was meant to establish collective responsibility. The decision to eliminate European Jews had already been made. No direct order from Hitler reflects this decision, but it is highly unlikely that he did not know and approve of the plans. Himmler took the lead in carrying out what he described as the Führer's wishes. The actual paper trail to Hitler only goes as high as a memorandum from Goering authorizing Reinhard Heydrich (1904–1942), an official in the SS, to take steps necessary "for the Total Solution of the Jewish Question within the realm of German influence in Europe."

The Nazis established six killing centers in Poland, the largest at Auschwitz (Oswiecim). Trains came from all over Europe to Auschwitz, which was actually a complex of camps and contained industrial enterprises as well as the death camp. After leaving the trains, people were separated into those headed for the gas chambers and those headed for the labor camp. The Nazis ran the operation with a kind of grotesque efficiency, a terrible parody of a rationalized industrial enterprise. They instructed those intended for the gas chambers first to go to the showers, after which they would receive new clothing and further instructions. Though the gas chambers were constructed in such a way as to resemble showers, it did not take long for people to understand what was happening. Death came quickly, but people nonetheless experienced panic and intense agony during the few minutes the process took.

Inmates of Buchenwald, a Nazi concentration camp, in April 1945. The young man seventh from the left in the middle row is Elie Wiesel who would later write *Night*, a memoir of his experience, and become a Nobel Prize laureate. National Archives and Records Administration (ARC no. 535561)

Evidence of this still exists in the grooves clawed into the concrete ceiling and walls of the chamber.

The Germans made efforts to run the killing centers as productive enterprises. They collected anything of value—mounds of human hair, warehouses full of shoes, handbags, and dresses. They removed gold crowns from the corpses before wheeling them into the crematoria. The economic irrationality of this enterprise was all too apparent. In the middle of a war beginning to go badly for Germany, vital resources were being squandered for the purposes of the slaughter. From the perspective of the Nazis who shared Hitler's racial beliefs, however, the extermination of Jews and other so-called undesirables (gypsies, homosexuals, and others) was precisely the point of the war.

The Holocaust produced a number of acute moral dilemmas. For example, if the perpetrators did not share Hitler's racial fantasies, then how did they justify their participation? Some, of course, insisted they were only following orders. Many were active participants in the Holocaust because they saw the war in the east as a crusade against communism. It is now recognized that the army played a larger role in the mass deaths outside the camps than was earlier believed to be the case. Some soldiers simply wanted to remain part of their unit, taking the bad with the good. More frequently than one might wish to think, participation in the mass killings hardened people; others found they actually enjoyed it. To the extent that the victim appeared to be weak, different, or alien, it was possible to consider that person less than human and, therefore, easier to kill. Certainly in the camps, where the system operated in such a way as

Werner von Braun and other members of the group that developed the V-2 rocket during World War II shortly after their surrender to American soldiers in 1945. Von Braun is wearing a cast from injuries suffered in an earlier automobile accident. He later played a crucial role in the development of the United States space program. National Archives and Records Administration (ARC no. 531328)

to degrade people and deprive them of any dignity, it was possible for guards and supervisors to see the prisoners as undeserving of life. Some of the perpetrators and many of the observers were appalled by what they witnessed but generally felt there was little they could do except on an individual basis.

For the inmates of concentration camps and death centers, ethical questions also existed. A few survived by losing every shred of humanity and taking part in crimes against their fellow prisoners. Most survivors, however, depended on solidarity with others. Invariably, there would come a time when even the strongest and most resourceful would find himself or herself lost without the help of a group. Much has been made of the inmates' passivity, of their failure to do anything to protest. To a large extent, this is unfair. First, the system worked in such a way as to disguise what was happening until it was too late. Second, there were uprisings and protests, even though the odds against their success were impossibly high. Perhaps the most serious moral questions came before people reached the death camps, in villages and towns before deportation orders came. Too many refused to heed the warnings or organize in their defense. By the time people had been placed in a ghetto, it was too late for escape in most cases. The Jewish councils the Nazis created to administer some aspects of ghetto life had to make agonizing decisions about compliance or resistance. Nonetheless, there were Jewish partisan groups and a few spectacular if also ultimately futile examples of resistance in the ghettos. The Warsaw Ghetto Uprising in April–May 1943 was only the largest and most famous of these acts of defiance.

Finally, there is the question of the many who knew about the Holocaust but did nothing to stop it. While some extraordinarily brave people worked to help Jews hide or escape to a neutral country, most tried to avoid any involvement in or knowledge of the scheme. By the middle of the war, Allied leaders knew the broad outlines of the Nazi plan to eliminate all European Jews, yet they took no direct action against it, military or otherwise. In part, this reflected a determination to get on with the war as the surest way to deal with a broad range of problems. In other cases, it reflected a global level of anti-Semitic prejudice that was much higher than many cared to admit. In the United States, for example, influential figures in both the State Department and the Congress blocked attempts to bring in large numbers of Jewish refugees before and during the war.

The Holocaust demonstrated the full range of human behavior. Its scale and the cold-bloodedness with which it was carried out set it apart. Between five and six million Jews were killed, approximately two-thirds of Europe's prewar Jewish population. Most of those killed came from Poland (3 million) and the Soviet Union (1.5 million). Sizable groups also came from Hungary, Romania, and Germany (Table 7.1).

Table 7.1 Jewish Victims of the Holocaust*

Country	Pre-Final Solution Population	Estimated Deaths
Poland	3,300,000	3,000,000
USSR	3,103,000	1,480,000
Baltic countries	253,000	228,000
White Russia	375,000	245,000
Ukraine	1,500,000	900,000
Russia (RSFSR)	975,000	107,000
Romania	600,000	300,000
Czechoslovakia	180,000	155,000
Hungary	650,000	450,000
Germany/Austria	210,000	240,000
Netherlands	140,000	105,000
France	350,000	90,000
Yugoslavia	26,000	43,000
Greece	70,000	54,000
Belgium	65,000	40,000
Italy	40,000	8,000
Norway	1,800	9,000
Luxembourg	5,000	1,000
Bulgaria	64,000	14,000
Denmark	8,000	—
Finland	2,000	—
Total	8,861,800	5,933,900

*The table is based on Dawidowicz (1975)

The End of the War

The Holocaust now seems like a crucial element in any consideration of the nature and impact of World War II, but in the minds of those working in 1944 and 1945 to establish the bases of the postwar world, it was a relatively unimportant factor, even when there was some conception of the dimensions of the event. Uppermost in the minds of the leaders of the Allied Powers by 1944 was the war in the Pacific. By then, it seemed apparent the Nazi Third Reich was doomed. Planners thought the war in the Pacific might easily continue another year or more, resulting in hundreds of thousands of further casualties for the Allies. A second crucial consideration involved political arrangements for European countries that had been either belligerents or occupied territories during the war. For various reasons, it did not seem possible simply to return to the boundaries of 1938 and out of the question to allow some regimes to continue in power unaltered.

At the time of the Yalta Conference in February 1945, the American, British, and French forces had recovered from the Battle of the Bulge, but they had yet to cross the Rhine River. The Soviet Union by that time was approximately 100 miles from Berlin and had occupied most of the major capitals of Eastern and Central Europe. The military situation at that time had obvious political implications. Americans continued to resist the idea of using military means to achieve political objectives. Still, a certain context for the discussions had already been established.

Yalta has often been viewed as either a failure of American diplomacy or a triumph of Russian duplicity. It should not be seen as either, but rather as an agreement that made sense in the context of the times, yet also one badly flawed by misunderstandings. In part, the agreements were shaped by the desire to involve the Soviet Union in the war in the Pacific. While this represented a considerable concession on the part of the Soviet Union in that it had borne the brunt of Allied efforts in the war in Europe, Stalin was eager to capture the parts of the Japanese empire that had once been Russian. The major problem, however, concerned Eastern Europe and Russian interests there. Beginning with the Nazi–Soviet Nonaggression Pact, the Soviet Union had worked consistently to make sure the states along its western borders were sympathetic to its interests and nonthreatening to its security.

Poland formed a major focus of concern. The Soviet Union desired a postwar government in Poland that was at least friendly toward the Soviet Union and willing to accede to its wishes, including incorporation by the Soviet Union of territory that had been disputed by the two states between the wars. The government, seemingly, did not have to be a communist one. The Soviet Union believed it had a natural right to act in its interests and had been encouraged in this belief by Anglo-American practices in Italy, where policies based on American and British institutions and values had been put in place. The so-called percentages deal in October 1944 between Churchill and Stalin, dividing Central and Southeastern Europe into areas in which the Soviet Union or Britain would have predominant influence, was of limited importance but certainly accorded with the Soviet perspective on postwar arrangements.

The problems associated with Yalta came later when the Soviet view, pragmatic and hard-nosed, began to clash with the American view, also pragmatic but colored by ideals drawn from such documents as the "Atlantic Charter," which had been issued by Roosevelt and Churchill in August 1941. Part of the problem lay in definitions. Phrases such as "free elections" or "democratic governments" might be understood in different ways. From the Soviet point of view, an election was not free or a government democratic if the result was a state hostile to Soviet interests.

The final and most important issue concerned plans for Germany after the war. Proposals to destroy German industrial capacity were not accepted, but it was agreed that reparations could be extracted. Reparations could come from current production of various enterprises or could be an enterprise itself, which was then dismantled and shipped back to the Soviet Union. It was further agreed that the country and its major city, Berlin, were to be divided into four sectors, each to be run by one of the occupying powers but all to cooperate economically. The fate of Germany was the dominant issue for the Soviet Union and the failure of the other Allies to understand this fully created much of the basis for the Cold War that followed the end of World War II.

Between Yalta and the next meeting of the Allied leaders at Potsdam in July and August 1945, the war in Europe ended. In March, the Americans crossed the Rhine, the last major obstacle to the conquest of Germany. In the latter part of April, American and Russian troops met at Torgau on the Elbe River. Hitler committed suicide in his bunker in Berlin on April 30, the day after marrying his mistress, Eva Braun (1912–1945). It was left up to the German military commanders to surrender early in May to the Allied forces.

The war in the Pacific ended a little more than three months after the German surrender. American forces in the latter part of 1944 moved in two directions. One involved the invasion and reconquest of the Philippines. On October 20, 1944, General Douglas MacArthur waded ashore on the island of Leyte and announced that he had returned as promised. It was March of the following year, however, before the United States managed to complete the retaking of the Philippines.

The second, "island hopping," campaign followed up the conquest of Saipan in the Mariana Islands with the invasion of the island of Iwo Jima in February 1945. After two months of fierce combat, scarcely any of the 21,000 heavily fortified Japanese defenders of Iwo Jima remained alive. More than 6,000 American marines had died and another 17,000 had been wounded in the taking of the island. This engagement was followed by another bloody campaign, from April through June, to take the island of Okinawa.

As US forces neared Japan's home islands, American planners contemplating the invasion of Japan suggested various estimates of casualties the United States might suffer, some as high as one million men. It seemed possible that war would continue to the spring of 1946. When the atomic bomb finally became available for use, there was a limited discussion of the possibility of a demonstration of its immense power before actually using it on a target, but a series of objections to this option was raised. The decision was made to use the bomb against Japan in the hope of forcing their surrender and ending the war as soon as possible.

Table 7.2 Deaths in the Europe/North African Theaters in World War II

Country	Military deaths	Civilian deaths	Total
Soviet Union	8,660,000	16,900,000	25,560,000
Poland	123,000	6,028,000	6,151,000
Germany	3,500,000	1,600,000	5,100,000
Yugoslavia	305,000	1,200,000	1,505,000
Romania	520,000	300,000	820,000
France	253,000	350,000	603,000
Czechoslovakia	246,000	294,000	540,000
Great Britain	397,000	93,000	490,000
Italy	347,000	93,000	440,000
Hungary	136,000	294,000	430,000
Greece	17,000	325,000	342,000
U.S.A.	309,000	9,000	318,000
The Netherlands	8,000	200,000	208,000
Belgium	9,000	76,000	85,000
Finland	80,000	3,000	83,000
Canada	34,000	—	34,000

The table is based on tables found online in Necrometrics 2013.

On August 6, 1945, the United States dropped an atomic bomb on the Japanese city of Hiroshima, killing 100,000–150,000 people. Three days later, it dropped a second atomic bomb on the city of Nagasaki, killing 60,000–80,000 people. Also that day, the Soviet Union entered the war in the Pacific. On the 14th, the emperor stated the war should end and recorded a radio message to the Japanese people. The following day, the message was broadcast, the first time most Japanese had heard the emperor speak (Table 7.2).

References

The Avalon Project: Documents in Law, History and Diplomacy. 2013. "Treaty of Nonaggression Between Germany and the Union of Soviet Socialist Republics." Accessed January 29, 2013. http://avalon.law.yale.edu/20th_century/nonagres.asp. The following document is the "Secret Additional

Protocol." The document before the "Treaty of Nonaggression…" is the "Memorandum of a Conversation Held on the Night of August 23rd to 24th, Between the Reich Foreign Minister, on the One Hand, and Herr Stalin and the Chairman of the Council of People's Commissars Molotov, on the Other Hand."

Davidowicz, Lucy B. 1975. *The War Against the Jews, 1933–1945*. New York: Holt, Rinehart and Winston.

Kennedy, David M. 1999. *Freedom from Fear: The American People in Depression and War, 1929–1945*. New York and Oxford: Oxford University Press.

Necrometrics. 2013. "National Death Tolls for the Second World War" Accessed April 23, 2013. http://www.necrometrics.com/ww2stats.htm

Roberts, Andrew. 2011. *The Storm of War: A New History of the Second World War*. New York: HarperCollins Publishers.

Weinberg, Gerhard L. 1994. *A World at Arms: A Global History of World War II*. New York and Cambridge: Cambridge University Press.

Wright, Gordon. 1968. *The Ordeal of Total War, 1939–1945*. New York: HarperCollins Publishers.

Further Reading

Bartov, Omer. 1986. *The Eastern Front, 1941–1945: German Troops and the Barbarization of Warfare*. New York: St. Martin's Press. Bartov's study is an important revisionist account of the war between Germany and the Soviet Union that provides evidence that the German army was complicit to a far greater degree in the Holocaust than had been thought previously.

Beevor, Anthony. 1998. *Stalingrad*. London: Viking Press. A comprehensive history of one of the turning points of World War II by a historian who has written widely on World War II in Europe.

Browning, Christopher. 1992. *Ordinary Men: Reserve Police Battalion 101 and the Final Solution in Poland*. New York: HarperCollins Publishers. A groundbreaking study of the Holocaust that has disturbing implications about human behavior.

Browning, Christopher. 2004. *The Origins of the Final Solution: The Evolution of Nazi Jewish Policy, September 1939–March 1942*. Lincoln. The University of Nebraska Press. The best study available of this crucial topic.

Dower, John W. 1987. *War without Mercy: Race and Power in the Pacific War*. New York: Pantheon Books. One of the most controversial and important books written about World War II in the past few decades, it asserts that both Americans and Japanese soldiers were deeply prejudiced toward one another.

Frank Anne Frank, and The Netherlands State Institute for War Documentation. 2003. *The Diary of Anne Frank: The Revised Critical Edition.* New York: Doubleday. A worldwide bestseller, it is undoubtedly the most famous book from World War II.

Fulbrook, Mary. 2012. *A Small Town Near Auschwitz: Ordinary Nazis and the Holocaust.* Oxford: Oxford University Press. How ordinary German civilian authorities who were neither perpetrators nor resisters dealt with the Holocaust.

Hastings, Max. 2011. *Inferno: The World at War, 1939–1945.* New York: Alfred A. Knopf. A recent, well-received book by the author of many books on World War II.

Jackson, Julian. 2001. *France: The Dark Years, 1940–1944.* New York: Oxford University Press. An exhaustive history of occupation, resistance, and liberation in France.

Kennedy, Paul. 2013. *Engineers of Victory: The Problem Solvers Who Turned the Tide in the Second World War.* New York: Random House. A careful discussion of the part played by scientists, business leaders, and others who provided essential but little-known contributions to the war effort.

Marrus, Michael. 1987. *The Holocaust in History.* Hanover: Brandeis University Press. A brief but very useful introduction to the topic.

Milward, Alan S. 1977. *War, Economy and Society, 1939–1945.* Berkeley: University of California Press. A scholarly study of the economic side of war.

Mulisch, Harry. 1985. *The Assault.* New York: Pantheon Books. A powerful novel about moral dilemmas in the Resistance in the Netherlands.

Paxton, Robert O. 2001. *Vichy France: Old Guard and New Order, 1940–1944.* New York: Columbia University Press. A careful examination of this controversial topic.

Rhodes, Richard. 1987. *The Making of the Atomic Bomb.* New York: Simon & Schuster. A lengthy but fascinating history of the Manhattan Project.

Spiegelman Art. 1986 and 1991. *Maus,* 2 Vol. New York: Pantheon. An emotionally gripping personal narrative of the Holocaust using the comic book form. It was awarded the Pulitzer Prize.

8

Cold War and Decolonization, 1945–1961

Chronology

1945	Formation of the United Nations
	Yalta Conference
	Potsdam Conference
1946	George F. Kennan's "Long Telegram"
1947	Truman Doctrine launches the era of containment in the Cold War
	Marshall Plan offers economic aid to Europe
	Communists forced out of coalition governments in France and Italy
	Formation of the Communist Information Bureau (Cominform)
1948	Communist coup in Czechoslovakia
	Berlin blockade and Berlin airlift (June 1948–May 1949)

Twentieth-Century Europe: A Brief History, 1900 to the Present, Third Edition.
Michael D. Richards and Paul R. Waibel.
© 2014 John Wiley & Sons, Inc. Published 2014 by John Wiley & Sons, Inc.

1949	Federal Republic of Germany (West Germany) founded
	German Democratic Republic (East Germany) founded
	North Atlantic Treaty Organization (NATO) created
	Soviet Union becomes an atomic power
	People's Republic of China (PRC) founded
1950	Korean War (1950–1953)
1953	Death of Stalin
	Uprising in Germany
1954	French defeat at Dien Bien Phu marks the end of the war in Indochina
	Vietnam divided into two states at Geneva Conference
1955	West Germany becomes a member of NATO
	Creation of the Warsaw Treaty Organization (WTO)
1956	Khrushchev's speech denouncing Stalin at the Twentieth Party Congress of the Communist Party of the Soviet Union
	Worker unrest in Poland
	Hungarian Revolution and Soviet intervention
	Suez Crisis
1957	Soviet Union opens a space race with the launching of *Sputnik*
1961	Construction of the Berlin Wall

ON MONDAY, JULY 16, 1945, there was a break in the conference at Potsdam and President Harry Truman (1884–1972) decided to take a look at Berlin. Sitting in the back seat of an open Lincoln with James Byrnes (1882–1972), his secretary of state, and Admiral

William Leahy (1875–1959), President Truman was driven past miles of burned-out buildings and rubble. The motorcade went down one of Berlin's best-known streets, Unter den Linden, now stripped of its famous Linden trees, past the Reich Chancellery, the Brandenburg Gate, and the Reichstag. That night, he wrote in his diary (as quoted in McCullough 1992):

> I thought of Carthage, Baalbek, Jerusalem, Rome, Atlantis, Peking . . . [of] Scipio, Rameses II . . . Sherman, Jenghiz Khan. . . . I hope for some sort of peace—but I fear that machines are ahead of morals by some centuries and when morals catch up there'll be no reason for any of it. (p. 415)

Churchill also toured Berlin that afternoon. Stalin, who had arrived on his armored train only that day, did not. Of course, neither he nor Churchill really needed to see the ruins of Berlin in order to know the destructiveness of World War II. They had only to look at the great cities of their own countries.

More than 40 million people were killed in the European part of the war. Civilian deaths were nearly three times the number of military deaths. Millions survived with disabilities of one kind or another. Millions more fled before advancing armies or were forced to migrate after the war. The largest group of the latter were Germans forced to move west from what had been East Prussia.

Material losses were enormous. The estimate, in 1945 dollars, was between $2 and $3 trillion. This included damage to farmland, destruction of cattle and other livestock, and the devastation of villages, towns, cities, bridges, railroads, and highways. Not only Germany but every country that had been involved in the war faced the need to rebuild its economy and to repair the social fabric. Some countries suffered more than others, of course. Denmark was, comparatively speaking, unmarked by the war. The Netherlands, by way of contrast, endured many hardships, particularly in the "Hunger Winter" of 1944–1945. The Soviet Union, victorious and powerful, had nevertheless incurred enormous losses. And, of course, it seemed Germany could not possibly recover.

There was much pessimism; some believed Europe had been hopelessly weakened.

This assessment gained force not only from the emergence of two enormously powerful countries on either flank of Europe, the United States, and the Soviet Union but also from the grave weakening of the colonial empires. In different manners, in some cases quickly and in others slowly and painfully, the empires collapsed and disappeared (see the discussion of this process later in this chapter).

Finally, the spiritual cost of war and its aftermath was enormous. Europe had fallen back into a barbarism during World War II that contradicted the previous decades of progress or perhaps simply effaced them. The magnitude of the cruelty largely defied understanding. The "Final Solution" naturally was the premier example of barbarism in the war, but other events, such as the firebombing of cities such as Hamburg and Dresden in Germany and Tokyo in Japan, also were seen as barbarous acts, even if not on the same scale and done with the stated intention of ending the war as soon as possible. Additionally, the use of atomic weapons in the case of Hiroshima and Nagasaki was seen by some as beyond cruel and unnecessary, even if others claimed it had been done in the interest of forcing Japan to surrender as quickly as possible. All the claims of cultural or moral superiority Europeans had ever made now seemed hollowed out by the events of the war. A spiritual malaise accompanied military impotence and economic devastation.

Additionally, as Keith Lowe (2012) notes:

> . . .the war did not simply stop with Hitler's defeat. A conflict on the scale of the Second World War with all the smaller civil disputes that it encompassed, took months, if not years, to come to a halt and the end came at different times in different parts of Europe. (p. xiv)

In Poland, for example, Polish Communists with the aid of the Soviet Army hunted down members of the Polish Home Army, the major Polish resistance force in the war. In Greece, a savage civil war broke out. Everywhere, collaborators were punished. In Poland and Czechoslovakia in particular, ethnic Germans were forced to leave. Ukrainians expelled Poles from the newly acquired territory. Poles returned the favor for those Ukrainians who found themselves still in Poland even after the border had moved west. In a terrible irony, in Eastern Europe, many of the old concentration camps filled up again with political prisoners. And superimposing itself on the anarchy and chaos was the beginnings of a decades-long struggle between the two "superpowers" the war had produced: the Soviet Union with its massive army and devastated economy and the United States with its unique atomic arsenal and hugely productive economy. The contest that developed between these two giants in the wake of the war would reshape Europe and the rest of the world in fundamental ways.

Origins of the Cold War

Some observers take the long view and see the Cold War as first appearing with the Allied intervention in the civil war after the Russian Revolution. Others prefer to begin with the issue of the second front and other controversial matters in World War II. In both cases, the Soviet Union and the West had reasons for suspicion and distrust of each other. Still, at the end of the war in Europe, both sides seemed to want to believe the wartime alliance could be continued in some fashion.

When the Allied leaders met between July 16 and August 2, 1945, at Potsdam, a suburb of Berlin, the intention was to continue the alliance. The end of the war in the Pacific was now in sight, but estimates of when this would actually happen ranged between several weeks and several months. The leaders of the Allies had changed. Stalin continued to speak for the Soviet Union, but Roosevelt died on April 12, 1945, shortly after returning from the Yalta Conference in February. In his place was Harry Truman, inexperienced but determined. Both Winston Churchill from the Conservatives and Clement Atlee (1883–1967) from the Labour Party came to Potsdam to represent Britain. The parliamentary elections, the results of which were only announced on July 26, brought a stunning defeat to Churchill and Atlee took over for Britain.

By midsummer of 1945, serious differences of opinion had already begun to surface with regard to postwar Europe. The most important disagreement concerned the composition of the Polish government and the question of the administration of occupied Germany. What ensued stemmed largely from a series of misunderstandings. The Soviet Union saw no reason to tolerate a Polish government unreceptive to its ideas about the reordering of Eastern Europe. Therefore, the Soviet Union contended that if it were to install in Poland a government it sponsored, and largely excluded one backed by Britain, this would be the same thing the Soviet Union believed the United States was doing in Italy and Britain was doing in Greece. In occupied Germany, now divided into a Soviet, an American, a British, and a French zone, the Soviet Union had begun a policy of wholesale confiscation of materiel and facilities in its zone and also in the other three zones. The United States feared this would lead to the economic collapse of Germany and require greatly expanded American aid. The American government could see no point in American taxpayers subsidizing German reparations to the Soviet Union.

Truman took a more aggressive stance at Potsdam than Roosevelt had in earlier meetings. Roosevelt had sometimes been as suspicious of British imperialism as of Russian communism. Truman mainly distrusted the Russians. Some scholars hold out the possibility that Truman wanted to use the American monopoly of atomic weapons to force the Russians to make concessions, but there is no hard evidence in support of this view. Truman did practice a blunt, no-nonsense kind of diplomacy, and he may have hoped the announcement of the new and devastatingly powerful "A-bomb" would give him some leverage with Stalin. Atomic blackmail would not have worked in any case. Stalin already knew a good deal about the American efforts to build the bomb through reports on the Manhattan Project sent to the Soviet Union by spies. He wanted the Soviet Union to have similar weapons and had already ordered Lavrenty Beria (1899–1953), Stalin's chief of the secret police, to set up a crash program to build an atomic bomb. He also believed the United States was unlikely to use atomic weapons in most circumstances.

Potsdam, together with Yalta, had created a volatile situation but not one fated to lead to confrontation. After all, the details of treaties with Germany and its allies were yet to be worked out. Whatever problems might appear could be resolved in the various forums now available. The main forum for discussion was the newly created United Nations, in particular, the Security Council, on which both the Soviet Union and the United States had permanent seats. The UN was never the kind of obsession for Roosevelt that the League of Nations had been for Wilson, but it was important to him. And he was not alone in placing great hopes in it. In addition, there were meetings of the foreign ministers of the Allies and, on a more local level, meetings of the Allied Control Council in occupied Germany.

There was no Cold War yet in 1946. Churchill, however, gave a speech at little Westminster College in Fulton, Missouri, President Truman's home state, on March 5, 1946, "The Sinews of Peace." In it, he famously stated, "From Stettin in the Baltic to Trieste in the Adriatic, an iron curtain has descended across the Continent" (as quoted in the online Britannia Historical Documents 2013). Developments were taking shape that would rapidly move Europe toward the grimness of the Cold War.

The two main problem areas, occupied Germany and the new Poland, had become even more intractable. In occupied Germany, there were already signs that a common occupation policy was not going to be established. In 1946, the United States and Britain no longer allowed the Soviet Union to take reparations from their zones. In September of 1946, Secretary of State James Byrnes called for a revival of the German economy in a speech that signaled a decisive shift in American policy vis-à-vis Germany. Soon after that, on January 1, 1947, the British and American zones fused into a single economic and administrative unit, "Bizonia." In Poland, the Soviet Army had in 1945 installed the "Lublin Poles" (Polish communists sponsored by the Soviet Union) in power. A few "London Poles" (Poles who had worked with the United States and Britain during the war) had been added later to form a coalition government. In 1946, Polish communists worked diligently to break apart the Peasant Party, potentially the most powerful political party in Poland, and gain control of another popular political force, the Polish Socialist Workers Party. The elections scheduled for January 1947 did not look promising for the democratic forces.

Elsewhere, American diplomatic pressure led the Soviet Union to withdraw troops from the northern part of Iran by early May of 1946, but Soviet pressure on Turkey continued. The Soviet Union did not try to influence the civil war in Greece between Greek communists and Greek monarchists, but, even so, by the end of 1946, the British were experiencing difficulties sustaining the monarchists. In all parts of Western Europe, there was no sign of economic recovery taking place soon. The communist parties in France and Italy took part in the coalition governments in those two countries, but they seemed likely to be the main beneficiaries if the economies could not be restarted. In February 1946, George F. Kennan (1904–2005), an American diplomat stationed in the Soviet Union, sent an 8,000-word telegram, the "Long Telegram," detailing his sense of how Russians viewed their history and the present moment. Kennan believed Russia's historic sense of insecurity, exacerbated by communism's idea of the inevitability of war with capitalism, led Stalin always to seek to improve the country's situation. The Soviet Union, however, did respect strength. A firm response would force Stalin and the Soviet Union to back down (The National Security Archive 2013). From this essay came the idea of "containment" (of communism), of meeting every Soviet move with a countermove and, later, of anticipating possible Soviet moves in order to preempt them.

Crisis Years, 1947–1948

In 1947, the Cold War began to take shape. The immediate origins lay in the situations in Turkey and in Greece. Turkey had been under considerable pressure from the Soviet Union to allow a Soviet military presence near the straits between the Black Sea and the Mediterranean. Greece was still involved in a civil war between Greek communists and Greek monarchists. Early in 1947, Britain informed the United States it could no longer afford to supply aid to the two countries.

The United States now faced the task of maintaining Anglo-American interests in the eastern Mediterranean. Truman, however, in his remarks to a joint session of Congress in March 1947, asked for an open-ended commitment by the United States to help any government threatened by invasion from without or subversion from within. This became known as the Truman Doctrine, and although the Soviet Union was not specifically mentioned in his address, his sentiments were widely regarded as an expression of hostility to Russia and to communism more generally. In effect, the address became the opening salvo of the Cold War (Harry S. Truman Library & Museum 2013).

In the months after Truman's speech, Secretary of State George C. Marshall (1880–1959) and others in the State Department concerned themselves with the economic and social problems of Europe. George Kennan, by then the head of the new Policy Planning Staff at the State Department, quickly put together a report on the European situation recommending American aid. It would, he thought, be up to the Europeans to draw up the plans. Aid should be offered to all of Europe. Any decision leading to a division of Europe should stem from the Russian response to the American offer rather than the offer itself. In large part, the aid would be directed at German economic recovery, which Kennan saw as "a vital component of the recovery of Europe as a whole."

Although Marshall had planned to attend the Harvard commencement ceremonies in the spring of 1947, where he was to be awarded an honorary degree, and had been invited to give a speech, it was virtually at the last minute that he decided to use the occasion to launch what became known as the Marshall Plan. In his talk, Marshall indicated he was advocating economic measures to meet economic and social problems. (George Marshall's speech can be found on the internet in the *Internet Modern History Source Book*.)

> Our policy is directed not against any country or doctrine but against hunger, poverty, desperation and chaos. . . . Any government that is willing to assist in the task of recovery will find full cooperation, I am sure, on the part of the United States Government. Any government which maneuvers to block the recovery of other countries cannot expect help from us.

Later seen as the economic counterpart to the Truman Doctrine, the Marshall Plan (or the European Recovery Program as it was formally known) was viewed by Marshall as a means of speeding European economic recovery. He saw, of course, the political implications of social and economic stability in Europe. He was also aware of the importance to American business of an economically viable Europe.

On December 10, 1953, George C. Marshall, Chief of Staff of the United States Army during World War II and Secretary of State from 1947 to 1949, was awarded the Nobel Peace Prize for his work with the Marshall Plan, the massive postwar program of American aid that helped rebuild Western Europe after the war. To the left is Carl Joachim Hambro, President of the Norwegian Storting. AP/Press Association Images

Although the Marshall Plan was not an American maneuver in the rapidly emerging Cold War, the Soviet Union saw it that way. It walked out of the conference the British and French had called to discuss the initiative and pressured the Poles and Czechs to drop their interest in the plan as well. Stalin saw the plan simply as a means whereby the United States could gain control of the European economies. In particular, he had no intention of revealing the extent to which the war had damaged the Soviet economy.

By the end of 1947, many of the major elements of the Cold War had fallen into place. In May, the communist parties in France and Italy had been forced out of the coalition governments. In September, the Cominform (Communist Information Bureau), the successor to the Comintern, was established with headquarters in Belgrade, Yugoslavia. This was seen in the West as evidence of the existence of a monolithic communist movement, controlled by Moscow and dedicated to the subversion of democratic governments everywhere. Actually, the main task of the Cominform was to tighten Soviet control over Eastern Europe and in particular to try to gain a greater measure of control over communist Yugoslavia.

The Two Germanies

During all this time, the Allied Powers found themselves growing farther apart in their ideas about the administration of occupied Germany. The status of Germany was the most important issue in relations between the Soviet Union and the other Allied Powers. The Soviet Union wanted to make sure Germany could not threaten it again in the twentieth century. The United States was more concerned about feeding Germany and the connection between its economic recovery and the recovery of the rest of Europe. Neither side seemed to understand very fully the position of the other side. Each side had apparently learned different lessons from the peacemaking process after World War I.

As mentioned, the Soviet Union set out first to strip its zone of Germany of raw materials and factories. It also exercised its rights to take reparations in kind from the other zones. This was in line both with its concerns about security issues and its concerns about its own economic recovery. Initially, the French also followed a policy of extracting reparations from their zone. They began to see, however, as the British and Americans already had, that it was not to their advantage to destroy the German economy if this meant later they would have to send food, goods, and money back into Germany to prevent social unrest and instability.

In the American and the British zones, an effort was made to carry out a program of de-Nazification, demilitarization, and democratization, but the programs were only partially successful. In particular, the process of de-Nazification moved slowly and was not especially effective. Many high-ranking Nazis escaped trial because the often cumbersome process attempted to comb through the entire population. Other Nazis managed to escape trial because they were regarded as useful by the United States either for scientific projects or for espionage. The Americans and the British also made efforts to find Germans who had administrative experience but had not been tainted by association with the Nazis for positions of leadership. One such a person was Konrad Adenauer (1876–1967), former lord mayor of Cologne, then already 77 years old.

Russian practices differed considerably. In 1946, the Soviet Union virtually eliminated political parties in its zone and put intense pressure on the old Social Democratic Party (SPD) to unite with the Communists (KPD) to become the Socialist Unity Party (*Sozialistische Einheitspartei Deutschlands* or SED). The Soviets also carried out an extensive program of land reform and nationalization of industry. This was based in part on the idea that destruction of capitalism would eliminate the basis for fascism since fascism was a product of "monopoly capitalism."

Two distinct zones were being created. One was composed of the American and British zones, which formally merged economies in January 1947, and, as mentioned, became known as "Bizonia." (The French did not, at first, accept the invitation to join.) The other was the Soviet zone. When, in 1948, the three Western powers announced the introduction of currency reforms, a necessary prelude to economic recovery and the functioning of the zones as an economic unit, the Soviet Union closed down rail, road, and water traffic between Berlin and the west. The Berlin blockade, which lasted from June 23, 1948, to May 12, 1949, and the Berlin airlift countering it were the most visible signs of increasing Cold War tension.

On June 26, the United States and Britain responded to the Soviet blockade by starting an airlift to supply the city. A proposed plan to break the blockade by sending an armored column down the autobahn to Berlin was ruled out as too confrontational. Although Soviet pilots sometimes harassed incoming transport planes, the

Soviet Union did not attempt to counter the airlift by shooting down the supply-laden Allied aircraft.

After the airlift was reorganized by General William H. Tunner (1906–1983), it was successful in supplying the more than two million residents of the allied sectors of Berlin for the 11 months during which the Soviet blockade remained in effect. Even after the Soviets ended the blockade, the airlift continued until September 30, 1949. The airlift supplied Berlin with 2,323,738 tons of food, fuel, and other supplies. The successful response to the Soviet challenge contributed greatly to the growth of West European support for American efforts in the Cold War duel with the Soviet Union.

In 1949, the division between western Germany, which became known as the Federal Republic of Germany (FRG or West Germany), and eastern Germany, the German Democratic Republic (GDR or East Germany), was officially set. West Germany quickly began to move from the status of former enemy to that of potential ally of the Western powers. A divided Germany had not been the intention of any of the Allied Powers at the end of World War II, but in the new context of the Cold War, it suited each of them well enough and in time came to be seen as the normal state of affairs.

The Cold War Launched

The postwar world in 1949 presented a new, ominous look. In addition to the quarrel over the status of Germany and its division into two separate states, there was the phenomenon of tightening Soviet control in Eastern Europe. This was symbolized most vividly by the Czech coup in February 1948. In the process of replacing a democratic coalition government with a communist one, Jan Masaryk (1886–1948), Czech foreign minister and son of the founder of the Republic, died in a mysterious fall from his office window. Czechoslovakia, when Eduard Beneš (1884–1948) had been president and Masaryk foreign minister, seemed the exception to the rule in Soviet-controlled Eastern Europe, a sign of hope that a democratic, freely elected government might be allowed to exist within a sphere of influence dominated by the Soviet Union.

West Europeans and Americans, faced with the events of 1947 and 1948, responded by forming the North Atlantic Treaty Organization (NATO) in 1949. NATO grew out of an earlier pact, the Brussels Treaty (1948), signed by Britain, France, Belgium, Luxembourg, and the Netherlands. In effect, these West European countries invited the United States to participate in an alliance that it would naturally dominate. Europeans agreed to, actually encouraged, the formation of an informal American empire in the interests of collective security. By way of contrast, the Soviet Union imposed its empire on Eastern Europe in the interests of the national security of the Soviet Union.

Three developments in Asia also contributed to the shaping of the emerging Cold War world. These were the American occupation of Japan, the victory of the Chinese Communists over the Chinese Nationalists in 1949, and, finally, the Korean War.

Rioters in East Berlin throw stones at Red Army tanks in June 1953 to protest the increase in work norms set by the government of the German Democratic Republic. Cracks appeared every decade after the formation of the Soviet bloc, but the Soviet Union held its empire together until 1989. DPA DEUTSCHE PRESS-AGENTUR/DPA/Press Association Images

The United States exercised complete control over the occupation of Japan. General Douglas MacArthur (1880–1964), commander of the occupation administration, used his authority to reshape Japanese political life, firmly reestablishing a tradition of parliamentary democracy while allowing Emperor Hirohito (1901–1989) to remain as a national symbol. MacArthur had less impact on the contours of economic and social affairs, although he did much to improve the status and rights of women. The Japanese themselves decisively rejected militarism. Although they placed themselves under the American security umbrella and became an important economic component of the Cold War, they did not join, as did West Germany, an Asian equivalent of NATO.

The victory of the Chinese Communist Party under Mao Zedong (1893–1976) shaped the Cold War in two important ways. The People's Republic of China was an enormous addition to what American and other observers now regarded as a monolithic world communist movement. In reality, Chinese national interests often clashed with Russian national interests. This would not surprise anyone familiar with the long history of contacts between the empires dating back to the seventeenth century, but this perspective seemed to have disappeared in the face of concerns about the newly expanded communist movement. In addition, Mao's ideas and the revolutionary romanticism associated with his past accomplishments heightened a fear that every national liberation movement would end up as a victory of the supposedly monolithic world communist movement.

Of the three developments, the Korean War (1950–1953) had the greatest impact on the development of the Cold War. At the end of World War II, the Soviet Union occupied the northern half of the Korean peninsula and the United States the southern half. In the next few years, each power created a Korean administration that conformed more or less to the occupying power's political system. In North Korea, Kim Il Sung (1912–1994), a Korean communist and nationalist, believed his country could easily reunite the peninsula. Additionally, he thought an invasion of the south would lead to a popular uprising. Finally, the Americans seemingly had written Korea off as an area of strategic interest. In any case, they would not have time to intervene. This was the scenario Kim Il Sung presented to Stalin. Although Stalin was generally quite cautious about support for ventures of this sort, he appeared to believe the plan involved little risk. Kim Il Sung then persuaded Mao to lend support as well.

The invasion was initially successful, pushing the South Korean army down the peninsula. The United States intervened at the head of an international force under United Nations' sponsorship. This was possible because the Soviet Union had temporarily boycotted meetings of the UN Security Council. Had the Soviet delegate been present when the matter came up, he would undoubtedly have vetoed intervention.

Initially, the intervention did not go well, but by August, UN forces outnumbered the North Korean forces. General MacArthur pushed for an amphibious landing at the port of Inchon near Seoul and far to the north of the UN perimeter around the southern port of Pusan. This was a daring but also risky plan. Despite the risks, the landing on September 15 worked as MacArthur had hoped and the UN forces surprised the North Korean forces, retaking Seoul and trapping nearly half the North Korean army. From there, the UN forces drove the North Korean army out of South Korea and all the way up to the Yalu River, the boundary between North Korea and the People's Republic of China. At this point, an alarmed China did more than lend lip service to its support of the North Koreans and counterattacked, forcing the American troops into a disastrous retreat. After this, the war settled eventually into a costly stalemate, the front lines of which lay near the middle of the peninsula, more or less on the old borders between the two Koreas, North and South.

Early in 1950, the US National Security Council, an agency created in 1947 to help manage America's response to the Cold War, issued a report entitled "NSC 68: United States Objectives and Programs for National Security." This position paper recommended that the United States oppose the Soviet Union in virtually any situation that might work to the benefit of the latter.

According to "NSC 68," the Soviet Union was "animated by a new fanatical faith . . . and seeks to impose its absolute authority over the rest of the world" ("NSC 68" can be found in the online Federation of American Scientists 2013). The document further recommended greatly increased military spending and foreign-aid programs. President Truman initially did not act on the document when he received it in early April. Instead, he requested an economic analysis of the proposal. If the Korean War had not begun shortly after the report was presented, it is possible that no action would have been taken.

Aid to the French in Indochina (see the discussion below) and intervention in the Korean War contributed greatly to the militarization of American foreign policy. In addition, over the next several years, American leaders thought not simply of containment, but increasingly of "rollback," a policy that would lead, they hoped, to a weaker Soviet Union and to the liberation of some of the areas now under its control.

The Soviet Union, meanwhile, saw itself as weak and vulnerable. In the late 1940s, it was desperate to gain security. At the same time, domestic politics played a great role in the conduct of foreign policy. Two developments were crucially important. First, Stalin's health was failing. World War II had been extremely stressful. In the postwar years before his death in 1953, Stalin probably suffered from arteriosclerosis, hardening of his arteries, which reduced the flow of blood to his brain and might account for lapses of judgment, such as in the Korean War; memory loss; and the need for extended vacations. The second factor was the vicious infighting among Stalin's top lieutenants; he manipulated and controlled these men to some extent, but could not completely dominate them.

Initially, Stalin turned on Vyacheslav Molotov (1890–1986), long one of Stalin's most trusted lieutenants, because he had been too soft in his dealings with the allies in postwar Europe. He also took away control of the secret police from Beria, who, as a fellow Georgian, had been extraordinarily powerful, and assigned him the risky task of developing a Soviet atomic capacity as rapidly as possible. Stalin demoted Beria's ally, Georgy Malenkov (1902–1988), a secretary of the Central Committee and an expert on missiles, leaving as the temporary winner Andrei Zhdanov (1896–1948), "the Pianist" as he was called by Stalin's inner circle. Zhdanov, whose power base was in Leningrad, was placed in charge of cultural matters after the war. He launched what became known as the *Zhdanovshchina*, which set forth the idea of two hostile camps, and also called for a thorough Russification of the Soviet Union.

Zhdanov, in even worse health than Stalin, died August 31, 1948. Beria and Malenkov used this opening to attack Zhdanov's associates and again rise to power. Nikita Khrushchev, who was head of Ukraine after the war, and Nikolai Bulganin (1895–1975), minister for the armed forces, were two additional survivors and rounded out the inner circle. Stalin, however, who did not trust Beria, moved toward what might have been a new version of the Great Terror with the addition of virulent anti-Semitism in the so-called Doctors' Plot. Only the death of Stalin, March 5, 1953, made it possible to avoid a return of terror on a large scale.

Among all the maneuvers of Stalin and his inner circle, the Soviet Union responded to the many foreign policy challenges. Although it apparently did not believe the United States would again act on its monopoly of atomic weapons, the Soviet Union spared no effort to create its own nuclear weapons. Its viselike grip on Eastern Europe was another effort to enhance security. Most important of all, its policies toward the two states of East Germany and West Germany betrayed an obsessive, almost irrational, fear of German potential. At the same time, the Soviet Union viewed the United States as an immensely wealthy, powerful, and also hypocritical nation, one that denied the Soviet Union those very items essential to its security while reserving for itself the right to act as it saw fit. Paradoxically, the Soviet Union also feared revolution. Although it gave lip service to national liberation movements in other nations, it offered little real help, and in the case of the Chinese Communists probably hindered their efforts to come to power. In the last years of Stalin's life, the Soviet Union sponsored purges in Eastern Europe designed to place communists loyal to Moscow solidly in power. It also attempted to destroy the power of Marshal Tito and other

Yugoslavian communists who were attempting to follow a national (read independent) line of development.

Dismantling the Colonial Empires

The postwar dismantling of the colonial empires took place in two large waves. Most of Asia gained independence in the initial wave of national liberation movements in the first several years after the war. Nationalist movements, some heavily influenced or even dominated by communists, had existed throughout the colonial world before World War II. In some cases, and here India is the best example, these movements had made considerable progress toward the achievement of self-government if not independence. In most areas, however, the effects of the war had created the conditions that made the taking back of power by nationalist movements a distinct possibility.

In those areas where the Japanese had smashed colonial regimes in the process of takeover, a power vacuum existed into which nationalists might move at the end of the war. One such place was the Dutch East Indies, where Indonesian nationalists under Ahmed Sukarno (1901–1970) declared independence in 1945. Although the Dutch returned after the war and attempted to regain control of the islands by use of armed force, they lacked the resources necessary for that task. The United States was not only unsympathetic to the Dutch cause but actually put them under considerable pressure to grant the Indonesians independence. In 1949, the Dutch recognized the independence of Indonesia. Of the Dutch empire, originally one of the great empires of the world, there now remained only a few fragments. The Dutch had regarded the empire as a very important factor in the economy. They were surprised that its loss had little effect on their ability to recover prewar economic levels and then to surpass them.

The Vietnamese, like the Indonesians, took advantage of the destruction of the colonial government during the war. They did not, however, as the Indonesian nationalists did, work with the Japanese during the war. In August of 1945, they declared their independence in words taken from the American Declaration of Independence. Ho Chi Minh (1890–1969), affiliated between the wars with the Comintern, had created the Viet Minh, a broadly based nationalist movement heavily influenced by Vietnamese communists. He and the Viet Minh took control of the northern part of the peninsula after the Japanese surrender. The British prevented the Viet Minh from establishing control in the southern part of the peninsula. Instead, they worked with the French to restore the colonial regime. An uneasy truce existed between the north and the south, but it broke down finally in December 1946 after a French attack. Over the next several years, the Viet Minh defeated French efforts to reestablish control over all of Indochina. At first, they used guerrilla tactics similar to those employed by Mao Zedong in China. Later, they moved to conventional warfare. The French by the early 1950s counted on large-scale American aid. The United States, still smarting from the victory of the Chinese Communists in 1949, was eager to assist the French in their struggle in Vietnam, in sharp contrast to policies followed earlier in connection with Dutch efforts to regain control of Indonesia. The United States did, however, draw the line at sending American troops to help. When the French attempted to defeat the Viet Minh decisively at the Battle of Dien Bien Phu in 1954 and instead were shocked to suffer a major defeat, the Americans debated various possibilities, including the use of atomic weapons, but, ultimately, refused to intervene directly in the conflict. At the Geneva Conference in 1954, the Russians and the Chinese pressed the Viet Minh to accept a division of Vietnam at the seventeenth parallel. The northern part of the peninsula would remain under the control of the Viet Minh, and the southern part under a noncommunist Vietnamese government. Elections were to be held by 1956 to determine the government under which Vietnamese people wished to unite. However, unification came only in 1975, when North Vietnam finally conquered South Vietnam. The Vietnamese Communists spent much of the two decades after the Geneva Conference struggling against the military forces of the United States, which had been increasingly drawn into attempts to support South Vietnam (see the discussion of American policy in Vietnam in Chapter 9).

Ho Chi Minh speaking to an audience in Paris following the breakdown of negotiations in 1946. Seated behind him is Admiral Thierry d'Argenlieu, the French governor of Vietnam. Later in 1946, the French attacked Ho's forces and began an eight-year war that ended in the defeat of the French in 1954. AP/Press Association Images

Other attempts at national liberation were less successful. The British were able to withstand a challenge in Malaya primarily by Chinese inhabitants influenced by communism. Malaya, which became independent in 1957, merged with other nations in 1963 to form Malaysia. Singapore, inhabited mostly by Chinese, became an independent city-state in 1965. The United States granted the Philippines full independence in 1946. The Philippines under the charismatic leadership of Ramon Magsaysay (1907–1957) instituted land reforms and successfully ended a guerrilla insurrection by 1951.

India was the major exception to the pattern of national liberation movements and the most important of all the Asian nations gaining independence in the first wave of decolonization. The British had

Europe During the Cold War

reluctantly agreed to Indian independence after the war. The major problem concerned whether a separate state should be established for the Muslim population of India. Despite the efforts of Mohandas Gandhi (1869–1948) to keep India intact, the British carved Pakistan out of India and granted the two nations independence in 1947. Gandhi had been the inspirational leader of the Indian National Congress in the 1920s and 1930s and was the chief exemplar of a nonviolent approach to political and social change in the twentieth century. Although he was assassinated shortly after India became independent, he had a powerful influence on politics in the remainder of the century, not the least on Martin Luther King Jr. and other leaders of the American Civil Rights Movement.

The British rather abruptly brought the two states into existence with the passage by the British Parliament of the Indian Independence Bill in July 1947. Although India (predominantly Hindu) and Pakistan (predominantly Muslim) had not had to fight for their independence, many thousands of civilians were killed in the aftermath of the partition, as Muslims fled from newly Hindu-controlled areas and Hindus fled from the newly Muslim-controlled territory. Not long after India and Pakistan gained independence, Ceylon (now Sri Lanka) and Burma (now Myanmar) gained independence as well.

In North Africa and the Middle East, where most of the population was Muslim, two crucial situations took shape in the late 1940s and early 1950s. First, in the British mandate of Palestine, Jewish settlers successfully established Israel as a Jewish state. Palestine had been partitioned in 1947 by the United Nations into a Jewish state and a Palestinian state. When the British left the area, neighboring Arab states attempted to destroy Israel in the Arab–Israeli War of 1948–1949. Israel not only defeated the Arab coalition but enlarged its own territory. Arab defeat led to military revolts in Egypt, Syria, and Jordan and to war and waves of terrorism over the next several decades. British and French influence in the area disappeared; an ill-fated effort to regain influence in the joint attack with Israel on the Suez Canal in 1956 misfired (see the discussion of this event in Chapter 9).

The United States became a major factor in the politics of the area over the next half century with mixed results. On the one hand, it was a major supporter of Israel. On the other, the United States worked with most of the other states in the Middle East, making Iran in particular into a major power in the area by the 1970s. The Soviet Union attempted to play a role in Middle Eastern affairs, but generally without success except in the area of terrorism (see Chapter 10 for comments on terrorism). Israel, heavily influenced by the influx of European Jews and the historical legacy of the Holocaust, became the strongest and most successful state in the area, in no small part because of US foreign and military aid.

In North Africa, the French faced a major challenge in Algeria when the National Liberation Front (FLN) began a revolution in 1954. Although the French had considerable success militarily against the FLN, they steadily lost ground in the court of world opinion. The revolution grew increasingly brutal in the methods used by the two sides. For the French, it was particularly troubling since they could not help but note they were using many of the same methods the Gestapo had used in World War II against the French Resistance. Both Tunisia and Morocco gained independence in 1956, but a similar move for Algeria was out of the question, first of all because the one million Europeans, or colons, living in Algeria controlled its economy and government and considered it a part of France. For the French army, holding on to Algeria had become a question of honor, of redeeming itself after humiliating defeats in 1940 by the Germans and in 1954 by the Vietnamese. It was only after the coup in Algiers, the capital of Algeria, and a close brush with civil war, which brought Charles de Gaulle to power in 1958, that a way was found to extricate France from Algeria in 1962 (see Chapter 9 for discussion of de Gaulle's efforts to resolve the Algerian crisis).

By the mid-1950s, in what might be seen as the second wave of independence movements, the British and the French both began moving to grant their African colonies independence. In 1960, the French granted full independence to their African colonies, which had earlier been given autonomy within the French community of nations. The French dream of assimilation, of transforming the inhabitants of colonial areas into people whose culture and heritage were French, had not prepared the former colonies well for independence. Only a tiny elite had been able to follow the path opened up by French education. Most of the population of the new nations was simply unprepared for life in the modern world.

The British did somewhat better in terms of training a large group of Africans to take over the task of governing themselves. Several areas of the former colonies, however, contained large numbers of white settlers. In those places, there was resistance to independence and considerable violence. In Kenya, the Mau

Mau movement (1952–1956) struggled for independence. Most of its terrorist tactics were directed against Africans reluctant to support independence against the British, but white settlers were also killed.

Rhodesia, controlled by white settlers, declared its independence in 1965, but after more than a decade of struggle, Rhodesia became Zimbabwe in 1980 and power was handed over to the black majority. The Union of South Africa left the Commonwealth in 1961 and became the Republic of South Africa, a state characterized by an elaborate system of *apartheid* or state-mandated segregation. Only after adopting a new constitution in 1993 and holding free elections in 1994 did South Africa leave behind the destructive system—in which the white majority lived vastly better than the black majority it controlled—that had shaped its society and economy for most of the twentieth century.

The Belgians, who had not done much better in managing the Congo after taking it away from the Belgian king in 1908, badly mismanaged the granting of independence. In 1960, with very little advance preparation, the Belgians simply withdrew from the Congo and granted it independence. This led to a five-year period of civil war in which the United States, the Soviet Union, and the People's Republic of China intervened at one time or another. Between 1971 and 1997, the nation was known as Zaire and ruled by Mobutu Sese Seko's (1930–1997) brutally corrupt and inept regime.

By the mid-1960s, the second wave of independence movements had ended. Only a few white settler regimes and the Portuguese colonies remained in Africa. Elsewhere, a handful of colonies in the Western Hemisphere and in the Pacific still existed. To all intents and purposes, imperialism in the sense of colonial empires had disappeared from the face of the earth.

Many of the newly independent nations retained ties to their former colonial powers. They did not always, however, follow the political traditions of the ex-colonial powers. The United States, especially, and also the Soviet Union maneuvered for influence in the new nations but with only limited success. A major movement of the 1950s and 1960s was nonalignment, an effort by new nations to avoid a unilateral commitment to either major superpower.

Many Europeans had spent most or all of their lives in the colonies and after independence found it difficult to return to their home country. They felt considerable bitterness in many cases. Probably, the Dutch did the best job of making room for people returning from the old empire. The French, particularly in the difficult case of the colons from Algeria, did the worst job. The British fell somewhere in the middle. Europeans as a whole, however, once they had recovered from the trauma of decolonization, found the loss of colonies offset by the freedom from responsibilities the colonies had brought with them. In many cases, they discovered new possibilities. Some countries, the Netherlands may be the best such example, built up a far more prosperous and stable economy than they had ever achieved with colonies.

The emergence of dozens of new nations in the 1950s and 1960s began to change the nature of international relations. Now, European nations, like all other industrialized and modern states, had to contend with the claims of the so-called Third World. Political independence was only the first step. The next was to provide, in the form of foreign aid, a fair share of the wealth Europeans had gained over the many years from the operations of the modern world economy. Europeans wrestled with this issue and by and large did far better by the emerging nations than either the United States or the Soviet Union.

References

Britannia Historical Documents. 2013. "The Sinews of Peace." Accessed January 28, 2013. http://www.britannia.com/history/docs/sinews1.html.

Federation of American Scientists. "NSC 68: United States Objectives and Programs for National Security (April 14, 1950)." Accessed January 29, 2013. http://www.fas.org/irp/offdocs/nsc-hst/nsc-68.htm.

Harry S. Truman Library & Museum 2013. "Address of the President to Congress, Recommending Assistance to Greece and Turkey, March 12, 1947." Accessed January 28, 2013. http://www.trumanlibrary.org/whistlestop/study_collections/doctrine/large/index.php.

Internet Modern History Source Book. 2013. "Marshall Plan Speech." Accessed January 28, 2013. www.fordham.edu/Halsall/mod/1947marshallplan1.asp.

Lowe, Keith. 2012. *Savage Continent: Europe in the Aftermath of World War II.* New York: St. Martin's Press.

McCullough, David. 1992. *Truman*. New York: Simon & Schuster.

The National Security Archive. 2013. George Kennan's "Long Telegram." Accessed January 28, 2013. www2.gwu.edu/~nsarchiv/coldwar/documents/episode-1/kennan.htm. The National Security Archive is an independent non-government research institute and library located at The George Washington University in Washington, DC. It is a basic resource for the study of the Cold War.

Further Reading

Ansprenger, Franz. 1989. *The Dissolution of Colonial Empires*. London and New York: Routledge. A comprehensive examination of the end of empire.

Applebaum, Anne. 2012. *Iron Curtain: The Crushing of Eastern Europe, 1944–1956*. New York: Doubleday. An excellent comparative study of Soviet efforts in East Germany, Hungary, and Poland to create states and societies in the Soviet image.

Eisenberg, Carolyn.1996. *Drawing the Line: The American Decision to Divide Germany, 1944–1949*. New York: Cambridge University Press. A careful look at efforts by the United States to deal with the German question in the 1940s.

Gaddis, John Lewis. 2005. *The Cold War: A New History*. New York: Penguin Books. An excellent review of significant aspects of the Cold War.

Gaddis, John Lewis. 2011. *George F. Kennan: An American Life*. New York: Penguin Books. A full account of the life of a central figure in the Cold War.

Hammer, Ellen J. 1966. *The Struggle for Indochina 1940–1955*. Stanford: Stanford University Press. An excellent discussion of French efforts to maintain Indochina as a colony after World War II.

Hogan, Michael J. 1987. *The Marshall Plan: America, Britain and the Reconstruction of Western Europe*. Cambridge and New York: Cambridge University Press. The best single book on the Marshall Plan.

Horne, Alistair. 2006. *A Savage War of Peace: Algeria 1954–1962*. New York: New York Review of Books. A fascinating account of a very important national liberation movement.

Internet Modern History Source Book. "The Marshall Plan, 1947." Accessed October 3, 2013. www.fordham.edu/halsall/mod/1947marshallplan1.htm.

Leffler, Melvin P. 1994. *The Specter of Communism: The United States and the Origins of the Cold War, 1917–1953*. New York: Hill and Wang. A brief but very insightful discussion of the many factors contributing to the emergence of the Cold War in the first decade after World War II.

McMahon, Robert J. 2003. *The Cold War: A Very Short Introduction.* Oxford and New York: Oxford University Press. A useful entry in the excellent Oxford University series of very short introductions.

Montefiore, Simon Sebag. 2004. *Stalin: The Court of the Red Tsar.* New York: Alfred Knopf. An eye-opening account, based on extensive research in the archives, of Stalin's career as leader of the Soviet Union.

Patterson, James T. 1996. *Grand Expectations: The United States, 1945–1974.* Oxford and New York. Oxford University Press. A well-informed and judicious account of the United States, both domestic events and foreign policies, in the first three decades after World War II.

Shlaim, Avi. 1983. *The United States and the Berlin Blockade: A Study in Crisis Decision-Making.* Berkeley: University of California Press. A detailed analysis of this pivotal event.

Zubok, Vladislav and Pleshakov, Constantine. 1996. *Inside the Kremlin's Cold War: From Stalin to Khrushchev.* Cambridge, MA: Harvard University Press. The most detailed and authoritative discussion of the role of the Soviet Union in the Cold War from 1945 to 1962.

9

Out of the Ashes
From Stunde Null *(Zero Hour)*
to a New Golden Age, 1945–1967

Chronology

1945	Nazi Germany defeated; Japan surrenders
	Labour party wins elections in Britain
1946	Constitution of French Fourth Republic approved
	Italy becomes a republic
	National Health Service established in Britain
	Beginning of the Indochina War between France and the Viet Minh
1947	British rule in India ends
	Truman Doctrine
	Marshall Plan
	Communists forced out of coalition governments in France and Italy

Twentieth-Century Europe: A Brief History, 1900 to the Present, Third Edition.
Michael D. Richards and Paul R. Waibel.
© 2014 John Wiley & Sons, Inc. Published 2014 by John Wiley & Sons, Inc.

1948	Communist coup in Czechoslovakia
	Christian Democrats win elections in Italy
1949	Federal Republic of Germany (West Germany) founded
	German Democratic Republic (East Germany) founded
	Dutch rule in East Indies ends
1950	Schuman Plan
1952	European Coal and Steel Community (ECSC) established
1953	Death of Stalin
1954	France defeated at Dien Bien Phu
	Vietnam divided into two states at the Geneva Conference
1956	Khrushchev's speech denouncing Stalin at the Twentieth Party Congress of the Communist Party of the Soviet Union
	Worker unrest in Poland
	Hungarian Revolution and Soviet intervention
	Suez Crisis
1957	European Economic Community (EEC) established by the Treaty of Rome
1958	Charles de Gaulle becomes president of France
	French Fifth Republic established
1959	European Free Trade Association (EFTA) established
1961	Construction of Berlin Wall begins
1962	Cuban Missile Crisis
1963	De Gaulle vetoes British membership in the EEC
	Franco-German Treaty signed
	West German Chancellor Konrad Adenauer retires after 14 years in office

1964	Khrushchev forced to retire—replaced by Brezhnev
1966	Grand coalition of the CDU and SPD in Germany ends 17 years of conservative government
	De Gaulle announces French withdrawal from NATO
1967	Military seizes power in Greece
	EEC, ECSC, and Euratom combine to become the European Community (EC)

IN 1950 LAURENCE WYLIE, then a professor of French at Haverford College, took his wife and children to the commune of Roussillon for his sabbatical year. Situated in the southeastern part of France, Roussillon contained only about 800 people. At that time, about half the population of France lived in similar rural communes (a rural commune is defined as containing fewer than 2,000 people). And, as Wylie later realized, many other French had lived in such communes at one time or another before moving to larger towns or cities. As the 1950s began, a large number of French men and women shared the same values and approach to life as the people Professor Wylie encountered in Roussillon.

In 1950, many farmers planted wheat instead of the fruit trees they knew to be better suited to the soil and climate. As one of them put it to Wylie (1974, p. 33): "Plant an apricot orchard so the Russians and Americans can use it as a battlefield? Thanks. Not so dumb." His comments reflected the fear common to many Europeans in the early 1950s that a third world war might well break out.

Eleven years later, Roussillon had changed considerably. Upon revisiting in 1961, Wylie noted he could see fruit orchards in every direction from his vantage point atop a hill overlooking the commune. More than agricultural practices had changed. Roussillon had become a resort town, a fashionable place to live. A construction boom was underway. Television had made its entrance by the late 1950s and with it the idea of buying on the installment plan.

Roussillon by the early 1960s was representative of one aspect of the new Europe, a Europe more urban, more affluent, more egalitarian, and more confident than it had been only a decade before. By the early 1960s, with only a few exceptions, it had left colonial empires behind, if not all the legacies of colonialism. There was also a loosening of the two great blocs, the East led by the Soviet Union and the West led by the United States, and indications of détente, a relaxation of tensions between the two great powers. The economy continued to grow and there seemed to be no end in sight for what was increasingly being called a golden age.

Reconstruction

Certain factors worked to make the post-World War II reconstruction easier than was initially expected. First, war damage had sometimes been exaggerated. In addition, in some cases, the wartime demolition had a "positive" side. A factory destroyed in the war became an advantage if the factory was replaced by a more efficient plant. In other situations, the economies of the belligerent nations had expanded during the war and were nearly as large, or even larger, than their prewar versions, even after wartime damages had been taken into account. A largely intact productive capacity that could be modernized where damaged, together with a great shortage of goods of all kinds, created a basis for a rapid recovery. The crucial missing factor was the capital needed to finance economic growth.

The United States provided much of the capital needed for recovery through the Marshall Plan (1947) and other smaller programs. Before the Marshall Plan, America had already made available to postwar Europe nearly $15.5 billion in aid, about $7 billion of that in outright gifts. From 1947 to 1952, the United States provided Europe with about $13 billion in aid under the European Recovery Program. After that, Europe financed recovery largely through the expansion of exports.

The Marshall Plan was based on national plans that the Organisation for European Economic Co-operation (OEEC) helped to coordinate. These national plans gave Americans some assurances as to how their money would be spent as well as encouraged participants to use all resources in the most constructive manner.

In many ways, the Marshall Plan's main contribution was a psychological one. It demonstrated American faith that European economies could be successfully reconstructed and gave Europeans reason to cooperate with one another in the process. Other factors involved in the recovery included an increase in trade worldwide and several demographic factors in Europe. First, there was a rising birthrate. Additionally, the influx of refugees and, later, the arrival of large numbers of foreign "guest workers" added to the capacity to produce goods relatively cheaply. Heavy consumer demand, especially in areas of housing and automobiles, was vitally important in maintaining a long-term economic growth.

A new kind of capitalism, one characterized by extensive state intervention in national economies through the use of devices such as planning and nationalization, also played an important role in recovery. Governments often used their control of central banks and government investment to determine both the rate of growth of an economy and the direction of that growth. Governments extended their activities beyond areas having to do with welfare—unemployment, retirement, working conditions, public health, and housing—to the workings of the economy itself. In some cases, housing, for instance, welfare and economic expansion went hand in hand. Efforts to make the economy function effectively and equitably followed patterns that had developed in each of the two world wars. All the factors taken together enabled most Western European countries not simply to recover but also to develop at a rapid rate through the first two decades after World War II.

Reconstruction in the West: British Problems

Three major developments characterized Britain in the first decade after the war. The most basic was the distressingly slow recovery of the economy and Britain's failure to share fully in the rapid economic growth of the 1950s. Britain was initially handicapped by an enormous war debt and by foreign policy crises in areas such as India, Palestine, Greece, and Malaysia. Even after relinquishing responsibilities around the world, however, Britain still faced a severe balance of payments problem. It had become less competitive on the world market because of a variety of factors. The industrial plant was aging, the labor force more concerned with benefits than productivity, and the management reluctant to modernize facilities and encourage innovation. The loss of markets and the sell-off of investments to help finance the war increased the difficulty of balancing imports by exports. Despite economic difficulties, Britain resisted the idea of long-term economic planning and restricted governmental interference in the private sector. Nationalization was regarded more as a rescue operation than as a tool for restructuring or directing the economy.

The expansion of the welfare state formed the second development. This expansion drew on the famous 1942 report by Sir William Beveridge (1879–1963). The Labour Party erected a comprehensive social security system and a socialized medical care program, beginning with passage of the National Insurance Act and the National Health Services Act in 1946. Criticism was heavy at the time and continued long after Labour had lost power, but both measures quickly became accepted as integral parts of British life. Even during Labour's long absence from power between 1951 and 1964, there were no serious attempts to dismantle the welfare systems.

Finally, Britain spent most of the postwar period in a somewhat inglorious "retreat from empire." The attempt to reassert its old position in world affairs, the conspiracy with France and Israel to take over the Suez Canal in 1956, failed miserably when the United States and the United Nations forced Britain and its allies to back down.

Labour presided over the initial period of recovery and the elaboration of the welfare state. The party became bogged down, however, by infighting. Badly divided between left and right wings by 1951, it lost power to the Conservatives in that year's elections. Winston Churchill returned to serve as prime minister until his retirement due to ill health in 1955. Anthony Eden (1897–1977) thereafter served as prime minister for a short time before the Suez

Canal debacle forced him to resign. He was followed by Harold Macmillan (1894–1986), "Supermac," the most able of the three Conservative prime ministers of the immediate postwar years. In the 1950s, Britain enjoyed a modest economic recovery and the easing of international tensions. By the end of the decade, its economy was prosperous if still vulnerable. Heavily dependent on exports, it nevertheless remained relatively uncompetitive because of the factors previously discussed.

Reconstruction in the West: French Success

The general pattern of economic recovery outlined above fits the French experience closely. Wartime destruction and social dislocation demanded strong economic measures. Social and economic programs based on discussions in the resistance movement during World War II and on the experiences of the Popular Front in the 1930s also had an impact. While some industries were nationalized, the more important factor was the emphasis placed on economic planning. Jean Monnet (1888–1979), the architect of French economic recovery and later of European economic integration, put together a four-year plan that went into effect in 1948. Initial efforts were designed to channel investments into such basic areas of the economy as coal, electricity, steel, and farm machinery. Later plans were directed toward consumer goods, housing, and farm production.

The idea of a national economy with a large public sector, planned and guided from above, was a radical departure from past French policy. Owners of small businesses and farmers resisted it, but, nonetheless, during the 1950s and 1960s, a "silent revolution" took place, making France industrially and technologically competitive with other nations. At the same time, large numbers of people moved into urban areas and agriculture was thoroughly modernized. In little more than a decade, the French economy changed drastically, despite tenacious rearguard actions.

The French version of the welfare state was not as comprehensive as the British system, but it was a greater break with the past. Aside from some efforts by the Popular Front in the 1930s, French governments had done virtually nothing in the way of welfare reform before the 1940s and 1950s. The new French system provided not only health, maternity, and old-age benefits but also family allowances paid to families with two or more children. It was meant to provide the population with benefits in such important areas as health services, education, and family life, which would, first, improve the quality of people's lives and, second, protect them from the effects of catastrophes such as long-term illness, accidents on the job, or unemployment.

Success in the social and economic spheres made it possible for the French to ignore for a time the conspicuous political failure of the Fourth Republic. Its initial efforts, after its establishment in 1944 by General Charles de Gaulle, were directed to the writing of a new constitution. While the Communists and Socialists favored a strong legislature (National Assembly), the Popular Republican Movement (MRP) and de Gaulle favored a strong executive. The constitution passed in November 1946 called for neither a strong national assembly nor a strong executive. Instead, it resembled to a large degree the system of the Third Republic.

By the middle of 1947, mounting Cold War tensions forced France to take sides. Shortly after the announcement of the Truman Doctrine, the French Communist Party stopped supporting government efforts to regain Indochina. In April, the Communist Party felt compelled to support a strike in the government-owned Renault automobile plant. The premier won a vote of confidence and then demanded the Communists resign from the coalition.

The end of coalition government based on three major parties created nearly impossible political conditions. Coalitions had to be constructed from several different parties and could survive only by doing as little as possible. Any controversial effort might destroy the government. This created the "immobilism" in politics that was the hallmark of the Fourth Republic.

Colonial questions caused the major dilemmas in the 1950s, leading to frequent cabinet changes. Premier Pierre Mèndes-France (1907–1982) was successful in 1954 in ending French involvement in Indochina. Unfortunately for France, the simmering Algerian crisis exploded that same year.

By 1958, France was on the verge of civil war over Algeria. In Algiers, the French army and the colons (European settlers in Algeria) seized power. Next, the army and colons seized Corsica and made plans to attack metropolitan France, intending to bring to power a government that would keep Algeria French. Charles de Gaulle, then in self-imposed political exile, appeared the only national figure acceptable to all groups. The French army officers and colons willingly accepted de Gaulle as the one person who could keep the country united and Algeria French. At the time, de Gaulle hoped to keep Algeria attached to France, although not necessarily in the same manner as the army and colons wished.

De Gaulle was successful in the next several years both in constructing the type of government he had wanted earlier and in resolving the Algerian crisis. In large part, success in creating a Fifth Republic dominated by a powerful executive allowed him to deal successfully with the colonial impasse. Working quickly in 1958 and 1959, de Gaulle supervised the writing of a new constitution and the referendum approving it. His prestige and force of personality allowed him over the next several years to pursue a number of goals. Absolutely vital was bringing the Algerian crisis to a close. Initially, de Gaulle tried to keep Algeria attached to France in some way, but when he saw this would not work, he pushed through Algerian independence. For some in the French military, this was completely unacceptable. Although some officers resorted to revolt and assassination attempts, de Gaulle prevailed. France by the early 1960s enjoyed both a strong, rapidly developing economy and a stable, confident government.

Reconstruction in the West: German *Wirtschaftswunder*

The Federal Republic of Germany was a creation of the Cold War, a version of Germany acceptable to the United States, Britain, and France once it became clear no agreement could be reached on uniting all of Germany. Although an artificial construct, West Germany proved to be remarkably successful, both politically and economically, going mostly from strength to strength over the

40 years of its existence. Even today, the united Germany is in the main an enlarged version of West Germany.

As a product of the Cold War, West Germany almost by definition excluded the left from politics. The Communists were formally banned in 1956. On the right, the neo-Nazi Reich Party was also banned. The Social Democrats found acceptance only after adopting a new party program (Godesberg Program) in 1959, with which the SPD abandoned Marxist rhetoric and became a party of reform. The mostly conservative resistance in Germany had not been interested in radical social and economic change. Instead, the major emphasis was on reconstruction of the economy and on establishment of a political system that would not make West Europeans or Americans nervous.

The founding father, or perhaps grandfather, of West Germany was Konrad Adenauer, leader of the Christian Democratic Union (CDU). Adenauer, who had been lord mayor of Cologne before the Nazis came to power in Germany, was one of the few German politicians with experience and without the taint of association with the Nazis. He also had good connections with the British and the Americans. Elections in 1949 gave the CDU and the Free Democratic Party a majority. Adenauer became chancellor and remained in that office until 1963, governing in a paternalistic fashion and excluding the *Bundestag* (parliament) whenever possible from discussion of political questions. His style of government, featuring a strong executive and a restricted democracy, has been called "chancellor democracy." It was acceptable in the 1950s, despite its authoritarian overtones, primarily because of Germany's economic success but also because of the nation's delicate situation in international affairs. Adenauer seemed indispensable in the latter area.

Adenauer's lieutenant, Ludwig Erhard (1897–1977), emphasized economic recovery and expansion. Much was left up to the private sector. A combination of good business management, including efforts by industry to channel investments and to control prices; government intervention when necessary; and a long period of labor peace enabled German business to become highly competitive in the world market. An expanding economy eventually led in the 1960s to high wages and a comprehensive welfare system. Some commentators believe Erhard's "socialmarket" approach placed an undue burden on the workers. Others emphasize labor cooperation as an essential factor in the robust economy of the 1950s and 1960s.

Although basically a laissez-faire economy, it always experienced some level of government intervention, a good deal of cooperation within industry, and sizable efforts by the larger banks to direct the workings of the economy. While no four-year plans on the French model existed, a good deal of planning took place in the private sector. To a large extent, however, German business simply needed to do what it had done so well before. The factors that had worked to make it successful earlier—concentration of capital and other resources, economies of scale, reduction of competition—worked again in the postwar period to make it successful. Economic success, in turn, helped make political questions less significant. One question, however, unification, would not go away. Millions of Germans, displaced from their homes after the war, kept it on the political agenda in the 1950s and the 1960s. Unification, then and for many years later, was, however, out of the question. No other European state, especially not France or the Soviet Union, wanted a reunited Germany. Adenauer understood this and worked to place West Germany in European and Atlantic political and economic structures (e.g., NATO). At the same time, he paid lip service to the desire for unification. As German war refugees were integrated into the new West German society, contributing vital skills and labor, some of the tension surrounding this issue and the even more explosive issue of recovery of lands lost to Poland began to diminish. West Germany by 1961 was divided from East Germany in a very physical way, especially after the construction of the Berlin Wall in August of that year. By then, however, the economy was booming, and many West Germans were beginning to live very well indeed. For these people, politics no longer seemed to matter all that much.

Reconstruction in the West: Other Countries, Other Stories

Immediately after the war, Italy was governed by a coalition of the Christian Democratic Party (DC), the Communists (PCI), and the Socialists. The 1946 referendum on the monarchy resulted in the creation of the Republic of Italy. The coalition broke up the following year because of increasing Cold War tensions and disagreements over plans for social change.

The United States played a large role in Italian politics in the late 1940s. In the 1948 elections, American officials let it be known that the wrong kind of government from the American point of view would lead to a cutoff in Marshall Plan aid. The DC won a working majority and governed over the next decade in coalitions, usually with the Social Democratic Party, a splinter from the old Socialists. The Social Democrats were distinguished primarily by their refusal to cooperate with the Communists.

Coalition government, in which the most influential politician was Alcide De Gasperi (1881–1954) from the DC, worked reasonably well at first and restored Italy to economic and social stability by the late 1940s, largely with the help of the Marshall Plan. In the 1950s, the coalitions grew weaker and less able to take initiatives. A curious political trend developed in which the left gained increasing numbers of votes with each election while at the same time becoming more moderate in its approaches. In particular, the PCI, under the leadership of Palmiro Togliatti (1893–1964), moved toward the center under the influence of moderate trade unionists and in reaction to the Soviet suppression of the Hungarian Revolution in 1956. The Socialists (not to be confused with the Social Democrats) moved away from the Communists and openly sought a coalition with the DC.

By the 1950s, Italy enjoyed a high rate of economic growth, becoming a major supplier in Europe of automobiles, refrigerators, office machinery, and other goods. It was an unusual mixed economy. The government-controlled holding company, the Institute for Industrial Reconstruction, and the government energy concern were both administered by private enterprise. Together with FIAT, the giant automobile manufacturer, they contributed concentration of capital, reduction of competition, and economies of scale to economic success. Another major element was formed by sources of cheap labor, particularly in the underdeveloped south. Overall, the south gained little from Italy's reconstruction after the war other than the possibility of employment in the factories and other enterprises in northern Italy.

Each of the smaller countries in Western Europe had unique political and economic situations that, with the exception of Spain, Portugal, and Greece, they had considerable success in overcoming. Finland and Austria resolved the problem of relations with the Soviet Union in differing ways: Finland by keeping its foreign policy in line with Soviet wishes and Austria in the form of a treaty in 1955 that ended occupation but obligated Austria to remain permanently neutral. Sweden and Switzerland, both neutral during World War II, achieved standards of living fully comparable with that of the United States by the early 1960s. Both Belgium and the Netherlands faced divisive religious–political problems after the war. In the Netherlands, where an elaborate system guaranteed equity for Protestants and Catholics, rapid economic growth helped to smooth out many of the differences. A rapidly growing and changing economy also helped the Dutch weather the loss of empire.

Reconstruction in the East: The Stalinist Legacy

The Soviet Union had suffered enormously in what it termed "The Great Fatherland War," in which roughly 25 million Russians had died. Great stretches of European Russia had been devastated by Nazi and Soviet scorched-earth policies. Nonetheless, Russians were hopeful a new era was at hand, one in which wartime sacrifices would be rewarded. Instead, Soviet citizens were bitterly disappointed by a return to the Stalinist practices of the 1930s. The fourth Five-Year Plan, introduced in 1946, stressed heavy industry and armaments.

By 1950, the Soviet Union had reached prewar levels in industry and agriculture through the utilization of its own resources, reparations from some nations, and one-sided economic arrangements with its East European satellites. A major industrial power in terms of basic categories like coal and steel production, and closing the gap between itself and the United States in some areas, it nevertheless lacked the technological range of a truly modern industrial society. Much of its production in the 1950s was inferior in quality or outmoded in design. There were serious shortages from the consumer point of view. Agriculture, despite the vigorous efforts of Khrushchev, was inefficient and had not recovered from the effects of collectivization in the 1930s.

By 1952 and early 1953, there were ominous signs that Stalin, aging and in poor health, intended to reinstitute the purges of the 1930s. One major piece of evidence was the "Doctors' Plot," supposedly a plot by several prominent physicians to murder important party and government officials. Any plans that may have existed to restart the purges were cut short by Stalin's death in March 1953 (see Chapter 8 for a detailed discussion of Soviet politics from the end of World War II to Stalin's death).

Many Soviet citizens were despondent, believing they had lost the strong ruler who, if sometimes harsh, had kept them from a worse fate and had made the Soviet Union a powerful and respected state. Collective leadership was emphasized since no one dared to claim the ability to fill Stalin's role. Georgy Malenkov (1902–1988) became premier. The secretariat of the Central Committee, Stalin's old source of power, was reorganized by abolishing the office of general secretary. Khrushchev simply became first among equals on the list of secretaries. Lavrenty Beria either made a play for power or his colleagues feared he would. Arrested in June 1953, he was unceremoniously shot. The NKVD was reorganized to curtail its independence and renamed the KGB.

Infighting continued, but methods changed. Malenkov, identified with the "new course," which had emphasized production of consumer goods, resigned his post in 1955. The other leaders saw his ideas as endangering security. The old survivor Vyacheslav Molotov (1890–1986), long Stalin's closest associate, remained a very important figure, but the dominant political force increasingly was Khrushchev.

In 1956, at the Twentieth Party Congress, Khrushchev made a so-called secret speech in which he severely criticized Stalin for his cult of personality, his leadership in World War II, and many of his actions in the 1930s. This was the beginning of a process of de-Stalinization, which had several goals. By blaming Stalin for many past wrongs, Khrushchev and his colleagues deflected a good deal of the criticism of the existing situation. Criticizing Stalin was also a way to improve relations with those communist movements that had resented Stalin's autocratic behavior toward them. Finally, distancing the present government from Stalin made the relaxation of Cold War tensions more likely. In a sense, Khrushchev was only trying to find a way to get around Stalin's legacy.

In 1956, Khrushchev also faced difficult situations with Poland and Hungary. Ironically, the Soviet Union was trying not only to reestablish a good working relationship with Tito and Yugoslavia but also to treat countries in the East Bloc as sovereign states. Thus, the Warsaw Treaty Organization (WTO, commonly called the Warsaw Pact) came into being in 1955, partly in response to West Germany joining NATO but additionally as a way of establishing proper relationships between the Soviet military and the armed forces of the East European states. In the case of Poland, the Polish leader Wladyslaw Gomulka convinced the Soviets of the loyalty of the Polish Communists and the stability of the political situation in Poland. Hungary, for its part, appeared about to leave the WTO, and the Russians resorted to force to end the Hungarian Revolution. (These events are covered in greater detail later in the chapter.)

Although Stalinism had been heavily criticized, the Stalinists were still a powerful force in Soviet politics. In 1957, they nearly succeeded in deposing Khrushchev. Khrushchev, ever the resourceful politician, took his case to the Central Committee, the members of which mostly owed their careers to him. He also had the backing of the military, in particular Gregory Zhukov (1896–1974), the great Soviet military leader of World War II. It now became clear Khrushchev was the leading figure in the party, even if not all powerful.

From 1957 until Khrushchev was successfully deposed in 1964, he tried many schemes to create conditions for a more productive, efficient, and technologically sophisticated economy in the Soviet Union. In some respects, he was remarkably successful. The Soviet Union took an early lead in space exploration with the launching of *Sputnik I*, the first orbiting satellite, in 1957, and with Yuri Gagarin (1934–1968) as the first man in space (1961) (Table 9.1). On the

Table 9.1 Major Events in Humanity's Journey into Space

1957	*Sputnik I* (USSR), first earth-orbiting satellite
1958	First dogs in orbit (USSR)
1959	First monkeys sent into space (USSR)
1961	Yuri A. Gagarin (USSR), first man to orbit earth
1963	Valentina V. Tereshkova (USSR), first woman to orbit earth
1965	Alexei Leonov (USSR), first man to leave spacecraft and float in space
1966	*Luna IX* (USSR), first soft landing on moon
	Gemini VIII (USA), first linkup in space
1968	*Apollo VIII* (USA), first manned mission to orbit moon and return
1969	*Soyuz IV* and *V* (USSR), first experimental space station
	Apollo XI (USA), first manned landing on moon
1971	*Salyut I* space station (USSR)
1973	*Skylab* space station (USA)
1975	*Apollo XVIII* (USA) and *Soyuz XIX* (USSR) dock while in earth orbit
1984	First untethered space walk (USA)
1986	*Mir I* (USSR), first space station meant to be permanently manned but closed in 1999
	Shuttle *Challenger* (USA) explodes just after takeoff
1989–1993	Magellan mission to Venus (USA)
1989–2003	Galileo mission to Jupiter (USA)
1990	Hubble space telescope (USA) launched (repaired 1993, 1997, and 1999)
1995	Cooperation between US shuttles and Russian *Mir* space station begins
1997–1998	Mars *Pathfinder* mission (USA)
1997	Cassini–Huygens launched—bound for Saturn
2000	First crew in International Space Station
2003	Mars Rover (USA) launched, landed 2004 and still active at present
2005	Huygens probe (USA) landed on Saturn's moon Titan
2012	Nuclear-powered NASA rover lands on Mars to seek out life clues

other hand, the Virgin Lands campaign, an effort to put into cultivation vast new areas that were fertile but lacked sufficient rainfall, was initially successful but disastrous over the long run. Similarly, efforts to reorganize the bureaucracies of the Soviet Union were well meaning but not sufficiently thought out. Ultimately, Khrushchev's downfall came from a streak of adventurism in foreign policy. In particular, the Cuban Missile Crisis between the Soviet Union and the United States in 1962, during which the world ventured to the edge of a nuclear holocaust, prompted his colleagues to bring in someone less erratic. (See "Détente" for a discussion of Khrushchev and the Cuban Missile Crisis.) Ironically, they had to delay deposing him because the Chinese Communists had been extremely critical of him, and at the height of the Sino-Soviet split, the Soviets would not admit the Chinese were right about anything.

Reconstruction in the East: The Seemingly Successful German Democratic Republic

The Soviet Union was ambivalent in its relations with the German Democratic Republic (GDR) or East Germany. For many years, it exploited the GDR economically in order to build up its own economy. Set against this, however, was the need to offset the propaganda value of West Germany and, in particular, West Berlin. Additionally, the Soviet Union feared any kind of German resurgence, even if it seemed to be contained by a divided Germany.

Many Germans had returned to the GDR because they had an idealistic vision of what communism might achieve. From their perspective, capitalist West Germany was little better than Nazi Germany. In the first years after the GDR's founding, it was forced to follow the Soviet economic and political model closely and to join in the witch hunt for national deviationists or Titoists. Trials in the GDR, however, did not result in executions, and on the whole, there was less brutality there than in Czechoslovakia or Romania.

Crucial events for the later evolution of the GDR took place in 1953. It was a classic case of mixed signals. The SED (Socialist

Unity, or Government Party), with Walter Ulbricht (1893–1973) as its most influential figure, agreed to follow a Soviet line emphasizing social and economic concessions. Coupled with the concessions, however, were increases in some work norms, which led construction workers in Berlin to begin protesting on June 16, 1953. The following day the protests spread to all the major cities and towns. It was a large-scale protest but probably should not be seen as an uprising. Only toward the end of the day did the Soviets send in tanks to help restore order.

The irony of 1953 is that it reinforced Ulbricht's position. Over the next few years, he triumphed over a variety of voices within the SED, closing off discussion. The SED became a neo-Stalinist party at precisely the time Khrushchev was launching his de-Stalinization campaign. For the Soviet Union, however, particularly after 1956, it seemed more important to have a strong figure in charge in the GDR than to advance the cause of political reform.

By the late 1950s, the GDR was suffering from the effects of a massive depopulation process. Hundreds of thousands of people each year were flowing out across the border. Almost all the border was sealed off by the end of the decade, but there remained the problem of Berlin, where thousands of people each day crossed from East to West or vice versa to go to work, to shop, or to visit friends. West Berlin was a hole in the dike threatening to drain the GDR, particularly of young, talented, and well-educated people. Khrushchev attempted to resolve the Berlin issue in the late 1950s on several occasions. He threatened to conclude a treaty with the GDR, leaving it responsible for all of Berlin, if the United States, Britain, and France were not willing to renegotiate the status of the city. The East German leaders finally came up with a crude but workable solution to the problem: the Berlin Wall. Construction of the wall, under the supervision of Ulbricht's eventual successor, Erich Honecker (1912–1994), began on August 13, 1961. Well into the fall of that year, Berlin threatened to become a flash point with, for example, American tanks driving full speed right up to the border to face their Russian counterparts only a few feet away. The crisis passed, however, and East Germans resigned themselves to life behind the wall.

A portion of the Berlin Wall as it had developed by the early 1970s. Note that the wall is actually a series of obstacles, fences, and open spaces, as well as walls. From the collection of Paul Waibel

Reconstruction in the East: The New Poland

Next to Germany, Poland was the country in Eastern Europe about which the Soviet Union worried most. By 1948, Poland was on its way to becoming a carbon copy of the Soviet Union. People like Wladyslaw Gomulka (1905–1982), who emphasized a national approach to communism, were arrested, imprisoned, and in some cases even executed.

By 1956, Poles began to believe the situation was improving and things could be somewhat different. At the end of June, riots began in Poznan, protesting the low standard of living of the working class. The Polish United Workers' Party (PUWP), the official name for the Communist Party, split between the Stalinists and those who wanted to improve the lot of the workers. Neither the police nor the army would attempt to stop the riots. The government promised the end of collectivization and reforms for the workers. Gomulka was released from prison and returned to power.

Gomulka and his supporters worked hard to convince the Soviet Union of two things: Poland would remain in the Soviet Bloc and PUWP would continue to exercise power. The Soviets agreed, not relishing the prospects of fighting the Poles. Aside from abolishing collectivization and de-emphasizing heavy industry, relatively little changed in Poland. Gomulka and the Poles were able to avoid the fate of the Hungarians who, in October and November of 1956, became involved in revolution.

Reconstruction in the East: Hungary and Revolution

Hungary became a People's Republic in 1949 and followed the Stalinist path of economic development over the next four years to the point of economic collapse. Four months after Stalin's death, Imre Nagy (1896–1958), seen as a moderate, was appointed premier. His policies mirrored Malenkov's new course and included diversion of resources to light industry and an end to forced collectivization. Malenkov's fall from power in the Soviet Union in 1955 led to his protégé, Nagy, being ousted from the premiership. The following year, however, the Hungarian government ran into trouble. In October 1956, it made a fundamental error in calling in the Soviet Army to deal with Hungarian demonstrators. Throughout Hungary, councils were formed demanding free elections, the withdrawal of Soviet troops, and an end to the security police.

At first, it appeared the Hungarians had won the day. Nagy established a new government on October 28, and Soviet troops began to leave. On October 31, Nagy went too far by declaring Hungary's neutrality. After that, Soviet leaders believed they had to crush the revolution by force. The Soviet Union smashed the Nagy government and installed János Kádár (1912–1989) as the new leader. This action had several far-reaching consequences. For one, it played an important role in the Stalinists' attempt to oust Khrushchev in 1957. It complicated efforts by the Soviet Union to establish relations with countries in the East Bloc that provided for autonomy and national sovereignty. Communist movements elsewhere in Europe reassessed Soviet

A crowd of Hungarians gathers around a large statue of Stalin that had been knocked off its base in Budapest, October 1956. The Soviet Union used force to suppress the Hungarian Revolution and regain control over the People's Republic of Hungary. ARPAD HAZAFI / AP / Press Association Images

Communism and in some cases moved to more independent positions. The West reacted very unfavorably, but involved in the Suez Crisis and in no case wishing to challenge the Soviet Union directly, it could only criticize and find places for the large numbers of former Hungarian freedom fighters now refugees.

Throughout the 1950s, the Soviet Union dominated the affairs of East and Central European countries with the exception of Yugoslavia. The Soviet Union not only shaped the political systems but also the social and economic systems. This meant, leaving aside Czechoslovakia and the GDR, an emphasis on industrialization and urbanization in what had been countries with large peasant populations and small industrial bases before the war. In each nation, the pattern was roughly the same: centralized planning, rapid economic growth, and the development of heavy industry at the expense of the production of consumer goods.

On the Way to a United Europe

The division of Europe into two great blocs was both unexpected and unfortunate in the postwar period. Within each bloc, however, there existed considerable interest in European unity. In the East Bloc, the Soviet Union limited and distorted any expression of interest in unity. It also repressed expressions of nationalism. In the West, movement toward unity built on ideas and concepts coming from the experience of World War II and followed three parallel paths, two of which reached dead ends by the mid-1950s.

The first path involved political union. In May 1948, a Congress of Europe took place. Among the participants were such leading Europeanists as Churchill, De Gasperi, Robert Schuman (1886–1963) of France, and Paul-Henri Spaak (1899–1972) of Belgium. The Congress proposed the political and economic unification of Europe and established the Council of Europe to that end. The power of decision lay in the hands of the foreign ministers of the member states, organized as the Committee of Ministers. But they guarded the sovereignty of their respective nation states jealously. Political integration was not in the cards.

A second effort at integration concentrated on military matters, specifically the rearmament of West Germany. In 1950, the French proposed to create a European army as a means of circumventing the problem of German rearmament and enhancing the defensive capabilities of Western Europe while the United States was embroiled in the Korean War. Before the European Defense Community (EDC) could be organized, however, events passed it by. Stalin's death, the end of the Korean War, and the easing of Cold War tensions in the mid-1950s all worked to remove some of the more pressing reasons for the EDC. The French themselves had second thoughts about such a drastic turn toward supranationalism. The British finished the plan off by declining to participate. Instead, a German military force was created and made part of NATO in 1955. NATO remained a collection of armies with some provision for an integrated command structure.

The third path toward unity evolved from the cooperation called for under the European Recovery Program (the Marshall Plan) and from earlier efforts at economic cooperation among Belgium, the Netherlands, and Luxembourg. Two Frenchmen, Commissioner of Planning Jean Monnet and Foreign Minister Robert Schuman, proposed a pooling of coal and steel resources in Europe in what became known as the Schuman Plan. Perhaps the most important aspect of the plan is that it included West Germany. The Germans, for their part, welcomed the opportunity to take part on equal terms in an international organization. According to Judt (2005), Adenauer stated, "Das ist unser Durchbruch" (this is our breakthrough). The plan went into operation in 1952 with France, West Germany, Italy, and the Benelux countries (**Be**lgium, the **Ne**therlands, and **Lux**embourg) working together in the European Coal and Steel Community (ECSC).

The ECSC was a great success. Its members pressed on to further economic integration in part because of the obvious potential economic advantage. They were also painfully aware of their vulnerability and weakness as individual states. The failure of the French and British to regain control of the Suez Canal in 1956 only served to underline this. In 1957, the Treaty of Rome established the European Economic Community (EEC) or Common Market. The EEC set out to eliminate customs barriers among its member states and to create a common tariff structure for the rest of the world.

Three significant events affected the development of the EEC in the 1960s. First, French President de Gaulle, worried that Britain's entry into the EEC would weaken French dominance of the institution, vetoed Britain's application in 1963. Second, the Luxembourg Agreement in 1966 resolved clashes between those who favored the Commission, the executive body of the EEC, and those who wanted the Council of Ministers, which represented the individual states, to retain control of the EEC. It required the Commission to consult individual states before making major proposals and noted that no nation could be overturned in the Council of Ministers if it were a matter of national interest. Finally, the so-called Merger Treaty of 1967 combined the EEC, the ECSC, and Euratom (the European Atomic Energy Community) into a single institution, the European Community (EC). Despite these various developments, however, by the end of the 1960s, the EC had not realized the promise many saw in it at the beginning of the decade.

The British sponsored a seven-nation European Free Trade Association (EFTA), a much looser arrangement than the EEC. In Eastern Europe, the Council for Mutual Economic Assistance (variously referred to as Comecon, CEMA, or CMEA), in existence since 1949, took on a new life. Originally constructed as a counter to the Marshall Plan, but actually little more than a cover for Soviet exploitation of the Eastern European economies, Comecon became directed more toward mutually advantageous economic relations. In this, it reflected not only the example of the EEC but also the desire for autonomy and national sovereignty, which had been dampened in some ways by 1956 but also paradoxically accelerated by events of that year.

Although the widespread interest in European unity in the postwar period gave way quickly to political realities like the Cold War and concerns for national interests, it did result in some important steps toward unity on social and economic policies. It also produced processes, particularly in the EEC, by which more could be achieved. It was one of the most significant and characteristic developments of the first two decades after the war.

A Consumer Economy in Western Europe

The main characteristic of this period in Western Europe was the extent of prosperity. There was, to be sure, considerable difference between the more industrialized and affluent north and the less developed south. Even within countries, there was considerable regional difference. The Italian case offers the best example. The north contained most of the industry and employment opportunities, the south millions of urban and rural poor. But overall, Europe was prosperous to an extent never before realized in its history.

One means of measuring the development of a consumer economy is to examine the composition of the work force. A work force in which the agricultural sector shrinks while the industrial sector remains largely stable and the service sector grows was considered to be moving in the direction of a modern economy, in postwar terms. For the 1950s, using France, West Germany, and Italy as examples, the industrial sector and service sector both increased in size, while the agricultural sector declined. In the 1960s, the agricultural sector continued to decline, with less than 10 percent of the West German work force engaged in agriculture and related activities. In that same period, the industrial sector declined slightly in France and grew slightly in West Germany and somewhat more in Italy, while the service sector grew substantially in each state. Each economy was becoming increasingly modern.

As the nature of the economy changed, the work force gained larger amounts of disposable income, that is, more money to spend on food, clothing, and other goods after paying fixed expenses such as rent and taxes. Per capita disposable income increased 117 percent in the United States between 1960 and 1973, but this was greatly exceeded by European figures for the same period: France, 258 percent; Germany, 312 percent; and Denmark, 323 percent. Disposable income increased more rapidly in nearly every Western European country than it did in the United States, although only Denmark, Germany, Switzerland, and Sweden were close to (or actually higher than in the case of Sweden) the total figure for per capita disposable income in the United States. The rates in France and Belgium, despite large increases, remained substantially below the American figure, while those of Britain and Italy were considerably below.

Old patterns of national affluence also shifted in this period. Britain, the wealthiest country in Europe at the start of the century, continued to lag behind most other Western European nations. The beginnings of this trend went back to the interwar period. The French, and especially the Italians, moved dramatically in the opposite direction, constructing much stronger and more affluent economies than they had enjoyed before World War II.

The range of consumer goods and the increasing levels of consumption in this period provide not only a graphic illustration of how much more disposable income Europeans enjoyed but also of a major sociocultural shift in this period. Not just refrigerators, washing machines, and televisions, but automobiles and houses

Table 9.2   Automobiles in 1957 and in 1965

	1957	1965
France	3,476,000	7,842,000
West Germany	2,456,288	8,103,600
Italy	1,051,004	5,468,981
The Netherlands	375,676	1,272,898
Sweden	796,000	1,793,000

Table 9.3   Televisions in 1957 and in 1965

	1957	1967
France	683,000	6,489,000
Germany	798,586	11,379,000
Italy	367,000	6,044,542
The Netherlands	239,000	2,113,000
Sweden	75,817	2,110,584

came to be items Europeans might aspire to own in the 1960s. The rapid increase in ownership of automobiles is a particularly sensitive indicator of ways in which the economy and people's habits were changing. By 1969, 2 of every 10 people in Britain, Sweden, West Germany, and France owned automobiles. The United States was still considerably ahead with a figure of 4 in 10, but the gap was closing.

Television, a shaper as well as a symbol of a consumer society, provides an even better index of change (Table 9.2 and Table 9.3).

Along with the acquisition of goods came considerable changes in lifestyles and attitudes. The American-style supermarket began to spread in the late 1960s, competing with the neighborhood butcher, greengrocer, baker, and retail grocer. The number of people running routes through neighborhoods selling milk, bread, coal, or sundries began to decline. Once- or twice-weekly markets became smaller and less important in some areas and disappeared in others. It would be easy to exaggerate the extent of the changes, yet the trends were clear by the late 1960s. While most Europeans welcomed the new prosperity, some viewed it with horror as a kind of Americanization of European society.

Social Change

Social change was perhaps most conspicuous among the farming populations of Western Europe. First of all, the number of farmers shrank in the 1950s and 1960s, while production both per capita and overall increased. This was due to what some have termed an "agricultural revolution." Primarily, it involved greater use of machinery and more attention to scientific techniques in areas such as breeding of livestock, selection of seed, use of fertilizers, and utilization of land. In general, it was connected with market-oriented and capital-intensive rather than labor-intensive farming methods. These changes, together with policies favorable to agriculture in the EEC and elsewhere, led to a decline in the number of marginal, self-sufficient farmers and a growing level of prosperity among those who approached farming as if it were an industry. This approach often robbed farm life of some intangible benefits that many prized, such as a feeling of kinship with nature, but it also helped to close the gap between urban and rural lifestyles. Improvements in transportation and communication also brought the farmer closer to life in the mainstream. The European peasant, long a distinctive social type, had, for better or worse, virtually disappeared.

The working classes were also changing, although not as dramatically as farmers. In some countries, a process of "embourgeoisement" was far advanced. This meant that Swedish and German workers, for example, differed less and less from members of the middle classes in terms of housing, clothing, leisure activities, and the like. In other countries, Britain, for example, class distinctions continued to remain strong. Practically everywhere in Western Europe, however, the working class had sufficient income to participate in the consumer economy. Advertising and the mass media between them created a lifestyle that most of the population, workers or middle class, desired. A common, mass culture began to take shape.

With some reservations and criticisms, workers accepted industrial capitalism by the 1960s in Western Europe. They were increasingly interested in gaining an equitable share of the national income together with better working conditions, expanded fringe benefits, and an extension of the welfare state.

The generally more cooperative attitude was most fully developed in Sweden and Germany. In Britain, expectations were similar, but relations between workers and employers remained somewhat antagonistic. While in France and Italy unions became more reformist in the 1960s, they achieved fewer improvements for workers than unions in Britain, Germany, and Sweden. In part, working-class satisfaction with its situation had to do with the role played in the economy by guest workers, laborers brought in from Yugoslavia, Greece, Turkey, Spain, Portugal, and North Africa to take the lowest-paying, least-desirable jobs. These groups, especially important in Germany, Switzerland, and the Netherlands and present in large numbers in Sweden and France, provided European economies with greater flexibility. In good times, they were available to work cheaply. In bad times, they could in theory be shipped back home. Neither for the indigenous working class nor for the other elements of the population was the situation of the guest workers a source of much concern in the 1960s.

By the 1960s, the middle classes could be divided into two large groups. On the one hand, a large number of white-collar employees worked as clerks, technicians, sales personnel, lower-ranking professionals (e.g., teachers and nurses), and supervisory and lower-level managerial personnel. On the other, a relatively small number of higher-ranking professionals (lawyers, doctors, university professors), upper-level bureaucrats and managers, and technocrats made up an upper segment. The upper segment in the 1960s still controlled a disproportionate share of wealth, political power, and status in European society. It constituted a new elite, composed of the remnants of the older elites and some segments of the traditional middle classes. The aristocracy had either disappeared or was regarded as a quaint anachronism. In Britain and France, the new elite was essentially still a continuation of the old establishment. Elsewhere, the new elite was more open. Education, especially a specialized or technical education, increasingly was a necessity. Family ties still played a role, if a declining one. The new elite, like the older upper class, could be generally characterized not only by educational attainment and social background but also by an attachment, genuine or not, to high culture and by distinctive patterns in housing and leisure-time activity. The role of the very rich differed from country to country; it was, for example, very important in Germany and Italy but minimal in Sweden. The difference had to do mostly with taxation and other income distribution policies. Class differences remained strong in Europe in the 1960s despite the efforts to democratize life. In fact, most of the social tension in Western Europe in the 1960s concerned the degree to which social and cultural institutions continued to work to the advantage of those already a part of the elites and against able and ambitious people lower down the social hierarchy.

Détente

Détente was the product of two crises. One, the Berlin Crisis, was actually a series of crises culminating in the construction of the Berlin Wall in August 1961. Between the formation of the German Democratic Republic in 1949 and August 1961, about three million East Germans, approximately 16 percent of the country's population, went through Berlin in order to leave the country. Many of the emigrants were young and well educated. Although Khrushchev may have been worried primarily about the possibility of the United States providing West Germany with atomic weapons, the East German regime worried about the survival of the state if the flow of citizens to the West were to continue.

The second, the Cuban Missile Crisis, edged the world very close to a thermonuclear war. A series of confrontations in the late 1950s and early 1960s, including not only the Berlin Crisis but also the U-2 spy plane incident in 1960 (in which the Soviet Union shot down an American high-altitude spy plane), the failed summit meeting between Nikita S. Khrushchev and US President John F. Kennedy in 1961, along with the construction of the Berlin Wall, had left the two great powers edgy. Khrushchev decided in 1962 to take a chance on installing missiles in Cuba as a means of gaining advantage at little cost. There were several reasons why he pursued this risky policy. One reason, of course, was to back up his guarantee to Fidel Castro to protect Cuba from American threats. A second was probably domestic. A cheap but dramatic victory in the Cold War competition would reinforce his position in the Soviet Union. Various disasters in domestic policy and reservations about the de-Stalinization campaign had eroded Khrushchev's power. Other reasons may have played a part, too. Khrushchev may still have hoped to revise the situation in Berlin. He apparently thought it might be possible to trade removal of missiles in Cuba for removal of American missiles in Turkey.

Kennedy, for his part, badly needed a diplomatic success after the Bay of Pigs fiasco in 1961 (the failed attempt by Cuban exiles trained by the US Central Intelligence Agency (CIA) to invade Communist Cuba and overthrow Castro; Kennedy had had to take responsibility for it) and the inability of the United States to stop construction of the Berlin Wall. President Kennedy's decision to set up a naval quarantine of Cuba was probably the best move once the crisis had become a matter of public knowledge. Within the small group that Kennedy assembled at the White House to discuss how to respond to Khrushchev's gambit, there were those who believed an air strike at the missile sites offered the best approach. Since representatives of the air force could not guarantee complete success, however, members of the committee discussed the need for a US invasion of Cuba and removal of Castro and his Soviet advisors.

Both the United States and the Soviet Union saw the seriousness of the situation and acted to defuse it. There was a great deal of behind-the-scenes consultation, particularly on the part of the Americans. A serious dilemma arose when Khrushchev's first letter, an emotional and personal appeal from one veteran of World War II to another (Kennedy), was followed by a second, tougher letter probably authored by the Politburo and signed by Khrushchev.

The dilemma was resolved when Kennedy and his advisors decided to respond to the first letter while simply ignoring the existence of the second letter.

Khrushchev agreed to remove the missiles in return for a pledge by the United States that it would not invade Cuba and an agreement, not publicized at the time, that the United States would remove its missiles from Turkey. After the crisis, the two powers moved rapidly in the direction of détente. A direct telephone line, the "hot line," was installed between the White House in Washington, DC, and the Kremlin in Moscow. In 1963, the Nuclear Test Ban Treaty was signed originally by the United States, the Soviet Union, and Great Britain and later by most other nations. Even when America began to play an active role in the conflict in Vietnam, détente continued. The Soviet Union continued to support the forces of North Vietnam but did what it could to prevent the war from widening. The United States, for its part, supported the forces of South Vietnam while pursuing policies designed to keep the Soviet Union as well as the People's Republic of China (PRC), loosely known as "Communist China," from taking a more active role in the war. The United States was caught in a particularly delicate situation wherein certain measures that might lead to military victory over the North Vietnamese had to be rejected for fear they would inadvertently bring the Soviet Union or the PRC directly into the war.

Conclusion

By 1967, Europe had recovered from the war and had broken much new ground. Industry had become the major factor in almost every European economy, even in Eastern and Southern Europe. The nature of industry was changing as well, especially in north-western Europe, where the emphasis was on the production of consumer goods, the development of new products, and the use of new machines and techniques. Standards of living had surpassed prewar levels. Societies were becoming more homogenous, even in Western Europe, where ideology did not work toward egalitarianism as such.

In politics, both east and west, governments became more involved in social and economic issues, resulting in the creation or extension of some kind of welfare state. Greater governmental intervention in economic matters meant not only increased regulation but also government-owned sectors of the economy in most states. Of course, in Eastern Europe, the private sector was almost completely squeezed out.

The changing political spectrum had resulted in the virtual disappearance of the prewar type of liberal or conservative party. Two major developments were the emergence of Christian Democratic parties, which dominated the first two decades of politics in Italy and Germany, and reform-minded, nonrevolutionary Socialist parties in several states. In many ways, the Christian Democratic parties, attracting members with widely differing interests, replaced the old conservative parties. The Socialists were a partial replacement for the liberals, although far more enthusiastic about government intervention. Politics was less polarized than in the period between the wars. Even the large number of votes given to Communist parties in Italy and France and occasional appearances of right-wing protest movements did not alter the essential moderation of West European politics.

Politics had changed drastically in Eastern Europe with communist states subservient to Moscow (with the exception of Yugoslavia and, later, both Albania and Romania), taking the place of the mostly authoritarian right-wing governments that had existed in the 1930s. In the west, parliamentary democracies existed in all states but Spain and Portugal, which still had 1930s-style authoritarian governments, and Greece, which had a military dictatorship for a brief period.

Europe writ large had not yet made itself into a third great power. In fact, it was actually losing rather than gaining ground in world affairs, as its steadily eroding colonial situation demonstrated. But it had managed to find its own way. European civilization had done far more than merely survive. It had undergone something of a renaissance, becoming by the late 1960s both a guide and an example, in terms of social policy and relations with Third World countries, for the United States and the Soviet Union.

References

Judt, Tony. 2005. *Postwar: A History of Europe Since 1945*. New York: The Penguin Press.

Wylie, Laurence. 1974. *Village in the Vaucluse*, 3rd ed. Cambridge, MA: Harvard University Press.

Further Reading

Fulbrook, Mary. 2009. *A History of Germany 1918–2008: The Divided Nation*, 3rd ed. Malden: John Wiley & Sons. An up-to-date history of Germany by one of the leading scholars in the field.

Ginsborg, Paul. 2003. *A History of Contemporary Italy: Society and Politics, 1943–1988*. New York: Palgrave Macmillan. An excellent overview.

Hoffman, Stanley, et al. 1965. *In Search of France*. New York: Harper Torchbooks. A classic discussion of many aspects of French life after World War II.

Judt, Tony. 2005. *Postwar: A History of Europe since 1945*. New York: The Penguin Press. A masterful discussion of postwar Europe, full of penetrating insights.

Milward, Alan. 1984. *The Reconstruction of Western Europe 1945–1951*. London: Methuen. An excellent study of the difficult first several years after the war in Western Europe.

Rothschild, Joseph and Nancy M. Wingfield. 2007. *Return to Diversity: A Political History of East Central Europe since World War II*, 4th ed. New York: Oxford University Press. A scholarly, country-by-country survey of the history of postwar Eastern Europe.

Turner, Henry Ashby. 1992. *The Two Germanies Since 1945: Germany from Partition to Reunification*, rev. ed. New Haven: Yale University Press. A succinct, instructive review of the parallel histories of West Germany and East Germany.

Wegs, J. Robert and Robert Ladrech. 2006. *Europe Since 1945: A Concise History*, 5th ed. New York: Palgrave Macmillan. A dependable, well-informed survey.

Part 4

Overview: 1968–Present

THE REVOLUTIONARY YEARS of 1968 and 1989 were bookends for a period of consolidation and attempted reform in response to dissatisfaction with the political, economic, social, and cultural arrangements in both Eastern and Western Europe. The period also featured efforts to deal with rapidly changing geopolitical, economic, and technological realities on a global scale. In the aftermath of the Cold War in the 1990s, Europe worked with considerable success to overcome the divisions that had characterized it for the first four decades after World War II and to build on previous accomplishments. It also experienced new and unexpected difficulties, discovering once again that human history is full of surprises.

In the year 1968, at the onset of which everything seemed possible, the radicalism of the 1960s peaked, both in Europe and in the United States. In Western Europe, radicalism reached a high tide in the events of May 1968 in France. For a brief moment, it seemed students and workers would unite to defeat the government of Charles de Gaulle. Not surprisingly, style and youthful enthusiasm were not enough, and de Gaulle and the Fifth Republic prevailed. In Czechoslovakia, Alexander Dubček attempted to renew communism in a reform movement known as the "Prague Spring." Widespread national support and earnest attempts by the Czechs to mollify other members of the

Twentieth-Century Europe: A Brief History, 1900 to the Present, Third Edition.
Michael D. Richards and Paul R. Waibel.
© 2014 John Wiley & Sons, Inc. Published 2014 by John Wiley & Sons, Inc.

Warsaw Treaty Organization failed to prevent the Soviet Union, strongly backed by East Germany and Poland, from crushing the movement in August. The 1960s in the United States featured widespread protest against the Vietnam War and a massive Civil Rights Movement. In 1968, the assassination of the civil rights leader Martin Luther King Jr. and presidential hopeful Robert F. Kennedy, race riots in major American cities, and widespread protest against the US participation in the Vietnam War on college campuses across the country left the American people badly divided and influenced the foreign policy of the nation throughout most of the 1970s, but it was the Civil Rights Movement that brought about fundamental change in American society.

By way of contrast, 1989 was a year in which the impossible suddenly—and surprisingly quite simply—happened. Large numbers of people in several Eastern European countries responded publically and courageously to economic and political systems that were visibly failing. The disproportionate emphasis on heavy industry had locked communist economic systems into an economic strategy that resisted innovation and failed to match the levels of material comfort achieved in Western Europe. Hollowed out economically and led in many cases by gerontocracies, the Eastern European satellite nations of the Soviet Union either gave way to popular discontent, as was the case in Poland and Hungary, or resisted ineffectively before completely losing control, as in the case of East Germany, Czechoslovakia, and Bulgaria. Government efforts to hold on to power in Romania led to considerable bloodshed, ending in the trial and televised execution of Nicolae Ceaușescu (1918–1989) and his wife. Perhaps the single most important result of the revolutions was the unification of the two Germanies the following year. This event not only signaled a definitive end to World War II but also marked a resolution of the German Question, one that had haunted Europe since the formation of the German Empire in 1871.

Between the revolutionary years of 1968 and 1989, Western Europe experienced a period of economic dislocation and political turmoil. The oil price shocks of the 1970s caused considerable problems in the West, but the economic crisis of this period had more deeply rooted causes. By the late 1960s, the postwar boom had played itself out. The continuous growth of the welfare state by this time had become a burden to the economy. The economy itself shifted from an industrial focus to one of service. It also shifted to reflect the increasingly global nature of economic affairs. The flexibility of Western European economies and the advantages provided by institutions like the European Community (EC) helped bring about recovery in the 1980s. Government policy, particularly that developed in Britain under Prime Minister Margaret Thatcher, also helped. Her neoconservative policies of privatization, union busting, and downsizing of government were mirrored by President Ronald Reagan's approach in the United States and adopted in varying ways on the continent. Along with economic recovery, however, came a more clear division of society into winners and losers, as reflected in particular in the persistence of high rates of unemployment, even after economic recovery.

The Cold War featured first a period of détente in the 1970s that continued and expanded developments from the previous decade, and then a brief revival of its worst features. The Soviet Union bore the major share of responsibility for said revival, primarily because of its military intervention in Afghanistan. President Ronald Reagan, an old Cold Warrior, took a hardline approach in the early 1980s. The activities of his administration, highly visible in the Caribbean and Central America, also worked in the Middle East and Central Asia to create the foundations of twenty-first-century foreign policy dilemmas in those regions. Under the circumstances, it was nothing short of miraculous that Soviet Premier Mikhail Gorbachev succeeded by the late 1980s in convincing Western leaders to work on defusing what by the 1980s was a more than four-decade-old Cold War.

The end to the Cold War came as a result of two events: the revolutions of 1989, which transformed the former satellites of the Soviet Union, and the collapse of the Soviet Union itself in 1991. In the Soviet Union, Mikhail Gorbachev tried a variety of new policies, principally *glasnost* (openness) and *perestroika* (restructuring), to open up a new era. The fundamental contradiction between perestroika and a powerful and conservative bureaucratic establishment, together with the desires of several of the republics in the Soviet Union to gain independence, created a stalemate that probably could not have been resolved. The attempted coup in August 1991 by communist hardliners led to the collapse of the Soviet Union and the emergence of Boris Yeltsin, the hero of the resistance to the coup, as the leading political figure in the Soviet Union.

In the 1990s, four quite different developments shaped the European experience. The disintegration of Yugoslavia, while not entirely unexpected, had deeply tragic results. It stemmed to a large extent from the political ambitions of one man, Slobodan Milosevic, but played additionally on nationalist passions and ethnic rivalries. The result was a series of wars and civil wars, ethnic cleansings, and interventions by NATO forces leading to an uneasy peace, particularly in Bosnia–Herzegovina and Kosovo.

Less obviously tragic but much more central to the future of Europe was the failure of the Russian Republic, the major successor state to the Soviet Union, to find its way. Under Yeltsin, Russia fell increasingly under the power of the oligarchs. They took advantage of the new economic circumstances to amass enormous wealth and political power. At the same time, Russia squandered resources and good will in failed military campaigns that attempted to restore Russian dominance in the breakaway Chechen Republic. The record under Vladimir Putin, now in his third term as president, has been mixed. Putin has provided leadership and profited from the improved economic picture created by the high price of oil, but this has come at the expense of a somewhat stunted democracy.

On the plus side, in 1993, the European Community transformed itself into the European Union (EU), which moved simultaneously toward wider and deeper versions of the old institution. At the end of 2004, the EU had grown to 25 members, with several other prospective members in the wings. It had also become far more carefully integrated. In many respects, the EU as it passed its 50th anniversary looked to be the most outstanding European achievement since World War II. Recent events, such as the Greek debt crisis and problematic economies in Italy and Spain, have, however, called this achievement into question. It may be that the EU will need to develop even deeper integration in order to deal with the fiscal crisis. Interestingly, Germany lies once more at the center of the question. As by far the most powerful European economy, it will have to agree to and largely fund the fiscal oversight for the Eurozone that appears to be necessary.

Finally, the 1990s and the early years of the twenty-first century witnessed the development of a new kind of terrorism, one based on Islamic fundamentalism. To some extent, the new terrorism stems from the continuing quarrel between the Israelis and the Palestinians. Another and more important source derives from American involvement in the Iran–Iraq War of the 1980s, the Soviet intervention in Afghanistan in the same period, and what may now be seen as the First Gulf War ("Desert Storm") in 1991. The highly visible presence of the United States in the Middle East in the 1990s led to a series of attacks on the United States in that decade and the first part of the twenty-first century, culminating in the tragic events of September 11, 2001. The American response to date has included invasions of Afghanistan and Iraq and a continuing effort to destroy the terrorist group *Al-Qaeda* (The Base). Although the war in Iraq has come to an end and the United States has determined to turn the fight against the Taliban (Islamic fundamentalist) forces over to the Afghanis (with some continuing presence of NATO forces), the current situation in the Middle East with the Arab Spring of 2011 and the current civil war in Syria makes it likely that problems in the region will continue to require the attention of Europe and the United States for years to come.

The development of a worldwide terrorist movement based on Islamic fundamentalism underscores the global context within which Europe now operates. Faced with its own internal difficulties, which include the problems of the Russian Republic, the continuing efforts in Eastern Europe to transform the political and economic spheres, demographic changes that include both an increasingly aging population and large-scale immigration in Western Europe, and the economic challenges the EU faces in a global economy, Europe must also contend with the tides of world affairs. These include, among others, the threat of nuclear proliferation in Iran and North Korea; the emergence of new economic powers such as the People's Republic of China, India, and Brazil; and the large question mark of environmental trends, in particular climate change.

Europe has long since ceased to dominate world affairs, yet it clearly still plays an important, even crucial, role in them. Most European countries have now achieved levels of political stability and economic prosperity that will allow their populations to take on the roles of wise counselors and arbitrators. Even if the European house is not completely in order, its inhabitants have the wherewithal to help the rest of the world contend with its problems.

Europe's altered role in the world a little more than a decade past the end of the millennium is mirrored in its intellectual and cultural history since the end of World War II. In many ways, the changes that have occurred in both elite and popular culture grew out of changing assumptions about the nature of reality that were under way already before and after World War I.

War I. The shifting philosophical sands after World War II from existentialism through structuralism to deconstructionism resulted from the attempt to make sense out of a world in which all of the old values and certainties had either failed or vanished. To the philosophers, a universe that rejected the existence of God or any other absolute truth that might provide meaning was a universe increasingly without meaning, either for the universe itself or the people who inhabited it.

As with the philosophers, postwar culture, whether high or popular, struggled to make sense of recent events that included war, a great depression, the Holocaust, and the threat of nuclear annihilation. The artists, musicians, poets, and writers displayed in their creative output the growing sense of alienation and despair and the fragmentation that characterized European civilization in transition. Whether in the fine arts or popular culture, influences from the United States tended to dominate. In the fine arts, this was due in part to the interwar flight of creative individuals before the tidal wave of Nazi and communist oppression. The economic dominance of the United States and the presence of American military forces in Western Europe assured that European popular culture and world popular culture would mimic American trends. American trends continue to have great influence, but the world of culture and intellectual life has become truly global. The ubiquity of the Internet is but one of many factors in this process.

In this globalized world, it is more important than ever to understand in some detail key areas of that world—Europe most definitely being one of them.

10

Metamorphosis
An Era of Revolutionary Change, 1968–1988

Chronology

1968	Events of May in France
	Prague Spring in Czechoslovakia and the Soviet intervention
1969	De Gaulle resigns as president of France
	Willy Brandt forms an SPD-FDP coalition in West Germany
1971	Erich Honecker replaces Walter Ulbricht as party leader in East Germany
1972	Basic treaty between East Germany and West Germany
	Strategic Arms Limitation Treaty (SALT I)
1973	Britain, Ireland, Denmark join the EC
	OPEC creates an oil crisis
1974	Return of democracy in Greece
	Portuguese Revolution

Twentieth-Century Europe: A Brief History, 1900 to the Present, Third Edition.
Michael D. Richards and Paul R. Waibel.
© 2014 John Wiley & Sons, Inc. Published 2014 by John Wiley & Sons, Inc.

1975	Death of Franco and beginning of the return of democracy in Spain
	Helsinki Accords
	First Group of Seven (G-7) meeting
1976	Worker unrest in Poland
1978	Former Christian Democratic premier of Italy Aldo Moro kidnapped and murdered by the Red Brigades
1979	Conservatives under Margaret Thatcher win in Britain
	Soviet military forces invade Afghanistan
1980	Solidarity (Solidarność) gains recognition in Poland
	Death of Tito
1981	Greece joins the EC
	Martial law declared in Poland; Solidarity outlawed
1982	Britain defeats Argentina in the Falklands War
	Brezhnev dies, replaced by Andropov
1984	Andropov dies, replaced by Chernenko
1985	Chernenko dies; Gorbachev becomes the new leader of the Soviet Union
1986	Spain and Portugal join the EC
	Chernobyl nuclear accident

AFTER THE REVOLUTIONS OF 1989, jokes circulated to help explain why the events of that year had such a significant impact on European history in comparison with the radical developments of 1968. As is usually the case, the jokes provided insight into what was otherwise a somewhat mysterious process. One joke asked: "What is the difference between 1968 and 1989?" The answer: "Twenty-one years." While not particularly funny, especially to those who had lived through those 21 years, the joke helped make plain that the events of 1968, at least in the Soviet Bloc, were premature. The time was not yet ripe for something like the Prague Spring.

Another joke asked: "What was communism?" The answer: "The stage of transition from capitalism to capitalism." While it did not turn out to be so simple to reestablish capitalism, much less democratic governments, in Eastern Europe, it was clear that communism had never taken root, not even in East Germany. When given a choice, most people in the Soviet Bloc opted for free enterprise and free elections.

In Western Europe, there was no equivalent to the revolutions of 1989 in Eastern Europe, yet there were significant changes in both politics and the economy. Perhaps the most significant change involved the rise of Thatcherism and its equivalents on the continent. Conservative politicians (and, in some cases, socialist politicians as well) worked to end the continuous growth of the welfare state and to decrease the role of government in the economy. At the same time, Western Europe survived a period of combined economic stagnation and inflation ("stagflation") and moved at the end of the 1980s toward an expanded and more fully integrated European Community.

Radicalism in Western Europe in the Late 1960s

At the end of the 1960s, most Western European countries seemed virtually besieged by radicals questioning political frameworks, social institutions, economic arrangements, and even cultural assumptions. Radicals accused governments of ruling in an authoritarian style at home and of aiding "imperialism" and counterrevolution abroad. They viewed social and economic institutions as consciously contrived to perpetuate political and economic power in the hands of ruling cliques while keeping the masses both ignorant of the true situation through manipulation of the media and satisfied through the production of inexpensive consumer goods. Some saw themselves as part of a worldwide revolutionary movement answering the call of the Cuban revolutionary Che Guevara (1928–1967) for "One, Two, Three . . . . Many Vietnams!" Few identified with the established socialist or communist parties. Some called themselves Maoists or professed to be anarchists. Many had quite limited aims and concentrated in particular on the reform of what they saw as an undemocratic, elitist educational system designed to reinforce and perpetuate the inequities of the larger political and socioeconomic systems. The organized radical movements, much smaller than the number of protesters who might appear at a demonstration, were mostly students and young intellectuals. They varied widely in terms of their impact on existing systems. France was affected far more than any other Western European country. Germany and Italy both confronted large-scale movements but escaped major crises. Britain and the Netherlands had important, if not greatly influential, movements.

In Germany, the German Socialist Student Federation (SDS) protested against the established system with great seriousness. The first major protest was directed against the Shah of Iran, Mohammad Reza Pahlavi (1919–1980), during his visit to West Berlin in 1967. The next focus of SDS attacks was the publications empire of Axel Springer (1912–1985), the influential newspaper and magazine publisher widely regarded as a pillar of conservatism or even counterrevolution. After one of the SDS leaders, Rudi Dutschke (1940–1979), was shot and seriously wounded in April 1968, protests against the Springer empire intensified. Events in Germany in the spring of 1968 were highly dramatic but the government escaped serious challenge. The SDS lacked circumstances similar to France in May, where de Gaulle's policies were widely criticized and student demonstrations brutally suppressed. Student radicals in Germany found themselves isolated from a general public largely satisfied with existing political and economic arrangements.

France in May 1968

What happened in France in May 1968 can scarcely be understood unless the influence of Charles de Gaulle in French affairs between May 1958 and May 1968 is taken into account. The structure of the Fifth Republic gave de Gaulle a position of considerable power. In addition to his constitutional powers, and somewhat like Adenauer in West Germany, de Gaulle overstepped the boundaries, taking actions that no politician without his force of personality and moral stature would have been allowed to carry out. While de Gaulle was preoccupied with foreign affairs and contacts with communist bloc and Third World leaders, domestic problems began to surface. One was the odd contrast between the sophistication of French technology and science and the backwardness of some aspects of life in France, two prime examples being the telephone system and housing. Second, society, if increasingly democratic, was still stratified. The different strata were determined in large part by educational achievement, but the way to an appropriate education was paved with money, family background, and connections. The very bright were co-opted into the system, but the system worked here as in other areas mostly to perpetuate the elites.

The 1965 presidential elections furnished one glaring indication of the level of domestic dissatisfaction. François Mitterrand (1916–1996), leader of the leftist coalition of socialists and communists, forced de Gaulle into a runoff. After prevailing in that contest, de Gaulle continued to govern virtually unchecked, seemingly deaf to the rising clamor of opposition.

The events of May 1968, although based on widespread dissatisfaction and on student grievances, began as a spontaneous reaction to a specific event of little significance: the arrest of a number of students demonstrating against the involvement of the United States in Vietnam. On March 22, a meeting to protest the arrests took place at the University of Nanterre, one of the new universities in the French system. A radical movement called the March 22 Movement came out of the meeting. On May 2, "Anti-Imperialist Day," members of the March 22 Movement, finding themselves locked out of Nanterre, went to the Sorbonne, the best-known part of the University of Paris. The following day, the police violated traditions of academic freedom by coming into the Sorbonne and arresting hundreds of students. This was the beginning of a series of demonstrations and confrontations between students and police in the Latin Quarter of Paris. A climax of sorts came on May 10, the "Night of the Barricades," when events in the streets were described minute-by-minute on national radio. On May 13, more than a million people demonstrated in Paris against the government. The day after, workers seized the Sud Aviation plant. More workers followed their example until, eventually, 10 million were on strike.

Toward the end of May, the government, which had been almost completely ineffective up to that point, dissolved the National Assembly and set a date for elections. De Gaulle, who had been mysteriously out of the country for several hours and had gained the backing of the French military, appealed for "civic action" against a "totalitarian plot." Many French began to worry about the possibility of anarchy or a communist takeover. Even in Paris, where sympathy for the students had been widespread, people were tired of the confusion and the disruptions caused by the ongoing demonstrations and strikes. There was, meanwhile, no consensus among the student radicals as to specific aims and goals. Workers generally wanted only moderate changes, in particular a substantial pay hike. Still, almost no one in the general public liked the idea of a genuine revolution.

French students clash with police in Paris during the events of May 1968 in Paris that came close to bringing down the government of President Charles de Gaulle. AP/Press Association Images

France, closer to revolution in 1968 than any other Western European country, was not, actually, all that close. Government inactivity, coupled with some blunders, had resulted in a situation in which the overthrow of the government seemed possible. Nevertheless, the government still maintained a strong position. It had capable leadership in de Gaulle and, especially, in the premier, Georges Pompidou (1911–1974). In the military and the police, it had an overwhelming monopoly of force. Even the social and economic strains were not as severe as they appeared at first. Despite the drama and color of events, the government could only fail by losing its nerve.

The radicals had little chance. The "system" was the enemy, but there was no agreement as to how to define the system or what program to follow in order to combat or replace it. While people like Daniel Cohn-Bendit (1945–), "Danny the Red" (so named for his hair as much as his politics), actually a German studying in France, caught the imagination of many, most radicals distrusted leaders and ideas about strategy. Operating almost exclusively on the level of tactics, the radicals were lost once the government took the initiative. Additionally, the radicals did not understand the aspirations of those temporarily allied with them, whether those of the working class or the middle class.

The major results of the radical movement were changes in the education system, principally possibilities for revised curricula, less elitist student bodies, and less authoritarian structures of university administration. In reaction to the events of May, many turned back to moderate or conservative parties. Parties on the left tried to appear moderate in order to distance themselves from the radicals. The Communist Party in France, which had done nothing to aid the radicals, found itself simultaneously distrusted by moderates and under heavy fire from the radicals. The year 1968, particularly as it played out in France, was the high point of postwar radicalism in Western Europe. Radicals had gained a hearing, but the sweeping, comprehensive changes they envisioned were not acceptable to most Europeans. Most found life all right as it was and worried more that the economy would cease growing or something else might happen to prevent them from achieving goals they had come to see as realistic possibilities. The contrast with the situation in the United States, where two issues, civil rights and the war in Vietnam, could not be ignored, was striking. (See a discussion of the 1960s in the United States later in this chapter.)

Brezhnev's Russia

In the 1960s and early 1970s, Leonid Brezhnev (1906–1982) ruled the Soviet Union as president and first secretary of the Communist Party in tandem with the premier, Alexei Kosygin (1904–1980). They had to acknowledge, however, the importance of several groups within the Soviet system, the military, the KGB, the governmental bureaucracy, and, of course, the party. Brezhnev and Kosygin wrestled with basically the same kinds of problems that had plagued Khrushchev, an unresponsive and overly centralized economy, unproductive agriculture, and elements in Russian society that enjoyed privileged positions.

Brezhnev, Kosygin, and other members of the Communist Party's Politburo (Executive Committee) steered a course in the 1960s between the arbitrary terror of Stalin and the adventurism of Khrushchev. Although they experimented briefly with ideas calling for a socialist market approach, that is, some attention paid to questions of demand and supply and also profitability of enterprises, their policies were largely conventional and followed two major paths. One emphasized highly concentrated efforts to succeed at particular tasks, most of which had a military payoff. A good example would be the Soviet space effort, which was not intended to race the United States to the moon but rather aimed at a different goal: creating a space station. The second approach emphasized increasing the number or amount of various components of an industry: more capital, a larger number of workers, a greater supply of energy, and so forth. The first approach achieved some amazing successes but at a high cost. The second worked well as long as larger numbers of workers or greater amounts of capital could make a tangible difference in a particular industry. What doomed the second approach by the 1960s were, first, the rapid increases in productivity outside the Soviet Bloc and, second, the rapid changes in technology, which quickly began to alter the very definition of a modern economy.

By the early 1960s, the position of the Soviet consumer had begun to improve, with refrigerators and television sets now being items people might finally be able to afford to purchase. The improvements over earlier periods in Soviet history were heartening, but to those able to make comparisons with the consumer economies of Western Europe or the United States, the contrast was startling. Soviet consumer goods tended to be scarce, expensive, and of poor quality. Housing in the cities was difficult to find even 20 years after the war; most of what was available was cramped and poorly constructed. Long lines to purchase almost anything were customary. One estimate is that Soviet women spent as much as two hours a day waiting in lines.

Some had it better. The "new class" of party officials, high-level bureaucrats, military personnel, technocrats, scientists, ballet and movie stars, world-class athletes, and some literary and intellectual luminaries had not merely higher incomes, which actually was not that much of an advantage, but a range of privileges unavailable to the ordinary citizen. These included a *dacha* (a cottage or even a rather large house in the countryside) for use on weekends or vacations, special stores with a wider selection than ordinary stores, special clinics for medical treatment without crowds and long waits, official cars for private use, and an "old boy" network that opened up educational and career opportunities to the sons and daughters of the prominent.

Growth rates began to fall in the 1950s and 1960s. By the early 1970s, the Soviet economy was scarcely growing at all. Agriculture remained a major problem despite a sizable investment by the state in the early 1970s. To some, the answer seemed to lie in technology transfers from the West. Certainly, part of the motivation for détente was the idea that if the Soviet Union played by the "rules," it could expect to receive help from Western Europe, the United States, and Japan in helping it bridge technological gaps and overcome obstacles to rapid economic growth.

In addition to economic problems, the Soviet Union faced growing problems with dissidents, some of which emerged in response to the neo-Stalinism that characterized the Soviet Union by the end of the 1960s. Although the Stalin cult of personality and the practice of arbitrary terror were not revived, Brezhnev became increasingly the center of Soviet politics, and Yuri Andropov (1914–1984) as head of the KGB worked out sophisticated methods utilizing the criminal justice system and mental health facilities to deal with anyone considered troublesome by the regime. A major dissident was Aleksandr Solzhenitsyn (1918–2008), whose short novel *One Day in the Life of Ivan Denisovich* was a revelation to many Russians in the early 1960s. The "one day" of the novel took Ivan Denisovich, who was a *Zek* or political prisoner, through his experiences in a labor camp in the GULAG, the Soviet prison system. Solzhenitsyn drew on personal experiences and revealed to many Russians who might have only heard rumors about the GULAG what a brutal institution it was. Other than *One Day* and a few short stories, Solzhenitsyn was not allowed to publish in the 1960s. He was also not permitted to accept the Nobel Prize for literature in 1970. Finally, he was deported from the Soviet Union in 1974.

Andrei Sakharov (1921–1989), an eminent Russian physicist and father of the Russian H-bomb, was even more important because of his work with the Committee for Human Rights, an unofficial nongovernmental organization (NGO) that monitored human rights violations in the Soviet Union. Dissidents were restricted generally to *samizdat* (literally "self-publishing"—hand- or typewritten manuscripts circulated illegally) or to occasional interviews with western journalists as ways to spread their views. Critics of the Soviet system as such were relatively isolated and unimportant in Soviet politics, despite the attention paid them by the West. More important, and treated even more harshly, were representatives of the nationalist movements in Lithuania, the Ukraine, and elsewhere. Also, some groups were suspect because of their religious beliefs, among these Russian Baptists and Jehovah's Witnesses. Finally, Soviet Jews were often harassed and their efforts to emigrate were generally not well received.

The Prague Spring

Elsewhere within the Soviet Bloc, there were attempts to make the Soviet model of communism work better than it did in the Soviet Union. In some cases, mild deviations from the model had been allowed. Poland had retreated from collectivized agriculture in the 1950s and enjoyed in the 1960s a much more productive agricultural sector. Hungary, in part to help people forget the events of 1956, was allowed to experiment with different economic structures and to seek some trade ties with Western Europe. East Germany, despite Soviet restrictions on the economy, had made considerable economic progress in the 1960s, in part because people realized after the construction of the Berlin Wall that there was no alternative to life in East Germany.

Czechoslovakia was a major disappointment. It had been an urbanized, industrialized state even before World War II. By the early 1960s, the Czech economy had deteriorated badly and the political system was regarded as repressive and ineffective. Communist leadership, particularly that of Antonín Novotný (1904–1975), first secretary of the party, increasingly came under criticism. Questions about the fairness of the political trials held between 1949 and 1954 kept coming up within the Czech Communist Party. Slovak communists, who believed, as did Slovaks generally, that Slovakia had been neglected, were especially active in pressing for party reform and a change in leaders.

In January 1968, Novotny was replaced as first secretary by Alexander Dubček (1921–1992), a Slovak and a leader of the moderate reform impulse. Dubcek moved first to liberalize the economy by decentralizing it, increasing the emphasis on consumer goods and on investments in Slovakia, and establishing more trade with the West. He also lifted censorship and encouraged cultural and intellectual life. Actually, the Prague Spring, a political reform effort that initially appeared in the Communist Party, owed its existence in large part to a kind of renaissance in the cinema, theater, and literature starting in 1966. Czech writers and filmmakers in particular had drawn the interest of avant-garde circles in Europe by the mid-1960s. By 1968, this renaissance and the impetus for reform within the party had come together in an impressive, seemingly irresistible, movement for change.

By late spring, the reform movement began to get out of hand. The growth of clubs and discussion groups threatened the communist monopoly of political power. The government granted freedom of speech and press. In a preview of the Russian experience with *glasnost* or openness in the late 1980s, Czechs began to explore their recent history. Dubĉek sketched a path to democratic socialism over several years and called for "socialism with a human face." Ludvík Vaculík published a frank criticism of the Czech Communist Party in late June, *The Two Thousand Words*. Some Czech communists began to have second thoughts about the Prague Spring even as others looked to the Party Congress scheduled for September, at which a reform program was to be presented. In contrast to the events of May, there were no crowds on the streets or barricades but, instead, sustained and intense discussion.

Meanwhile, the Russians, East Germans, and Poles grew apprehensive about the movement. Essentially, they had to decide whether the Czechs resembled Poland or Hungary in 1956. The Czechs held two meetings in the summer of 1968, the first with the Soviet Union and the second with representatives of most of the member nations of the Warsaw Pact. Finally, the Soviets, Poles, and East Germans invaded Czechoslovakia on August 20, paratroopers landing on the tarmac of and taking over the Prague airport and long lines of tanks and trucks driving over the border into Czechoslovakia. Czechs tried to block the invasion by such acts as removal of road signs. Demonstrations followed and a few people even set themselves on fire in protest, but no one wanted a repetition of the Hungarian Revolution. Brezhnev tried to justify the action by stating that socialist countries had an obligation to come to the aid of a brother socialist country when it was threatened by "counterrevolutionary forces," the so-called Brezhnev Doctrine.

The Prague Spring was a turning point that was not allowed to turn. It is debatable, of course, that even the Czechs could have taken their Soviet-style political and economic system and formed it into a real democratic socialism. Nonetheless, they were more likely to be able to do so than any other satellite country. Dubček did not have the same vision or capacities as Mikhail Gorbachev would have in the late 1980s, but Czechoslovakia might have been a better country in which to attempt Gorbachev-style reforms (see the discussion of Gorbachev and the Soviet Union later in this chapter).

The Soviet Union removed Dubcek and other reformers from power. By the spring of 1969, an orthodox communist regime under Gustav Husák (1913–1991) controlled the country. Ironically, efforts by the Czech communists to construct what some termed "socialism with a human face" failed in part because of the enthusiasm of many participants in the reform movement. They did not sufficiently take into account the rising anxiety of the leaders of the Soviet Union, East Germany, and Poland. Mainly, however, the leaders of these states feared infection from the Czech reform virus. Husák, moderate in comparison to the pro-Soviet hardliners, was successful in establishing pragmatic policies in Czechoslovakia in the early 1970s. He was not very successful, however, in causing Czechs and Slovaks to forget the promise of 1968. The most prominent group that continued to keep the spirit of the Prague Spring alive was Charter 77, which produced a document early in 1977 that criticized the government for failing to implement the human rights provisions of documents that it had agreed to previously. The regime punished those involved through a range of actions from dismissing people from their jobs to imprisoning them. A leading member of Charter 77 was the Czech playwright Vaclav Havel (1936–2011), who became president of Czechoslovakia after the Velvet Revolution of 1989.

Ironically, the leadership in both East Germany and Poland changed soon after the Soviet invasion ended the Prague Spring. Walter Ulbricht was replaced by Erich Honecker (1912–1994) in 1970 and Wladyslaw Gomulka by Edward Gierek (1913–2001) that same year.

Willy Brandt and *Ostpolitik*

If the Prague Spring might be seen as a turning point not taken, the *Ostpolitik* (Eastern policy) instituted by Willy Brandt in the early 1970s created a small but important bridge between East and West that both could accept with some degree of comfort. Brandt had been the Social Democratic mayor of Berlin at the height of the Berlin Crisis at the end of the 1950s. In the 1960s, he led the party into a grand coalition with the Christian Democratic Union (CDU).

In 1969, in a coalition with the Free Democrats (FDP), the SPD (German Social Democratic Party) became the governing party. The Ostpolitik, part of the larger détente between East and West, established a dialogue between West Germany and East Germany. In 1970, Brandt negotiated treaties with Poland and the Soviet Union and then in 1972 an agreement that led to East Germany and West Germany according each other diplomatic recognition. In particular, West Germany recognized the Polish–German boundaries. A related agreement in 1971 among the four powers that had occupied Germany after the war protected the rights of those powers in Berlin and also West Germany's particular interest in the city. All of the agreements taken together stabilized the status of both West Germany and East Germany and eliminated a major cause of the Cold War, that is, the failure to reach a postwar settlement that would prevent the possibility of German militarism reviving.

Brandt, who was awarded the Nobel Peace Prize for the Ostpolitik and what it had led to, enjoyed less success in terms of progress toward social reform in Germany or European unification. Ironically, given Brandt's success with the Ostpolitik, he felt compelled to resign in 1974 after it came to light that a trusted adviser had all along been an East German mole.

The 1960s in the United States

As dramatic as the 1960s had been in Europe, events in the United States were not only equally dramatic but also far more consequential. One, the Civil Rights Movement, changed basic aspects of American life profoundly. The other, the Vietnam War and the protests against it, was enormously divisive at the time but had fewer lasting effects.

The Civil Rights Movement in the United States

World War II, with the emphasis on liberating peoples from National Socialism and Japanese militarism, made the maintenance of segregation difficult to justify, but it was nevertheless successfully defended. In the late 1940s and early 1950s, African Americans and their white supporters undertook brave but largely ineffective efforts to challenge both informal and de jure forms of racial segregation, in the US South and also in other parts of the country. Then, in the mid-1950s, two events transpired that began to create conditions in which the practice of segregation could be successfully challenged. The first was the Supreme Court decision in the case of *Brown v. the Board of Education of Topeka* in 1954. Segregation in public schools had been based on the doctrine of "separate but equal." Chief Justice Earl Warren (1891–1974), as quoted in Patterson (1996), declared, "In the field of public education, the doctrine of 'separate but equal' has no place. Separate educational facilities are inherently unequal." The second event was the Montgomery, Alabama, bus boycott in 1955 and 1956 and the emergence of Martin Luther King Jr. (1929–1968) as a charismatic national leader of the Civil Rights Movement.

Desegregation of schools proceeded slowly and King's Southern Christian Leadership Conference (SCLC) seemed to lose momentum at the end of the 1950s. The Civil Rights Movement was re-energized by the nonviolent, "civil-disobedience" tactics of sit-ins beginning with the sit-in at the lunch counter of a Woolworth department store in Greensboro, North Carolina, on the afternoon of February 1, 1960, by four freshmen from the nearby all-black North Carolina A&T College. More such sit-ins in other parts of the country led later that year to the formation of the Student Nonviolent Coordinating Committee (SNCC). In 1961, the federal government began to be drawn into desegregation issues when another activist civil rights organization, CORE (Congress of Racial Equality), sent volunteer riders on interstate buses through the South to desegregate bus terminals. The question now became how the administration of President John F. Kennedy would respond to the Civil Rights Movement. The administration not only included John Kennedy (1917–1963) as president but also his brother, Robert Kennedy (1925–1968), as attorney general.

The turning point came in Birmingham, Alabama, in 1963. There, Reverend Fred Shuttlesworth (1922–2011), a courageous local civil rights leader, aided King in his latest protest, in which he encouraged the black citizens of the city to boycott downtown stores during the Easter shopping season. (African American protest could not hurt local politicians, because blacks were largely disenfranchised through "Jim Crow" voting regulations, but local merchants would feel the sting of the boycott.) Inadvertent assistance came from Eugene "Bull" Connor (1897–1973), the public safety commissioner of Birmingham. Connor eventually turned fire hoses on the peaceful demonstrators, which included women and children, and even let his police officers menace them with their police dogs. This made for particularly disturbing images that found their way into not only newspapers throughout the nation but also onto the nightly TV news programs. Birmingham galvanized the Kennedy administration into preparing a civil rights bill.

Some months afterward, on August 28, 1963, the Civil Rights Movement reached a high point in the March on Washington, DC, and King's famous "I Have a Dream" speech at the culmination of the march on the steps of the Lincoln Memorial. Toward the end of the speech, King departed from his prepared text and began to preach. What followed were lines that galvanized the large crowd:

> I have a dream that one day this nation will rise up and live out the true meaning of its creed: "We hold these truths to be self-evident—that all men are created equal."

> I have a dream that one day on the red hills of Georgia the sons of former slaves and the sons of former slaveowners will be able to sit down together at the table of brotherhood.

> . . . when we let freedom ring. . .we will be able to speed up that day when all God's children, black men and white men, Jews and Gentiles, Protestants and Catholics, will be able to join hands and sing in the words of that old Negro spiritual, "Free at last! Free at last! Thank God almighty, we are free at last!" (as quoted in the online American Rhetoric 2013.)

Although King's speech was widely admired, the legislation the Kennedy administration had prepared probably would not have been passed by Congress. Instead, Kennedy's assassination on November 22, 1963, created a situation in which his successor, Lyndon Baines Johnson (1908–1973), one of the most skilled legislators of the twentieth century, was able to push through the Civil Rights Act of 1964 and the Voting Rights Act of 1965. Although the Civil Rights Movement was far from done, these two landmark pieces of legislation did much to change American assumptions and behavior related to race relations. The United States in the early twenty-first century, while far from being a postracial society, is a completely different society from that of the segregated 1940s and 1950s.

King, shortly before he was assassinated in 1968, had begun to speak out against the Vietnam War. Other Americans, too, began to have reservations about the American involvement in what was essentially a civil war in a tiny country in Southeast Asia. This involvement had begun as support of the French efforts in the 1950s to defeat the Viet Minh. After the French departed, leaving Vietnam divided between North and South Vietnam, the United States stepped in to support the ostensibly "democratic" government of the republic of South Vietnam in its conflict with the communist government of North Vietnam under its charismatic leader, Ho Chi Minh. Under the Eisenhower and Kennedy administrations, support for South Vietnam had consisted of the sending of American military "advisers" and military supplies. President Kennedy had greatly increased the number of advisers, which by the end of 1963 numbered approximately 17,000. It is impossible to know how Kennedy would have gone on to handle the evolving Vietnam situation, especially if he had been elected to a second term. There are tantalizing indications that he was considering ending American involvement in his second term.

There was, however, no second term for President Kennedy. An assassin's bullet had seen to that. Instead, President Johnson, who was elected to a full term in 1964, pursued the war in Vietnam under the assumption that if the South Vietnam "domino" were to fall to a communist rival, then other such Southeast Asian dominos were sure to follow suit. Reading what he thought were the lessons of history, Johnson, as quoted in Patterson (1996), said, "I am not going to lose Vietnam. I am not going to be the President who saw Southeast Asia go the way China went."

The issue in Vietnam involved not only what some saw as American imperialism but also the impact of the military draft. Between 1964 and 1973, the years the United States was most heavily involved in the war in Vietnam, nearly 12 million Americans served in the armed services, slightly more than 2 million servicemen went to Vietnam, and 1.6 million of them saw combat. This was out of a total of 26.8 million Americans who came of draft age during this period. Although the number in harm's way was a small minority of those eligible for the draft, it created great uncertainty among those eligible and great anxiety among a much larger portion of the American population. It also appeared that the draft operated unfairly in that the white sons of the middle class and the wealthy could get deferments or safe appointments in the National Guard. Those who served in the American army in Vietnam were disproportionally poor and minorities. This made the issue of the Vietnam War an especially divisive issue in the late 1960s and early 1970s.

The issue reached a peak of sorts in 1968 in the aftermath of the Tet Offensive, an unsuccessful effort by North Vietnamese military forces and their Viet Cong allies in the south to challenge the United States and South Vietnam in the cities. Although militarily a defeat, the Tet Offensive was a propaganda coup in that it had caught the combined US–South Vietnamese forces by surprise and rendered hollow all the pronouncements US brass had recently made about lights at the end of the tunnel in the war. In the war of "search and destroy," a war of attrition, the North Vietnamese and their allies were far from beaten. The "credibility gap" seemed impossible to close. The so-called wise men, foreign policy experts from past administrations, advised President Johnson that Vietnam was a sinkhole with no end in sight. On March 31, 1968, he ended a speech on Vietnam by indicating that he would not seek or accept the nomination of his party for president in the upcoming elections of 1970. It was left to Johnson's successor as president, Richard Nixon (1913–1994), and his national security advisor and later secretary of state, Henry Kissinger (1923–), to come to terms with the Vietnamese, North and South, in 1973. Although Nixon had campaigned in 1968 claiming that he had a plan to end the Vietnam War, he actually had no such plan. Instead, he spent almost his entire first term trying to find what he called "peace with honor." In so doing, he expanded the war with an incursion into neighboring Cambodia in 1970, which had as a side effect the rise to power in Cambodia in 1975 of the brutal Pol Pot regime. Altogether, more than two million people, mostly Cambodians and Vietnamese, died while Nixon and Kissinger delayed the inevitable.

Where the Civil Rights Movement had undoubtedly changed the United States for the better, the Vietnam War and the fierce protest against it had weakened the United States both domestically and in terms of foreign policy. President Johnson's domestic agenda known as his Great Society legislation, particularly the passage of the Medicare and Medicaid bills in 1965, did accomplish much good, but involvement in the Vietnam War was an important distraction and the cost and divisiveness of the war a severe burden on the economy and the social fabric of the nation. The Vietnam War itself resulted in a hesitant approach to foreign policy questions in the 1970s, as leaders were reluctant to risk another large commitment of men and materiel.

The Price of Oil

The oil price shock of 1973 acted as a catalyst to set off a decade of economic problems that explains much of the pessimism and lack of political will marking the 1970s and early 1980s. The Yom Kippur War of 1973 between Israel and several Arab states (Egypt, Syria, Jordan, Iraq) provided the context for the first oil price shock. OPEC (Organization of the Petroleum Exporting Countries), founded in 1960, had lacked influence until the Arab-nation members of the organization persuaded the other member nations to impose an oil embargo on states that supported Israel in the 1973 war. Soon after the announcement of the embargo, oil prices worldwide increased to four times the previous level, and the evening news began to fill with images of long lines at gas stations and deserted highways, both in Western Europe and in the United States.

Even before the oil price shock of 1973, the western part of Europe had experienced some problems with inflation. By 1973, inflation was rampant, and the oil crunch simply made it worse. It was a prime example of one in a series of structural problems European economies faced. The end of the long postwar boom was perhaps the main contributing factor. Reconstruction was largely complete in the west, and people had bought their fill of houses, automobiles, and durable goods like refrigerators. Consumption could not, however, continue to expand indefinitely, especially after the increase in prices of all kinds of manufactured items caused by the jump in the price of energy.

The growth of the welfare state was another important factor. In most countries in Western Europe, it had reached a point at which it was straining national economies. As the economy slowed down, unemployment, which had been very low in the 1960s, began to rise. Western Europe was caught in a paradox: an inflation meant high prices and interest rates, a recession meant large-scale unemployment. Stagflation was the ungainly term some used to describe the situation of an economic downturn combined with spiking inflation. Finally, if the situation were not complicated enough, Europe and other parts of the urbanized, industrialized world experienced a technological revolution in the 1970s and 1980s, which by the end of the period had created an economy radically different from the postwar industrial economy based on heavy industry.

The Welfare State

Leo Tolstoy's opening lines in *Anna Karenina* might be applied to European welfare states in the 1970s: "All happy families are like one another; each unhappy family is unhappy in its own way." Welfare states by the late 1970s were all unhappy families.

As mentioned in Chapter 9, the welfare state system has deep roots in the Germany of the 1880s and the Great Britain in the decade before World War I. The prototype of the modern welfare state, however, was Sweden in the 1930s. After World War II, there was consensus in most European countries about the need to ensure the basic necessities of life (food, clothing, shelter, education, and health care) and to guard against catastrophes such as unemployment, injury, and illness. There was particular concern about mothers, infants, and children on the one hand and the retired on the other. While the aims of most nations were similar, the means to accomplish them diverged considerably.

The British system has become synonymous with the welfare state. This is not, however, accurate, since not every European country has a National Health Service or a social security system operated entirely by the state. Still, most Western European countries offered citizens free or virtually free health care and family allowances. Workers' income was covered in case of injury or other disability and in case of unemployment. Some provisions were made for the construction of low-cost or public housing. Education, which by the 1970s had become far more widely available even at the university level, was either free or provided for nominal fees.

A major difference among the various systems concerned who paid for services. In Britain and the Scandinavian countries, the state, that is, taxpayers, paid most of the costs. In West Germany, employers and employees covered 80 percent of the costs. In France and Italy, employers were responsible for about two-thirds of the costs.

By the 1980s, the welfare state not only existed to ensure an adequate foundation for people's lives and to guard against the unexpected disaster but also to provide a range of amenities that included parks, libraries, cultural facilities, and subsidies for artists and writers. Additionally, each generation growing up in the system considered what had been offered to them all their lives as an entitlement and expected the system to be further improved.

A final factor that convinced many that the welfare state had to be revised might be subsumed under the term "permissive society." Many critics of the welfare state regarded it as having robbed large groups of people of initiative and self-reliance. Others unfairly blamed the welfare state for new attitudes toward sex and drug use and for problems such as increasing rates of juvenile delinquency. The apparent rise in taxes was more a product of life in a highly industrialized and urbanized society than the existence of the welfare state as such, but whatever the real deficiencies of the welfare state, it became in the 1980s a major target for a new breed of conservative politicians determined to meet head-on the social and economic ills of modern society in Western Europe.

Terrorism

Adding to the complicated mix of social and economic issues confronting Europe in the 1970s, at that point, a new and highly disturbing phenomenon emerged and had the effect of making the situation appear a good deal worse than it was. Not only did the terrorists themselves seem to be an affront to constitutional systems, but governments in their response to the challenges terrorist attacks presented on occasion did more damage to civil and human rights than had the terrorists.

Terrorism on the left was largely an outgrowth of the failures and frustrations of the 1960s. When revolution had not occurred at the end of that decade, some radicals turned to terrorism: bombing, kidnapping, and murder. The best known of these groups were the *Brigade Rosa* (the Red Brigades) in Italy and the RAF (the *Rote Armee Fraktion* or Red Army Fraction) in West Germany. They were aided by the existence of what some fearfully saw as a terrorist international on the order of the old Communist International. The reality was less dramatic than this but still lethal. Centers of terrorist activity existed in the Near East, where the main players were the Palestinian Liberation Organization (PLO), backed by enormous amounts of petrodollars from sympathetic OPEC members. To this mix could be added the activities of the KGB and other East Bloc intelligence services and the existence of independent nationalist movements like the Irish Republican Army (IRA) in Northern Ireland and the Basque separatists in Spain. The latter appeared about the same time as the Red Brigades and the RAF but for different reasons. On the periphery were terrorists and revolutionaries from Japan and Latin America. While these groups aided one another in securing weapons, in locating sites for training, and with other matters, they seldom worked together on operations. Each group had its own agenda and cooperated with other terrorists only when this served its purposes. The idea of a terrorist conspiracy coordinated by Moscow was simply another variation on Cold War themes.

So far as the Red Brigades and the RAF were concerned, the late 1970s marked the end of any possibility that they would play a major role in national politics. By this time, the RAF had largely moved away from the ideals that had once characterized it to nihilism and criminality. The Red Brigades had also moved in the same direction. In 1978, however, it carried out its most spectacular operation when it kidnapped and later murdered a former premier of Italy, Aldo Moro (1916–1978). The national reaction against this senseless killing was the beginning of the group's downfall; nevertheless, it took the Italian police another five years to destroy the organization. Sporadic right-wing terrorism, particularly in Italy, continued in the 1980s, and disquieting instances of anti-Semitism also appeared. Most of the terrorism of the 1980s, however, was state terrorism sponsored by countries like Libya and Iran. In most cases, this form of terrorism was directed against dissidents from those countries; Western Europe merely furnished the location of the action.

Overall, Western Europe weathered the outbreak of terrorism in good fashion. While there was much discussion of antiterrorist legislation in West Germany, particularly a 1977 law requiring a political litmus test for civil servants that reminded many of the Nazi *Berufsverbot* (prohibition against entering a profession) used against Jews and others in the 1930s, both West Germany and Italy came through difficult times with their constitutional systems intact.

Recovery

While the economic and social problems of Western Europe were genuine and serious, the political problems were more apparent than real. Looked at another way, however, politics seemed to offer a solution to economic and social problems. Certain issues, the welfare state in particular, required rethinking. There was the clear impression among many conservatives that a government willing to divest itself of government-owned operations and to reduce controls and regulations could help create a climate favorable to business. US President Ronald Reagan (1911–2004) became the person most closely identified with this political position through his uncanny ability to project an image that matched what large numbers of Americans believed they wanted. It was the British

Prime Minister Margaret Thatcher (1925–), however, who most successfully translated this approach into national policy.

Thatcherism

Margaret Thatcher, probably the most influential woman in Europe in the last half of the century, inside or outside of politics, served as British prime minister between 1979 and 1990, transforming the Conservative Party and Great Britain in the process. As a young woman, she had studied at Oxford and worked as a research chemist. After her marriage in 1951, she studied law and in 1959 entered the House of Commons. Thatcher rose rapidly in the ranks of the Conservative Party and in 1975, at the age of 50, became its leader. Four years later, she led the party to victory in the elections of 1979.

British Prime Minister Margaret Thatcher delivers the final communiqué of the London Economic Summit, June 9, 1984, as other leaders look on. From the left, Japanese Prime Minister Yasuhiro Nakasone, Canadian Prime Minister Pierre Trudeau, and United States President Ronald Reagan. AP/Press Association Images

Over the next 11 years, "Maggie" Thatcher became very popular with the public but much disliked by her political opponents. She quickly came to be seen as the "Iron Lady," tough, decisive, strong-willed, and no-nonsense. Her main contribution to British recovery came in the area of economic policy. That policy had three main components: "privatization," reduction of inflation, and weakening of trade union power. The "privatization" of nationalized industries and national utilities received a great deal of press, but it is difficult to say whether it contributed much to overall economic recovery. Probably more important were the largely successful efforts to reduce the power of the trade unions. Trade unions in Britain had contributed to the lack of competitiveness of the economy by a series of regulations regarding work and seniority that made it diffi-cult for companies to reorganize production for greater efficiency. The new political climate favoring business and trade and the greatly weakened trade unions allowed many British firms to take maximum advantage of opportunities to secure profits. The reduction of inflation, which stood at nearly 22 percent in 1979 but had fallen dramatically to 3.7 percent in 1983, created favorable conditions for investment and economic growth. The Thatcher government was also blessed by the discovery of oil deposits in the North Sea.

For many British, the 1980s was a period of new prosperity. In most respects, the economy was stronger than it had been since the early years of the century. One major downside, however, was the rate of unemployment. At 6.1 percent in 1980, it rose to 11.6 percent in 1985 and then returned in 1989 to about the same level it had been in 1980, 5.3 percent. However, some sections of the country, the north in particular, did not share in the general prosperity. Generally, the Thatcher years had created a class of big winners, a large group of people who were doing somewhat better or at least okay, and "everyone else," a layer of people who were doing very badly with little prospects of improvement.

Part of Margaret Thatcher's popularity early in her tenure as prime minister and vital to her reelection in 1983 was Britain's successful defense of the Falkland Islands, an archipelago of islands near the coast of Argentina that was a contested British territory, from invasion by the Argentines. The Argentine regime that launched the minor engagement that became known as the Falkland War (between Argentina and Britain) had few friends. Many observers focused on what was, in retrospect, Britain's last imperial hurrah. The spectacle of Britain successfully conducting a long-distance war against Argentina caught the imagination of many Europeans and North Americans. South Americans and Third World countries, not surprisingly, tended to disapprove of British efforts to defend a new world territory of little value to them.

Finally, in the realm of international relations, Thatcher could count on friends in high places. In addition to President Reagan, her ideological twin, she enjoyed good relations with prominent European leaders such as Helmut Kohl and François Mitterrand. She also became, despite her reflexive anti-Communism, an early champion of Mikhail Gorbachev, whom she recognized as "someone she could do business with." All in all, Margaret Thatcher put her stamp on the last quarter of the twentieth century in a way no other European leader other than Gorbachev could match.

France

François Mitterrand served as president from 1981 to 1995. He spent much of the 1960s and 1970s rebuilding and strengthening the Socialist Party. When he and the Socialist Party came to power in 1981, he set in motion an ambitious wave of nationalization involving nine industrial groups including steel, aerospace, armaments, electronics, banking, and insurance. In an era when governments and businesses increasingly strived to become both leaner and meaner, Mitterrand was something of an anachronism. Within two years, the government quietly abandoned the socialist policies. Thereafter, a more conventional approach, one paying more than merely lip service to Thatcher's ideas, came to the fore.

After the 1986 elections, Mitterrand remained as president of France but had to share power with Jacques Chirac (1932–), a Gaullist, as prime minister. Chirac reflected the new rightist majority in the National Assembly. Mitterrand returned in 1988 to win one more term as president.

Over the 1980s, the power and appeal of the French Communist Party declined considerably. It gained only 9.7 percent of the vote in 1986, in contrast to the past when it regularly won 20–25 percent of the vote. A less powerful Communist Party on his flank allowed Mitterrand to moderate his positions to some extent, even if he and Chirac could not reach full agreement on domestic policies.

To some extent, the decline of the Communist Party was reflected in the growth of Jean-Marie Le Pen's (1928–) *Front National* in the 1980s. The Front National is a political movement based to a large extent on hatred and fear. It is racist, chauvinistic, and well to the right in terms of French politics. It is possibly more dangerous than neo-Nazi movements in Germany or Austria, but people do not automatically connect it with Hitler and the Nazis.

Le Pen, an astute and charismatic political leader, knows how to play on the fears of ordinary French men and women. Persistent high rates of unemployment in the 1980s nonetheless helped to convince many that Le Pen's perspective was worth taking seriously.

By the end of the 1980s, which saw the celebration of the bicentennial of the French Revolution, the French were doing well, despite the ongoing political controversy and nagging unemployment. For the majority, the standard of living had greatly improved since the 1960s. France also was characterized at the time by a greater degree of egalitarianism, especially in terms of equality of opportunity as reflected in such areas as education and health care.

West Germany

Helmut Schmidt (1918–) was a worthy successor to Willy Brandt and governed West Germany well in the 1970s and early 1980s. He successfully weathered the challenges of the Red Army Faction (RAF) and the economic downturns. He was unable, however, to maintain the previous coalition with the Free Democrats after the 1982 elections. Helmut Kohl replaced him as chancellor and based his government on a new coalition between the Christian Democrats and the Free Democrats.

Helmut Kohl (1930–) liked to say that his generation was fortunate in that it had not had to take part in World War II or the Holocaust and therefore was not burdened with the guilt felt by the generations that had. Critics quickly pointed out, however, that his generation, having grown up in the Nazi era, had undoubtedly absorbed much of the Nazi outlook and therefore had as much to overcome as earlier generations. From time to time, Kohl made particular comments that have marked him as something of an opportunist, eager to put the Nazi past behind him for good. Nevertheless, he endured as chancellor for quite some time, from 1982 until 1998.

In the 1980s, the Kohl government was successful in leading West Germany to a strong recovery, in part because of policies it introduced and also because of policies Schmidt had set in motion. Additionally, West Germany's powerful central bank, the *Bundesbank* (Federal Bank), and German business leaders made important contributions. The Kohl government largely followed policies West German governments had been following since the 1950s and 1960s. The major exception was an effort to stop the growth of the welfare state. Businesses were also encouraged to slow the growth of wage-and-benefits packages to prevent labor costs from pricing German exports out of the market. By the end of the 1980s, inflation had disappeared as a threat (6 percent in 1981 but −1 percent in 1986) and exports had shown strong growth. The major disappointment for West Germany was the continuing high unemployment figures, especially in a country that had long enjoyed full employment.

The major political development of the 1980s was the growing appeal of the Greens, an outgrowth of the Extraparliamentary Opposition (APO) of the late 1960s. Formed as a party in the 1970s, the Greens were interested primarily in environmentalism but diverse in outlook. Many in the movement disliked the idea of becoming a political party and participating in institutions like the Bundestag. Green members of the Bundestag introduced new styles of dress and behavior, but they also learned in the course of the 1980s how work was accomplished in that body and in many cases became quite proficient at advancing the Green agenda. In the 1987 elections, the Greens elected 47 members to the Bundestag. The Christian Democrats lost ground but continued to govern in coalition with the Free Democrats. The Social Democrats remained polarized between a radical left wing and a moderate center. They were also hampered by the lack of an effective standard bearer. Despite the opposition's weaknesses and the relative success of the Kohl government, Kohl's political prospects at the end of the 1980s were not particularly good. As it turned out, however, he stood on the eve of his finest hour.

Some Other States

In the 1970s and the 1980s, the Italian Communist Party (PCI) provided a major political story. Under the leadership of Enrico Berlinguer (1922–1984), the secretary-general of the PCI from 1972 to 1984, the party undertook a "historic compromise" in 1979 when it explicitly accepted the rules of the parliamentary system. It fared well in the elections in 1976, gaining 34 percent of the vote, and became part of an informal coalition between 1977 and 1979. In addition, the PCI controlled most of the major cities and 7 of the 16 regions, which meant it was often the leading political force on a local or regional basis. In the 1980s, even though the party continued to move rapidly away from Stalinism and even Leninism, its vote totals dipped. Meanwhile, the Christian Democrats turned their attention back to the Socialists.

The Reichstag Building as it appeared in 1985. Although in West Berlin, it was located quite close to the Berlin Wall and had no official function. After the unification of the two Germanies, it was completely renovated. From the collection of Michael Richards

In the 1980s, Italians enjoyed a decade of progress. The Christian Democrats continued to dominate national political life but had to concede in the mid-1980s the position of premier to Bettino Craxi (1934–1999), the leader of the Socialist Party. Craxi's government, which lasted from 1983 to 1986, was actually one of the more effective governments in Italian political history. Craxi hoped to emulate the French Socialists, but he was not able to duplicate Mitterrand's successes.

For Portugal and Spain, the events of the 1970s spelled release from decades of dictatorship and the beginning of efforts to catch up with other Western European countries. Portugal began to change after the death in 1970 of Antonio Salazar (1889–1970), dictator since 1932. Marcello Caetano (1906–1980) followed Salazar as prime minister in 1968. Caetano and the remnants of the dictatorship were overthrown by revolution in 1974. Army personnel, radicalized by the long and frustrating struggle to retain the empire, carried out the revolution and established the Supreme Revolutionary Council, which ruled in 1974 and 1975. In 1975, military personnel close to the Portuguese Communist Party attempted a coup, which was unsuccessful. The following year, a new constitution was promulgated. In the late 1970s and in the 1980s, the major figure in Portuguese politics was Mario Soares (1924–), a reformist socialist. Soares became president in 1986, the same year Portugal joined the European Community.

The death of Spain's dictator, General Francisco Franco (b. 1892), came in 1975. Franco made arrangements for restoration of the monarchy, with Juan Carlos (1938–), the heir apparent, succeeding to the throne. Despite serious problems with the ETA (the Basque separatists) and an attempted coup in 1981, which Juan Carlos I played a major role in thwarting, Spain enjoyed in the late 1970s and in the 1980s both a successful transition to democratic politics and impressive economic growth. Spain entered the NATO alliance in 1982 and the European Community in 1986. The major political figure in Spain in the 1980s and 1990s was Felipe Gonzales (1942–), who led the Socialist Workers Party to victory in the 1982 elections. He was 40 at the time. Gonzales served as prime minister from 1982 to 1996.

The East Bloc in Decline: The Soviet Union

If Western Europe experienced something of a roller coaster ride in the 1970s and 1980s, it was all downhill compared to the smashups that Eastern Europe (1989) and the Soviet Union (1991) faced. The Soviet Union maintained strict control not only domestically but also in Eastern Europe in the 1970s, with the important exception of the small opening provided by the Helsinki Process. The Soviet Union was itself a terrible kind of paradox, a world power finally, but also failing visibly in terms of the most vital indices of national well-being: infant mortality rates, life expectancy (especially for males), incidence of alcoholism, and accident and suicide rates. By the late 1970s, the Soviet Union seemed to have embarked on a kind of Cold War adventurism in Afghanistan, the Horn of Africa, and other trouble spots as a way of denying its economic problems and the disintegration of its social fabric. Leonid Brezhnev, old and ill, had become little more than a parody of a Soviet leader. Trotted out for important state occasions, he had to be helped on and off the podium and often lost his place in speeches.

After Brezhnev's death in 1982, Yuri Andropov, who had played a dark role in Soviet politics as the mastermind of the KGB through the 1970s and early 1980s, appeared ready to make sweeping changes in the Soviet Union. Andropov, as first secretary of the Communist Party from 1982 to 1984, presented to the credulous West as a jazz-loving, Scotch-drinking, spy-novel-reading liberal, never had much of an opportunity to demonstrate what he intended to do. His principal contribution to the 1980s was his sponsorship of Mikhail Gorbachev. Gorbachev had to wait his turn, however, until after the mercifully brief reign of Konstantin Chernenko (1911–1985) as first secretary in 1984 and 1985. Chernenko was rewarded for his utter loyalty to Brezhnev and will probably be best remembered as an example of the tendency of a decaying system to push to the top those totally incompetent figures who will finally destroy it.

Gorbachev replaced Chernenko in 1985. Unlike Andropov, he was truly a different sort of Soviet official. A graduate of Moscow

University in law, he had come up rapidly through the system, becoming a member of the Politburo in 1980 at the age of 49 and in 1985 secretary-general of the Communist Party. Although Gorbachev was a communist, he saw the need for far-reaching changes in the Soviet system and believed that Leninism provided an adequate basis for those changes. There is some similarity in what Gorbachev attempted to do and actions taken in the Prague Spring. One major difference is the extent to which the Soviet bureaucracy was deeply entrenched and determined to protect its prerogatives. What might have succeeded in Czechoslovakia had not the Soviet Union intervened was not very likely to succeed in the Soviet Union itself, even given the passage of time and growing awareness that the system was failing.

Gorbachev advanced several important general propositions: glasnost or transparency, perestroika or reformation, and new thinking. Glasnost was perhaps the easiest of the new approaches to institute. Censorship was gradually abandoned, and people were encouraged to present the past as accurately as possible in magazines, films, plays, and books. Perestroika was the most difficult to put into practice and ultimately Gorbachev's undoing. Economic reform, particularly the encouragement of modest levels of private enterprise, was stymied by bureaucratic obstructionism, which Gorbachev sought to counter through political reform. This, however, brought into question the primacy of the Communist Party. New thinking was Gorbachev's most successful initiative, perhaps because it was directed mostly at the West and offered a way out of the Cold War impasse. Although President Reagan was initially suspicious, he began to see possibilities in Gorbachev's proposals. In fact, at the summit meeting between the Soviet Union and the United States at Reykjavik, Iceland, in 1986, Reagan had to be restrained by his advisors from responding too enthusiastically to Gorbachev's overtures. The following year, the Intermediate-Range Nuclear Forces (INF) Treaty was signed, eliminating from the arsenals of both super powers all ground-based intermediate-range nuclear missiles. Enormously popular in the West ("Gorby Mania" was an extraordinary phenomena both in Eastern and in Western Europe),

Gorbachev experienced increasing difficulty in the Soviet Union in maneuvering between Communist Party hardliners and proponents of radical change.

Solidarity in Poland

The contribution of Poland's Solidarity (*Solidarność*) movement to the unraveling of the Cold War can hardly be exaggerated. It grew out of the politics of the 1970s. First, in 1970, strikes protesting increases in food prices led to the replacement of Wladyslaw Gomulka by Edward Gierek. Gierek pushed a policy of economic growth based on foreign loans. By 1976, however, it was apparent that unfortunate choices had been made in pursuit of economic growth (e.g., construction of huge steelworks at a time when demand for steel products was declining). Again, attempts to increase food prices led to strikes.

In the next few years, two developments helped to change the terms of confrontation between workers and the government. In one development, an organized intellectual opposition, KOR (Committee for the Defense of the Workers), made contact with workers' groups. Jacek Kuron (1934–2004), the leader of KOR, was a product of student movements in the 1960s. It had, however, been isolated from the workers. Worker protests in the early 1970s suffered from their isolation from students and intellectuals. Coming together in 1980 made a substantial difference in the possibility of resisting government pressure.

In the other development, the Catholic Church in Poland gained enormously in prestige from the election of a Pole, Karol Cardinal Wojtyla (1920–2005), as Pope John Paul II in 1978. The following year, Pope John Paul II made a triumphant tour of Poland and was welcomed by millions of the faithful.

In 1980, for the third time in a decade, the government tried to raise food prices. The strikes this time had a center in the Lenin Shipyards in Gdansk and a leader in Lech Wałęsa (1943–), an electrician at the shipyards and a participant in the events of 1976. In the negotiations between the workers and the government, the workers pressed for and won the right to organize an independent trade union movement, Solidarity. It began to take on a life of its own in 1981, becoming an enormously large and powerful trade union movement. Although there was no place for Solidarity in the communist system, it began to exercise a kind of de facto power, challenging the authority of the Polish Communist Party (technically the Polish United Workers' Party or PUWP). The upshot of this was the appointment of General Wojciech Jaruzelski (1923–) as prime minister and the proclamation of martial law. Wałęsa and other Solidarity leaders were imprisoned and Solidarity was outlawed.

Wałęsa, who won the Nobel Peace Prize in 1983, was eventually released from prison. He was able to maintain Solidarity's existence as an organization throughout the 1980s, first as an underground organization and later as an organization unofficially tolerated by the government. As problems mounted for the Polish government and PUWP, the power and influence of Solidarity began to increase. Finally, in 1989, talks between Solidarity and the government began, leading to events that formed one of the most important triggers of the revolutions of 1989.

Erich Honecker's East Germany

East Germany in the 1970s and 1980s seemed to be a success story. There was, first, the connection to West Germany that Brandt's Ostpolitik had developed. For Honecker, it was a double-edged sword. On the positive side stood the prestige involved in formal recognition by West Germany. In addition, entry fees paid by people entering East Germany, West German subsidies of various kinds, and access to the European Community produced income. The negative side was the public's greater contact with the realities of life in West Germany. This, of course, was difficult to avoid, given the widespread availability of West German TV programs. Honecker tried to offset Western influences through efforts to encourage East Germans to distance themselves from West Germany and to take pride in East Germany.

East Germany had about it in the 1970s and 1980s something of the atmosphere of bread and circuses. While it was drab and gray compared to the West, it offered its citizens the highest standard of living in the East Bloc. In effect, this was Honecker's agreement with East Germans. Work hard and you will be rewarded with better housing, good food and clothing, refrigerators, TVs, and the Trabi (the Trabant, the basic East German automobile). As bonuses, the East German regime offered an active cultural life and good health care and educational opportunities. Finally, the government sponsored an amazingly successful sports program, modeled on but surpassing that of the Soviet system.

Behind the bribes was an extensive system of surveillance and repression administered by the Ministry of State Security or the Stasi. The Stasi consisted of a sizable bureaucracy that carried out activities both abroad (principally in West Germany) and at home. It was assisted by thousands of people who either volunteered to help or were seduced or coerced into doing so. In some cases, husbands spied on wives and friends informed on friends. Even some pastors became agents of the Stasi, informing on members of their congregations. The amount of data gathered was staggering, miles of files. An argument could be made that the Stasi by the late 1980s could no longer see the forest for the trees. In any case, it failed to present the East German Politburo with a realistic picture of the country at the very point when one was desperately needed.

A realistic picture would have emphasized an economy rapidly becoming uncompetitive, starved for investment capital, and dependent on technologies that were causing enormous ecological damage. The system had never provided the kind of life it had promised. While small protest groups existed precariously under the umbrella of the Lutheran Church, thousands of other East Germans had decided it was time to leave. Thousands more were ready to jump at any realistic chance of leaving, should it present itself. It is no small irony that East German leaders directed almost all of their attention to the impending fortieth anniversary of the founding of the state and failed to see how badly those foundations had been eroded.

Conclusion

Both Eastern and Western Europe changed in significant ways in the 1970s and 1980s. Western Europe weathered difficult times in the 1970s and early 1980s. At the end of the 1980s, it seemed more economically and politically mature. Though Europe still looked to the United States for leadership, it was increasingly willing to forge its own path. Particularly in the case of the European Community, Western Europe appeared poised to break new ground. Eastern Europe, although it could not know it, stood in 1989 on the brink of fundamental changes.

Europe in the 1990s

References

American Rhetoric. 2013. "I Have a Dream." Accessed January 28, 2013. www.americanrhetoric.com/speeches/mlkihaveadream.htm.

Patterson, James T. 1996. *Grand Expectations: The United States, 1945–1974.* New York and Oxford: Oxford University Press.

Further Reading

Branch, Taylor. 1988. *Parting the Waters: America in the King Years 1954–63.* New York: Simon and Schuster. Two subsequent volumes (1999 and 2007) complete Branch's magisterial biography of King.

Carr, Raymond and Juan Pablo Fusi. 1990. *Spain: Dictatorship to Democracy,* 2nd ed. New York: HarperCollins. A thorough discussion of Spain's remarkable transition after the death of Franco.

Fulbrook, Mary. 2005. *The People's State: East German Society from Hitler to Honecker.* New Haven: Yale University Press. A view of what life was like in the German Democratic Republic by a leading student of twentieth-century Germany.

Ginsborg, Paul. 2003. *Italy and Its Discontents: Family, Civil Society, State, 1980–2001.* New York: Palgrave Macmillan. Up-to-date and highly recommended.

Kotkin, Steven. 2001. *Armaggedon Averted: The Soviet Collapse, 1970–2000.* Oxford and New York: Oxford University Press. A deeply informed overview of the collapse of the Soviet Union.

Kurlansky, Mark. 2004. *1968: The Year that Rocked the World.* New York: Ballentine Books. A fast-paced but reliable study.

Lacouture, Jean. 1992. *De Gaulle: The Ruler 1945–1970.* New York: HarperCollins. The major biography of the most important European political figure in the 1960s.

Marwick, Arthur. 2000. *The Sixties: Cultural Revolution in Britain, France, and Italy, and the United States, c. 1958–c. 1974.* New York: Oxford University Press. An exhaustive discussion of this watershed era.

Maxwell, Kenneth. 1995. *The Making of Portuguese Democracy.* New York: Cambridge University Press. The best book on the Portuguese Revolution and its aftermath.

Moore, Charles. 2013. *Margaret Thatcher: From Grantham to the Falklands.* London. Allen Lane.. The first of two volumes, this is a highly detailed but also fresh look at the Iron Lady.

Turner, Henry Ashby. 1992. *The Two Germanies Since 1945: Germany from Partition to Reunification*, rev. ed. New Haven: Yale University Press. A succinct, instructive review of the parallel histories of West Germany and East Germany.

Williams, Kieran. 1997. *The Prague Spring and Its Aftermath: Czechoslovak Politics, 1968–1970*. New York: Cambridge University Press. Includes new archival material.

11

Searching for Meaning in a Multicultural World

Chronology

1940s–1950s	Heyday of existentialist writers, e.g., Albert Camus and Jean-Paul Sartre
c. 1945–1950s	New York School of abstract expressionist art promoted by Peggy Guggenheim's Art of This Century gallery
1949	George Orwell's *1984*
1950s	"Pop Art" emerges in England as a reaction to abstract expressionism
1952	John Cage, leading figure in "music of chance," performs *4'33"*

Twentieth-Century Europe: A Brief History, 1900 to the Present, Third Edition.
Michael D. Richards and Paul R. Waibel.
© 2014 John Wiley & Sons, Inc. Published 2014 by John Wiley & Sons, Inc.

1950s–1960s	Theater of the Absurd popularizes existential philosophy
1954–1963	"Golden Decade" of "rock 'n' roll"
1955	Claude Lévi-Strauss's *Tristes Tropiques* marks the appearance of structuralism
1964	The Beatles appear on the *Ed Sullivan Show*, launching the "English invasion" of American popular music
1970s	Minimalism displaces Pop Art as the current fad
1973	"Aloha from Hawaii" with Elvis Presley is beamed live around the world on television
1980s	Deconstructionism, or postculturalism, flourishes
1982	Maya Ling Lin's *Vietnam Veterans' War Memorial* opens
1990s	"Postmodernism" becomes a popular description for the contemporary view of the universe as random chaos
2005	Christo and Jeanne-Claude de Guillebon's *The Gates* exhibited in New York City's Central Park
2012	Harvard University begins offering select courses free online

ON THE NIGHT OF FEBRUARY 13–14, 1945, the Tuesday night before Ash Wednesday, more than 800 RAF bombers dropped incendiary and high explosive bombs on the beautiful city of Dresden, Germany. American bombers, 300 on the following day and 200 the day after, stoked the flames of the burning city. A total of 650,000 incendiary bombs, more than one for each of the city's normal population of 630,000, were dropped during the raids. A firestorm of colossal force reaching temperatures of 800–1,000 degrees centigrade engulfed the city, converting more than 4,200 acres and 135,000 men, women, and children to ashes.

Dresden was of no strategic importance. It was known as a center of the arts, especially renowned for its beautiful Rococo architecture. Because it had escaped attention from the bombers previously, Dresden had become a center for refugees fleeing the oncoming Russian juggernaut. The decision to firebomb Dresden remains one of the most controversial Allied military decisions of World War II, perhaps second only to the subsequent decision to unleash nuclear bombs on Hiroshima and Nagasaki, Japan. Historians agree that the destruction of Dresden and its artistic treasures was one of the war's greatest cultural loses. To obtain some appreciation of the extent of the destruction of Europe's cultural heritage during World War II, one need only view old newsreels or old photographs of Europe's, especially Germany's, bombed-out cities. Many of Central and Eastern Europe's great cultural centers were almost totally destroyed.

The damage done to the psyche by the war was far greater than the ruin of the physical landscape. The disintegration of the Enlightenment tradition, which had begun before the Great War, now appeared complete. Faith in reason, the innate goodness of human beings, and the inherent value of the individual, like the belief in universal truths, values, or principles upon which to construct a humane world, all fell victim to apparent reality. Were reasonable people responsible for such devastation? Were the concentration camps, the firebombing of cities, and the atomic bombing of Hiroshima and Nagasaki the acts of reasonable people? The evil of Nazism in Germany and militarism in Japan were finally overcome, but by whom? Stalin, next to Hitler, was the other great villain of the twentieth century. It was the United States, the historical embodiment of the hope created by the Enlightenment philosophes, that released from Pandora's Box the frightening prospect of a future thermonuclear holocaust. There seemed little hope for the future of civilization viewed from the immediate postwar years.

In their attempt to make sense out of a world in which all the old values and certainties had either failed or vanished, a universe that rejected the existence of God or any other absolute truth that might provide unity and meaning, the intellectuals of the immediate postwar years embraced the philosophy of existentialism. Existentialism appeared to provide a means by which the individual could find (or create) meaning for his or her existence in a universe that seemed increasingly meaningless and frightening. By the 1960s, existentialism was giving way to structuralism, which shifted the focus away from the individual as the creator of meaning to universal thought processes that were to provide an underlying structure, or unity, to fragmented reality.

By the 1980s, structuralism had mutated into deconstructionism, sometimes referred to as poststructuralism. Deconstruction is a radical rejection of the whole Western tradition, especially as found in the Enlightenment tradition. It embraces the notion of total fragmentation and denies the possibility of discovering any truth or meaning in the universe. We are back to Nietzsche's assertion in his parable of the madman (*The Gay Science* [1882]) that if God is dead, then mankind is adrift in a universe without meaning. By the end of the twentieth century, many appeared to have embraced nihilism, at least intellectually and culturally.

The changing views about truth and reality found expression in the works produced by the purveyors of both elite and pop culture. An increasingly fragmented world view during the interwar years was mirrored in the art, music, and literature of the period (see Chapter 5). As the fragmentation of world view continued in the West, even increased, during the second half of the twentieth century, the message and technique of cultural expression changed. By the end of the twentieth century, there was no longer any accepted standard by which to judge works of art, literature, or music. Terms such as "good," "bad," "beautiful," or "ugly" were meaningless, when anything, no matter how outlandish, could qualify as art. This itself was an expression of the new consensus on the nature of man and the universe and whether that consensus itself had any meaning or relevance.

Existentialism

The roots of existentialism reach back into the nineteenth century with the writings of Søren Kierkegaard (1813–1855), Fyodor Dostoevsky (1821–1881), and Friedrich Nietzsche (1844–1900). Although most of the existentialists were atheists, or at least ignored the question of God's existence, some were Christians, some were religious—but not Christian—and at least one, Martin Buber (1878–1965), was a believing Jew. Existentialism is not easily defined, for there is no systematic dogma to which all its leading exponents adhered. In general, existentialists asserted that the individual must affirm and give meaning to his or her existence by struggling against the absurdity of a universe that is silent and indifferent to the individual's existence. By choosing to act, the individual gives meaning to his or her existence.

Postwar existentialism was born in the French resistance to German occupation during World War II. Albert Camus (1913–1960), French born and reared in French-ruled Algeria, was the premier example of the existentialist writers who came out of the French resistance. Camus confronted the predicament of the individual in a world without God that was silent and indifferent to the individual's existence. Having rejected both suicide and a fatalistic acceptance of nihilism, Camus likened the individual's task to that of the Greek mythic figure of Sisyphus. Like Sisyphus, who was condemned to repeatedly roll a great rock uphill, only to have it roll back down again, the individual is condemned to struggle against the absurdity of the universe, knowing all along that his struggle is in vain. Before his death in an automobile accident in 1960, Camus's ideas received wide exposure in three novels—*The Stranger* (1942), *The Plague* (1947), and *The Fall* (1956)—and two philosophical works, *The Myth of Sisyphus* (1942) and *The Rebel* (1951).

Perhaps the best-known and most controversial of the postwar French existentialists was Jean-Paul Sartre (1905–1980). Sartre's ideas were popularized primarily through works written during the war. Again, as with Camus, it was through a series of novels, especially *Nausea* (1938) and *The Age of Reason* (1945), and plays, such as *The*

Many individuals at the end of the twentieth century felt as though they were adrift alone in a world where the future was filled with uncertainty and the present haunted by symbols of the past. Photo courtesy of Elizabeth Waibel, private collection

Flies (1943) and *No Exit* (1944), rather than serious philosophical studies, like *Being and Nothingness* (1943), that Sartre's ideas achieved renown and influence.

For Sartre, an atheist, the starting point is the existence of the individual. There is no reference point in the universe or in time to which the individual relates that validates one's existence. The individual creates his or her own essence, that is, defines his or her own being. The individual is neither the product of environmental forces nor unconscious drives. To be a human being is to bear the burden of being one's own creator. One thing that the individual can do, indeed must do, is make authentic choices. By doing so, one takes on the role of what Nietzsche called a superman (übermensch), the creator of one's essence. In Sartre's own words:

> Not only is man what he conceives himself to be but he is also only what he wills himself to be. . . . *Man is nothing else but what he makes of himself* [emphasis added]. . . . existentialism's first move is to make every man aware of what he is and to make the full responsibility of his existence rest on him. (Sartre 1947)

Sartre found it impossible to live consistently by the philosophy he espoused. In 1960, he joined with other French intellectuals in signing the Algerian Manifesto, which said that the war in Algeria was morally and ethically wrong. By doing so, Sartre seemed to destroy his own philosophical position. There was a standard (an absolute?) by which human behavior could be judged and the individual could use reason to measure human actions against that standard. Similarly, Sartre's flirtation with Marxism between 1951 and 1955 appeared to place this prophet of radical individualism on the side of a radical mechanical materialism that denied individual freedom. Sartre broke with the Communist Party in 1956 and denounced the Soviet suppression of the Hungarian revolt, once again a moral judgment based upon reason. The contradiction was not overlooked by fellow existentialists. Both Albert Camus and Maurice Merleau-Ponty (1908–1961) broke openly with Sartre. In 1956, before Sartre rejected communism, he was an honored guest in Moscow, where he embarrassed himself by his overindulgence in vodka. Merleau-Ponty voiced the opinion of other existentialists when he accused Sartre of the sin of "ultra-Bolshevism," a betrayal of existentialism's belief in individual freedom (Stromberg 1994).

The following verses by poet–screenwriter Kendrew Lascelles evoke the sense of isolation that many people felt in the late twentieth century:

"When All the Laughter Dies in Sorrow"

When all the laughter dies in sorrow
and the tears have risen to a flood,
when all the wars have found a cause
in human wisdom and in blood,

do you think they'll cry in sadness?

do you think the eye will blink?
do you think they'll curse the madness?
do you even think they'll think?

when all the great galactic systems
sigh to a frozen halt in space
do you think there'll be some remnant beauty
of the human race?

do you think there'll be a vestige
or a sniffle
or a cosmic tear?

do you think a greater thinking thing
will give a damn
that Man was here? (Lascelles 1973)

Structuralism

During the 1960s, just as existentialism was filtering down to the masses through the medium of popular culture, even though few of the masses would have been aware of it or able to define the term, the intellectual trendsetters were moving on to structuralism, as if hoping to restore some order to the increasing fragmentation. Once again, the birthplace was France, where its appearance is often associated with the publication of *Tristes Tropiques* by Claude Lévi-Strauss (1908–2009) in 1955. Structuralism entered the United States through Yale University in the late 1960s. By the mid-1970s, it was no longer fashionable among French intellectuals, who were turning to deconstruction, a more radical form, or mutation, of structuralism. Nonetheless, structuralism remained popular among intellectuals in the United States, England, and Germany through the end of the century.

Structuralism was antihumanist. Whereas the existentialists focused on the individual and the individual's need to find meaning, the structuralists assumed a universal structure, or a kind of hidden harmony, or universal code, that exists independent of human beings. They focused on these universal structures that are independent of humans and determine human behavior. This universal code could be found in the human mind, that is, in universal thought processes that are unconscious but determine consciousness. Since these thought processes are universal, the same for the uneducated native and the sophisticated university professor or corporate executive, there is an alleged unity to humanity that transcends all cultural, racial, and class distinctions. It even transcends history.

Structuralism was a rejection of all Western thought, at least since the Enlightenment. Human beings as the self-conscious creators of a meaningful history were abolished. They were merely the playthings of hidden mechanistic forces, like puppets in the hands of an unseen puppeteer. The autonomous individual, who controlled his or her environment and was master of his or her fate, gave way to the individual as a social creature controlled by his or her environment.[1] History as a linear process that implied progress over time was denied. History was meaningless, and the study of history a waste of time. The study of the past, the gathering of historical data, was a futile activity that could teach nothing of value. Its only result was a collection of factual trivia, empty of any meaning. For Lévi-Strauss, for example, what was important was "the comparative, the universal, the mythic, the immediate rather than the historical and the temporal."

Lévi-Strauss was an anthropologist turned philosopher. His success in spreading the gospel of structuralism was due in part to his beautiful, almost poetic, writing style. His books and other writings are said to resemble musical compositions. In addition to *Tristes Tropiques*, a kind of intellectual autobiography, *The Savage Mind* (1962), *The Elementary Structures of the Mind* (1969), and a host of other popular writings helped make Lévi-Strauss one of the leading intellectuals in France during the 1960s and 1970s. His ideas were further popularized by Roland Barthes (1915–1989), an existentialist who converted to structuralism. Barthes was the editor of *Tel Quel*, an influential Parisian intellectual journal during the 1950s and 1960s.

The ideas of Lévi-Strauss and Barthes became popular during the 1960s and 1970s in the United States, where they were applied to literary criticism. Once again, it was the hidden structure behind the words on the page that the structuralist literary critic was seeking. The author's intent was irrelevant to the study of his or her work. As with a newspaper, it was the layout of the newspaper, its structure, rather than the articles themselves that interested the structuralists. In the end, the structuralists failed to uncover the hidden universal

---

[1] Structuralism and its successor, deconstruction, were ideally suited for "a world integrated by identification and manipulation of the universal genetic code, computer programs, communications satellites, and multinational corporations, and the absence of major wars. . . . A world fragmented culturally and aesthetically, a world of sub-cultures, small-group choices [made] on aesthetic principles and idiosyncratic, nostalgic recapitulations of the past, but one in which a comprehensive, integrating cultural theory is lacking" (Norman Cantor. 1997. *The American Century: Varieties of Culture in Modern Times*. New York: Harper Collins, 434–435).

structures that were thought to control the human mind and hence all that human beings produced. By the late 1970s, structuralism was passing out of fashion and yielding the field to deconstruction. Roland Barthes and Michel Foucault (1926–1984) served as a bridge between the two philosophies.

Deconstruction

Structuralism, as one intellectual historian has put it, slid into deconstruction, sometimes called poststructuralism. It did so by assuming that everything had to be decoded in order to discover the hidden meaning of things, which led to the question of whether there was any one meaning or simply different meanings. It did so, too, by insisting that one's intellect is determined by hidden structures, that is, by linguistics (words). Also, the structuralists were characterized by a sense of alienation that compelled them to play the role of subverters of meaning.

Once again, the home of this intellectual movement was France. The leading deconstructionists were the French thinkers Michel Foucault, Jacques Lacan (1901–1981), and Jacques Derrida (1930–2004). Deconstruction was an open denial of the whole Western intellectual tradition with its emphasis on the individual, the individual's ability to reason, and through reason to arrive at a true understanding of reality, which in turn implied the capacity to make meaningful moral judgments, resulting in a reasoned reformation of society.

Deconstructionists held that there was no one hidden meaning to be arrived at as a result of decoding a literary text, for example. There are an infinite number of possible meanings, as many as there are "decoders." The author's intent is no help either, for there is no implicit relationship between the author's mind and the words of the text. The deconstructionist critic may interpret a literary text any way he or she wishes, having deduced that interpretation, not necessarily from what the author wrote down, but from what the author left out, what Lacan calls the "holes in the discourse." Whether what the deconstructionist said of a text had any meaning itself was questionable, for deconstruction itself could be deconstructed. Derrida admitted that by the criteria of deconstruction, his own writings were meaningless. Deconstruction had a definite tendency toward nihilism.

The implications of deconstruction for understanding civilization in general and modern European civilization in particular are obvious. When the deconstructionists finish their work, there are no "great books," no treasure trove of wisdom from the past that defines, inspires, or provides a standard for modern civilization. History itself is a text to be deconstructed, revealing what Foucault called "non-historical, or discontinuous history." Historical and cultural institutions and forms are revealed to serve the interests of those who rule, who dominate. They are the means whereby the dominant class (e.g., European males) exploits the lower classes. What events of the past are worthy of recording is determined by whatever class is dominant at any given time.

Deconstruction was a logical by-product of the disintegration of European culture and the growth of cultural pluralism or multiculturalism after World War II. Deconstructionists believe that agreement on a meaningful history was only possible during the nineteenth century when there was a cultural unity among the literate classes of Europe. Historians of different cultural backgrounds would naturally interpret history differently. How, for example, might the history of the nineteenth century appear if written by a middle-class European or an African immigrant? This "discovery" leads to the logical conclusion that one cannot justify requiring today's student to study the history of Western civilization. For the ever-increasing numbers of those whose cultural heritage is largely non-European and non-Western, European history is only the story of deeds done by "dead white males," told by their descendants who seek authority through perpetuating their memory.

Postmodernism

Of the *isms* that have enjoyed a vogue during the latter part of the twentieth century, none is more difficult to define than "postmodernism." The term is actually old, having been used historically to characterize various trends in the arts. Since the 1980s, it has become the topic of culture talk shows on educational radio and television and the subject of academic conferences in all of the various disciplines. By the end of the century, it took on the characteristics of, as one critic put it, "a trendy buzzword rapidly reaching its sell-by date" (Ward 1997). At the turn of the twenty-first century, postmodernism and postmodernity were being used commonly to refer to the third and most recent period in a tripartite division of Western intellectual history into premodernity (the Medieval Synthesis), modernity (the Enlightenment tradition), and postmodernity (the Enlightenment tradition in disarray).

The term "postmodern" first appeared during the 1870s, when it was used to refer to what was later classified as postimpressionist art. During and following the Great War, there was talk of a postmodern man emerging, that is, one who opted for nihilistic or amoral values, having rejected the established values of modern Western civilization. Arnold Toynbee in his monumental *A Study of History* (1947) and some cultural historians of the late 1950s used the term to describe the period after 1875, when the spread of industrialization challenged the established values of "modern" civilization. During the 1960s, the term was used most often in reference to Pop Art.

The term really became fashionable during the last quarter of the twentieth century. Applied to the arts and architecture, it describes whatever is at the moment considered avant-garde, an eclectic style that combines elements of earlier, and seemingly incongruous, styles that mirror the diversity and pluralism of the contemporary world. Postmodern art and architecture is a kind of collage in which the diverse elements have no unifying theme. It is similar to modernism in that it presents a fragmented view of reality. However, in contrast to modernism, which lamented the loss of unity and meaning while holding forth the hope that such could be restored, postmodernism celebrates the fragmentation and loss of meaning. Beginning with the conviction that the world is meaningless, postmodernism sees no value in pretending otherwise. Rather, it revels in the chaos and absurdity of everything.

Applied to the areas of thought and history, postmodernism is synonymous with posthumanism. It is a fundamental break with the Enlightenment tradition (modernity) and the humanism at its core. Whereas the Enlightenment tradition (some would go back to the Renaissance) emphasized the individual, reason, order, and meaning, postmodernism rejects all of the fundamental assumptions of Enlightenment thought as no longer tenable. Thus, postmodernism includes structuralism and deconstruction, or poststructuralism.

As a term commonly used to refer to a contemporary view of reality, postmodernism is best understood when contrasted with premodernity and modernity. During premodernity, roughly the period from the High Middle Ages to the Enlightenment (c. 1000–c. 1700), reality was an orderly universe in which there was meaning and purpose for both the individual and history. The individual was understood to be capable of understanding oneself and the universe he or she inhabited, because the individual was a special creation created in the image of his or her creator, that is, God. The experts were the theologians and philosophers who interpreted God's revelation in Scripture and in nature.

According to modernity, roughly the period from the Enlightenment to the mid-twentieth century (c. 1700–c. 1950), reality was an orderly universe of cause-and-effect natural law but in a closed system, for God, the creator, was now a great architect or watchmaker. God created the universe machine, but was not involved in its operation. His continued existence as creator, however, kept at bay the troubling questions of why anything exists and whether or not there was any meaning for the individual or history. The experts were the scientists who could discover, interpret, and exploit natural law. Thus, mankind had faith in progress and was optimistic about the future.

In postmodernity, reality is a universe of random chaos, without meaning for either the individual or history. There is no creator, no God, either as the God of biblical revelation or the great architect of Deism. There is only the illusion of order. The ultimate reality is impersonal matter. There are no experts to interpret reality, for reality is only what anyone says it is at any given moment. Any attempt at a metanarrative (a "big story" that explains the meaning of all that is, e.g., the Bible) to explain reality is only the flawed expression of a particular subculture. Another way of looking at the contrast is to understand premodernity as the house that God built, modernity as the house that man built, and postmodernity as the house that never got built.

Culture

War is never kind to the physical manifestations of humanity's cultural achievements. History is impoverished by the loss of cultural monuments of all sorts due to wars. What wonders of human creativity have disappeared in the flames of warfare? Barbarian hordes put fire and sword to classical civilization in Western Europe, and the Vikings did likewise to the early centers of Western Christendom, often leaving behind only written memories. When the dust of World War II had settled and rebuilding began, cultural monuments were not neglected. Reconstruction of the great opera houses and concert halls were sometimes given priority over providing housing for the many homeless refugees. And such reconstruction was made as close to the original as possible. Postwar Europeans seemed to recognize that houses of culture were, like the cathedrals, reservoirs of the national spirit.

As with the philosophers, postwar culture, whether high or popular, struggled to make sense of recent events. The artists, musicians, poets, and writers displayed in their creative output the growing sense of alienation and despair and the fragmentation that characterized European civilization in transition. It was a continuation of trends already present at the beginning of the century, with perhaps a new reality. Whether in the fine arts or popular culture, influences from the United States tended to dominate. In the fine arts, this was due in part to the prewar flight of creative individuals before the tidal wave of Nazi and communist oppression. The economic dominance of the United States and the presence of American military forces in Western Europe assured that European popular culture would mimic American trends.

Art

The dominant artistic style after the war was what became known as abstract expressionism. Its roots lay in the surrealism of the interwar era. Like the surrealists, the abstract expressionists looked to the psychoanalytic theories of Sigmund Freud and Carl Jung (1875–1961). Believing that faith in reason and rationalism had guided European culture and politics into the horrors of two world wars, they were seeking a truth beyond reason in the realm of the unconscious. Perhaps, what was most characteristic of this artistic style, or concept, was the individualism of the artists associated with it. To really understand and appreciate it, one would need to study the output of each individual artist. Such a task is beyond our attempt to identify and describe trends in postwar culture. Hence, we note that abstract expressionism was characterized by a lack of recognizable content and an emphasis upon gesture and/or color. The artist intended to communicate a reality that he or she felt by means of the unconscious, rather than the conscious will.

Abstract expressionism is often referred to as the "New York School," because many of its practitioners were European expatriates and formerly leading figures in surrealism in Europe. Among these were the Spaniard Salvador Dali (1904–1989), the Dutchman Piet Mondrian (1872–1944), and the German artists Josef Albers (1888–1976), Max Ernst (1891–1976), Hans Hofmann (1880–1966), and George Grosz (1893–1959). Max Ernst's third wife (for a period of three years) was the influential art collector and patron, Peggy Guggenheim (1898–1979). Ms. Guggenheim exhibited the works of the European expatriates, as well as new artists whom she "discovered," in her Art of This Century gallery in New York City. Among the latter was Jackson Pollock (1912–1956), arguably the best-known abstract expressionist. Pollock might produce a work of art by merely walking around on a canvas stretched out on the floor while dripping paint from cans.

It was perhaps inevitable that some artists would react against the abstract expressionists' emphasis on nonrepresentationalism. That reaction came in the mid-1950s with a return to representation.

Salvador Dali A, or Dali Atomicus, a portrait of surrealist artist Salvador Dali, explores the concept of suspension. A collaborative effort between Dali and American photographer Philippe Halsman, wires and even the hand of an assistant (holding the chair) can be seen in this unretouched photo, published in *Life* magazine in 1948. Library of Congress (LC-DIG-ppmsca-09633)

This artistic movement became known as "Pop Art." For these artists, art should depict the real postwar world, one obsessed with commercialism and mass culture. Influenced by Dadaism, the Pop artists looked to everyday objects and images of mass production for their subject matter—soup cans, comic strips, advertisements of consumer goods, and photographs of movie and rock stars. Although the Pop Art movement originated in England, America was once again the primary home of this movement that was in vogue during the 1960s and early 1970s. Among the leading Pop artists were Jasper Johns (1930–), Robert Rauschenberg (1925–2008), Roy Lichtenstein (1923–1997), and Andy Warhol (1930–1987), "The Prince of Pop."

When one thinks of Pop Art, the name Andy Warhol immediately comes to mind. He burst onto the Pop Art scene in 1962, with an exhibition of paintings that depicted Campbell's soup cans and Brillo soap boxes. The difference between abstract expressionism with its nonrepresentation and Pop Art's return to representation was noted by Warhol: "Pop artists did images that anybody walking down Broadway could recognize in a split second—comics, picnic tables, men's trousers, celebrities, shower curtains, refrigerators, Coke bottles—all the great modern things that the Abstract Expressionists tried so hard not to notice" (Danto 2010). Unlike the abstract expressionists who were tuned into the problems of alienation and anxiety inherent in the postwar world as expressed by the existentialists and other philosophers, the Pop artists both celebrated and condemned the middle-class values of the consumer culture of the prosperous 1960s.

By the late 1960s and into the 1970s, minimalism displaced Pop Art as the current fad. The minimalists tried to avoid all emotional content or personal meaning. Minimalist painters produced geometric patterns of color, as, for example, in Ellsworth Kelly's (1923–) *Red, Orange, White, Green, Blue* (1968), a succession of color stripes on canvas. Likewise, minimalist sculptors emphasized simple, symmetrical sculptures. The *Vietnam Veterans' Memorial* (1982) designed by Maya Ying Lin (1960–), and consisting of two polished black granite walls with the names of the 58,000 Americans who died in the Vietnam War, is perhaps the best representation of minimalist sculpture.

In the 1980s and 1990s, artistic expression went in various directions, characterized by eclecticism. Some artists probed the limits of abstraction, while others chose a style known as the "new realism," reproducing objects with near photographic exactness. Eclecticism, a kind of "premeditated chaos," is one of the major characteristics of postmodern culture, which borrows at random from the past but only to revive the past in fragments without any unifying continuity with the past or link to the future.

Europe at the beginning of the twenty-first century is no longer the center of the world, replaced as it is by a faceless, soulless internationalism. In the postmodern "Global Village," there is no accepted historic community or tradition to validate knowledge or artistic experience. Multiculturalism does not allow for a common historical tradition upon which an aesthetic standard can be established. Therefore, the definition of what is good art or bad art disappears. Is graffiti sprayed on a wall or the side of a railroad car art or anti-art? When does dabbling on canvas or the wall of a public restroom become art?

Divorced from any historical continuity, postmodern art is transient and dependent upon the viewer interacting with it. Lacking any content or meaning, postmodern art has often become more spectacular in order to hold the viewer's attention. The Bulgarian-born Christo Javacheff (1935–) invented *empaquetage*, a technique by which he wrapped anything capable of being wrapped—for example, the Pont Neuf, the Art Museum in Bern, trees along the Champs-Élysées in Paris, or the Reichstag building in Berlin. Christo and wife Jeanne-Claude de Guillebon (1935–2009) exhibited The Gates, 7,500 saffron-colored fabric panels hanging on 16-foot high frames along 23 miles of New York's Central Park walkways, in January 2005. As to its message, said Jeanne-Claude, there is none: "It's only a work of art." Roland Baladi (1910–1980) proposed transforming the Arc de Triomphe in Paris into a giant snow globe. He planned to enclose it in a plastic dome with artificial snow blowing around inside the dome. It was a piece of conceptual art that, fortunately perhaps, remained a concept.

What is called "performance art" of the 1990s was a postmodern version of post-World War I Dadaism. The performance artists meant to be outlandish, to shock, or even to offend the viewer. Some of their art was merely amusing, as, for example, Janine Antoni's (1962–) *Loving Care* (1993), in which she used "her own hair as a paintbrush to 'mop' a gallery floor with Clairol's Loving Care black hair dye," (Perry, Baker and Hollinger 2005) or Yves Klein's (1928–1962) use of "living paintbrushes." While an audience listened to a chamber orchestra play a single note for 20 minutes, Klein, dressed in a tuxedo, directed several naked women covered in blue paint (patented as "International Klein Blue") to smear their bodies on a canvas stretched out on the floor of the Galerie Internationale d'Art Contemporain in Paris. Artist Spencer Tunick (1967–) assembled more than 5,000 nude men and women on March 1, 2010, in front of the Sydney [Australia] Opera House for what he titled "Mardi Gras: The Base."

Not all postmodern art was amusing. Some artists used religious or patriotic symbols or objects in ways many considered offensive or blasphemous. Displays of Robert Mapplethorpe's (1946–1989) photographs of homoerotic and sadomasochistic subject matter were so controversial that some museums were forced to close their exhibits. Such provocative art brought forth a public outcry from conservatives for an end to the use of public funding to purchase or support the arts.

Literature, Drama, the Cinema, and Music

Postwar writers also tried to find meaning in a world that appeared increasingly without meaning. One of the themes, or issues, that they explored in light of the changing assumptions about truth and reality was the quest for social justice, a continuation of the preoccupation of such interwar writers as Bertolt Brecht and the American John Steinbeck (1902–1968). Although both of them continued to write after World War II, they did their best work during the interwar period. Another theme, especially during the Cold War era, was an indictment of the new authoritarianism (totalitarianism, in Cold War terminology) of the Soviet Union. Some of the more effective of these writers were among those who had embraced Marxism (socialism, communism) during the early years of the Soviet experiment and now tried to come to grips with their disillusionment. Among these were the Italian Ignazio Silone (1900–1978), the Hungarian Arthur Koestler (1905–1983), and, perhaps best known, the Englishman George Orwell (1903–1950).

George Orwell's two most memorable works were written right after the war's end and just before his premature death in 1950. *Animal Farm* (1945) and *1984* (1949) are the best-known and most widely read indictments of the Soviet Union and totalitarianism. Yet, both end in despair, for although Orwell was deeply committed to the defense of human dignity and freedom, it is "Napoleon" and "Big Brother" who triumph over "Boxer" and Winston Smith.

Clearly, Orwell saw those "eternal" values of Western civilization in grave danger of being extinguished.

During the 1960s and 1970s, criticism of the communist regime in the Soviet Union was expressed most effectively in the historical and autobiographical novels of the Russian author Aleksandr Solzhenitsyn (1918–2008). In a series of novels beginning with *One Day in the Life of Ivan Denisovich* (1962) that won him the Nobel Prize in 1970 and expulsion from the Soviet Union in 1974, Solzhenitsyn charged that the atrocities committed under Stalin were not his responsibility alone, but must also be attributed to Lenin. After the collapse of the Soviet Union in 1991, Solzhenitsyn returned to Russia in 1994 and became a harsh critic of the "new" Russia. In an address given at Harvard University in 1978 ("A World Split Apart"), and again in an address given when he received the Templeton Prize in 1983 ("Men Have Forgotten God"), Solzhenitsyn criticized the West in general for having lost the will to defend the values that had once made Western civilization the envy of the world.

In postwar Germany, the two Nobel laureates Heinrich Böll (1917–1985) and Günter Grass (1927–) explored the damage done to the values of European civilization by the war and the failure of the postwar generation to come to grips with its past or to resist the temptation to allow West Germany's economic prosperity to numb the nation's collective conscience. Böll was a prolific writer of novels, short stories, and nonfiction. The best known of his novels are *Adam Where Art Thou?* (1959), *Billiards at Half-Past Nine* (1959), *The Clown* (1968), and *Group Portrait with Lady* (1971).

Günter Grass, like Böll, wanted postwar Germans living amidst economic prosperity to remember that they once embraced the darkness of National Socialism. In three novels known as the Danzig Trilogy—*The Tin Drum* (1959), *Cat and Mouse* (1961), and *Dog Years* (1963)—Grass tried to understand the attraction that Nazism once held and the power of West Germany's postwar economic miracle to aid in suppressing and forgetting the past. *The Tin Drum* is a particularly disturbing novel that was made into an equally disturbing motion picture.

The struggle to understand postwar Germany lies at the heart of novels written by the East German writer Christa Wolf (1929–2011). She chose to remain in East Germany because she felt that the Nazi past was more thoroughly repudiated there than in West Germany. Initially, she saw hope for the future in socialism. At one point, she even served as an informant for the East German secret police, the Stasi. By the mid-1950s, Wolf was becoming increasingly disillusioned with the socialist experiment as the repression of artistic freedom increased. Still, she remained in the GDR until the unification of the two Germanies in 1989, a development she opposed. Her unique contribution was the ability to critique postwar Germany from both perspectives.

Like Christa Wolf, the Czechoslovakian writer Milan Kundera (1929–) hoped for a better future in a Communist-controlled postwar Czechoslovakia. He joined the Communist Party in 1948 and was expelled from the party in 1950, readmitted in 1956, and expelled a second time in 1970. In 1975, Kundera left Czechoslovakia for France, where he has resided ever since, having become a French citizen in 1981. Kundera has always insisted that he is not a dissident writer, but rather a novelist. His novels are not overtly anti-Communist, but many find in them a critique of the increasing repression of freedom under postwar Communism.

Art and literature were one means by which philosophical issues and changing world views were communicated to a mass audience. We have noted above how existentialism was communicated more through the novels of Camus and Sartre than through their nonfiction. The theater, the cinema, and music were also powerful means by which serious philosophical statements reached a wider audience. An example from the theater is what was known as the Theater of the Absurd.

The Theater of the Absurd took its name from Albert Camus's description of the human predicament as essentially "absurd." The message of these dramatists who enjoyed a vogue during the 1950s and 1960s was that of existentialism. They portray the individual as inhabiting a meaningless universe in which he or she feels increasingly alone, isolated, bewildered, threatened, and even terrified, by an all pervasive sense of angst, yet desperately hoping against all hope to find in oneself some meaning. Among those associated with the Theater of the Absurd were Eugene Ionesco (1912–1994), Fernando Arrabal (1932–), Arthur Adamov (1908–1970), and Samuel Beckett (1906–1989).

Samuel Beckett's *Waiting for Godot* (1952) is the best-known example of the Theater of the Absurd. The play portrays two tramps who spend their days waiting for the coming of one Godot, a mysterious individual who may not even exist. Is he like Nietzsche's god, only a belief, but one whose hoped-for appearance nevertheless gives the two otherwise hopeless tramps a reason to go on living? *Waiting for Godot* remains one of the most often performed plays of the postwar theater. Perhaps, this is so because it, like few others, communicates so well the dilemma of humanity adrift in a postmodern universe.

The European cinema, unlike the American film industry driven by the demands of a mass market, also served as a medium through which the search for meaning in an alienated world could be shared with a wider audience. European filmmakers like Ingmar Bergman (1918–2007), Alain Resnais (1922–), Michelangelo Antonioni (1912–2007), Federico Fellini (1920–1993), and Luis Buñuel (1900–1983) powerfully explored the complexities of life in a postwar, postmodern world. Bergman's films are said to be filled with "Nordic angst and gloom" (Winders 2001). The central characters in Bergman's films are individuals "who wonder whether they are in this world for some reason. They feel themselves alienated from others, meaningless entities walking around on the earth for a few years and then vanishing into endless night" (Janaro and Altshuler 2003). During an interview in which he discussed the making of *The Silence* (1963), Bergman said that he had reached the conclusion that God is dead, and therefore, the universe is silent.

Classical music after 1945 developed mainly in two directions. One school, sometimes called the "structuralists," emphasized ever greater complexity in their compositions. The second school, more in tune with the philosophical assumptions of postmodernism, sought to compose music involving a technique employing random chance. French composer Pierre Boulez (1925–) exemplifies the former, while the American John Cage is the best example of the latter.

Boulez's compositions are characterized by their extremely complex structure that gives the composer total control over every element of the music. Building upon the serialism and 12-tone technique pioneered by Arnold Schoenberg (1874–1951), Boulez aimed at creating a musical structure, the effect of which is "to eliminate any sense of traditional melody, harmony, or counterpoint along with the emotions they evoke" (Cunningham and Reich 2009). This effort to remove the human

The Seventh Seal, 1957, directed by Ingmar Bergman. Above: Bengt Ekerot as Death.

element from music led to compositions of "electronic music," beginning in the 1950s.

In electronic music, sounds are arranged, or "ordered," by a computer and then played on an electronic oscillator, rather than traditional musical instruments. The invention of the synthesizer in 1955 by engineers at RCA greatly simplified the composition (or production) of electronic music. Karlheinz Stockhausen (1928–2007), a major composer of electronic music, chose to combine electronic music with traditional orchestras in, for example, his composition *Mixtur* (1965). The structuralists, whether following the example of Boulez's complex serialization or the more "programmed" innovations of electronic music, remained faithful to the most basic premise of Western music, that is, composers create their music according to rules that enable them to communicate with their listeners. This was not true of the second school, which turned to creating musical compositions according to random chance.

The so-called music of chance may be illustrated by the career of John Cage (1912–1992). Cage was inspired by the artist Marcel Duchamp (1887–1968), known for his "ready-mades," and Zen Buddhism, especially the *I Ching*, or *Book of Changes*. Like Duchamp, Cage believed that art and music exist all around us. It does not necessarily originate in the artist's mind. Cage made use of "ready-made sounds" by simply recording the random noises in the surrounding environment. His best-known piece is one titled *4'33"* (1952). The pianist approaches the piano, sits down, and, without ever touching the keys, turns the pages of a nonexistent score at random intervals. The actual music of *4'33"* is the random noises produced by the audience. Cage believed that music should reflect the random chaos of the universe that we inhabit.

Popular Culture

Not surprisingly, American tastes and America's spirit of commercialism were major forces shaping popular culture after World War II. The fear, expressed already in the 1920s by novelist Wyndham Lewis (1886–1957), that European culture would become "decivilized" by its "Americanization" as the world became smaller appears to have become a reality at the end of the twentieth century. The reasons for American cultural "imperialism" are varied and perhaps not unexpected.

Post-World War II American popular culture offered a very seductive model when compared to the war-scarred landscape of postwar Europe. The mystique of America as a land of prosperity, opportunity, and an exciting, fast-paced lifestyle grew in influence during the 1950s. American consumerism was associated in the minds of the European masses with prosperity, youth, popularity, glamor, and the latest fashions. Increasingly, Europe's youth took their cue from what they saw in America's movies and television programs or heard in its popular music. The presence of American troops in Europe after 1945, and the broadcasts of the American Armed Forces Radio Network, meant that there was little, if any, real difference between the American hit parade and that of any European nation.

The extent to which postwar European society was shaped in response to the influence of American consumerism would be difficult to overstate. It was particularly true following the collapse of communism in Eastern Europe. As the former Soviet Union became a graphic example of the failure of communism, it no longer served as a model for Europeans wanting to build a new future. America, throughout the twentieth century the flagship of capitalism and, after 1989–1991, the apparent victor in the century-long struggle between capitalism and communism, became the model (for better or worse) for Europe's future. By the end of the twentieth century, the symbols of America's commercial dominance could be seen everywhere. The "golden arches" of McDonald's fast-food restaurants and other logos of American franchises, like Starbucks Coffee, dotted the European landscape and threatened to overwhelm national tastes, much as the franchising of America itself largely destroyed regional tastes. More tourists reportedly visit the Disney theme park built outside Paris in 1992 than visit the traditional monuments of France's cultural and historical heritage.

Rock music and the popular cinema were the two main vehicles for the Americanization of European (even world) culture. As with jazz, that other American musical import that swept across Europe between the two world wars, "rock 'n' roll" had roots in the African American subculture. It was a blend of a variety of popular American music genres, including rhythm and blues, jazz, gospel, country and Western, and folk music. However, it was two white performers, Bill Haley (1925–1981) and Elvis Presley (1935–1977), who made "rock 'n' roll" the music of the new international youth culture during its "Golden Decade" (1954–1963).

Europe's youth were attracted to American "rock 'n' roll" music just as Western Europe began to enjoy a measure of economic prosperity. A measure of economic independence allowed European youth to break free of traditional class restraints and indulge their taste for American popular music. What they found in "rock 'n' roll" was a spirit of revolt and overt sexuality. England's "rockers" donned black leather jackets and rode motorcycles in imitation of their new American idols like Elvis Presley, the "King," and movie star Marlon Brando (1924–2004).

In 1964, leadership in popular music passed temporarily to the English groups, epitomized by The Beatles, who emerged from the working-class bars of Liverpool, England, to chart a new course for popular music. The success of their song "I Want to Hold Your Hand" (1964), the most popular rock hit since Elvis' "All Shook Up" (1957), launched them into superstardom. In February 1964, they premiered on the *Ed Sullivan Show*, a kind of rite of passage for any popular entertainer, individual or group, who aspired to stardom in America. Fans around the world held a vigil in December 1964 when drummer Ringo Starr (1940–) underwent a tonsillectomy. The appearance of their album Sgt. Pepper's Lonely Hearts Club Band in 1967, the cover of which was believed to contain hidden messages about the alleged death of band member Paul McCartney (1942–), raised the group to enduring cult status. In 1985, Queen Elizabeth II bestowed upon each member of The Beatles the honor of MBE, Member of the British Empire.

The rock groups that followed The Beatles looked and openly lived the rebellious and promiscuous lifestyle they sang about. An example was the Rolling Stones, a rock group that debuted in February 1963 at the Crawdaddy in Richmond, England. Whereas The Beatles' public image was that of clean-cut musicians in mohair jackets with ties and neatly groomed hair, the Rolling Stones were antisocial outlaws in both appearance and behavior. They sang lyrics so explicit that they were sometimes banned from play on the radio. They openly smoked marijuana, abused drugs, hosted wild parties that included nudity, and even were alleged to practice Satanism. The Rolling Stones quickly achieved cult status in the world of rock music and, despite the questionable quality of their music when compared to that of The Beatles, were still touring and performing before large crowds in 2013.[2] Rock music spoke to, or one might say, expressed the soul of post-World War II's youth. The themes found in the lyrics of rock music were the themes of the postwar generation—feelings of isolation, hunger for love, and sexual liberation. By expressing those universal themes, rock music had a wide appeal that helped to restore

---

[2]   Paul McCartney (1942–) of The Beatles, Joan Baez (1941–), Bob Dylan (1941–), and Judy Collins (1939–) were among the "great ones" of the classic age of folk and rock music, who were still touring and performing before live audiences in 2013.

a sense of community for a generation of youth who felt acutely the increasing fragmentation of the postmodern world. Although there were "native" European clones for American and British rock stars, rock culture bore a definite "made in America" stamp.

The evolution of popular music reflected three cultural trends— the changing standards of public morality, the ever-increasing role of commercial hype, and a cross-fertilization of cultural influences from around the world that were absorbed into what was becoming by the dawn of the new millennium a popular music that reflected a global culture.

When Elvis Presley made his first television appearance in 1956, his gyrating pelvis was considered so risqué that viewers were allowed to see him only from the waist up. During the 1960s, The Beatles dared use only suggestive language in reference to the emerging drug culture and relaxed sexual norms. By the mid-1970s, British "punk rock" performers like the Sex Pistols were openly and deliberately offensive, even vulgar, in both their performance style and the lyrics of their songs. The 1970s also saw the birth among urban African American teenagers of rap music. Rap, a kind of chanted poetry that satirizes racism, black culture, and other rappers, generally spoke openly and graphically of life in the urban ghetto, of drug use, and of sexual promiscuity as if it were a competitive sport.

The Sex Pistols exemplified the commercialization of popular culture. They were "manufactured" by their promoters as a product to be marketed for profit. This vulgar commercialization was increasingly characteristic of popular music. Styles of music, like differing styles of jeans, were created and marketed with an attentive eye on what might sell. The names of groups or individual artists passed in and out of style like the logos on jean pockets.

Technological advances made possible the cross-fertilization and international marketing of different musical styles. Musical styles from around the world were imported and synthesized. Indian sitar music was popularized by Ravi Shankar (1920–2012). Reggae, a blending of electric bass and guitars with organ, piano, and drums that originated among the poor of Jamaica, introduced a Caribbean influence into popular music. The appearance of music videos and live transcontinental television broadcasts (e.g., *Aloha From Hawaii* with Elvis in 1973 and the famous Live Aid show in 1985) demonstrated that rock had become the world's choice in popular music and the chief medium of popular culture.

The cinema, like rock music, did much to create a common popular culture. European directors, often enjoying government subsidies, continued to dominate the motion picture genre commonly referred to as the "art film." These were "gourmet" films intended for a very small but discriminating audience. The popular cinema, like popular music, was dominated by American-made action films, comedies, and sentimental romances, heavy on the entertainment but making very little demand on the viewer's intellect. As the growing popularity of television lured more and more people away from the movie houses, Hollywood turned during the 1950s to blockbuster epics like *The Ten Commandments* (1956), *Around the World in 80 Days* (1956), and *Ben-Hur* (1957).

American dominance of the silver screen continued during the last quarter of the twentieth century and into the twenty-first century.[3] American filmmakers like Francis Ford Coppola (1939–), the *Godfather* (1972), and George Lucas (1944–), *Star Wars* (1972) and *Raiders of the Lost Ark* (1981), made lavish blockbuster adventure films that enjoyed international popularity. No filmmaker of the late twentieth or early twenty-first centuries could trump Steven Spielberg (1946–) in box office receipts or artistic achievement. Spielberg produced films such as *Raiders of the Lost Ark* (1981) and *E.T. The Extra-Terrestrial* (1982) that warmed the heart and reduced moviegoers to tears, as well as serious films such as *The Color Purple* (1985), *Schindler's List* (1993), and *Lincoln* (2012) that raised the social consciousness of his audience.

The rapid spread of television from the 1950s on and the development of new technology such as videotapes (VHS), digital video disks (DVD), and cable and satellite television networks assisted creation of a universal pop culture. Since American commercialism

---

[3]   Hollywood did not have total control of the world market in actions films. Britain's "James Bond, 007" film series based upon the best-selling fiction of Ian Fleming (1909–1964) achieved international success comparable to any American produced film series.

was the major driving force behind the new technology, the culture that it nurtured reflected that of middle-class American youth. American films and television programs were now available to virtually unlimited audiences, and American entertainment stars became international stars. Lucille Ball (1911–1989); Bill Cosby (1937–); Peter Falk (1927–2011), the bungling lovable detective; and many others were as familiar to Europeans as Mickey Mouse.

Videotapes, video disks, and compact disks (CD) were but a small part of a revolution in technology that both shrunk the world and at the same time greatly increased its complexity. According to the US National Aeronautics and Space Administration (NASA), there were approximately 3,000 artificial man-made satellites orbiting the earth at the beginning of 2013. The launch of Telstar 1 in 1962 made live television broadcasts possible between the United States and Europe. The Public Broadcasting System (PBS) began transmitting programs by satellite in 1978. Home satellite reception became possible in 1980, and by the mid-1990s, more than six million American homes had satellite dishes in their backyards or on the roofs of their homes. A Global Position Satellite (GPS) system was established in 1994. Before the end of the first decade of the twenty-first century, GPS navigation systems were a built-in, in some cases standard, feature of many new automobiles.

Technology made it possible for an individual virtually anywhere in the world to communicate live and visually with any other individual anywhere. Instant access to the contents of libraries, art museums, and an ever-growing number of databases was possible with a small device that could be held in the palm of one's hand. In 2012, Harvard University began to offer many of its lecturer courses online free to the public. One hundred thousand individuals registered for the initial course offerings. Soon other major universities including Stanford, Yale, and Princeton and smaller colleges like Hillsdale College followed Harvard's example. For anyone with access to the new communications technology, any great work of art, rare book, or recorded music or voice was instantly available.

We began this chapter with the postwar intellectuals searching for meaning amidst the physical ruins of European civilization at the

Author J. K. Rowling, surrounded by adoring fans, poses with a copy of Harry Potter and the Deathly Hallows at the Natural History Museum in London, July 20, 2007. © ALESSIA PIERDOMENICO/Reuters/Corbis

end of World War II. Those intellectuals, who pondered the meaning of history and of life, concluded that human beings were adrift, alone in a cold and meaningless universe. At the end of the century and the beginning of the new millennium, there were signs that the masses did not agree with that conclusion. There is evidence in the popular culture that people did not accept the conclusion that a human being is only a cosmic cipher in a cold, dark universe. This could be seen in the phenomenal popularity, in both book publishing and the cinema, of two mega myths—the *Lord of the Rings* trilogy by J. R. R. Tolkien (1892–1973) and the seven-volume *Harry Potter* series by J. K. Rowling (1965–)—both British authors.[4] Both the *Lord of the Rings* and the *Harry Potter* series are adventure stories centered on a cosmic duel between good and evil. Upon the outcome of each

---

[4]   *Left Behind* (1995), a science fiction series based loosely on the biblical book of Revelation may be cited as another example. Definitely a distinctively American product, and lacking any literary merit, it has been a phenomenal best-selling series internationally.

struggle, both of which affirm the ultimate triumph of good, hangs the future of the universe. Tolkien, an Oxford professor of medieval literature, conceived of his story and worked on it during the interwar years. He was a member of the Inklings, a group of writers associated with C. S. Lewis (1898–1963), a professor of medieval and renaissance literature at Oxford University. J. K. Rowling, who published her first *Harry Potter* novel in 1997, has acknowledged that she was influenced by her reading of Tolkien and Lewis. Both series have broken all sales records in the publishing industry worldwide. Both have been made into motion pictures that likewise have established new records for attendance. Clearly, though the intellectual dream spinners may be adrift in a fog, the average man or woman living under the influence of European civilization is living in a world of hope, a world in which the future is brighter than the past.

References

Cunningham, Lawrence S. and John J. Reich. 2009. *Culture and Values. Vol. 2: A Survey of the Humanities*, 7th ed. Independence: Cengage Learning.

Danto, Arthur C. 2010. *Andy Warhol*. New Haven, CT: Yale University Press.

Janaro, Richard and Thelma Altshuler. 2003. *The Art of Being Human*. New York: Pearson.

Lascelles, Kendrew. 1973. *When All the Laughter Dies in Sorrow*. New York: Saturday Review Press. Mediarts Music, Inc. Used by permission of United Artists.

Perry, Marvin, Wayne Baker, and Pamela Pfeiffer Hollinger. (2005). *The Humanities in the Western Tradition: Ideas and Aesthetics. Vol. 2: Renaissance to Present*. Independence: Cengage Learning.

Sartre, Jean-Paul. 1947. *Existentialism*, translated by Bernard Frechtman. New York: Philosophical Library. Quoted in Marvin Perry, *An Intellectual History of Modern Europe*. Boston: Wadsworth Publishing, 1992, 449.

Stromberg, Roland N. 1994. *European Intellectual History Since 1789*, 6th ed. Upper Saddle River: Pearson.

Ward, Glenn. 1997. *Teach Yourself Postmodernism*. Chicago: McGraw-Hill Trade.

Winders, James A. 2001. *European Culture Since 1848: From Modern to Postmodern and Beyond*. New York: Palgrave.

Further Reading

Barrett, William. 1990. *Irrational Man: A Study in Existential Philosophy*. New York: Anchor Books. Still regarded as the best introduction to existentialist philosophy, it discusses the views of Kierkegaard, Nietzsche, Heidegger, and Sartre.

Britt, David, ed. 2008. *Modern Art: Impressionism to Post-Modernism*. London: Thames & Hudson. Noted artists provide essays on every aspect of the visual arts from impressionism to pop art with 400 colored illustrations.

Cantor, Norman F. 1997. *The American Century: Varieties of Culture in Modern Times*. New York: Harpercollins. A provocative look at the cultural history of the twentieth century, which focuses on Europe and the United States.

Friedman, Thomas L. 2007. *The World is Flat: A Brief History of the Twenty-first Century*, 3rd ed. New York: Picador. A widely acclaimed look at how globalization has "flattened" the world we live in.

Giannetti, Louis and Scott Eyman. 2009. *Flashback: A Brief History of Film*, 6th ed. New York: Pearson. A well-written, richly illustrated, popular history of "fiction movies," which views film as "both art and an industry."

Guardini, Romano. 2001. *The End of the Modern World*. Wilmington: Isi Books. A contemplation of the condition of modern man in the wake of two world wars, the Holocaust, and other horrors of the postwar world.

Lukacs, John. 2002. *At the End of an Age*. New Haven: Yale University Press. Believing that we are living at the end of an age that began with the Renaissance and is often called "modern," Lukacs examines what it means to live in a new age of post-modernism.

Rolling Stone Magazine. 1992. *The Rolling Stone Illustrated History of Rock and Roll*. New York: Random House. A comprehensive history of the musical styles and artists of rock and roll.

Stromberg, Roland N. 1975. *After Everything: Western Intellectual History Since 1945*. New York: St. Martin's Press. A somewhat dated but very useful introduction to the main themes of Western thought after World War II.

12

Charting a New Course
Europe from 1989 to the Present

Chronology

1989	First free elections in Poland in the postwar period; massive gains by Solidarity
	Fall of the Berlin Wall
	End of communist regimes in East Germany, Czechoslovakia, Bulgaria, and Romania
1990	Unification of Germany; Helmut Kohl reelected chancellor in the first free all-German elections since 1932
1991	John Major replaces Margaret Thatcher as leader of the British Conservative Party and as Prime Minister
	First Gulf War
	Dissolution of the Warsaw Treaty Organization

Twentieth-Century Europe: A Brief History, 1900 to the Present, Third Edition.
Michael D. Richards and Paul R. Waibel.
© 2014 John Wiley & Sons, Inc. Published 2014 by John Wiley & Sons, Inc.

Attempted coup in the Soviet Union;
   Gorbachev resigns as president of the
   Soviet Union;
The Soviet Union is dissolved at the end
   of the year
Slovenia and Croatia leave the Yugoslav
   Federation; beginning of the
   disintegration of Yugoslav Federation

1992   Bosnia withdraws from the Yugoslav
           Federation
        Maastricht Treaty sets the process by which
           the European Community (EC) will
           become the European Union (EU)

1993   EC becomes the EU
        Czechoslovakia's "Velvet Divorce" results in
           the formation of the Czech Republic and
           the Republic of Slovakia

1995   Austria, Finland, and Sweden join the EU
        Dayton (Ohio) Agreement establishes a
           loosely federated Bosnia and ends the civil
           war in Bosnia (1992–1995)

1997   British Labour Party under Tony Blair wins
           the election

1998   Helmut Kohl defeated by Gerhard Schröder;
           Germany governed by Social-
           Democratic/Green coalition

1999   Introduction of the Euro
        NATO admits Poland, Hungary, The Czech
           Republic
        War in Kosovo

2000   George W. Bush becomes president of the
           United States in an election decided by the
           US Supreme Court
        Vladimir Putin becomes president of the
           Russian Republic

2001	9/11 attacks on the World Trade Center in New York and the Pentagon in Washington, DC, by members of Al-Qaeda
2002	US invasion of Afghanistan
	Rose Revolution in Georgia
	Chechen rebels seize theatre in Moscow
2003	Second Gulf War (United States invades Iraq and drives Saddam Hussein from power)
	Completion of the Human Genome project
	Space Shuttle *Columbia* destroyed on re-entry
2004	EU enlarged by the inclusion of 10 new members
	NATO adds seven new members
	Madrid train bombing
	Orange Revolution in Ukraine
	Boxing Day tsunami
2005	7/7 attacks on the London Underground
	Angela Merkel becomes the German chancellor
	Benedict XVI becomes pope
	Hurricane Katrina
2007	Beginning of the Recession in the United States
2008	Barack Obama elected president
	South Ossetia War between Russia and Georgia
	Independence of Kosovo
2009	Election protests in Iran
2010	David Cameron becomes prime minister in the United Kingdom
	Moscow Metro bombing

	Problems with the Greek economy set off the European sovereign debt crisis
	Arab Spring begins in Tunisia
2011	Arab Spring continues
	Earthquake and tsunami in Japan
	Official end of the Iraq war
	Osama bin Laden killed in a US Navy Seals raid
	World population reaches the seven billion mark
2011–2012	Russian election protests
2012	Diamond Jubilee of Queen Elizabeth
	Olympics held for the third time in London
	Barack Obama elected to a second term as president
2013	Pope Benedict XVI resigns as pope and Francis I, the first pope from the Western Hemisphere becomes pope

IN THE FALL OF 1989, the Monday evening prayer services held at the Nikolai Kirche (the St. Nicholas Church) in Leipzig, East Germany, became political events. Even more astounding in a system in which religion was carefully monitored, the crowds that filled the square next to the church after the service increasingly used the occasion to exchange information and to organize processions around the inner city. On October 2, more than 10,000 protestors marched past the train station and the Stasi headquarters (!) to the town hall, the kind of demonstration that had not been seen since the Berlin uprising in 1953.

On October 7 Mikhail Gorbachev, head of state of the Soviet Union, appeared in East Berlin to participate in the celebration of the fortieth anniversary of the founding of the GDR. He famously warned Erich Honecker "life punishes those who delay." That same weekend rumors abounded that any attempt to use the next Monday evening prayer services for political purposes would be met by a show of force. Hospitals were warned that they should be prepared to treat injured people. Factory militias were given orders to deploy to locations around Leipzig. The police presence around the city was beefed up. Alarmed by the possibility of a bloody clash between demonstrators and government forces, local government officials, prominent members of the community, and the local communist party leadership issued an appeal. Assurances were exchanged that neither side would offer provocation to the other.

On the 9th of October thousands of Leipzigers thronged the Nikolai Kirche, and other churches in Leipzig, for the Monday

A massive protest demonstration in front of Leipzig's main railroad station in 1989. The October 9 demonstration, immediately after the celebrations in East Berlin of the 40th anniversary of the founding of the German Democratic Republic (GDR), is often cited as the beginning of the Revolution of 1989 in the GDR. © STR/ Reuters/Corbis(42-48896253)

prayer services. Afterwards, thousands of demonstrators marched around the inner city proclaiming *Wir sind das Volk!* (We are the people!). The march was peaceful and the government did not attempt to break it up. From that moment on, it could be said that the East German government had lost the initiative and was never able to regain it.

The Revolutions of 1989

Many different factors contributed to the decisive events of 1989 in Eastern and Central Europe. They began in 1985 when Mikhail Gorbachev became the Secretary-General of the Communist Party of the Soviet Union. Gorbachev's policies of glasnost and perestroika created an attractive model that many in Eastern Europe wanted to emulate. Furthermore, Gorbachev began to indicate that the Soviet Union would no longer be willing or even able to intervene in the affairs of eastern European countries, as had been the case in 1953, 1956, 1968, and 1981. By 1989 Gorbachev was telling communist leaders of the satellite nations that they were on their own.

Another essential factor in the events of 1989 was the re-emergence of Solidarity as a major influence in Polish politics. In the partially free summer elections of 1989, Solidarity won all of the 161 seats in the *Sejm* (the lower house) it was allowed to contest. (The Polish Communist Party had tried to arrange the election so that it would secure a majority of seats.) In addition, Solidarity won all but one of the Senate seats. Both the Communists and Solidarity were surprised by the election results. Solidarity negotiated with the smaller parties that had been controlled by the Communist Party and the result was a new coalition government with Tadeusz Mazowiecki (1927–2013), a Solidarity activist, as premier. And in 1990, Lech Wałęsa was elected president.

About the same time the Polish Communist Party was losing its grip on Poland, its Hungarian counterpart was running into difficulties. In the summer of 1989, Hungarians were able, for the first time since 1956, to discuss the Hungarian Revolution of 1956 openly. In a moving ceremony, Hungarians reburied several of the martyrs of that event.

Hungary also contributed to the developments in the GDR. In the spring of 1989, Hungary removed the barbed-wire fence between it and Austria, symbolizing a new relationship with Western Europe. East Germans vacationing in Hungary began crossing the Hungarian border into Austria illegally during the summer. Once in Austria, they travelled, courtesy of the West German government, to West Germany and a new life. Early in the fall, Hungary stopped all efforts to prevent East Germans from crossing, despite its obligations under a treaty with the GDR. The flood of East German refugees over the border between Hungary and Austria, together with those East Germans who crowded into the West German embassies in Prague and Warsaw, pushed the East German government off balance. Then, as noted above, the uncontested march of East German citizens around Leipzig on October 9 began a process whereby the government responded to events rather than initiated them.

In Czechoslovakia, demonstrators in Prague filled Wenceslaus Square in November. At first, police tried to break up the demonstrations. Within a few days, however, the crowds grew to overwhelming numbers. The Czech government, like its counterpart in the GDR, found itself on the defensive, responding to events, always at least one step behind. The center of political gravity moved to the Magic Lantern Theatre, where Vaclav Havel and colleagues associated with Charter 77, a group of activists dedicated to monitoring abuses of human rights as defined by the constitution of Czechoslovakia, worked to give direction to the movement against the government. By December, the old government had resigned and a new government headed by Havel had formed. Alexander Dubček, the heroic figure of the "Prague Spring," emerged from long years of obscurity to lend his presence to the "Velvet Revolution." Tragically, Dubček died in November 1992 from injuries received in an auto accident.

The revolutionary wave also swept away the communist government in Bulgaria without violence. In Romania, however, Nicolae Ceauşescu, who had ruled in a harsh and increasingly arbitrary manner since the 1960s, attempted to hold on to power. Revolutionary forces arrested Ceaucescu and his wife. They promptly put the couple on trial, declared them guilty, and shot them. Pictures of the dead couple flashed around the world in television reports.

In a few short months, the unthinkable had taken place. The "Iron Curtain" had dissolved and was no more. Instead, a series of new governments eagerly began to experiment with the transition to a market economy and a democratic political system. In the euphoria of early 1990, some thought the transition was a matter of a few hundred days. Instead, years of trial and error lay ahead.

Prague on the eve of free elections in June 1990. Only a few months earlier, the "Velvet Revolution" had swept the communist government from power. Behind the statue of Tomáš Masaryk, the founder of Czechoslovakia, is the headquarters of Civic Forum, the party that won the election. From the collection of Michael Richards.

German Reunification

The fall of the Berlin Wall on November 9, 1989, symbolized for many the end of the Cold War. Pictures of happy East Berliners streaming past the Wall into West Berlin and being greeted by ecstatic West Berliners with champagne, flowers, and bananas flashed around the world. Within a year the German Democratic Republic no longer existed. At the end of 1991 the Soviet Union disappeared, replaced by 15 republics. The Cold War was over; statesmen supposedly were putting the New World Order in place.

The GDR was the best positioned of all the former Soviet satellites, whether it remained independent or chose to unify with the Federal Republic of Germany. Many within the old Socialist Unity Party, which renamed itself the Party of Democratic Socialism

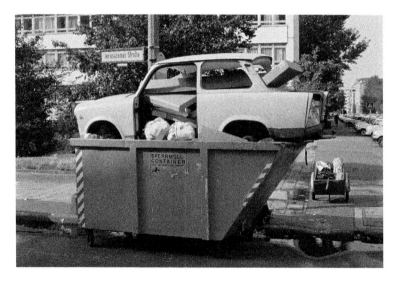

A gutted Trabant (or "Trabi") sits in a dumpster, symbolic of the initial turning away from anything connected with the old regime. Although East Germans were generally cautious with their money in the first months after unification with West Germany, many could not resist buying a West German or Swedish car. © Wim Wiskerke/Alamy

(PDS) in December 1989, wanted to remain independent and to reform the political and economic systems of the GDR. Most of those active in the citizens' movement, members of the New Forum or Democracy Awakening, for example, also hoped to reform the old systems. By December, however, the majority of those who participated in the demonstrations in Leipzig, Berlin, Dresden, and other cities and towns of the GDR were beginning to think about the possibility of quickly gaining a western standard of living. Even after the Wall opened, East Germans continued to leave in large numbers for West Germany. The average East German wondered why he or she should be part of a new socialist experiment when the tried-and-true West German approach was readily available.

To his credit, Helmut Kohl understood early on that a possibility existed to bring East and West Germany together in the very near future. He daringly decided to take the lead and to support a process of rapid unification early in 1990. With very little support from his west European colleagues and with Gorbachev and the Soviet Union still a question mark, this move by Kohl was a brave one. Kohl did have the backing of President George H. W. Bush (1924–) of the United States, who had succeeded Reagan. Kohl also felt the continued influx of East German refugees into West Germany would eventually work a hardship on the West German economy. Despite his vision and bold action, Kohl underestimated the difficulty of restructuring the East German economy and raising living standards to West German levels.

The first free elections in the GDR, in March 1990, were for the *Volkskammer* (the People's Chamber, the parliament of the GDR). The main issue was unification. West German politicians campaigned for their East German counterparts. The Christian Democrats (CDU) formed a coalition with several smaller parties and strongly supported the idea of rapid unification. They won a stunning victory over the Social Democrats, who had been lukewarm toward unification. The new government under Lothar de Maizière (1940–) plunged into negotiations for the introduction of the Deutschmark into East Germany in July. Kohl contributed a crucial element to the unification process through a meeting with Gorbachev. The meeting resulted in Germany agreeing to pay the

Soviet Union a large sum. The Soviet Union not only gave its blessings to unification but also agreed to a timetable for withdrawing its troops from the eastern part of Germany. Further negotiations between East and West Germans that summer led to unification in October and to the first free elections in all of Germany since November 1932. Kohl and the coalition of Christian Democrats and Free Democrats (FDP) easily beat the Social Democrats. In the east, only a few delegates from the PDS were elected. Almost no one from the citizen movements was elected. Although some Germans complained that the GDR had been "annexed," unification had been accomplished in less than a year from the beginning of the German Revolution of 1989. Germany began to pour billions of marks annually into the east to undo the damage done by the old regime and to bring the infrastructure up to West German standards.

The unification of Germany led also to full sovereignty. In addition to negotiations between East Germany and West Germany, there were the "2 + 4" talks involving the two Germanys and the four ex-Allies from World War II, the Soviet Union, Britain, France, and the United States. The major result was a treaty that formally put an end to any remaining rights held by the four powers in Germany.

The whole process changed Europe in profoundly important ways. In many respects, European history since 1990 has been an attempt to deal with the various ramifications of German unification. The new Germany was larger and far stronger economically than any other European state. A Franco-German partnership in Europe now depends not on the relatively equal weight of the two countries but more on Germany's conscious efforts to maintain it. More than ever before, it seemed important to Europeanize Germany in various ways.

During Kohl's fourth term as chancellor, Germany signed treaties with Poland (1990) and Czechoslovakia (1993) recognizing post-World War II boundary changes. Even more consequential, the government decided to move the capital from Bonn to Berlin in 1991. Berlin became the scene of new building projects as many companies moved their headquarters to the renewed capital city.

The most important efforts of Kohl's fourth and fifth terms (he was re-elected in 1994) concerned the reconstruction of what had been the German Democratic Republic. In part, this involved both deindustrialization, the removal of outmoded industrial facilities—and repair of the environment. East German efforts to develop a major industrial economy had resulted in extensive environmental damage, including pollution from the burning of sulfur-laden brown coal and the dumping of toxic waste products. Despite the transfer of nearly $2 trillion over two decades, however, projects meant to provide East Germans with a lifestyle comparable to that enjoyed by West Germans have been only partially successful. The Gross Domestic Product (GDP) per capita produced by a West German in 1990 was more than twice that produced by an East German. By 2012 East Germans were producing more than twice as much per capita as in 1990 while West Germans produced only about 50 percent more than earlier. They were, however, still producing 30 percent more per capita than East Germans. More than a million East Germans moved to the western part of Germany in search of employment. It is somewhat ironic that the infrastructure in East Germany, roads, bridges, airports, train stations, is in better shape than the infrastructure in the West because it has been recently built or rebuilt. Nonetheless, unemployment in 2012 on average remains higher in the East, nearly 10 percent, than in the West, just under 6 percent. This disguises the fact, of course, that the West has areas of nearly full employment and other areas where the rate of unemployment is higher than the average for the East. Now that a new generation that knows only a reunited Germany is coming of age, many differences will begin to fade. The government is, nevertheless, committed to plans to level any differences still existing for several more years.

The Federal Commissioner for the Stasi Archives, popularly known as the Gauck-Behörde (Gauck Agency), became one of the most important efforts to come to terms with the past of the former German Democratic Republic. Because the Stasi were such a pervasive influence in the GDR, it seemed necessary to preserve their files and to guard against their misuse. Under the first commissioner, Joachim Gauck (1940–), the archives were established. Anyone with a Stasi file was allowed to see it. Care was taken not to allow the files to be used for political purposes.

This aspect of reconciliation with the disappearance of the GDR has been relatively successful. For those who were 40 years of age

A remnant of the Berlin Wall at the East Side Gallery with a painting of Leonid Brezhnev, the General Secretary of the Central Committee of the Communist Party of the Soviet Union, bestowing a fraternal kiss on Erich Honecker, General Secretary of the Socialist Unity Party (SED). © Pierre Brumder/Alamy

and older in 1989, however, the changes have been difficult in many cases. To many it seemed they had spent their entire careers working for something now viewed as worthless. Especially for those who had retired or were about to retire, the newly reunited Germany was a bitter pill. Even among those who had not liked the old regime, there was a certain *Ostalgie* (nostalgia for the eastern way of life). Many valued, for example, the social guarantees, the slower pace of life, and the idea that people need their neighbors and could expect their help in difficult times.

Germany in the twenty-first Century

Gerhard Schröder (1944–) ended Kohl's long run of electoral success in 1998 and formed a coalition of Social Democrats and Greens. Although a Social Democrat, Schröder followed a domestic policy that resembled that of Margaret Thatcher or

Ronald Reagan. Schroder's Agenda 2010 reform program included cuts in various parts of the social welfare system, including national health care, unemployment benefits, and pensions. It also resulted in lower taxes and new regulations on employment. Especially controversial were what is known as Hartz I-IV, a series of recommendations regarding unemployment and social welfare benefits. Although Schröder's policies were controversial within his own party and in other quarters, they have been given some credit for Germany's relatively strong showing since the beginning of the economic recession in 2008.

The Schröder government was initially very supportive of the United States after the September 11, 2001, attacks at the hands of Al-Qaeda terrorists on targets in New York City and Washington, DC, and sent German troops to fight alongside US troops in Afghanistan—the first German soldiers used in combat operations since World War II. Schröder publically broke with President George W. Bush (1946–), however, over his decision to call for the US invasion of Iraq in 2003. Schröder also established a close relationship with Vladimir Putin (1952–) of Russia and took something of a pro-Russian line in foreign policy matters.

In the German elections of 2005, no clear winner emerged. Instead the leading parties formed a Grand Coalition of the Christian Democrats/Christian Socialist Union and the Social Democratic Party. Both Angela Merkel (1954–) and Gerhard Schröder wanted the chancellorship. Merkel prevailed in the contest, becoming chancellor, and the SPD was given 8 of the 16 cabinet posts. In the 2009 elections, the CD/CSU gained enough votes to form a coalition with the Free Democratic Party.

Merkel, although born in West Germany, moved with her family to East Germany as a child and grew up there. She entered politics in the wake of the 1989 Revolution and swiftly rose in the CD ranks. She is often compared to Margaret Thatcher. Her tough stance in the Euro crisis following the 2008 recession has also led commentators to compare her to Bismarck, the Iron Chancellor. In 2012, she was named by *Forbes* magazine as the second most powerful person in the world (President Barack Obama of the United States was first). She has played a crucial and controversial role in efforts to defuse the Euro crisis (see the latter part of this chapter for a discussion of the crisis).

The Soviet Union Disappears

For many in the Soviet Union, the events of 1989 and 1990 appeared only to underline the decline of the Soviet Union as a world power. President George H. W. Bush's "New World Order," as it took form in the crusade against Iraq (the first Gulf War in 1991) appeared to offer the Soviet Union only the role of junior partner. In the Soviet Union itself, Gorbachev had not succeeded in making perestroika work in the economy. In fact, the economy seemed stuck between two systems, communism and capitalism. The Soviet economy would probably have run into serious trouble even without perestroika, but Gorbachev's experiments gave people something highly visible to complain about.

While Gorbachev maneuvered politically, seemingly moving well to the right in 1990, Boris Yeltsin (1931–2007) emerged as a rising political star. Elected president of the Russian Republic, Yeltsin began immediately to enhance the power of the republics of the Soviet Union and to decrease the power of the central government. By the late summer of 1991, he and his fellow presidents of the republics of the Soviet Union appeared to have achieved success. A treaty setting up a federal arrangement that would have given the republics a good deal more authority was scheduled to be signed. Gorbachev had swung back to the left and looked ready in August to agree to the treaty.

Before the treaty could be signed, members of Gorbachev's own government staged a coup. They placed Gorbachev, on vacation in the Crimea, under house arrest. Yeltsin, in his capacity as president of the Russian Republic (which made up the major part of the Soviet Union), defied the coup from the [Russian] White House, the building housing the parliament, in Moscow. The coup leaders lacked direction and nerve. The military refused to move against Yeltsin and his supporters. Television coverage worldwide by the ubiquitous CNN (Cable News Network) worked against the coup and for Yeltsin.

After the collapse of the coup, Gorbachev returned to power in Moscow, but his days as president of the Soviet Union were numbered. By the end of the year, the Soviet Union had been dissolved. Several republics, Estonia, Latvia, and Lithuania, went their own way. The remaining republics grouped together in the Commonwealth of Independent States (CIS), but this organization did not develop into a strong association. Instead, the various republics played largely independent roles. The most powerful was the Russian Republic under Boris Yeltsin. Other important republics were Belarus, Ukraine, Georgia, and Kazakhstan.

Seventy-four years after the October Revolution, the Soviet Union ceased to exist. In many important ways, however, the Russian Republic continued to play the same role in the world. While it cooperated with the United States in the important task of disarmament, especially in the area of nuclear weapons, it regarded itself as a major power with its own set of interests and objectives. It has at times acted as if the old Soviet Union had never imploded, intervening on occasion in Georgian affairs and in the affairs of some of the Central Asian republics, putting pressure periodically on Ukraine, and fighting two bloody wars against the Chechens within Russia itself. It has been periodically upset by NATO's efforts to expand to the east, but it has also enjoyed playing a role in the G-8 (Group of Eight) meetings of the major industrial states. From the beginning of its independent existence, it replaced the Soviet Union as a permanent member of the United Nations Security Council.

Under Yeltsin, Russia made only limited progress toward a working democracy. President from 1991 to 1999, he soon tarnished the brave image he had established during the coup of 1991. In a bizarre turn of events, Yeltsin, in a quarrel with the Congress of People's Deputies in 1993, sent tanks to fire on the [Russian] White House in order to quash attempts by deputies to unseat him. Yeltsin also led Russia into a disastrous war against Chechnya, a former republic of the Soviet Union located in southwestern Russia.

Yeltsin's biggest problem was the attempt to lift price controls and establish a market economy in Russia. The existence of a very large defense sector made the transition to a market economy difficult. It was estimated that the defense sector accounted for about 25 percent of Russia's gross output. Defense expenditures could not be sustained nor was it easy to make the transition from defense products to consumer goods. A second and related problem was the existence of so-called "mono-industrial regions," areas in which a particular part of the economy had been concentrated. In addition, welfare functions were generally attached to industries rather than to local governments. All these factors helped to bring on a depression in the mid-1990s. In the late Soviet era, estimates of those in poverty stood at 1.5 percent of the population. By 1993, the estimates ranged from one-third to one-half of the population. Life expectancy for males plunged from 64 in 1990 to 57 in 1994 and only rose to 59 by 2009. Life expectancy for women dropped from 74 in 1990 to 70 in 2009.

The first Chechen War began in 1994. Chechnya resisted successfully for nearly a year, humiliating the Russian army in initial encounters. The Russians managed to take the capital city of Grozny in 1995. In August of 1996, a cease-fire was arranged and a peace treaty signed in 1997.

The elections of 1996, nonetheless, resulted in a victory for Yeltsin. His most serious competition came from the leader of the Communist Party, Gennady Zyuganov (1944–), who forced Yeltsin into a run-off election. Vladimir Zhirinovsky (1946–), a rabid nationalist and anti-Semite, gained serious support from the extreme right. Yeltsin emphasized that only he could prevent a return to a totalitarian system. Some observers of the elections believed that holding elections and running a parliamentary system, despite obvious ups and downs, constituted an important step forward. Others pointed to the corruption of the system and the arbitrary use of power as indications that democracy had not yet taken root.

A kind of robber baron capitalism characterized Russia in the 1990s. It was most successful in Moscow and a few other major Russian cities. The oligarchs, among them Boris Berezovsky (1946–2013) perhaps the best known of the group, were instrumental in Yeltsin's 1996 election. There was also the disturbing presence of a large, well-organized Russian mafia, which operated abroad as well as in Russia.

Under Yeltsin, insiders managed to grab valuable state holdings for pennies on the dollar. Russia, heavily dependent on the sale of oil, natural gas, and other commodities, was hard hit by the recession of 1998. That year, despite a large emergency loan from the International Monetary Fund (IMF), Russia defaulted on its international debt and its currency (the ruble) collapsed.

Russia in the Twenty-First Century

On the last day of 1999, Yeltsin resigned. He picked Vladimir Putin (1952–) the head of the Federal Security Service (FSB), the successor agency to the KGB, to replace him as temporary president. In the 2000 elections, Putin was elected president in part because of Russian success in the second Chechen War that had begun in September 1999. Putin remained in power even in the face of grisly incidents connected with the war in which the government response appeared inept and was heavily criticized. In October 2002, the Moscow theater hostage crisis took place. Some 40–50 Chechen rebels held more than 840 hostages. They demanded the withdrawal of Russian troops from Chechnya and an end to the war. Russian special forces stormed the building after firing into the building canisters of gas that was supposed to put the hostages and their captors to sleep. The gas in many cases proved lethal, killing more than 100 civilians. Less than two years later, in September 2004, Chechen rebels took more than 1,000 persons (including 770 children) hostage at the Beslan school. Russian troops used tanks, rockets, and other heavy weapons to storm the school. This tragic event ended with the death of nearly 400 people, including 186 children.

During his first term, Putin also staged a confrontation with another group that contested his power. This group included some of the oligarchs. Berezovsky went into exile but Mikhail Khodorkovsky (1963–), the head of Yukos, Russia's largest oil and natural gas company, was arrested in 2003, tried on fraud and tax charges, found guilty, and sentenced to nine years in prison. There is reason to believe these charges were politically motivated. He was later tried on additional charges and his sentence extended to 2017. Putin not only removed powerful and wealthy critics from the Russian political scene, but he also took over their extensive media holdings, thus eliminating a major source of opposition.

Putin won re-election in 2004. Much of his popularity was due to an economic recovery based largely on the rising price of oil, of which Russia had plenty. Relations with the West deteriorated first because of western support for the independence of the Serbian province of Kosovo in 2008 (see below) and secondly after the West criticized Russia's intervention in the quarrel between South Ossetia and Georgia. Russia was also criticized for its intervention in Ukrainian politics and its support of the autocratic government in Belarus.

In 2008, Dmitri Medvedev (1965–), an associate of Putin's, was elected president of Russia and named Putin as Prime Minister. Medvedev, perhaps somewhat more moderate than Putin, worked to modernize the Russian economy and to decrease its dependence on natural resources. Whatever the difference between the two men, they worked out an exchange of jobs with Putin again winning election for president in 2012 and Medvedev, who became the leader of the United Russia Party that year, accepting the post of Prime Minister. There were large protest movements against the results of the elections, but Putin will probably hold on to power, in one office or another, as long as the economy continues to perform well. Russia does, however, remain quite vulnerable to changes in the prices of various natural resources and particularly vulnerable to changes in the markets for natural gas.

The Disintegration of Yugoslavia

The disappearance of the Soviet Union was a more or less inevitable process. By contrast, the disintegration of Yugoslavia was largely the work of two political leaders willing to put their own power above the welfare of the people of their countries. The better known of the two and the first to fan the fires of ethnic hatred was Slobodan Milosevic (1941–2006), the leader of Serbia. The other was Franjo Tudjman (1922–1999), president of Croatia, someone not generally held responsible for his part in the Yugoslav tragedy.

It was perhaps remarkable enough that the delicate, complicated governmental system of Yugoslavia survived the death in 1980 of its founder, Marshall Tito, by more than a decade. By 1990, however, Milosevic, in order to maintain power in Serbia and also to begin turning Yugoslavia into a greater Serbia, played the nationalism card, that is, played on Serbian fears of other ethnic groups, first in Kosovo, an autonomous province of Serbia with an Albanian majority, and then in Vojvodina, another autonomous province of Serbia, in this case one with a large Hungarian population. Croatia and Slovenia met these challenges to the federal structure of Yugoslavia with their own versions of emotional appeals to ethnic separatism.

In June 1991, Slovenia and Croatia declared independence. Germany contributed to the developing conflagration by recognizing the two states diplomatically, despite the fact that other members of the European Community (EC) wanted to withhold recognition in the hopes of keeping Yugoslavia intact. Serbia's response was to use the Yugoslav army against the two republics. Slovenia, favorably situated both in terms of geographic location and a homogenous population, was able to defend itself and escape the civil war. Croatia and Serbia, not for the first time in the twentieth century, went to war with one another. For many Serbs, memories of World War II and the activities of Croatian fascists in the Ustasha were still strong.

The war became even more complicated the following year when Bosnia declared its independence. Bosnia had once been a model of the possibilities for a harmonious existence of Serbs, Croatians, and Muslims. The population spoke the same language, Serbo-Croatian, although Serbs would use the Cyrillic alphabet to write it while Croatians would use the Roman alphabet. They differed, of course, in terms of religion, with the Serbs belonging to the Orthodox faith, Croats to the Catholic religion, and the Bosnian Muslims to Islam. Up to 1992, however, despite differences, there had been a great deal of intermarriage and mixed neighborhoods were common.

The Serbian siege of Bosnian-Muslim Sarajevo, which only a few years before had been the site of a Winter Olympics, became the centerpiece of the Yugoslav tragedy. "Ethnic cleansing," an euphemism which meant in reality anything from forcibly driving a particular group away from an area to systematic and repeated rape of women to the torture and killing of men, entered as a disgraceful new term into the vocabulary of the world.

Efforts by the EC to negotiate a settlement or even to find a common position were for the most part unsuccessful. The United Nations sent a peacekeeping force, which was largely ineffectual to the extent that it did not actually work to the advantage of the Serbs. In 1994, however, Serbia distanced itself from the Bosnian Serbs because of the effects of economic sanctions against it. NATO began to weigh in with air strikes against the Bosnian Serbs. Finally, in 1995, the combatants reluctantly agreed to the Dayton (Ohio) Agreement calling for a loosely federated Bosnia. Troops from the United States and from other NATO nations arrived soon after to enforce the agreement.

The last act of the Yugoslav tragedy came in Kosovo. It was here, in 1987, that Milosevic had begun his nationalistic campaign. While civil war raged elsewhere in Yugoslavia, the Serbs stripped Kosovo of its autonomous status and worked to ensure Serbian control of every aspect of life in the province. A Kosovar (Albanian) resistance movement appeared. In 1991, a Kosovo parliament declared the independence of the province. Up to 1995, however, both the Kosovars and the Serbs avoided direct confrontation. In the meantime, the Kosovo Liberation Army (KLA) formed. The Dayton Agreement, which seemed to give Milosevic a free hand in Kosovo, galvanized the Kosovar resistance.

In 1996, the KLA went on the offensive. In response, in 1998 Milosevic stepped up the level of military actions, authorizing the use of helicopter gunships and armored personnel carriers against civilian targets and destroying homes and villages. This, in turn, radicalized the Kosovars.

The international community faced a dilemma. Although the KLA had initially been seen as terrorists, Serbian reprisals had created a humanitarian crisis that appeared patterned after Serbian ethnic cleansing campaigns in Bosnia. The United States and Western European countries threatened the Serbs with NATO air strikes and compelled them and the Kosovars to negotiate at Rambouillet, outside Paris, in February 1999. The Kosovars eventually agreed to a plan that would have brought NATO peacekeepers to Kosovo and forced Serbian troops to leave. Kosovo would have remained in the truncated Federal Republic of Yugoslavia as an autonomous province. The Serbs refused to sign.

NATO began bombing on March 24, 1999. Even before the bombs began to fall, the Serbs had embarked on a massive campaign of ethnic cleansing. Operation Horseshoe was designed to drive all the Kosovars from the province. By June 10, when NATO ended the bombing campaign, nearly 900,000 Kosovars, about half the Albanian population of Kosovo, had fled the province. The others were on the run within the province.

Once NATO began the campaign, it had to continue to victory or lose all credibility. Milosevic also faced a difficult decision. On the one hand, Serbian troops could only be dislodged by ground troops, which NATO was reluctant to introduce. On the other, NATO had not called off the air strikes and Russia had failed to stop them. The situation in Serbia itself was rapidly deteriorating. On June 10, 1999, Milosevic agreed to withdraw troops from Kosovo in return for an end to the bombing. He also agreed to the introduction of a NATO peacekeeping force. In the aftermath of the war, Kosovo Serbs became the victims. Nearly 200,000 fled the province by October.

Milosevic himself became a casualty of the Kosovo war. In September 1999, he failed to gain reelection as president. When he tried to falsify the results of the election, his former allies deserted him. Nearly two years later, on June 29, 2001, the Serbian government turned him over to the International Criminal Tribunal in The Hague to be tried for war crimes and crimes against humanity. Five years later, Milosevic died in prison, apparently of a heart attack.

The European Union

Before the revolutions of 1989, many observers of the European scene had predicted the 1990s would be the decade of the European Community. The 1985 report of the Delors Commission (Jacques Delors [1925–], a leading official in the European Community, president in 1990) called for the removal of all physical, technical, and fiscal barriers to the free movement of capital, goods, and people. This would create a single European market. The Single European Act (SEA-1986) legislated the necessary steps for implementing the report. By the time SEA went into effect, January 1, 1993, German unification and other changes in Eastern and Central Europe placed the European Union (EU—the new title for the EC) in somewhat of a quandary. Should it deepen, that is, become more fully integrated by pursuing a common fiscal policy and even a common foreign policy, or should it widen by taking in not only some of the old European Free Trade Association (EFTA) states but also some of the new democracies in eastern and central Europe?

Rather typically, the EU has tried to do both. Meeting in Maastricht, the Netherlands, in December 1991, what then was still the EC put together a treaty (Treaty on Economic and Monetary Union or "Maastricht Treaty") calling for further radical changes, among them a single European currency and a common foreign policy. The idea of a common foreign policy floundered on the inability of the EC to meet the Yugoslav crisis effectively. The idea of a single European currency, the Euro, was meant in part to integrate Germany even more tightly into the European framework. Those states wishing to join the monetary union had to meet a number of fiscal criteria, among them low inflation, budget deficits no more than 3 percent of Gross Domestic Product (GDP), and a government debt less than 60 percent of GDP. Progress toward these and other goals slowed in 1992–1993 as the result of an economic slowdown. In large part, the slowdown reflected soaring interest rates caused by Germany borrowing heavily to fund the reconstruction of the former East Germany. Europe began to pull out of the recession in 1994. In December 1995, the new currency received a name, the Euro. In 1998, 11 of the 15 members (Austria, Sweden, and Finland had joined in 1995) met the criteria for monetary union. Denmark, Britain, and Sweden had opted out earlier, and Greece failed to meet the criteria. In June 1998, the European Central Bank began operation. In 1999, the EU began using the Euro in business transactions. Finally, on January 1, 2002, the Euro became the sole currency of 12 EU states (Greece qualified for membership in 2001).

In 2004, the EU took in 10 new members: Cyprus, the Czech Republic, Estonia, Hungary, Latvia, Lithuania, Malta, Poland, Slovakia, and Slovenia. Bulgaria and Romania joined in 2007. Croatia is slated to join soon. Finally, Turkey, seemingly a perpetual

Table 12.1   European Community/European Union

1957	Treaty of Rome creating the European Economic Community (EEC) signed by original six member nations: Belgium, Federal Republic of Germany, France, Italy, Luxembourg, and the Netherlands
1967	EEC merged with the European Coal and Steel Community (1951) and EURATOM (1957) to become the European Community (EC)
1973	Denmark, Republic of Ireland, and United Kingdom joined the EC
1981	Greece joined
1986	Portugal and Spain joined
	Single European Act passed
1992	Treaty on the European Union (Maastricht Treaty) called for movement toward economic and monetary union and intergovernmental cooperation in some areas
1993	EU formally in existence
1995	Austria, Finland, and Sweden joined the EU
1999	Euro introduced for business transactions
2002	Euro became the sole currency of 12 of the 15 members of the EU (Denmark, Sweden, and the United Kingdom opted out of the monetary union)
2004	Ten new members joined: Cyprus, the Czech Republic, Estonia, Hungary, Latvia, Lithuania, Malta, Poland, Slovakia, and Slovenia
2007	Bulgaria and Romania join the EU
2009	Treaty of Lisbon goes into effect
2010	Problems with the Greek economy lead to a crisis of the Euro
2013	Croatia joined the EU

candidate, remains in limbo. Although it is a member of NATO, it has not been able to move very close to membership in the EU. While there are many obstacles in the way of membership for Turkey, the key issue may be that its population is mostly Muslim (Table 12.1).

In 2004, the European Union presented a constitution that, if it had been approved, would have resulted in a more centralized federal system. The proposed constitution failed, however, to gain the unanimous support required for it to take effect. Although there were clear benefits to be had in a more unified organization, these were weighed against fears of losing national sovereignty. A new Treaty of Lisbon replaced the old draft treaty in 2007. The Treaty of Lisbon kept much of the old treaty but adjusted the political structure to address concerns about national sovereignty. In 2009, the Treaty of Lisbon had been ratified by all the EU states and went into effect. By that time, however, the Greek debt crisis was threatening to destroy the Euro zone and all that had been done to integrate the European economy.

The Global Economic Collapse of 2008

The widening and deepening of the EU took place within the context of a global economy that had already experienced severe challenges in the late 1990s and the early part of the first decade of the new century. These challenges paled, however, in comparison with the economic collapse of 2008, one caused by fundamental flaws in the American mortgage industry and in securities based on mortgages. Simply put, it became clear by 2007 and 2008 that a large number of mortgages issued by American banks, both big and small, should never have been offered in the first place. These loans, with little or no down payments required, were provided to people who simply lacked the income to pay their mortgage payments. This became increasingly obvious once the initially low interest rates on so-called ARMs (adjustable-rate mortgages) were replaced by dramatically higher interest rates. To compound the problem, large US banks and investment houses bundled these unsound mortgages and offered them as the basis for securities they marketed and sold as highly secure financial products based on highly rated mortgages. As the US housing market slowed and investors found it difficult to "flip" houses, that is, sell them to other investors for a profit shortly after having purchased them themselves, the number of foreclosures began to climb, then spike. As the US housing bubble burst, companies and individuals that held large numbers of securities based on bad mortgages or had insured those securities began to lose great sums of money. Early in 2008, one major investment house collapsed, another was sold at a great loss, and the American government made the unprecedented decision to bail out several large banks and other financial institutions. The American economy went into deep recession and, despite stimulus efforts by both the Bush administration and the Obama administration, only slowly began a weak recovery in 2010.

The EU experienced its own recession and an even slower comeback during the same period. Complicating the situation for the EU was the possibility, the widespread realization of which started to become apparent to all parties in 2009, that Greece would have to default on its sovereign debt and leave the Euro zone. The Greek government, as was the case with several other governments, had taken advantage of cheap credit early in the twenty-first century to fashion an extensive and generous welfare package. When the global economy began to contract in 2007 and 2008, the Greek government found it increasingly expensive to borrow the funds necessary to maintain its benefits system. Since the Greek economy was a very small percentage of the EU economy, there was speculation that it could simply default on its debts. The problem with this, aside for the hardships that would result for the Greeks themselves, was that such a move might fatally weaken confidence in the larger economies of Italy and Spain.

Over the next two years, the EU pushed Greek governments to agree to austerity measures, fewer benefits, and higher taxes, and worked to reassure holders of Greek bonds and to keep interest rates low. It also worked with the Italian and the Spanish governments to pursue a similar course of austerity and financial support for their bond markets. Protests against austerity measures and complaints about both increasing rates of unemployment and the lack of economic recovery caused some observers to question this approach to the resolution of the EU crisis.

By 2012, the question seemed to be one of surrendering some aspects of national sovereignty to the EU in order to promote a sounder and more coordinated approach to fiscal policy. Many saw the European Central Bank (ECB) as the crucial institution. If it could use its power to oversee banking in the different EU countries and intervene where needed to purchase bonds or to provide bailout funds, the Euro zone could be preserved. The catch here is that the one country essential to the success of such an approach is Germany. Although Chancellor Merkel and her finance minister, the influential Wolfgang Schäuble (1942–) appear to favor the approach, they have yet to make a definitive statement to that effect. In any case, Germany finds itself once again at the center of an area of vital concern to Europeans. The German economy is a crucial part of the EU economy, often seen as the locomotive of that economy. The EU economy, in turn, forms the world's largest single economy, and thus is of vital concern to other players in the world economy.

The Revival of Terrorism

On September 11, 2001 ("9/11"), terrorists sponsored by Al-Qaeda (Arabic for "the base," an international terrorist network that wants to end western influence in Muslim countries and to create fundamentalist Islamic governments) flew two commercial airliners it had hijacked and taken the controls of into the twin towers of New York's World Trade Center. Another hijacked airliner flew into the Pentagon in Washington, DC, and a fourth plane, supposedly meant to target the White House or the Capitol, crashed instead in a field in Pennsylvania, this after the passengers of the doomed aircraft thwarted their hijackers' plans. These horrific attacks, in which almost 3,000 people died, followed a decade of terrorist actions by Al-Qaeda directed against the United Sates including, among others, the truck bombing of the World Trade Center in 1993, an attack on American troops in Saudi Arabia in 1996, attacks on American embassies in Africa in 1998, and the attack on the U.S.S. *Cole* in the Yemen in 2000.

The American government reacted to 9/11 by first demanding that the Taliban government in Afghanistan surrender Osama Bin Laden (1955–2011), thought to be the mastermind behind 9/11. When the Taliban refused to do so, the United States and its allies, including Afghan groups already fighting the Taliban, invaded the country and destroyed the Taliban government. The invasion forces failed, however, to find Bin Laden.

In 2003 the United States, together with its chief ally, Britain, and several other countries, decided to invade Iraq. In effect, this was a continuation of the First Gulf War ("Desert Storm," 1991). Critics wondered what the invasion of Iraq had to do with the war on terrorism. In particular, France, Germany, and the Russian Republic opposed the American effort. No weapons of mass destruction (WMDs) were found. Close ties between Saddam Hussein (1937–2006) and Al-Qaeda could not be established. It also became clear that Saddam Hussein had not lent support to the attacks on September 11, 2001.

Iraq was defeated with relative ease, but occupation was another matter. By 2006 the United States faced not only continued opposition to its control of the county but also a civil war between Sunni and Shiite factions. That year the Bush administration began what came to be known as the "Surge," an infusion of troops to attempt to regain control of the country and to end the sectarian violence. This effort, under the leadership of General David Petreus (1952–) resulted in decreased sectarian violence and progress by the United States in preparing Iraq to regain sovereignty and responsibility for its security. Under the terms of an agreement with the newly elected Iraqi government, the United States ended the occupation of Iraq in 2011. Many questions about the future of Iraq remain unanswered. They include the extent to which Al-Qaeda may be re-establishing itself in Iraq, Iranian influence among the Iraqi Shiite population, and the three-way contest for power among the Sunni, the Shiites, and the Kurds in Iraq.

As the situation in Iraq was reaching a kind of resolution, American policy makers became increasingly aware of unfinished business in Afghanistan. The Obama administration followed up on initial efforts by the Bush administration to defeat a resurgent Taliban with a firm commitment to assist a notably corrupt Afghan government in creating a workable democracy and gaining the capacity to manage its own security needs. Part of the commitment involved announcing a 2014 date for withdrawal of coalition forces.

One crucial factor in the attempt to establish a strong, secure Afghan government is the US–Pakistan relationship, one that has remained, for a number of reasons, problematic. One point of contention in the relationship is the American reliance on drone warfare, the use of unmanned airplanes to strike at targets in the western borderlands of Pakistan, attacks that invariably result in collateral damage, that is, the death of innocent civilians. Tracking down Osama bin Laden, who had been hiding in plain sight in a Pakistani city, and assassinating him in 2011 also increased tensions. The American raid clearly infringed on Pakistan's sovereignty. There was, however, no possibility of a joint raid given the hostility to the United States of some elements within the Pakistani government and security apparatus.

In many ways, the United States has been supremely fortunate in the years from 9/11 to the present. Although Al-Qaeda has not necessarily been removed as a source of global terrorism, it is at least possible to point to the limited success of various attempts at terrorism on American soil since the horrific 2001 attacks. One incident, the killing of 13 people at Fort Hood, Texas, November 5, 2009, has been classified as an act of workplace violence, although many would consider it an act of terrorism. Another incident, two bombs set off at the finish line of the Boston Marathon on April 15, 2013, killed 3 and wounded more than 200. There have been several unsuccessful attempts at terrorism in the United States.

Terrorism in Europe

There have been two major instances of terrorism in Europe since 9/11, one in Britain and one in Spain. The commuter train bombing in Madrid on March 11, 2004, killed 191 people on four different trains. It was the largest terrorist action in Europe since the 1988 bombing of a passenger jumbo jet en route from London to New York that went down in Lockerbie, Scotland, resulting in the loss of 259 persons onboard and 11 more on the ground. This attack was determined to be the work of Libyan nationals. Officially, the Madrid bombing is regarded as an Al-Qaeda action, possibly in retaliation for Spanish involvement in the war in Iraq. The initial response by the Spanish government, however, was to blame the attack on the ETA, the Basque separatist terrorist organization. Rumors have continued to circulate that the ETA together with Muslim terrorists were involved. It may well have as much to do with Spanish political problems as with global terrorism.

The other major terrorist bombing consisted of coordinated suicide attacks during the rush hour in London on the morning of July 7, 2005. In these incidents, four Islamic "home-grown" terrorists set off bombs on three trains in the Underground and one bomb on a double-decker bus. In addition to the terrorists, 52 civilians were killed. The terrorists were protesting against the American war on terror. In addition to Afghanistan, Palestine, and Iraq, the terrorists mentioned Chechnya. While the bombing was clearly connected to Al-Qaeda and the wars in Afghanistan and Iraq and the bombers were inspired by people identified with Al-Qaeda, it is not clear how much help or direction the bombers obtained from outside sources.

The US-led "War on Terror" has done much to reshape the world since 9/11. After the death of Osama bin Laden, many assumed that the leadership of Al-Qaeda had been decimated and scattered. This may have been an overly optimistic assumption. Al-Qaeda is still active in the borderlands between Pakistan and Afghanistan, in Somalia and Yemen, once again in Iraq, and also in northern Mali. People claiming to be connected with or inspired by Al-Qaeda appear frequently in countries like the United States Great Britain, Spain, and Russia. Funding for the terrorist organization, in particular from individuals and families in Saudi Arabia, is plentiful. Sadly, the current period is much like the 1970s, when international terrorism, at that time in a variety of different forms, appeared to be going strong. Perhaps, just as earlier, this era of international terrorism will eventually fade.

European Demographics

European societies are growing older. Nineteen of the twenty countries with the highest share of people over the age of 60 are European (Japan is the exception). Fertility rates are low, in many cases well below replacement level. The situation is similar in the United States except for the very large number of immigrants coming into the United States and the fact that these people are disproportionately young adults. In the United States and in Europe, this difference aside, the questions being asked are the same. How will the benefits be paid for when the number of workers supporting those benefits is no longer adequate to pay for them? Various schemes have been discussed to get around this problem. They involve reductions in benefits or increases in taxes or increased privatization of benefits. Additionally, there are occasional calls for greater labor market flexibility so that economies can grow and thus relieve problems. The noted historian Tony Judt notes in *Postwar* (2005, p. 793) the existence of "a broad international, cross-class consensus about the duty of the state to shield citizens from the hazards of misfortune or the market." It is this consensus, even after the powerfully influential model constructed by Margaret Thatcher, which may make it difficult for Europeans to find a way forward economically and socially.

Compounding the difficulties of modifying the consensus will be European attitudes toward immigrants. The immigrant populations of the various European nations are young, fertile, and increasingly restless. Many are second and third generation, they speak and write the language of the country fluently, and possess good educations. It is a vast resource, not always put to good use.

Perhaps the main problem is that most of the immigrants are Muslim. In a Europe that is more and more only nominally Christian or Jewish, Muslim immigrants, most of whom consider themselves devout, tend to stand out. There seems to be no easy way to assimilate these immigrant populations into the existing society. France can be seen as a case in point. A series of riots broke out in the suburbs of Paris in 2005 and in 2009, mostly involving French youth of North African heritage. The riots appeared to reflect frustration with high unemployment and police harassment and brutality. Religious ideology appeared to have little to do with the melees. Nonetheless, public opinion reflected fear that immigrant communities would never accept European values or integrate into existing society. A sophisticated version of the anti-immigrant and anti-Muslim rhetoric can be found in the ideas put forth by the National Front in France, which is now run by the daughter of the founder, Marine Le Pen (1968–). The government has added to the controversy by banning the wearing of headscarves by Muslim women in educational institutions. Some Muslim commentators recommend full participation in French society and politics. Others counsel remaining apart from French institutions. Finally, there are observers who see immigrants, the "other," as a vital addition to French life. Given the demographic and economic problems, immigrants can furnish a crucial resource in working toward a better future for all of France. Similar observations could be made about several other European countries and, of course, about the United States.

Conclusion

Europe remains an important part of the world. The European Union, despite the Euro crisis, is a powerful part of the global economy. In recent years, however, Europe has failed to find common ground for either a foreign policy or a defense policy. In these cases, nationalism is still too strong a force for Europeans to hope to pursue common objectives. Also a factor in this case, Europeans tend to wait to see what the United States will suggest or do. Paradoxically, Europeans now may find themselves refusing to follow the American lead or, conversely, attempting to get the Americans to go along with projects they find important. In a post-Cold War World, this is probably only to be expected. Recent examples of Europeans taking the lead include French efforts to establish a no-fly zone during the Libyan civil war and calls for intervention in the Syrian civil war.

The world in the twenty-first century is interconnected but far from integrated. In the long Cold War period between 1949 and 1989, differences within the two opposing camps were suppressed. Now, for better or worse, the many powerful players in global politics and economics are able to pursue their own interests and policies without paying too much attention to the needs and desires of other players. This takes place largely within a consensus that recognizes that competition should stop well short of war. Nonetheless, it is a world that the United States together with its European allies cannot expect to dominate. Individual European states may align themselves with the United States on occasion and the EU will probably see situations in similar fashion as the United States, but there are realities that must be honored. Depending on one's location and need for certain resources, Europeans will have to work with the Russian Republic and will have limited influence on its activities with respect to Ukraine, Georgia, or Belarus. The People's Republic of China not only will become a formidable competitor in Southeast and East Asia but also in Africa and the Middle East. India, while not so formidable in military or political terms, will continue to be important economically. It is a world in which perhaps as many as six or seven political-economic entities, one of them the European Union, will carry great weight. It is a world of vast potential and serious problems. Europeans, having moved perhaps further from the use of war or imperialism because of historical experience than any other people, have much to contribute. If the potential for good is to outweigh the tendency for problems to expand, it may well be Europeans who over the next few decades will show the way.

Reference

Judt, Tony. 2005. *Postwar: A History of Europe since 1945*. New York: The Penguin Press.

Further Reading

Caldwell, Christopher. 2009. *Reflection on the Revolution in Europe: Immigration, Islam, and the West*. New York: Doubleday. A thoughtful analysis of the various problems associated with Muslim immigrants in Europe.

Johnson, Lonnie R. 2010. *Central Europe: Enemies, Neighbors, Friends*, 2nd ed. New York: Oxford University Press. A review of Eastern Europe before and after the Revolutions of 1989.

Judah, Tim. 2000. *The Serbs: History, Myth, and the Destruction of Yugoslavia*. Excellent discussion of a complicated situation.

Judt, Tony. 2005. *Postwar: A History of Europe since 1945*. New York: The Penguin Press. A well-informed and wide-ranging history of all of Europe by one of the leading historians of his generation.

Kaplan, Robert. 2012. *The Revenge of Geography: What the Map Tells Us About Coming Conflicts and the Battle Against Fate*. New York: Random House. An insightful review of how geography shapes the current international political scene.

Patterson, James T. 2005. *Restless Giant: The United States from Watergate to Bush v. Gore*. New York: Oxford University Press. Another brilliant and deeply insightful review of American history, part of the Oxford History of the United States.

Pinder, John and Simon Usherwood. 2007. *The European Union: A Very Short Introduction*. New York: Oxford University Press. A concise but also comprehensive discussion.

Remnick, David. 1997. *Resurrection: The Struggle for a New Russia*. New York: Random House. Yeltsin's Russia by an astute and well-informed journalist.

Appendix

Abbreviations and Acronyms

THE TWENTIETH CENTURY produced a bewildering array of abbreviations and acronyms for the many political parties, committees, organizations, and institutions that have appeared over the years. No one can hope to remember all the relevant short forms used in European history in this century. The two alphabetical lists should help, however, in quickly determining what a set of initials stands for or how the name of a particular institution is commonly abbreviated. In some cases, the initials will not correspond to the English version of the name. This is because the initials are taken from the name as it appears in the language of the country. For example, the German National Socialist Workers' Party is abbreviated NSDAP, which stands for Nationalsozialistische Deutsche Arbeiterpartei.

Belgium, Netherlands, Luxembourg	BENELUX
British Union of Fascists	BUF
Cable News Network	CNN
Christian Democratic Party (Italy)	DC
Christian Democratic Union (West Germany; Germany)	CDU
Committee for the Defense of the Workers (Poland)	KOR

Twentieth-Century Europe: A Brief History, 1900 to the Present, Third Edition. Michael D. Richards and Paul R. Waibel.
© 2014 John Wiley & Sons, Inc. Published 2014 by John Wiley & Sons, Inc.

Commonwealth of Independent States (Former USSR)	CIS
Communist Information Bureau	COMINFORM
Communist International (Third International)	COMINTERN
Communist Party (Germany)	KPD
Communist Party (Italy)	PCI
Communist Party (Soviet Union)	CPSU
Conference on Security and Cooperation in Europe (*See also* the Organization for Security and Cooperation in Europe)	CSCE
Council for Mutual Economic Assistance	COMECON
East Germany (German Democratic Republic)	GDR
European Coal and Steel Community	ECSC
European Community (*See also* European Economic Community; European Union)	EC
European Defense Community	EDC
European Economic Community (*See also* European Community; European Union)	EEC
European Free Trade Association	EFTA
European Monetary System	EMS
European Recovery Program (Marshall Plan)	ERP
Federal Republic of Germany (West Germany)	FRG
Geheime Staatspolizei (Secret Police in Nazi Germany)	GESTAPO
German Democratic Republic (East Germany)	GDR
German National Socialist Workers' Party (Nazis)	NSDAP
German Social Democratic Party	SPD
Gross Domestic Product	GDP
Group of Seven (leading industrial democracies)	G-7
Independent Social Democratic Party of Germany	USPD
Kosovo Liberation Army	KLA
Kriegsrohstoffabteilung (War Raw Materials Administration)	KRA
League of Communists of Yugoslavia	LCY
Main Administration of Corrective Labor Camps (USSR)	GULAG
New Economic Policy	NEP

North Atlantic Treaty Organization	NATO
Organization for Economic Cooperation and Development	OECD
Organization for Security and Cooperation in Europe	OSCE
Organization of European Economic Cooperation	OEEC
Party of Democratic Socialism (formerly the Socialist Unity Party)	PDS
Polish Socialist Workers Party	RPPS
Popular Republican Movement (France)	MRP
Royal Air Force (United Kingdom)	RAF
Russian Social Democratic Labor Party (Bolsheviks; Mensheviks)	RSDLP
Schutzstaffel (Protective detachment—SS Nazi organization)	SS
Secret police (East Germany)	STASI
Single European Act	SEA
Socialist German Student Federation	SDS
Socialist Party (France)	SFIO
Socialist Revolutionaries (Russia)	SR
Socialist Unity Party (East Germany)	SED
Soviet Secret Police (1935–1953)	NKVD
Soviet Secret Police (1953–1992)	KGB
State Defense Committee (Soviet Union)	GKO
Strategic Arms Limitations Talks / Treaty	SALT
Strategic Defense Initiative ("Star Wars")	SDI
Sturmabteilung (Stormtroopers—Nazi organization)	SA
Trades Union Council (United Kingdom)	TUC
Warsaw Treaty Organization	WTO
West Germany (Federal Republic of Germany)	FRG
World Trade Organization	WTO

BENELUX	Belgium, Netherlands, Luxembourg
BUF	British Union of Fascists
CDU	Christian Democratic Union (West Germany; Germany)
CIS	Commonwealth of Independent States (Former USSR)
CNN	Cable News Network

COMECON	Council for Mutual Economic Assistance
COMINFORM	Communist Information Bureau
COMINTERN	Communist International (Third International)
CPSU	Communist Party (Soviet Union)
CSCE	Conference on Security and Cooperation in Europe (*See also* the Organization for Security and Cooperation in Europe)
DC	Christian Democratic Party (Italy)
EC	European Community (*See also* European Economic Community; European Union)
ECSC	European Coal and Steel Community
EDC	European Defense Community
EEC	European Economic Community (*See also* European Community; European Union)
EFTA	European Free Trade Association
EMS	European Monetary System
ERP	European Recovery Program (Marshall Plan)
FRG	Federal Republic of Germany (West Germany)
FRG	West Germany (Federal Republic of Germany)
G-7	Group of Seven (leading industrial democracies)
GDP	Gross Domestic Product
GDR	East Germany (German Democratic Republic)
GDR	German Democratic Republic (East Germany)
GESTAPO	*Geheime Staatspolizei* (Secret Police in Nazi Germany)
GKO	State Defense Committee (Soviet Union)
GULAG	Main Administration of Corrective Labor Camps (USSR)
KGB	Soviet Secret Police (1953–1992)
KLA	Kosovo Liberation Army
KOR	Committee for the Defense of the Workers (Poland)
KRA	*Kriegsrohstoffabteilung* (War Raw Materials Administration)
LCY	League of Communists of Yugoslavia
MRP	Popular Republican Movement (France)
NATO	North Atlantic Treaty Organization
NEP	New Economic Policy
NKVD	Soviet Secret Police (1935–1953)
NSDAP	German National Socialist Workers' Party (Nazis)
OECD	Organization for Economic Cooperation and Development

OEEC	Organization of European Economic Cooperation
OSCE	Organization for Security and Cooperation in Europe
PCI	Communist Party (Italy)
PDS	Party of Democratic Socialism (formerly the Socialist Unity Party)
RAF	Royal Air Force (United Kingdom)
RPPS	Polish Socialist Workers Party
RSDLP	Russian Social Democratic Labor Party (Bolsheviks; Mensheviks)
SA	*Sturmabteilung* (Stormtroopers—Nazi organization)
SALT	Strategic Arms Limitations Talks/Treaty
SDI	Strategic Defense Initiative ("Star Wars")
SDS	Socialist German Student Federation
SEA	Single European Act
SED	Socialist Unity Party (East Germany)
SFIO	Socialist Party (France)
SPD	German Social Democratic Party
SR	Socialist Revolutionaries (Russia)
SS	*Schutzstaffel* (Protective detachment—SS Nazi organization)
STASI	Secret police (East Germany)
TUC	Trades Union Council (United Kingdom)
USPD	Independent Social Democratic Party of Germany
WTO	Warsaw Treaty Organization
WTO	World Trade Organization

Index

Note: Page numbers followed by *il, n, p, t* indicate illustrations, footnotes, photographs, or tables respectively.

Twentieth-Century Europe: A Brief History, 1900 to the Present, Third Edition.
Michael D. Richards and Paul R. Waibel.
© 2014 John Wiley & Sons, Inc. Published 2014 by John Wiley & Sons, Inc.